# The Definitive Guide to the Microsoft Enterprise Library

Keenan Newton

Apress®

**The Definitive Guide to the Microsoft Enterprise Library**

**Copyright © 2007 by Keenan Newton**

Softcover re-print of the Hardcover 1st edition 2007

ISBN-13: 978-1-4842-2026-9

ISBN-10: 1-4842-2026-9

DOI 10.1007/978-1-4302-0315-5

Trademarked names may appear in this book. Rather than use a trademark symbol with every occurrence of a trademarked name, we use the names only in an editorial fashion and to the benefit of the trademark owner, with no intention of infringement of the trademark.

Lead Editor: Jason Gilmore
Technical Reviewer: Jason Hoekstra
Editorial Board: Steve Anglin, Ewan Buckingham, Tony Campbell, Gary Cornell, Jonathan Gennick,
    Jason Gilmore, Kevin Goff, Jonathan Hassell, Matthew Moodie, Joseph Ottinger, Jeffrey Pepper,
    Ben Renow-Clarke, Dominic Shakeshaft, Matt Wade, Tom Welsh
Project Manager: Beth Christmas
Copy Editor: Marilyn Smith
Associate Production Director: Kari Brooks-Copony
Production Editor: Katie Stence
Compositor: Gina Rexrode
Proofreader: Patrick Vincent
Indexer: Broccoli Information Management
Artist: April Milne
Cover Designer: Kurt Krames
Manufacturing Director: Tom Debolski

Distributed to the book trade worldwide by Springer-Verlag New York, Inc., 233 Spring Street, 6th Floor, New York, NY 10013. Phone 1-800-SPRINGER, fax 201-348-4505, e-mail orders-ny@springer-sbm.com, or visit http://www.springeronline.com.

For information on translations, please contact Apress directly at 2855 Telegraph Avenue, Suite 600, Berkeley, CA 94705. Phone 510-549-5930, fax 510-549-5939, e-mail info@apress.com, or visit http://www.apress.com.

The source code for this book is available to readers at http://www.apress.com.

# Contents at a Glance

# Contents

# About the Author

 **KEENAN NEWTON** was born in Canada and moved to the United States when he was 12 years old. He has been in the information technology industry for more than 10 years, working primarily as a software developer and more recently as an application architecture designer. As a software developer, Keenan has always been on the leading edge—sometimes bleeding edge—of industry trends and technologies. He is an active member of his local development communities, and has published various articles in *CoDe Magazine*. Keenan currently is a Senior Consultant for Microsoft Consulting Services. In his spare time, Keenan enjoys traveling, music, attending professional football games and landscaping.

# About the Technical Reviewer

**JASON HOEKSTRA** is an independent consultant who focuses on delivering solutions on the Microsoft .NET Framework and related platform products. With more than 10 years of experience, his efforts have helped businesses of all sizes turn business goals into deliverable products. His specialty of integrating open source and off-the-shelf tools (like Enterprise Library) has enabled teams to develop high-quality software in shorter time frames. In his spare time, Jason enjoys traveling with his wife, cooking, aviation, and videography.

# Acknowledgments

I could not have done this book on my own. My friends, family, and colleagues all assisted in some way. I would like to first acknowledge Timothy Murphy, a friend who helped with a good deal of research on the application blocks. Without his assistance, I doubt I would have completed this book. Next, I would like to acknowledge Jason Hoekstra, who is my technical reviewer for this book. He has been instrumental in being a second pair of eyes on everything. Next, I would like to acknowledge Tom Hollander and Eugenio Pace from the Microsoft patterns & practices group. Both of these gentlemen have been instrumental in answering whatever questions I had or in pointing me in the proper direction to get the answer I needed. I, of course, also want to acknowledge the exceptional staff at Apress for walking me through this process. Their patience and guidance is greatly appreciated. I can not forget Keith Franklin at Magenic Technologies, for encouraging my involvement in the development community. Finally, I would like to acknowledge Rod Paddock, the chief editor of *CoDe Magazine*. He opened the door for me getting into writing, and I would not be here today without him.

# Introduction

All developers are lazy. I don't mean lazy in a bad way, but in a good and efficient way. We are all looking for ways to crank out code faster so we can get to the next biggest thing. From the beginning days of computing with punch cards all the way to the modern-day managed applications created with the .NET Framework and relational databases like SQL Server 2005, developers have been looking for ways to cut corners efficiently without sacrificing quality. This is where Microsoft Enterprise Library comes into play. Enterprise Library helps cut out some of the routine tasks that developers need to perform while developing applications, and yet provides the best practices to ensure the application is designed and runs as efficiently as possible.

This book will provide the knowledge you need to get started and get comfortable with the Microsoft Enterprise Library application blocks. I will go over the design of each application block, how it is used, and how it can be customized. Throughout the chapters, you will find code samples for each application block that will be useful in getting a jump-start in your own applications.

The book also presents a reference implementation, which is a vertical component of a point-of-sales application. This implementation demonstrates how an application can use the different application blocks that are provided with Enterprise Library and how the application blocks themselves interact. The amount of detail devoted to the reference implementation in each chapter depends on the topic of that chapter and subsequent chapters. The complete application is available from the Apress website (http://www.apress.com).

As a reader, I am sure you may come up with questions. Please do not hesitate to post any questions that you may have on my blog at http://blogs.msdn.com/knewton.

# CHAPTER 1
■ ■ ■
# Enterprise Applications

From the beginning of time, people have been trying to make the quality of their lives better by finding new ways to do more tasks in less time with less effort. This is evident by the technological advances humans have made such as fire, the wheel, the telephone, and the computer. As each discovery is made, we then improve on that discovery to make it more efficient and cheaper to produce. This desire to make our quality of lives better is what drives us—it makes us who we are.

This desire is quite clear in the world of software development, where we continually try to discover better ways to create software so that it runs faster, is developed faster, is cheaper to produce, and can do more. One of the key strategies that the software development community discovered early on was the reuse of software code. Unfortunately, in many places, the same software code would be "copy and pasted" and used repeatedly within an application, making development and maintenance tasks a real challenge.

As time has gone on, many improvements, such as reusable methods, object orientation, service orientation, and so on, have been incorporated into the process of developing software. However, these software development techniques alone will not make software development easier. These are just the building blocks that you must build upon to ensure an ideal project outcome.

Understanding the architecture and needs of a software application will give the developer a better understanding of how the Enterprise Library can assist in developing an application framework. This framework could be the basic foundation of services for all applications within a particular organization. In this chapter, I'll cover the basic fundamental building blocks of today's software applications. The rest of the book will then show how the Enterprise Library can help ease the development of these application building blocks.

## The Needs of a Software Application

Successful software development is possible only through proper planning. Without doing so, you may find the application took longer to build, wasn't what you or the user expected, or worse yet was almost impossible to maintain. Proper preparation and design are integral to the creation of any software application regardless of its size and complexity.

When creating a new application, you first need to understand the type of business the application is for or in some cases who the audience of the application is if it is not specific to a business. Understanding the needs of the stakeholders and users is critical to the success of any application being built. For instance, a money management company responsible for securities trading would require applications to be very responsive because actions must be taken on a timely basis once a buy or sell decision has been made. However, if your application is tasked with working with batch processes, performance may not be as important as scalability. These two examples indicate that the audience will drive the design of the application indirectly based on what its needs are.

The end user's purpose will help define the general technical and design needs of an application; however, gathering the specific requirements from the business will determine the application's design requirements. From these business requirements, you should create a set of functional requirements detailing the specific functions required of the application. This is probably a good place to create use cases to define the actions and tasks that can be performed in the application. Finally, you can create the technical requirements for the application. This is where you get to create all the fun UML class diagrams and sequence diagrams as well as the data modeling. However, before you get to the technical specifications, you should consider some issues first.

The first elements to understand are the growth and current direction of the business. Is the business looking to expand its product line? Has the company been trending toward a 30 percent growth rate over the past five years, or is growth more along the lines of 300 percent? These types of questions are important to ask and understand, because it will help determine to what degree the application should scale. Although I'm aware that some professionals think you should never design an application beyond meeting the business and functional requirements, I think you should consider exposing certain interfaces so that future expansion can be done with less effort. However, such considerations should be balanced with the understanding that an application will not be able to account for every possible expansion scenario.

During the application design phase, you'll soon discover that you will be repeatedly implementing many of the same features and functions. The following are common examples of this recurring code:

- Retrieving, inserting, updating and deleting database data

- Logging application events

- Handling application exceptions to ensure that they are properly escalated

- Retrieving and updating application settings

- Improving performance by providing a caching mechanism to reuse static data performance

You can implement these common functions in a few ways, discussed in the next sections.

## Copy and Paste

One way to implement these examples is to copy and paste code throughout the application. Granted, this may seem extremely easy, but maintainability is nearly impossible. Think about an application that requires access to a database. Typically the creation of the connection object would be the same for all retrieve, insert, update, and delete functions. Assuming there are three tables used for this application, it would be safe to say there would be about 12 instances where a connection object would be needed. So, copying and pasting 12 times seems relatively easy. But if a change is required for one of the three tables to point to another database, you now have to go into the application and find the appropriate locations to change and modify them. To make matters worse, what if it became necessary to change the ADO.NET data provider? You would need to find all the connection object creation code and modify it. In short, although this approach results in short-term gratification, the long-term effects can be error prone and costly.

## Code Generation

Another way to handle this repetitive code is by creating it via a code generator. Code generators are very good at creating a lot of code quickly. But although they are adept at creating stable, bug-free code, code generators aren't without their own issues. First, modifying the generated code will prevent the developer from being able to regenerate the code using the code generator, since the code generator does not have the ability to incorporate the changes. This will effectively make development no easier than the copy-and-paste scenario described earlier. Second, they are applicable only given a certain set of conditions. If the code generator is unable to address a specific requirement, then it will be necessary to modify the code generator to address that need. Another issue with code generators is that typically all the code generated can be easily modified by the developer, and this can be problematic in environments where a specific technique is desired to handle a function such as creating a connection object. This is not to say that using a code generator is bad, and in fact, used properly, it can be a useful tool during the development of an application or component and can be used alongside other techniques of handling repetitive code such as frameworks.

## Frameworks

Another common technique is to create a series of components that can be reused throughout an applicationto perform the desired common functionality. These components can typically be used as is or subclassed to provide special implementations. The use of these components allows for cleaner, simplified code, which in turn allows for maximum maintainability while providing simplified interfaces for the developer to use. Together, these components create a foundation that an application can be built upon. Another common name for this collection of components is a *framework*.

# Common Framework Types

An application can utilize one of two types of frameworks: an *environment framework* (sometimes referred to as a *development and execution environment framework* or *system framework*) and an *enterprise framework* (also known as an *application framework*). These two frameworks work together to provide the services and interfaces necessary to develop software applications. I'll now introduce you to both types.

## The Environment Framework

Every mainstream operating system has a set of application programming interfaces (APIs) that expose its features and functionality. Generally, this API is quite robust and exposes interfaces that most applications may never use. Additionally, to utilize the features of the operating system API, a fair amount of repetitive code must be written in order to perform simple tasks such as creating a window. This is where an environment framework can simplify the utilization of system resources.

The environment framework typically provides a set of interfaces and features available within the operating system environment to a development environment. These interfaces and features hide all the necessary environment-specific code to implement specific tasks. Some examples of execution environment frameworks include the Java Virtual Machine, Visual Basic runtime, and the .NET Framework. These frameworks provide reusable code that makes tasks such as creating a window simple. With the environment frameworks, you typically do not have to worry about low-level tasks such as memory allocation, file handlers, windows handles, and so forth.

## The Enterprise Framework

It is great that we can take advantage of environment frameworks when developing applications, but most applications are going to have greater framework needs. Granted, when you are developing a Windows or web application, the environment framework can save you from disaster by giving you a friendly and relatively safe environment in which to create your masterpiece. However, if you are not careful, you will find yourself with unmanageable code that is hard to read.

The problem is that most development environments such as the .NET Framework provide more than one way to perform a specific task. Suppose a business is going to require a new reporting module that contains multiple reports, and three developers—Steve, Andrew, and Sue—have been assigned to create this reporting module. Since the three reporting module contains three separate reports, the three developers decide to develop one report each.

Steve determines that he needs to retrieve a table of lookup values that will be used to determine the proper criteria to create the report. Therefore, the first task Steve decides to do is create a data access class. And in this new class Steve creates a method called GetReportLookupData to retrieve a drop-down list of data needed for a report:

```
public class myLookupDataAccessClass
{
    public ReportLookUpData GetReportLookUpData()
    {
        //Some code...
    }
}
```

At first glance, it seems like a pretty simple implementation. Steve will write some data access code within the GetReportLookUpData method that is going to return a custom business entity called ReportLookUpData. Therefore, Steve decides to use a SqlReader to retrieve the lookup data. To create the SqlReader object, Steve must create a SqlCommand object to execute the SQL statement and a corresponding SqlConnection object to connect to the database. Now the SqlConnection object requires a connection string to determine specific parameters required by SQL Server in order to connect to it. In this particular case, Steve decides to just hard-code the string into the code:

```
public class myLookupDataAccessClass
{
    public ReportLookUpData GetReportLookUpData()
    {
        string myConn = "server=MyServer;database=MyDatabase;Integrated
```

```
                        Security=SSPI";
        ReportLookUpData lookUp = new ReportLookUpData();
        SqlConnection connection =  new SqlConnection(myConn);

        //Data retrieval code...
        return lookUp;
    }
}
```

While Steve was creating his data access component, Andrew was working on a data access component for another report. Andrew's experience told him that hard-coding the connection string would not be the best choice, so he decided to use the application's configuration file to store the connection string.

Finally, Sue was working on yet another data access component for the report she was creating, and she decided to store the connection string in the Windows registry.

From the developers' standpoint, the application is ready to be deployed in the production environment, with the connection strings hard-coded, stored in the Windows registry, and stored in the application configuration files.

A few months pass, and a new developer named Tim joins the company. Tim is tasked with changing database providers from SQL Server to Oracle. Tim immediately sees an issue with Steve's hard-coding of the connection string, so he opts to use a text file to store the connection string for the application.

Now Tim not only has to modify each data access component but he also must discover how the connection strings were stored and modify all the storage mechanisms in order to change the connection string between the development, integration, and production environments. For the very smallest of applications, this may not be a big deal. However, for very large applications, where there may be hundreds of data access components that require connection strings, this can become a maintenance nightmare.

Having a common, consistent way of handling connection strings is most beneficial from both the development and administrative points of view. To accomplish this, an organization might define a coding standard defining how to properly store and retrieve a database connection string. However, this technique will end up creating many coding rules that the development team will constantly have to remember and enforce. Even with a coding rule like this in place, the application developers would still have to create the code to retrieve the connection string, and this repetitive coding would eventually become mundane and time-consuming.

A better way to handle these kinds of development issues is through an enterprise framework. An enterprise framework builds upon the functionality available within a development environment, but it takes the most common code routines in an application and encapsulates the code into a more simplified implementation. Let's reconsider the previous example, this time revising it to use a framework component:

```
public class myLookupDataAccessClass
{
    public ReportLookUpData GetReportLookUpData()
    {
```

```
        ReportLookUpData lookUp = new ReportLookUpData();
        SqlConnection connection =  new
            SqlConnection(AcmeFramework.GetConnectionString());

        //Data retrieval code...
        return lookUp;
    }
}
```

Now Steve has used the GetConnectionString method in the AcmeFramework component to retrieve the connection string. Steve does not have to worry about the details of how the connection string is stored or how to retrieve it. The AcmeFramework will handle the details for him.

Now when the application is promoted to production, the production enterprise framework will handle the details of how to retrieve the connection string. Hence, it is not required to modify the application configuration file or Windows registry to add the new database connection string. In addition, the developers will typically be required to write fewer lines of code using an enterprise framework as opposed to writing a custom implementation.

Another benefit to using an enterprise framework is the ability to change the underlying implementation of the framework without having to always touch the public interfaces it exposes. For example, let's assume the AcmeFramework utilizes an XML file to store configuration data; however, company policies change, requiring all connection strings to be encrypted. Instead of having to change every data access component's connection string implementation, only the GetConnectionString method is concerned with decrypting the encrypted connection string inside the XML file.

Overall, an enterprise framework will help enforce consistent software development, require less code, require fewer bugs, and provide the use of best-practices implementations within an application. Other benefits of using an enterprise framework include freeing developers from having to code low-level tasks, such as opening and closing files, and allowing less experienced developers to develop an application. From a project management standpoint, this can lower a project's development costs and at times allow developers who have more business than technical skills to play a bigger role in the development of an application. In the end, an enterprise framework is not a silver bullet; it should provide the core common functionality and features needed for most, if not all, of your software application as well as allow for more project success stories by letting the developers focus on implementing the application's requirements as opposed to worrying about connection string management.

# Core Components of an Enterprise Framework

To understand the components of an enterprise framework, you first have to understand the components used to create an application. Each application has to perform certain functions in order to meet the needs of the user. These functions can range from accessing data to sending email messages to formatting a document. To perform these tasks, it makes sense to try to break them out into specific components. This breaking apart of the features allows for easier maintenance of the application, as well as the ability to scale out as needed.

Most business applications require some sort of user interface to interact with data, a mechanism to validate data entered in by the user, and the ability to read and write data. Typically, the components are called *separated tiers* or *layers*. I prefer the term *layers* when thinking of the logical separation of components and *tiers* when referring to the physical separation of components. The typical high-level layers of an application are the presentation layer, the business logic layer, and the data layer. However, the needs of an application do not stop with these components of an application. As previously mentioned, an application may also need components to handle security, application configuration, exception handling, logging, application deployment, and so forth. The specific application components will be determined based on the functional and technical requirements of the application. However, as an enterprise grows and applications are developed, it will soon become apparent that all these applications share common functionality between them. This common functionality is the perfect candidate for common enterprise framework components. Figure 1-1 shows the different components that are typically used in an application. In the following sections, I'll introduce several of the most common components.

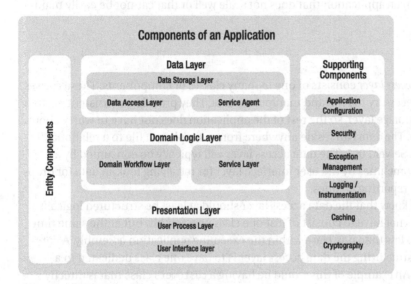

**Figure 1-1.** *Components of an application*

# Data Layer

The *data layer* can be broken into three sublayers in most applications. They are the data storage layer, the data access layer, and the service agent, as shown in Figure 1-1. The data storage layer provides the mechanism for storing and managing your application data, and the data access layer provides the logic needed to retrieve and manipulate data. The service agent is like the data access layer, but instead of accessing a data storage layer, the service will access another domain process such as a web service or COM+ component via DCOM. Together these three logical layers provide the mechanisms for gathering and manipulating data.

## Data Storage Layer

Typically, the data storage layer consists of a relational database server such as Microsoft SQL Server 2005 or Oracle. This layer can be shared between multiple applications, but there should be some logical or physical separation within the database server. One example would be having a database for each application that the database server is supporting.

The data storage layer provides a series of functionality to an application such as retrieving, inserting, updating, and deleting data. Not all data storage layers are relational database servers. An XML document utilizing an XML parser such as the MSXML DOM or a SAX parser could also be considered a data storage layer. Some other examples of data storage layers could be the Windows registry, a .NET application configuration file, or even a Microsoft Excel spreadsheet. However, relational databases are the most common for storing application data. They typically abstract the methods of "how" to retrieve data and instead expose functionality on "what" data to retrieve, which lets the database server figure out the "how." The most common language used for retrieving data is SQL or some derivative of it.

The data storage layer is typically called only by the data access layer; by reporting and analysis tools; or by other extraction, transformation, and loading (ETL) applications. Hence, you should not interact with the data storage layer from the user interface or business layers; doing this can result in an application that does not scale well or that cannot be easily maintained.

## Data Access Layer

Ordinarily, the *data access layer* consists of one to many classes or components. These classes handle all the work necessary to read and manipulate data. They provide a consistent abstract interface to the data storage layer, so the rest of the application does not have to worry about how to get at the data. The data can reside anywhere from a simple text file to a relational database such as SQL Server 2005. The data access layer will typically be consumed by a business logic layer, sometimes by the user interface layer for retrieving lookup data for dropdowns controls, or by reporting engines.

It is important to know that the data access layer should at least be structured logically. In other words, it does not have to consist of just one class or assembly, but at the same time, it should consist of no less than one class within the executing application assembly. A common way of logically structuring the data access layer is to have one class dedicated to a logical group of data. An example of this would be having a customers class that is directly related to a group of customer tables. The decision of whether you want to have your data access logic inside the main executing assembly or physically separated like in an *n*-tier application will be based on the scalability, maintainability, and performance needs of your application. By containing your data access logic with one or more classes, you will gain the advantage of being able to swap out a data access component with another one. For instance, suppose that the application your organization has been using currently is utilizing an Oracle database. Now with .NET 3.0 and SQL Server 2005 being the latest and greatest development technologies, the powers that be have made an executive decision to migrate all databases to SQL Server 2005. For the most part, all you would have to do is create a new class that now utilizes the SQL Server client provider (System.Data.SqlClient) as opposed to the Oracle provider. Then test the new component, and put it in production. From a high-level point of view, not all implementations may be as simple, especially when using SQL commands that are specific to a database provider.

The key to allowing this is that the public interfaces that were exposed by the Oracle data access component should match the new public interfaces exposed by the SQL Server data access component. Testing should be just as simple, and your original unit tests should work with the new data access component just as it did with the old data access component. Again, this is facilitated by the fact that the public interfaces did not change. Or at least you should not have to change the interfaces to swap out database providers. The following is an example of how two data access classes can each have the same interfaces yet each utilize a different database for its data:

```
public class myOracleDataAccess
{
    public DataSet GetSalesReport(DateTime beginDate, DateTime endDate)
    {
        DataSet myDataSet = new DataSet();
        string myConnString = "Data Source=Oracle8iDb;Integrated Security=yes";
        OracleConnection myDbConn = new OracleConnection(myConnString);
        OracleCommand myDbCmd = new OracleCommand();
        myDbCmd.Connection = myDbConn;

        //Oracle Data Adapter, command string, and parameters added here

        myDataAdapter.Fill(myDataSet);
        return myDataSet;
    }
}


public class mySqlDataAccess
{
    public DataSet GetSalesReport(DateTime beginDate, DateTime endDate)
    {
        DataSet myDataSet = new DataSet();
        string myConnString =
            "Server=SqlServerDb; Database=Northwind; Trusted_Connection=true";

        SqlConnection myDbConn = new SqlConnection(myConnString);
        SqlCommand myDbCmd = new SqlCommand();
        myDbCmd.Connection = myDbConn;

        //SQL Data Adapter, command string, and parameters added here

        myDataAdapter.Fill(myDataSet);
        return myDataSet;
    }
}
```

Examining the two classes, myOracleDataAccess and mySqlDataAccess, you'll notice each one has a method called GetSalesReport that returns a dataset. You will notice in both instances that the method signatures are the same; hence, you could pull out the Oracle data access class and replace it with the SQL data access class. You, of course, would want to make sure that the results returned are identical between the two classes for the given method.

### Service Agents

*Service agents*, also referred to as *proxies*, access information from another domain process. In very large organizations, it is beneficial to keep different applications loosely coupled. Thus, each application can utilize the best platform and technology to perform the necessary functions that it requires and yet provide interfaces to other applications to consume these functions. Service agents can also be used to retrieve data from a third-party vendor. An example of this is a retail application requesting a shipping cost from a courier by passing destination and pick-up ZIP codes to the courier, with the courier responding with a shipping cost.

Service agents are not a new concept; they have been around for years—from the crudest of interfaces such as passing an ASCII file from one server to the next to more elegant solutions such as DCOM and today's web services.

---

■**Note**  I prefer calling business logic *domain logic* because the word *business* implies the logic is for business purposes, and I prefer a more generic term to encompass any kind of problem or process that requires rule validation—business or not.

---

## Domain Logic Layer

The *domain logic layer* (more commonly referred to as the *business logic layer*) is where you will process all the rules and validation needed to perform an action. This layer, like the data access layer, should at least be its own class to allow for easy replacement if necessary, but it does not have to be a separate assembly.

---

■**Note**  I prefer the term *domain layer* because the term *business layer* should always refer to "business" rules. The word *business* is too narrow of a concept in the vast world of application development. A perfect example of this is an Internet email client validating that a user has entered a proper email address; this task is important, but it's not specific to a business purpose.

---

The purpose of the domain logic layer is to mimic what was once performed by another domain process whether it was done automatically in a software application or done manually by a person. For instance, in a retail point of sales (POS) process, a clerk would have to manually write each item being purchased on a sheet, then tally the total of all the items, and finally add any sales tax. In a POS application, listing the items being purchased, tallying them, and adding sales tax is all done by the application. The location within an application where this is done is typically the domain logic layer.

By keeping the domain logic together in one layer of your application, you are also going to simplify its maintenance. The domain logic layer typically sits in between the data access layer and the presentation layer. Hence, as a user enters data into the application, the data is validated against the domain logic and then passed to the data access layer to be saved into the database.

The domain logic layer, like the data access layer, should at least be a logical separation within your application. However, this does not prevent you from having multiple classes, assemblies, and so on, in your domain logic layer. Also keep in mind that not all domain logic components will necessarily communicate with a data access layer. Some of these components will be stand-alone such as financial math calculators; some typical names for these kinds of domain logic components are *common logic components* or *common domain logic components*.

Finally, when it comes to the domain logic layer, remember that not all of your domain logic will be able to reside solely in this layer. Yes, it is important to strive to get as much as your domain logic in one manageable location, but sometimes this is not practical. One good example of this is when performing business-specific calculations. It may make sense to perform these calculations within the domain logic layer, but it may also be practical to perform the same calculations while doing a bulk upload of data into the database. Therefore, you may have one component deployed to both the database layer on the database server and the business layer on either an application server in an *n*-tier environment or the workstation in a client/server environment. Again, you will have to balance out maintainability, scalability, and performance requirements based on your application needs.

## Domain Workflow Layer

This layer, a subcomponent of the domain layer, handles the processing of workflows. Typically, the components built in the domain layer should be very specific to a domain problem. Some examples of this are adding a new customer, adding a new order, requesting shipping costs, and calculating sales tax. The domain workflow layer would handle the process of creating a new order by orchestrating the domain logic calls and transactions.

The domain workflow layer is not for every application. Its use should be determined based on the application needs. For instance, a simple maintenance application that maintains a list of countries would probably not use a domain workflow layer. However, an application for an investment company may use a domain workflow to manage the process of trading securities.

## Service Layer

The *service layer*, also known as a *façade layer*, provides an entry-point mechanism for other applications to access specific domain functions or services of an application. It allows you to provide a black-box interface to your application so that the caller doesn't need to know the internal details of domain logic. Typically, service agents consume service layers, and some common implementations of service layers are web services, CORBA, and COM+. Service layers typically will perform necessary data mapping and transformations as well as handle processes and policies for communicating between the domain layer and consumer.

Interoperability between heterogeneous systems is not a requirement for a service layer; it is perfectly acceptable to support just one platform in your service layer implementation. Interoperability can introduce performance issues and system limitations. The need to provide an interoperable service layer will be based on the overall requirements of the domain. For third-party vendors, it is probably a great idea to utilize web services for its service layer.

For an internal application where all the applications are on one platform, utilizing .NET remoting or COM+ via DCOM might be a better solution.

---

**Note** It is important to note that the service layer doesn't necessarily imply the use of web services. Web services are just one implementation of service layers; other implementations might use .NET remoting, DCOM, CORBA, and so on.

---

## Presentation Layer

The *presentation layer* typically consists of one or two sublayers, namely, the *user interface layer* and the *user process layer*. In most smaller applications, it is necessary to have only the user interface layer. However, in large applications or applications with multiple types of user interfaces, a user process layer would prove beneficial. The user process layer would handle the common user interface processes such as wizards and the interfaces to the domain logic layer.

Like the data access layer, you will sometimes have to keep some logic in the presentation layer. However, this domain logic is very basic and is typically used for validating data types and formatting. A few examples of this would be validating that a phone is formatted correctly or that an entered credit card number contains only numbers.

Also keep in mind that it is fine to call a data access layer directly from the presentation layer; however, this should be done only for retrieving lookup values in a combo box or list box or for reporting purposes. All data manipulation should be done strictly through a domain layer. You also have to keep in mind that calling the data access layer from the presentation layer reduces your application's scalability.

### User Interface Layer

Most applications are designed with the intention that a user will interact with it. The user interface layer will contain all the user interface components such as web or Windows forms. These user interface components are then used to interact and communicate with the domain logic layer and sometimes the data access layer.

An important thing to remember about the user interface layer is that you should keep domain logic to a minimum. If you are using a user process layer in your application, you should have practically no domain logic whatsoever in the user interface. Any domain logic should then be part of the user process layer. The one exception to this rule is a web application; for performance and usability reasons, it may also be necessary to apply some domain logic in the HTML page as client script.

---

**Tip** In web applications, it is important to remember that even if some domain logic is being performed in the browser, you still have to perform it on the server to ensure the domain logic is applied. Not all environments can guarantee that the web browser has scripting turned on. This is very true for business-to-consumer applications.

---

### User Process Layer

With larger applications where you have rich, robust user interfaces or many types of user interfaces, it may become more critical to manage the processes or workflows of the user interface in a separate layer. This allows the abstraction of user interface components from the actual process that a user must undertake to complete a given task. The user process layer would also manage state and calls to the domain logic and data access components. Using a user process layer will help make your user interfaces very lightweight and ideally give you the ability to easily create multiple types of user interfaces without having to do much more than create your Windows or web form and drop some UI controls onto it.

The Model-View-Controller (MVC) design pattern is a good implementation of a user process layer. The model would manage the state and calls to the domain logic components. The view would be the user interface components themselves. Lastly, the controller would handle events, handle workflows, and make the necessary calls to the view and model. In this case, the model and controller are the components of the user process layer, and the view is the component of the user interface layer.

## Entity Components

An *entity component*, also referred to as a *business entity*, should represent an entity within a domain. A customer, sale item, employee, and sales transaction are all typical examples of an entity. Each one of these entities can be represented as an entity object. The entity component will contain all the attributes necessary to perform the tasks that it is related with. The entity component is typically shared between all the layers of an application, because the entity component is the primary way you would pass the application data around your application.

For example, an entity component that represents an employee in a retail application may contain the following attributes: first name, last name, Social Security number, employee number, and home address. The Social Security number, last name, first name, and address attributes are required for printing the employee's paycheck. The first name, last name, and employee number attributes are required during a sales transaction. In this case, one entity component can be used for sales transactions and employee payroll. However, sometimes when an entity has many attributes, these attributes are specific to certain domain tasks. It may be necessary to create more than one entity component to represent a domain entity.

One way to minimize the amount of redundant code is to use inheritance when designing your entity component. In this case, you would build a base component called person, and a person would have a first name, last name, and address. The inherited class would contain all the attributes the base class has plus any new attributes it would add. Since a customer and an employee both require a first name, last name, and address, you would inherit from the person base class and create a customer class and an employee class. The customer and employee classes can then add specific attributes for a customer or an employee. Therefore, a customer entity might add a preferred shipping method attribute and a birth date attribute. The employee entity might add a Social Security number attribute and employee number attribute.

Also, in some architectures, an entity component can be part of the domain layer. An example of this is in an object-oriented architecture; the entity object would also contain the necessary methods for performing data manipulation upon itself. Although this kind of implementation would be considered a good OO design, in some cases scalability and performance may be sacrificed while taking this approach. This is why most applications take a component-oriented architecture or service-oriented architecture approach and pass the entity component to a domain component where some action is taken on that entity component.

## Application Configuration Data

Every application needs to contain metadata that will define the application's execution environment. Some examples of metadata include a database connection string, FTP server addresses, file paths, and even sometimes branding information. To provide a way to set this configuration data in an application, most applications depend upon an INI or XML file to store that data. With .NET applications, it is easy to utilize the application configuration file to store your configuration data in an XML format. You can utilize the built-in `<appSettings>` element setting configuration settings, or for more complex scenarios where you have complex hierarchies of configuration data, you can create your own custom configuration section.

Some of the downsides of using the .NET application configuration file are that the files are read-only at runtime and it's not possible to centralize data between multiple applications. These limitations may force larger applications to come up with a custom solution to store the configuration data for an application. Also, currently it is not a good user interface for an administrator to configure the application configuration file. This can make administrating this file difficult and cumbersome when attempting to read and modify these files with a large amount of configuration data.

Some other options you can look at to store configuration data are the Windows registry, a file stored locally, or a file stored on a network file server; you can even use a database server to store application configuration data. The key thing you want to remember is to determine the features of the configuration data needs based on the current application requirements and the potential growth of the application.

## Managing Security

Another important application need is securing the data and features that an application provides to its users. To do this, an application must identify and then determine what data and application rights it can access. Another set of terms for this is *authentication* and *authorization*. Some of the challenges faced with application design are determining a simple way of managing security between the different layers and determining the different types of user interfaces that may be required for the application.

Another challenge is also determining what is the best way to implement the security management of an application. Some things to consider in this decision process are as follows:

- Is the application in-house, or are you a vendor building this application for your clients?

- How will the application be accessed? Will it be strictly internal, or will it be accessible via an extranet or over the Internet?

- What portions of the application will be exposed to whom? Will it be necessary to ensure that the sales group cannot access the executive manager's reports?

- Does the application have to worry about being platform or version independent?

- Do the security mechanisms have to be shared between heterogeneous applications?

Once you have determined the needs of your application, you can determine the best approaches for securing your application.

## Authentication

The first step you must perform to secure your application is to determine the identity of the person or system that is trying to access it. For .NET applications, you have two basic choices: you can authenticate either with Windows authentication or with non-Windows authentication. Both of these have their pros and cons.

When utilizing Windows authentication via Active Directory, you are allowing the operating system and domain to determine the identity of the person or system trying to access it. This usually takes place by a user or system supplying a username, password, and domain to the application. Once those are supplied, the application will call upon the operating system to verify the credentials presented. In a Windows application, this is done just by the fact the user has logged onto their desktop. A Windows service provides the credentials supplied to it to the operating system. For a web application, an Internet browser will attempt to utilize the credentials that the user is currently running the web browser with. However, if the web application server cannot verify the credentials, then the web server may give the user an opportunity to supply the correct credentials to access the web application. In the case of a web service application, the application calling the web service needs to have the credentials supplied. Depending on the design of the web service proxy component, this can be defaulted to the credentials that the user is logged in as, or another set of credentials can be supplied by the application to the web service.

In a non–Active Directory authentication scenario, the burden of verifying a user is put on the application. In Windows applications and Windows services, it is up to the application to look up the credentials provided and verify them against a custom implementation. One example might be taking a username and password and validating against a database table of usernames and passwords.

In web applications, you have a few more choices in how you can validate a user. You can do it manually like a Windows application, but then you are required to put in this authentication code for each web page of your application. This is to prevent someone from gaining access to your application by attempting to navigate to some web page other than your intended main entry or login page. Or a better solution would be to use ASP.NET forms authentication. Forms authentication takes users who are not validated and redirects them to a login page where they can supply their user credentials. Once authenticated, they are free to navigate the web application as they like. Forms authentication utilizes cookies to determine whether the user is known or unknown as they navigate the application. The credentials can be stored in the web application configuration file or can be a custom implementation such as the custom database scenario described for the Windows application.

In the scenario of a web service, the same issues that existed for the web application also exist for a web service application. However, they are harder to resolve. In a web application, forms authentication would redirect the user to a login page. In a web service, that is not practical, so it will be necessary to authenticate the user before taking any other action. This will require the application consuming the web service to call a login web method where the web service can authenticate and issue a cookie to the calling application. What makes matters more difficult is if the calling application is a web application, you have to manage state to retain the authentication cookie. You can do this by storing the cookies in a session variable. In all web services, you probably want to steer away from forms authentication. The good news is there are other technologies such as Web Services Enhancements (WSE) that specifically address security issues for web services.

## Authorization

Once you have authenticated a user or system process, the next task is to determine what features and functions they have access to in your application. The first choice you have to make is whether you want your application to authorize access on a per-user basis or whether you prefer to assign the user to a group and grant the group access to specific features.

In the scenario where you assign access to features and functions in your application on a per-user basis, you will find for larger applications that administration will soon become a nightmare. However, for very small applications, authorizing users directly might be acceptable. You will have to determine this during the design of your application.

Assigning groups of users to a specific feature or function, better known as *role-based authorization*, will prove beneficial in moderate to large applications. Once again, you have two high-level choices you can choose from when implementing role-based authorization: either the operating system can help manage it or you can build your own custom solution.

In allowing the operating system to help manage role-based authorization, you will probably be using Active Directory to manage your groups. Thus, you will assign an Active Directory group to a specific feature or function. Then you will assign users to active directory groups. When a user authenticates to the operating system, you can then determine which active groups the user belongs to and determine authorization to the features and functions of your application based on those active groups.

Some key points to remember when using Active Directory are as follows:

- You can use Active Directory only if the user is authenticated to the operating system and domain.

- When dealing with applications that are intended for public availability such as web applications, performance and maintenance of Active Directory may become an issue.

- Active Directory does not interoperate well with other heterogeneous systems like Unix servers.

Another approach to handling role-based authorization is to create a custom implementation. One example like the custom authentication scheme mentioned earlier is to utilize a database to store groups of users. This way you can have user credentials related to user groups and then have user groups related to application features and functions. This approach offers more flexibility than Active Directory in that it can be implemented for different operating system environments. It can use the operating system to authenticate a user while still using this custom implementation. Finally, a database will typically perform better than Active Directory, especially with large volumes of users and groups like in the scenario of a public web application.

The downside is that you have to implement this beforehand, so you will need to create the data structures to store the data. You also will probably want to implement a maintenance application to maintain the users and groups. Overall, like everything else, the requirements of the application will determine the best approach.

# Handling Exceptions

As much as we like to believe that we create bug-free applications, this is almost certainly an unrealistic aspiration. Sometimes it is because of a bug within a technology we are utilizing, but most of the times the exception will occur because we introduced a bug or error into the application. Handling exceptions is a critical task in an application; it provides a way for the application to inform the user when something goes wrong.

Out of the box, .NET provides a mechanism for reporting exceptions to the user; unfortunately, the messages are not user-friendly. On top of that, when a user sees an error, 90 percent of the time they will close the application and try to restart it. If the function they were trying to perform works after the restart, more than likely you will never know the exception occurred. Granted, some individuals believe that ignorance is bliss, but in this case an unhandled defect in an application can reduce confidence in the application as well as in the developer who wrote it.

This means as developers we have to anticipate the errors that can occur and try to gracefully recover from them. Sometimes you can do this without telling the user anything and simply log it to an exception log file. Other times, you have to notify the user and perform some kind of action such as canceling the task they are trying to perform or closing the application. When you are handling specific errors, you can then not only notify the user of the issue but also notify the developers via an exception log or possibly an email. This allows the developer to be aware of any issues regardless of whether the user opted to notify the developer.

In addition, we can't anticipate certain errors, such as the users attempting to use the application it was never intended for. These unanticipated exceptions should be handled globally. In this case, you may have to close the application, but you can still notify the user with a friendly message, as well as send a message to the support staff. This can give the support staff the opportunity to address the issue before it becomes widespread.

In either case, handling errors in your application will help you improve the quality of your application as well as save face in front of your users. Also, handling errors gives you the opportunity to cleanly close down an application or feature of an application, thus reducing the possibility of memory leaks.

# Logging

Along with handling exceptions, it can also be beneficial to log events within an application. Logging can help determine the application's performance, create audit trails, and log both application and process exceptions. These are just some of the benefits of implementing logging in your application.

You can implement logging utilizing a simple file-based approach such as the Internet Information Services (IIS) web logs. Another possible approach to logging application events might be to log data to a database. You should determine the exact storage mechanism based on the needs to query the log data. If you have to query the logged data, often a database may prove to be more beneficial. However, if your logged data is rarely looked at but must be done to satisfy the requirements of your application, then a simple text file may be sufficient. In addition, you can utilize the Windows event log features to log application events.

Other possible factors in determining the approach you use when logging application events can include the following:

- *Performance*: What is the minimum number of log entries that must be made within a given period of time?

- *Frequency*: At what interval will the log be added to?

- *Purging*: How long will it be before logged events can be purged out of the log files?

- *Readability*: Will you need to create a special application to view the log entries?

- *Scalability*: Does it make sense to contain the logs in a centralized location?

Another issue to consider is the configurability of the logging to be used in an application. For instance, should certain events be logged based on the environment that they're in? Should certain events be logged depending on whether the application is being debugged? Once you have determined the requirements of your application, you can then determine the best logging implementation approach.

## Other Application Needs

When designing your application, you may find that your application has other needs as well. Some of these needs might include handling a disconnected environment, caching data, and encrypting and decrypting information, as well as dealing with application deployment.

### Caching

Caching data can be useful in an application, especially when used to recall common lookup data often. Caching can provide the following benefits for an application:

- Improved application performance

- Improved scalability

- Reduced load on application and database servers

A perfect example of this is caching lookup data for drop-down list boxes in the user interface. In this case, an application would retrieve the lookup data on the initial load of the user interface and store that within the user interface so that it can be reused on subsequent loads for that particular user's UI component. This would save unnecessary hits to the database for that data that rarely or never changes.

When you cache data, you have to assess the data's volatility and determine how long you want to keep the cache around before expiring it and requiring the application to refresh the cache. Also, you must be aware of how much data is cached within a particular layer of the application, because caching can take up memory, and too much caching of data may unnecessarily take up too many resources from the running application. The use of caching must be balanced based on the amount of free local resources such as memory.

## Cryptography

If you find that your application needs the ability to encrypt and decrypt data, you have to consider which methods will meet your needs and yet still perform well. The .NET Framework offers many options for handling the encryption and decryption of data; you can also create your own custom implementations or use third-party implementations if they meet your needs. The important thing you need to do is provide a consistent common interface for your cryptography needs in your application, thus allowing simplified maintenance and ensuring best-practice implementations.

## Deployment

Another issue that you will more than likely have to address is the deployment of the application. For a web application, deployment is not as big of an issue as it would be for a Windows application. In a web application, you can simply deploy your application via Xcopy or an MSI to your production servers. However, a Windows application deployment can be a hair-raising issue, especially if you have many client workstations to which the application has to be deployed.

In many cases for large Windows application deployments, you must put a strategy in place for deploying the initial application and subsequent updates. The .NET Framework 2.0 had introduced a new technology called ClickOnce just for handling this kind of deployment.

---

■**Note**  ClickOnce is also present in the .NET Framework 3.0.

---

ClickOnce allows the deployment of applications over the Web. A user can click an application in the Start menu or use a link, and ClickOnce will determine based on a manifest whether the application should be updated. Although ClickOnce can handle some application deployment scenarios, it has some limitations. These limitations include the inability to modify registry settings, create custom installation directories, and share installations.

Another solution could be the use of a simple MSI installation package that a user can run themselves; however, even this scenario can have problems. Some of these problems can include the lack of rights, the user not performing the necessary updates, and installation problems such as prerequisite components not being present on the user's machine.

Another possible solution is to create a custom bootstrapper application for downloading updates to a desktop. In many cases, you can buy third-party packages to do this, or you can find open source implementations on the Internet. Although this approach removes the need to push installation packages each time an application requires an update, an initial installation will still have to take place to get the bootstrapper on the user's desktop.

# Summary

In summary, this chapter has gone over the key components most applications will need in order to create successful, reliable, and scalable applications. Remember to break apart the components of an application in at least a logical manner. Having one class file that handles all the application functionality can become a nightmare to maintain; plus, having the components logically separated will allow for future growth by allowing for the physical separation of layers into components to facilitate scalability.

Now that you understand these components, the next task is to figure out how to implement these different layers and to understand how the Enterprise Library Application Blocks can fulfill these necessary features in an application.

# CHAPTER 2

■ ■ ■

# Introducing the Enterprise Library Application Blocks

In the first chapter of this book, you learned about the various decisions and components that are involved in developing an application. Figuring out the requirements of your application is a critical and necessary step in the development of any application. Without this analysis, you will probably find that your application will be over budget, be difficult to maintain, and, worse yet, may not even satisfactorily meet the requirements of your users.

Once you have figured out these requirements, it is time to figure out how you're going to go about fulfilling them. This is where you get to exercise your creative thinking by keeping it as simple and to the point as possible while still keeping it extensible. Always keep in mind that all that matters to the client is whether you've met their expectations.

When it comes to figuring out the architecture and design of your application, you will have to decide whether to build the components yourself or utilize a general framework. Building it yourself will give you the freedom to create the architecture that best fits the application you are creating. The downside to this is that it can be time-consuming, and if you don't put enough thought into the process, you might find yourself with an architecture that is less than desirable.

Utilizing a general framework can mean two things: either using an open source architecture or purchasing one. Given the number of open source architectures that are available these days, it's difficult to justify purchasing an architecture. One of the reasons for this is that most commercial frameworks do everything under the sun, and accordingly, they can be difficult to incorporate into different business environments. The biggest reason commercial frameworks can be difficult in a specific business environment is that they often require an organization to adjust its software to work the way the framework wants the software to work. This is especially true for commercial frameworks where the source code is closely guarded. When evaluating a commercial framework or any framework that does not offer its source code to the public, it is important to not only evaluate whether the framework can meet the current needs but also to evaluate whether it will meet the needs of the future.

Not having the framework's source code introduces another risk. If the framework provider were to go out of business or simply stop providing support for that framework, then the organization would have to decide whether to modify its applications to use a new application framework or stay with the existing framework, knowing that the applications will eventually become outdated and limited by the legacy application framework.

With that said, this doesn't mean that commercial frameworks are all bad. I just urge you to at least evaluate them and determine that they will not hinder your application from a scalability and performance perspective; in addition, you should ensure that they incorporate the current industry best practices.

Open source frameworks, or frameworks that provide the source with them, are, in my mind, the better choice. First, most open source frameworks tend to be created and contributed to by developers who listen, respond, and implement the design based on feedback from the development community. Second, the source code is provided with the framework, so if there is something you do not like about a particular framework component, you can change it to your liking. Lastly, these types of frameworks do not try to consider every possible scenario; thus, they typically don't force you to have to consider changing the way you develop your applications. The end result is that they are simple to use and easy to expand upon. Granted, you may have to expand on the open source framework features, but this allows you to gain a deeper knowledge while trying to tackle the specific features you need in order to make your particular implementation of the framework complete.

# Microsoft Patterns and Practices

In recent years, Microsoft has made a strong push into the architectural and development guidance arena. It created the Microsoft patterns & practices group, which is responsible for the development and evangelism of best-practice recommendations for designing, developing, deploying, and operating architecturally solid solutions with Microsoft technologies and tools.

Microsoft patterns and practices contain knowledgeable, tested, and practiced guidance and source code based on real-world experience. Microsoft creates this guidance and source code by combining the minds, efforts, and feedback of leading software architects, developers, and consultants from internal sources, as well as community leaders and Microsoft partners. The offerings from the Microsoft patterns & practices group fit into four major categories: written guidance, reference implementations, software factories, and application blocks.

## Written Guidance

The written guidance, also referred to as *guides*, gives real-world best-practice guidelines for developing your application. You can view the guides online, or if you prefer, you can get them in a printed format. The guides cover topics such as data access, security, integration, design patterns, smart client development, and exception management. The guides are constantly evolving in order to keep pace with changing technologies and industry best practices. The guides are essentially the white papers used to create the reference implementations and application blocks.

### Examples of Guides

The following are some of the guides available on the website at
http://msdn.microsoft.com/practices/:

- *.NET Data Access Architecture*: Describes the best practices for accessing and storing data in a multitiered application environment

- *Application Interoperability: Microsoft .NET and J2EE*: Provides best practices in designing interoperable applications between Microsoft .NET and J2EE, thus allowing organizations to leverage these technologies together

- *Caching Architecture Guide for .NET Framework Applications*: Provides best-practice guidance for all aspects of caching within .NET applications

- *Data Patterns*: Contains industry best-practice methodology for handling common data problems such as the complex issues revolving around data replication within an organization

- *Deploying .NET Framework-based Applications*: Provides industry best practices in deploying your .NET applications as well as discussions about .NET-specific technologies that can assist in the deployment process

- *Designing Application-Managed Authorization*: Focuses on common authorization tasks that may come up in a typical application and how to best approach these tasks using the .NET Framework

- *Designing Data Tier Components and Passing Data Through Tiers*: Discusses best practices in exposing and handling data in between application layers or physical tiers in order to facilitate distributed applications

- *Enterprise Solution Patterns Using Microsoft .NET*: Provides guidance in applying enterprise solution patterns based on community-accepted patterns and solution patterns cooked up by Microsoft

- *Exception Management in .NET*: Provides best-practice suggestions in handling exceptions with a .NET application such as the centralization and notification of exceptions on an enterprise level

- *Integration Patterns*: Discusses 18 common integration patterns and implementations used within a specific sample scenario

- *Smart Client Architecture and Design Guide*: Describes how to overcome design issues and architectural challenges when building smart client applications as well as how to combine the benefits of rich client applications with the manageability of thin client applications

- *Testing Software Patterns*: Describes the best industry techniques in developing testing patterns

---

**Note** You can find the current Microsoft practices and patterns guides at http://msdn.microsoft.com/practices/guidetype/Guides/default.aspx.

---

## Guidance Explorer

Another new feature offered by the Patterns & Practices group that relates to guides is the Guidance Explorer. The Guidance Explorer is an application that allows an organization to easily organize best practices and application development policies into an easily navigable application. The best practices and application development policies come in two flavors: guidance and checklists. A *guidance* includes specific scenarios that define a potential problem and how to resolve the problem. A *checklist* defines how to look for a particular problem and how it can be fixed. The most common difference between the two is that a guidance is a proactive attempt at helping to ensure best practices are used such as during the beginning of developing an application, and a checklist is a reactive attempt at helping to ensure best practices are used such as during code reviews. Figure 2-1 shows the Guidance Explorer user interface.

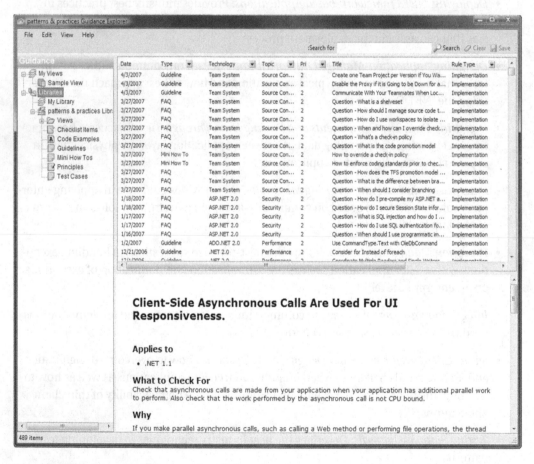

**Figure 2-1.** *Guidance Explorer user interface*

At the time of this writing, the Guidance Explorer was still in beta. However, the Guidance Explorer does contain many features such as the ability to search based on attributes such as topic, type, category, and source; the ability to filter and sort on specific columns in the grid view; and the ability to add guidance that can be defined by an organization or other industry sources. The guidance data is stored in an XML format that can easily be created, imported, and exported. The tool also allows for specific views of the data to be saved, imported, and exported, thus allowing specific views of the data to be recalled easily. This can be important for defining specific views of guidance depending on a specific person's role and responsibility within the application's development life cycle.

---

**Tip** The Guidance Explorer's import feature can be especially useful because it allows an organization to easily sort and share best-practice knowledge of not only technology but also of internal and industry-specific information throughout the development team.

---

## Software Factories

The software factories are a newer concept that allow an organization to develop end-to-end solutions for a particular type of application. At the time of writing this book, six software factories are available:

- Guidance Automation Toolkit
- Smart Client Software Factory
- Mobile Client Software Factory
- Web Client Software Factory
- Web Service Software Factory
- Application Block Software Factory

### Guidance Automation Toolkit

The Guidance Automation Toolkit (GAT) is an extension developed for Visual Studio 2005 that allows an organization to define specific assets to be used when developing an application. It essentially creates the necessary code using a guidance package that can dictate which specific assets are to be used when developing an application. These assets can include guidance (best practices), patterns, components, and frameworks. Generally, an architect will define the guidance packages for a specific organization and then distribute the guidance to the developer's development environments. The developers would then use these guidance packages when developing components for applications. You can find more information about GAT at http://msdn.microsoft.com/vstudio/teamsystem/Workshop/gat/.

### Smart Client Software Factory

The Smart Client Software Factory contains a specific GAT implementation that stubs out the creation of a smart client application. You can then customize this GAT to meet an organization's requirements for user interface design and the overall look and feel of an application. This software factory utilizes the Composite UI Application Block, which is discussed in Chapter 15, to create the user interface experience. You can use this software factory right out of the box, but most organizations will find it better suits their specific needs after making some tweaks.

### Mobile Client Software Factory

The Mobile Client Software Factory is a mobile version of the Smart Client Software Factory. It also contains a specific GAT implementation for creating mobile applications, but it contains special application block components specifically for a mobile device. The Mobile Client Software Factory also includes a special build of ObjectBuilder that is tailored to mobile devices.

### Web Client Software Factory

The Web Client Software Factory is much like the Smart Client Software Factory except that it is tailored to building web applications on top of the ASP.NET 2.0 platform. The offering includes two application blocks, one called the Web Composite Application Block and the other called the Page Flow Application Block.

### Web Service Software Factory

The Web Service Software Factory provides guidance, code, and patterns useful for creating web services using solid architectural guidance.

---

■**Note**  The application blocks included with the Smart Client Software Factory, Mobile Client Software Factory, and Web Client Software Factory are listed later in this chapter and are described in detail in Chapter 15.

---

### Application Block Software Factory

The Application Block Software Factory is a new factory that is included with Enterprise Library 3.0 - April 2007 release. This software factory allows for the development of new application blocks using predetermined guidance packages to help simplify the development process. Chapter 14 describes how to use the Application Block Software Factory.

## Reference Implementations

The reference implementations provide executable sample applications containing source code that can be used to show examples about the best-practice guidance. The reference implementations available at the time of writing this book are contained within the following four software factory offerings:

- Mobile Client Software Factory

- Web Client Software Factory

- Smart Client Software Factory

- Web Service Software Factory

# The Original Application Blocks

The application blocks are reusable, open source components that help developers resolve commonplace challenges found in applications of all varieties. These challenges can include dealing with the repetition of code and trying to figure out the best practice in implementing a specific Microsoft technology. The application blocks are essentially the implementations of the patterns and practices guides.

During the creation of an application block component, some careful considerations were made in the design. The Patterns & Practices group has four major design goals it has tried to achieve since the first release of the original application blocks: ease of use, consistency in design, integration, and extensibility. As with any project, some things don't always come out as perfect as one would hope; however, with each iteration of the application block components, the Patterns & Practices group has been achieving better success at accomplishing these goals.

The original application blocks were the initial Patterns & Practices group offerings for the .NET Framework 1.0 and 1.1 environments. They contained configurable components to handle data access, data aggregation, application configuration, exception handling, caching, asynchronous invocation, logging, application updates, and user interface handling. Together these components can create many of the support services required to complete an enterprise framework. All that is needed is to create your own domain layer, or if you hunt around on the Web, you can find some popular frameworks and components that specialize solely in the domain layer components and design.

Note that the application blocks are not considered a Microsoft "product"; they are considered a "guidance offering." This means application blocks are shipped "as is" and without warranty; however, it is possible to obtain support. It is suggested that the developer community should support each other. Also, there is no guarantee that one version of a guidance offering will be compatible with the next version, because guidance recommendations can change from one platform version to the next. The way you did something in the past might not be the most efficient way to do something today.

On the upside, a guidance offering adheres to the best practices that are available for a particular platform. You can extend a guidance offering via its extension points and configuration settings, and since it also comes with the source code, you can just modify the source directly.

Lastly, it is important to note that these guidance offerings will have a three- to six-month development life cycle. Hence, a new offering will be made every three to six months. This will help make sure you are getting the best possible guidance for your application development needs.

## Data Access Application Block

The Data Access Application Block implements a class called SqlHelper, which is a data access helper component. The SqlHelper class simplifies execution statements against SQL Server 7.0 and newer by exposing a set of static methods and reducing the amount of code required to perform the specific function. Another class, SqlHelperParameterCache, assists the SqlHelper class by caching the SqlParameter objects so that they can be repeatedly reused without having to be re-created. SqlHelperParameterCache even has the ability to query a stored procedure and return a SqlParameters collection, which is needed to interact with it. Although overall this does not increase the performance of the application, it does make it easier to accommodate minor changes made to stored procedures without having to change your code. An example of this might be modifying a parameter to be a varchar(20) as opposed to a varchar(10). No code modifications would be necessary; simply just restart the application to force a refresh of the SQL parameters.

There are two versions of this component: 1.0 and 2.0. Version 2.0 adds support for filling a typed dataset and has other minor improvements. One of the major limitations of this component is that it works only with the .NET SqlClient data provider; hence, it is useful only with Microsoft SQL Server.

---

■**Note** The Data Access Application Block was designed based on the recommendations made in the *.NET Data Access Architecture* guide.

---

## Exception Management Application Block

The Exception Management Application Block provides an easy-to-use and flexible infrastructure for publishing exception information in an application. This application block also supports filtering and creating your own custom exception publishers. The custom exception publishers along with the filtering support will allow you to publish specific exception data to different data storage locations such as a file system, email, and database. For example, if you're publishing a general exception to a database and the exception comes from the SqlClientException class, you could then publish the data to a local XML or text file on disk.

The Exception Management Application Block revolves around the ExceptionManager class. This class is responsible for taking an exception and publishing it to any location you want. It does this by using entries in the application configuration file to define custom publishers that you can write, or if there aren't any publishers created, it will use the built-in default publisher to write to the local machine's Application event log. In the application configuration file, you can specify which publishers you want to log to, and you can also specify specific exceptions to be published only to specific custom exception publishers. For example, say you use SQL Server to publish all of your exceptions. But what if SQL Server is the problem and you cannot connect to it? Well, then you can create a special publisher exception that can take all connection-related exceptions and publish them to a text file or the local event log. It does this by looking at the type of exception that is being published.

---

■**Note** The Exception Management Application Block provides the BaseApplicationException class from which it contains extra environment data that can be published as is, or you can derive from it, add your own exception data to it, and publish your custom exception class.

---

## Asynchronous Invocation Application Block

The Asynchronous Invocation Application Block is a dispatcher component that manages and dispatches background threads and then notifies the application when the threads have completed their tasks. In the .NET Framework 2.0 and 3.0 worlds, the need for this application block has been diminished by the new BackgroundWorker component, but if you are still developing or maintaining a .NET 1.1 or 1.0 application, you should take a look at this application block. This application block utilizes the Exception Management and Data Access Application Blocks. It can be used alone or with the Aggregation and Caching Application Blocks mentioned next.

## Aggregation Application Block

The Aggregation Application Block can complement the Asynchronous Invocation Application Block well. This block, utilizing the Asynchronous Invocation Application Block, dispatches multiple service agents that then go out and retrieve data back into a single XML document that is then returned to the application. This can be used in both Windows and web applications to give the appearance of a more responsive application. You can also use this component with the Caching Application Block for caching purposes as well as the Asynchronous Invocation Block for thread dispatching. Finally, note that this component utilizes the Exception Management Application Block for exception management.

## Caching Application Block

You can use the Caching Application Block alone or with the Aggregation and Asynchronous Invocation Application Blocks. This block provides the mechanisms to manage relatively static information for an application via a cache manager. The cached data can be stored as memory-mapped files, within a singleton object, or even in SQL Server. You can also force refreshes of the cached data as well as expiration timeouts of the cached data. Underneath the hood, like the Asynchronous Invocation Application Block, this block uses the Exception Management and Data Access Application Blocks. You'd typically use this application block only for Windows forms, Windows services, and other non-ASP.NET applications, since ASP.NET already provides its own cache mechanism.

## Configuration Management Application Block

The Configuration Management Application Block excels in storing, managing, and securing application configuration data and metadata. This component essentially abstracts how and where the data is stored, thus allowing an application to store data in any format necessary. Examples of data storage types include the following:

- XML document
- Microsoft SQL Server
- INI file

This component also encrypts configuration data, caches configuration data, and handles application exceptions that can occur. Thus, you can protect sensitive information such as usernames and passwords used for databases or web services, and you can cache frequently used information. The cache mechanism also contains expiration features. The nicest feature of this component is that it has the ability to write data, not just read it. With all these features comes a slight price; it is not as easy as using `System.Configuration.AppSettings` to store data in the configuration file, but after a little practice, using this component should not be a problem.

## Updater Application Block

The Updater Application Block is a component that can be used to download new versions of applications. It includes a manifest to specify which files to download, it ensures the entire application is downloaded properly, and it contains optional file verification mechanisms. This component comes with a Background Intelligent Transfer Service (BITS) downloader component, but it can be extended to support custom verification and downloading components. It is important to note that this application block utilizes the Exception Manager Application Block to manage exceptions.

■**Note** BITS provides for the uploading and downloading of files between two computers. You can use it in the foreground or background to exchange files asynchronously while allowing other network applications to be responsive. It also has the ability to restart a file transfer automatically in the event it was prematurely interrupted.

## User Interface Process Application Block

The User Interface Process Application Block provides a base class called `ControllerBase` and the User Interface Process Manager component; these allow you to separate the logic and state of the user process from the user interface. This in theory allows for application navigation, application state, and data validation to be performed independently of the type of user interface used. This component also includes multiple persistence managers that allow you to save the state of the process in a SQL Server database, save it in an ASP.NET session, or store it in a custom component.

## Smart Client Offline Application Block

The Smart Client Offline Application Block is a component that allows you to create applications that are connected to online servers only some of the time. Basically, it allows the application to function normally even when disconnected. A perfect example of an application requiring this kind of capability is a CRM application or a personal information manager such as Microsoft Outlook. You want the salesperson to be able to download new contacts, messages, and appointments. Then the salesperson can disconnect from the application servers, go to his clients, and update contact information. Finally, at the end of the day, the salesperson can connect to the application servers and synchronize contacts, messages, and appointments.

# Enterprise Library for .NET Framework 1.1 Overview

The original set of application blocks was a successful set of components widely used in the .NET development community; they are still used to this day. Like the original application blocks, the core design requirements of Enterprise Library for .NET Framework 1.1 revolved around four major goals: ease of use, consistency in design, integration, and extensibility. The Patterns & Practices group also wanted to make sure that Enterprise Library was not designed for any one specific architecture.

The development community has evolved some of the components such as the Data Access Application Block, and the Microsoft patterns & practices group has updated others such as the Updater Application Block. However, like anything else, once something is built and used by others, feedback and suggestions start rolling in. Soon it is easy to see what the strong points are and what the weak points are of a particular product.

One of the more common requests made by the development community with the first set of application blocks was to make the overall design more consistent. Yes, the first set of application blocks used best-practice techniques and offered a lot of value, but the detailed designs and architectures between the different components were sometimes different. Another request made was to offer a better way to configure the components; most of the time you had to go into the application configuration file, and after a while, the application configuration file got very big and difficult to maintain. This was very apparent when trying to manage environment-related settings.

In January 2005, a new set of application blocks was introduced to the public. This time the application blocks were designed as a joint effort between Microsoft and Avanade (http://www.avanade.com), and many things had changed in the design of them. These new sets of application blocks are now called the Enterprise Library application blocks. These Enterprise Library application blocks (sometimes referred to as simply Enterprise Library) are the next evolution of application blocks for the Microsoft patterns & practices group. The Enterprise Library was built with the intention of offering a consistent design, simpler configuration, and robust extensibility all the while still utilizing the industry's best practices. Currently, there are four versions of Enterprise Library: Enterprise Library for .NET Framework 1.1 (January 2005 and June 2005 releases), Enterprise Library for .NET Framework 2.0 (January 2006), and Enterprise Library for .NET Framework 3.0 (January 2007).

## January 2005 Release

The first version of Enterprise Library (also sometimes known as the 1.0 version) was first released in January 2005. In this release, the number of application block components was actually reduced from the original blocks. The components excluded with the 1.0 release were the User Interface Process, Updater, Asynchronous Invocation, Aggregation, and Smart Client Offline Application Blocks. However, Enterprise Library 1.0 has added two new components: the Cryptography Application Block and the Security Application Block. The reasoning behind reducing the number of application blocks came from the desire to change the focus of Enterprise Library.

---

■**Note**  The Updater Application Block has been ported to leverage Enterprise Library for .NET Framework 2.0.

---

For the User Interface Process, Updater, and Smart Client Offline Application Blocks, the Patterns & Practices group wanted Enterprise Library to be a generic application framework that could be used in any type of architecture, whether it was service-oriented, object-oriented, or some other architecture. With this in mind, the group opted to focus on the business tiers of the application for the core set of application blocks. This, however, does not mean you will not be able to find application blocks for the presentation tier, but they will not be part of the core set of components that will come with Enterprise Library 1.0.

As for the Asynchronous Invocation and Aggregation Application Blocks, there was never a strong demand for these components when they were released as part of the original application blocks. Even though these components could make sense as part of the core Enterprise Library application blocks, the Patterns & Practices group decided to stay focused on the more common needs and leave these two components out of the core set of components.

The following is a list of components provided in Enterprise Library 1.0:

- Configuration Application Block

- Data Access Application Block

- Caching Application Block

- Exception Handling Application Block

- Logging and Instrumentation Application Block

- Security Application Block

- Cryptography Application Block

The January 2005 release included these seven application blocks, and it also introduced some new utilities to ease the management of Enterprise Library throughout the different stages of application development. This utility is called the Enterprise Library Configuration Tool, and it allows you to configure the application blocks to properly fit your application and environment needs.

## June 2005 Release

The June 2005 release (also sometimes known as the 1.1 version) did not introduce new components into Enterprise Library. Instead, this version made Enterprise Library compatible with the .NET 2.0 Framework and included a few bug fixes and performance tweaks. Because of the bug fixes made in the June 2005 release, the January 2005 release is no longer available for download from the Microsoft website. The good news is you should be able to upgrade the January 2005 release without any major issues to the June 2005 release. If you would rather keep the January 2005 release, just make sure you go to the Enterprise Library community website and download the patches available for the January 2005 release.

---

■**Note**  You can find the Enterprise Library community site on GotDotNet.com's website
(http://www.gotdotnet.com).

---

It is important to note that although version 1.1 will work with the .NET Framework 2.0, it
was not specifically tuned or designed for .NET 2.0. Testing had not occurred with this release
and the .NET Framework 3.0. The purpose of this upgrade was to allow for a smoother transition of existing application components that were written in the .NET Framework 1.1 into the
.NET 2.0 world. However, any new development with the .NET Framework 2.0 or 3.0 should
utilize the next version of Enterprise Library as opposed to the June 2005 release.

---

■**Note**  Although the 1.1 June release may work with the .NET Framework 3.0, since testing was not
performed with 1.1 and .NET Framework 3.0, issues might arise.

---

# Enterprise Library for .NET Framework 2.0 Overview

With any major upgrade of the .NET Framework, there is no doubt that Enterprise Library will
also need to undergo extensive changes. The Patterns & Practices group's answer to the .NET
Framework 2.0 is Enterprise Library for the .NET Framework 2.0.

The application blocks that were available in version 1.0 and version 1.1 are here in some
form or another; however, don't expect the same code underneath the hood. A lot of the application blocks have been overhauled to leverage the new features of the .NET Framework 2.0.
In fact, how you use some of the components has changed. If you are currently using Enterprise Library for .NET 1.1, you might have to make some changes within your application to
be able to utilize them. Even more important in the end, the Patterns & Practices group made
sure Enterprise Library for .NET Framework 2.0 application blocks fully utilized .NET 2.0 best
practices and development techniques.

The Enterprise Library for .NET Framework 2.0 now truly contains only six core application blocks. The Configuration Application Block is no longer a separate application block,
and the instrumentation features in Enterprise Library for .NET Framework 1.1 of the Logging
and Instrumentation Application Block have been relocated.

The Configuration Application Block in Enterprise Library for .NET Framework 2.0 has
had some major overhauling. The .NET Framework 2.0 introduced some major changes in the
System.Configuration namespace. These changes have allowed for greater configuration flexibility in all applications and components based on the .NET Framework 2.0. With these
changes to the System.Configuration namespace, it was decided for all the Enterprise Library
application blocks to utilize these new configuration features in .NET 2.0. However, this does
not mean the Enterprise Library Configuration Tool has gone away, and you can still use the
configuration helper classes in the Common assembly.

The Logging and Instrumentation Application Block is now just referred to as the Logging Application Block. The instrumentation features have been pulled out of this component and put into the Common assembly. In Enterprise Library for .NET Framework 2.0, instrumentation has been enhanced, and it now allows you to control which types of instrumentation to enable and disable. By default, all instrumentation features are disabled for the application blocks and need to be manually turned on by the Enterprise Library Configuration Tool, also known as the *configuration console*.

## Data Access Application Block

The Data Access Application Block has gone through some retooling. In this version, more has been done to allow for improved consistency and ease of use. Here are a few important changes:

- You can utilize your application configuration file to store connection strings, or you can specify connection strings in your code.

- The API has been simplified to utilize the ADO.NET's DbCommand class, as opposed to the DbCommandWrapper class of prior versions.

- You can use the Data Access Application Block with any ADO .NET 2.0 data provider via the GenericDatabase class.

The changes made to the Data Access Application Block helped simplify and improve efficiency when working with data storage providers.

This application block is meant to handle a majority of your data access needs. Another way to put it is that you will probably find situations were it might be difficult and/or cumbersome to actually use the Data Access Application Block in a particular scenario. If you find yourself in this predicament, you will have to ask yourself three questions:

- Is this a one-off situation, or will this situation occur repeatedly during application development?

- How much effort will it take to enhance the Data Access Application Block to accommodate your specific scenario?

- Will the new features added actually improve productivity, efficiency, or performance?

Each application development environment will have different answers to the previous questions. Based on those answers, you will have a solid understanding of whether you really need to modify the application block or just code using the native features of ADO .NET 2.0 to handle your specific situation.

## Caching Application Block

The Caching Application Block has mostly gone through performance and design tweaks in Enterprise Library. Like its pre–Enterprise Library predecessor, data can be persisted to a database or other storage mechanism to help survive application restarts. The Caching Application Block is also thread-safe, ensuring that the in-memory cache and the persisted data store stay synchronized. In addition, your multithreaded applications can call the cache without all the potential issues that can arise from calling a single object from multiple threads.

When using the Caching Application Block, note that you should use it only if you need to persist data to some permanent data store; otherwise, the Patterns & Practices group recommends, and I agree, that you should use the built-in caching features found in the System.Web.Caching namespace. Hence, in .NET 2.0+, you can use the System.Web.Caching namespace outside ASP .NET 2.0.

## Exception Handling Application Block

Enterprise Library has introduced many new features into the world of exception management in the .NET environment. The pre–Enterprise Library Exception Management Application Block essentially just logged an exception to a specific sink such as a database, a text file, or the Window's Application event log. This time the Patterns & Practices group has opted to shift the focus of the Exception Handling Application Block in Enterprise Library. Now this application block is focused more on the handling aspect via policies as opposed to simply logging them.

## Logging Application Block

The Logging Application Block has become more inline with .NET 2.0 by simplifying the design to allow for easier integration with System.Diagnostics features. Also, many performance enhancements have been added to this application block. Here is a list of some of the new features:

- It's configurable via the Enterprise Library Configuration Tool.

- It can be used with any .NET TraceListener or Enterprise Library Listener, or you can build a custom listener.

- One LogEntry instance can have multiple categories as opposed to one.

These enhancements plus others provided in the Logging Application Block allow for greater flexibility and ease of use.

## Security Application Block

The Security Application Block when originally released in Enterprise Library for .NET Framework 1.1 provided functionality to simplify and handle authentication, authorization, role management, profile management, and caching principles. In the .NET Framework 1.1, these features were not readily available or simple to use out of the box.

The Security Application Block in Enterprise Library for .NET Framework 2.0 has also been trimmed down. These new features in the 2.0 version of the .NET Framework make the interfaces, factories, and providers for authentication; role management; and profile management features that were provided in Enterprise Library for .NET Framework 1.1 obsolete. However, the authorization and security caching interfaces, factories, and providers are still present in Enterprise Library for .NET Framework 2.0 and 3.0.

## Cryptography Application Block

In Enterprise Library for .NET Framework 1.1, the Cryptography Application Block was included to help simplify the developers' need to handle encryption in their applications, while still providing a consistent, simplified approach. The Cryptography Application Block supports all .NET cryptography algorithms out of the box, and it is possible to create your own cryptography components. The block even can handle the Data Protection API (DPAPI) provided by the Win32 API.

# Enterprise Library 3.0 Overview

Now here comes Enterprise Library 3.0; as you have probably guessed, it is intended to take advantage of the new .NET Framework 3.0 features, but may be used with the .NET Framework 2.0 as well. This new version of the .NET Framework is not a major overhaul like from version 1.1 to 2.0. Instead, this version adds a lot of new features without changing much of the existing components of the .NET Framework 2.0. Some of these new features include the following:

- Windows Presentation Framework

- Windows Communication Framework

- Windows Workflow Foundation

- Windows CardSpace

Enterprise Library 3.0 adds new functionality and integration to go with these new features of the .NET Framework 3.0. It also does not introduce any breaking changes from Enterprise Library for .NET Framework 2.0. Currently there are two versions of Enterprise Library 3.0. Enterprise Library 3.0 - April 2007 release and Enterprise Library 3.1 - May 2007 release. The 3.1 version includes some fixes to the original 3.0 and an enhancement to the Policy Injection Application Block. For simplicity sake all versions of Enterprise Library 3.x will be referred to as simply Enterprise Library 3.0 in this book.

## Validation Application Block

The Validation Application Block will allow developers to create validation rules that can be applied in the code to implicitly or explicitly validate properties and parameters. It will even support named validation, which allows a validation rule to be defined in the application configuration file and allows it to be applied to wherever the named validation rule is enforced within an application. This can give the application the flexibility to change rules applied to many fields in one central location without having to rebuild the application.

## Policy Injection Application Block

The Policy Injection Application Block enables the policy-driven externalization of functionality and behaviors. You can specify policies (through configuration) that invoke functionality such as validation, exception handling, or logging, and you can attach these policies to specific types and methods in your applications through predicates, such as "All classes in the My.Application namespace" or "All methods with MyClass objects as parameters."

This allows the developer to create an application and then define which tasks or polices will be applied to the code via configuration data. This can be useful for specifying specific types of policies for different stages of the application's life cycle.

# Application Blocks That Are Not Core

In addition to the core application blocks in Enterprise Library for .NET Framework 2.0 and Enterprise Library 3.0, the Practices and Patterns has created other application blocks. Some of these application blocks are available as separate downloads, and others are part of software factory offerings. The other application blocks include the following:

- *Composite UI Application Block*: This application block provides a framework based on .NET 2.0 that allows you to build complex UIs using industry best practices. The application block is part of the Smart Client Software Factory, or it can be downloaded independently.

- *Updater Application Block*: The Updater Application Block provides a mechanism for updating smart client applications.

- *Composite Web Application Block*: This application block allows you to create complex web client applications that are built upon ASP.NET 2.0. This application block is part of the Web Client Software Factory offering.

- *Page Flow Application Block*: This application block provides a mechanism for managing page-flow processing for simple or complex workflow scenarios. This application block is included with the Web Client Software Factory offering.

- *Mobile Composite Application Block*: This provides a framework for building mobile UI clients on mobile devices. This application block is part of the Mobile Client Software Factory.

- *Mobile Data Access Block*: Like its Enterprise Library counterpart, this provides functionality for simplifying data access on a mobile device. You can find this application block within the Mobile Client Software Factory offering.

- *Mobile Configuration Block*: This is included with the Mobile Client Software Factory offering, and it provides functionality for managing configuration data on a mobile device.

- *Mobile Connection Monitor Block*: This application block provides functionality for monitoring network connections and services to allow mobile application to switch from online to offline mode. This application block is also part of the Mobile Client Software Factory offering.

- *Mobile Data Subscription Block*: This application block helps create SQL Mobile replication scripts. This application block is included with the Mobile Client Software Factory offering.

- *Mobile Disconnected Service Agent Block*: This application block provides a mechanism for storing offline web service requests and later executing them when the mobile device can connect to the web service. This application block is included with the Mobile Client Software Factory offering.

- *Mobile Endpoint Catalog Block*: This application block provides features that help manage the physical address and associated metadata with remote services that can be consumed by a mobile application. This application block is included with the Mobile Client Software Factory offering.

- *Orientation Aware Control Block*: This application block helps build mobile device user interfaces by assisting the user interface in handling screen orientation, form factors, resolutions, and cultural settings. This application block is included with the Mobile Client Software Factory offering.

- *Password Authentication Block*: This application block is included with the Mobile Client Software Factory offering and provides functionality to authenticate users, encrypt data, and store data.

All of the application blocks that were created outside Enterprise Library still use the same fundamental concepts as the core Enterprise Library application blocks. In fact, some of these noncore application blocks such as the Composite UI Application utilize the same core components such as ObjectBuilder.

**Note**  You can find more in-depth details about these application blocks in Chapter 15.

# Using Enterprise Library

To continue with the rest of this book, it is important to install Enterprise Library for .NET Framework 3.0. The following sections guide you through the installation process.

**Note**  It is possible to install Enterprise Library only for .NET Framework 2.0; however, you will not be able to utilize Enterprise Library 3.0–specific features such as  WCF support in the Exception Handling Application Block.

## Before You Install

Before installing Enterprise Library, it is important to make sure that the operating system and software on the target computer meets the following requirements:

- *All environments*:

  - Microsoft Windows 2000, Microsoft Windows XP, or Microsoft Windows Server 2003

  - Microsoft .NET Framework 3.0

  - Microsoft SQL Server or another database is required for some application blocks that require database interaction

- *Development environments*:

    - Microsoft Visual Studio 2005 Standard Edition or greater

    - Microsoft Visual Studio 2005 Team System role-based editions, Microsoft Visual Studio 2005 Team Suite, or NUnit 2.2 for unit testing.

## Installing Enterprise Library

For the development environment, the first step is to download Enterprise Library 3.1 - May 2007 release from the MSDN Patterns & Practices website (http://msdn.microsoft.com/practices/). Once you've downloaded them, you can go ahead and execute the MSI setup program. The only major options you have in the installation are to choose the installation location, which components to install, and whether you want to include the source code during installation. Generally speaking, you will always want the source code installed and want to have the installation program compile it for you. Even if you don't use all the application blocks in your own applications, it is a good idea to have the source as a reference. Also, so that it is easier to follow along with this book, please install all the components, and select the Compile option.

---

■**Note** If you find yourself having any issue during installation, or for that matter any issues with Enterprise Library, visit http://www.codeplex.com/entlib for the latest known issues and community support.

---

Deploying Enterprise Library 3.0 in production environments can easily be accomplished with Xcopy deployment techniques, even in low-level privilege environments such as ASP.NET applications. ClickOnce is another viable option for Enterprise Library distribution. Of course, if you want a pretty install package, you can still create an MSI project in Visual Studio 2005 and add Enterprise Library as one of the dependencies for your application as you would any other installation dependency.

## Getting the ACME Cosmetics Point-of-Sales Application Setup

Now that all the necessary software including Visual Studio 2005 and Enterprise Library have been installed on your machine, it will help to download and compile the ACME Cosmetics Point-of-Sales Application source code to follow along with the samples in this book. The samples within the book will not always contain all the code necessary to make a particular component compile. Hence, without the source code, trying and testing the samples will be difficult.

---

■**Note** You can find the current source for the ACME Cosmetics Point-of-Sales Application on the Apress website (http://www.apress.com).

---

# Summary

In summary, this chapter went over the past and present Microsoft offerings from its Patterns & Practices group. This includes the guides, reference implementations, software factories, and application block components. Because this book primarily focuses on Enterprise Library 3.0 application block components, the other offerings are just as important and are worth understanding and possibly implementing within your own environment. Also, although this book concentrates on Enterprise Library 3.0, there are no breaking changes between the 2.0 and 3.0 versions of Enterprise Library. Most of the content on the application blocks will also apply to Enterprise Library for .NET Framework 2.0, unless otherwise noted.

The next chapter will provide a high-level overview of the application block components contained in Enterprise Library 3.0. Reading the next chapter will help you determine which application block components could be useful in your applications. This way, you can skip to the chapters that you have a specific interest in. However, if you plan on going through the sample application provided with this book, you should read each chapter in order; the application adds components in each chapter, so it might have dependencies on a prior chapter's components.

# CHAPTER 3

■ ■ ■

# The Design of the Enterprise Library Application Blocks

**S**ince the inception of the original application blocks that Microsoft released over a period of several years beginning in 2002, many changes have taken place. These changes have made Microsoft's current Enterprise Library one of the best practices and patterns offerings yet. It contains the industry's best and standard practices, and the Microsoft patterns & practices group has been taking direct community feedback on the overall design of the components within the Enterprise Library.

This chapter describes some of the specific patterns and design considerations used in creating the Enterprise Library application blocks. It is important to understand the different patterns and designs used in order to fully appreciate the Enterprise Library architecture. This chapter will also cover the extensibility features and services provided for the Enterprise Library, the application block conceptual architecture, unit testing, and migrating from earlier versions of Enterprise Library. Finally, you'll set up the sample application we'll use in this book.

## Overall Design of the Enterprise Library

The Enterprise Library developers have set out to kill two best-practice birds with one stone. First, best practices are demonstrated in the overall design of the application blocks. Second, Enterprise Library provides context-specific guidelines in the design of the individual application blocks. Thus, you not only get to see how to create an overall infrastructure to support the application blocks, but you can also see the Microsoft patterns & practices group's suggested best practices for each application block. The upcoming chapters devoted to the specific application blocks will detail the best practices used to create them. This chapter will go into some of the reasoning behind the overall practices to create the infrastructure for the application blocks.

Enterprise Library uses a series of design patterns to support the design of the overall application block offering. Patterns provide common solutions to needs that come up repeatedly throughout the development cycle of an application. Using patterns makes the development cycle more productive by allowing for simple solutions that do the job, provide a common "language" that can be shared among developers and architects, allow for consistency in the developed solution, and enable reuse.

The three major patterns used in Enterprise Library are the Factory pattern, Plug-in pattern, and Dependency Injection pattern. The application blocks also use many other patterns, but these three are common themes throughout the Enterprise Library components.

## Factory Pattern

Software developers spend a lot of time considering the design and modeling of objects, and in a lot of scenarios, it is common to instantiate these objects directly. Although this is perhaps the easiest method to create an object, it is not always the best way.

In the industry of technology and software development, change is a common occurrence. Although this can lead to exciting times, it can also create havoc when you need to update existing software applications. One way to mitigate the challenges of modifying an existing application is to abstract the different components used within an application. The *Factory pattern*, a creational pattern, is used to create concrete objects through an abstract object. Another way to look at it is that the "client" will use the "factory" to retrieve a final "product."

You can find the Factory pattern used extensively within the .NET Framework, such as the CreateDomain method of the System.AppDomain class and the CreateInstance method of the System.Array class. Listing 3-1 shows an example of the Factory pattern.

**Listing 3-1.** *Factory Pattern Example*

```
//interface that all concrete classes must implement
public interface IDemo
{
    string DemoType
    {
        get;
    }

}

//implementation of IDemo interface
public class AlphaDemo :IDemo
{
    private string m_Type;

    public AlphaDemo()
    {
        m_Type = "Alpha";
    }

    //should return Alpha
    public string DemoType
    {
        get
        {
```

```csharp
            return m_Type;
        }
    }
}

//BetaDemo implementation of IDemo interface
public class BetaDemo : IDemo
{
    private string m_Type;

    public BetaDemo()
    {
        m_Type = "Beta";
    }

    //should return Beta
    public string DemoType
    {
        get
        {
            return m_Type;
        }
    }
}

//DeltaDemo implementation of IDemo interface
public class DeltaDemo : IDemo
{
    private string m_Type;

    public DeltaDemo()
    {
        m_Type = "Delta";
    }

    //should return Delta
    public string DemoType
    {
        get
        {
            return m_Type;
        }
    }
}

public class MyDemoFactory
{
```

```
    public static IDemo CreateInstance(string instanceType)
    {
        IDemo myDemo;

        switch(instanceType)
        {
            case "beta" :
                myDemo = new BetaDemo();
                break;

            case "delta" :
                myDemo = new DeltaDemo();
                break;

            default :
                //alpha type
                myDemo = new AlphaDemo();
                break;
        }

        return myDemo;
    }
}

public class MyDemo
{
    [STAThread]
    public static void Main(string[] args)
    {
        IDemo currentDemo;

        currentDemo = MyDemoFactory.CreateInstance("alpha");
        //should return Alpha
        Console.WriteLine(currentDemo.DemoType);

        currentDemo = MyDemoFactory.CreateInstance("delta");
        //should return Delta
        Console.WriteLine(currentDemo.DemoType);
        Console.Read();
    }
}
```

This example will output Alpha and then Delta in a console window, as shown in Figure 3-1.

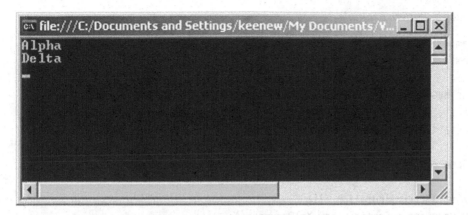

**Figure 3-1.** *Factory pattern example console output*

As you can see, you could have many variants of a particular interface and determine which variant of a class you want to return. This could be useful for developing a data access layer for an application and ensuring that the data access layer abstracts the specific data access provider through a Factory pattern implementation. The example in Listing 3-1 also uses an interface to provide the different invariant interfaces to the MyDemo class. It is possible to use an abstract class to perform the same function. In fact, abstract classes could provide common functionality and provide a better mechanism for handling versioning over an interface.

## Plug-in Pattern

Another pattern that is used in Enterprise Library application blocks is the *Plug-in pattern*. This pattern allows for extending the behavior of an existing class to suit a specific need by defining the correct instance outside the existing class.

Reconsidering Listing 3-1, suppose that the appropriate IDemo instance returned is to be determined by an environment variable. Say there are ten environments that need ten different instances of IDemo. To support that, ten different case statements would be required within the switch state of the CreateInstance method. Although this wouldn't be that difficult to handle in this scenario, imagine an enterprise scenario where there could be hundreds of factories returning different instances. One way to prevent this type of maintenance headache is to use the Plug-in pattern. Now the correct component can be determined at runtime, based on a configuration file provided for the specific environment. In this case, a Factory pattern could still be used, but a demoType would not be passed in as a parameter of the CreateInstance method. Instead, the CreateInstance method would look at a configuration file to determine the appropriate IDemo instance to create. Listings 3-2 and 3-3 show an example of this.

**Listing 3-2.** *Plug-in Pattern Configuration Example*

```
<myDemoConfig>
    <object type="MyDemo.AlphaDemo" assembly="MyDemo"/>
</myDemoConfig>
```

**Listing 3-3.** *Plug-in Pattern Example*

```
using System.Reflection;
using System.Xml;

public class MyDemoFactory
{
    public static IDemo CreateInstance()
    {
        IDemo myDemo;

        //Get XML configuration file
        XmlDocument myConfig = new XmlDocument();
        myConfig.Load("c:\\myConfig.xml");
        XmlElement objectElement =
            myConfig.DocumentElement.FirstChild as XmlElement;

        //Get assembly and create instance
        Assembly myAssembly =
            Assembly.Load(objectElement.GetAttribute("assembly"));
        myDemo =
            myAssembly.CreateInstance(objectElement.GetAttribute("type")) as IDemo;

        return myDemo;
    }
}
```

As shown in this example, now it is possible to determine the correct instance to return IDemo by retrieving the proper assembly and type from the configuration file and using reflection to create an instance of that type.

## Dependency Injection Pattern

The Inversion of Control (IoC) principal—also referred to as the Hollywood Principle ("Don't call us; we'll call you.")—is defined as classes that do not direct the flow of executing code. Essentially, the classes are passive and are called upon when needed. Lately, IoC has been receiving a lot of attention; however, it is not a new concept. In fact, it is an old object-oriented programming principle that has been around for years. The original implementation of IoC was the creation of reusable white-box frameworks that were extendable through plug-in classes. In white-box frameworks, a new class that is created does not call the framework; instead, the framework calls the new class. One reason for the recent buzz around IoC is that it is considered a good technique to make applications easier to test in test-driven development, and it also makes an application more extensible.

Another key principle of IoC is that classes should have no knowledge of other services or dependencies that might act upon them. This principle is also referred to as the *Dependency Injection pattern*. The Dependency Injection pattern allows the injection of objects into a class without the class needing to create the object. Although many individuals use the terms *IoC* and *Dependency Injection*, interchangeably, Dependency Injection is really a specific flavor of

IoC. Generally, when implementing Dependency Injection, there are two important rules of thought:

- You can create highly cohesive modules with well-defined interfaces.

- The determination of module interaction can be performed at runtime.

These two rules of thought together make an application declare the dependencies and let some other "container" component figure out the details of location, initialization, sequences, and other references the objects' dependencies may need at runtime.

# How Dependency Injection Works

A good way to demonstrate how Dependency Injection works is to describe it with a real-world scenario. Then we'll look at Dependency Injection and factories, Dependency Injection and containers, and Dependency Injection implementation.

## A Real-Life Analogy of Patterns

We'll actually look at two scenarios here, to give you an idea of the usefulness of Dependency Injection.

### Scenario 1: Game Day

You and your friends are avid football fans. On game day, you get up, load the fridge with your favorite frosty beverage, invite your friends over, and call the local pizza delivery establishment. So, the typical game-day preparation events would look like this:

1. Load the fridge with favorite frosty beverage.

2. Call your friends.

3. Call the pizza delivery establishment.

Listing 3-4 represents the game-day scenario 1 as code.

**Listing 3-4.** *The Game-Day Scenario 1 Code*

```
public class Pizza
{
    public string PhoneNumber;

    public void Load(string toppings)
{
    //Call for a "toppings" Pizza with the specified phone number
    }

}
```

```csharp
public enum Location
{
    Garage,
    Kitchen,
    LivingRoom
}

public class ContactCollection
{
    public string Message;

    public Contact Add(ContactMethod contactMethod, string name,
        string contactMethodAddress)
    {
        //Add contact to friend collection
    }

    public void SendInvite()
    {
        //Send invite message to friends via their specified contact method
    }

}

public class FrostyBeverage
{
    public Location HomeLocation;

    public void Load(object BeverageContainer)
    {
        //Load into BeverageContainer from specified location
    }
}
public class GameDayPrep
{
    private Pizza m_pizza;
    private ContactCollection m_Contacts;
    private Beverage m_FrostBeverage;

    public void DoGameDayPrep()
    {
        //Create instances
        m_Pizza = new Pizza();
        m_Friends = new FriendCollection();
        m_Beverage = new Beverage("Frosty");

        //Load fridge with frosty beverage
```

```
    m_Beverage.HomeLocation = Location.Garage;
    m_Beverage.Load(Fridge.Get());

    //Invite friends
    m_Contacts.Add(ContactMethod.Call, "John", "551-555-1212");
    m_Contacts.Add(ContactMethod.Call, "Joe", "552-555-1212");
    m_Contacts.Add(ContactMethod.IM, "Sam", "sam123");
    m_Contacts.Add(ContactMethod.Call, "Carolyn", "554-555-1212");
    m_Contacts.Message = "Come watch the game with me.  " +
        "I got pizza and frosty beverage. ";
    m_Friends.SendInvite();

    //Order Pizza
    m_Pizza.PhoneNumber = "555-555-1212";
    m_Pizza.OrderPizza(" Sausage");
    }
}
```

In this scenario, you must know the phone numbers of your friends, as well as the number of the pizza delivery establishment. You also need to know where in the house you have stored the frosty beverage. Now what happens if the pizza delivery place closes down and you need to call someone else? What happens if your friends change their phone numbers or you make new friends? And what if the usual spot where you store your frosty beverage has been relocated?

These changes would require changing and learning a new routine to call a new pizza delivery place, knowing your friends' new numbers, and finding the new location of the frosty beverage. Sure, it may not seem like a big deal for you to learn these new techniques, but think about if all avid football fans had to go through this process. How much time would be lost because of relearning?

## Scenario 2: Significant Other

The second scenario twists scenario 1 around a bit. In this scenario, your affectionate "significant other" has graciously agreed to assist you with the game-day preparations. Now, your significant other will find and get the frosty beverage for you, so that you can load it in the fridge. Your significant other will contact your friends and pass along your invite message for you. Finally, your significant other will call the pizza delivery establishment and give you the handset so you can place your order. Listing 3-5 takes scenario 2 and represents it as code.

**Listing 3-5.** *The Game-Day Scenario 2 Code*

```
public interface IFood
{
    void Load(string toppings);

}
```

```csharp
public interface IBeverage
{
    void Load(object BeverageContainer);
}

public interface IContactCollection
{
    string Message { get; }
    IContactCollection GetContacts(string);
    void SendInvite();
}
public class Food : IFood
{
    private string m_PhoneNumber;

    public static GetFood(string foodType)
    {
        // Using the foodType string get the correct PhoneNumber from metadata
    }

    public void Load(string toppings)
    {
        //Call for a "toppings" Pizza with the specified phone number
    }

}
public class ContactCollection : IContactCollection
{
    private string m_Message;
    public string Message
    {
        get { return m_Message; }
        set { m_Message = value; }
    }

    public static IContactCollection GetContacts(string contactType)
    {
        //Get Contacts from metadata based on contactType
    }

    public void SendInvite()
    {
        //Send invite message to friends via their specified contact method
    }


}
```

```
public class Beverage
{
    public static IBeverage GetBeverage(string beverageType)
    {
        //Get beverageType from location specified in metadata
    }

    public void Load(object BeverageContainer)
    {
        //Load into object from specified location
    }
}

public class GameDayPrep
{
    private IFood m_Food;
    private IContactCollection m_Contacts;
    private IBeverage m_Beverage;

    public void DoGameDayPrep()
    {
        //Create instances
        m_Food = Food.GetFood("Pizza");
        m_Contacts = Contact.GetContacts("Friends");
        m_Beverage = Beverage.GetBeverage("Frosty");

        //Load fridge with frosty beverage
        m_Beverage.Load(Fridge.Get());

        //Invite friends
        m_Contacts.Message = "Come watch the football game with me.  " +
            "I got pizza and frosty beverage. ";
        m_Contacts.SendInvite();

        //Order Pizza
        m_Food.Order("Sausage");
    }
}
```

Now if a new pizza place opens, you no longer need to worry about the details of where to locate and how to initiate the call. All you have to do is tell the person on the other end of the line what you want your pizza. Also, finding and retrieving your frosty beverage is handled by your significant other, so the only thing you need to do is place the beverage in the fridge. As for your friends, all you have to do is tell your significant other what the message is, and that person will handle the details of to whom and how to deliver that message. So, even if you make new friends or your friends get new phone numbers, the process of you telling your significant other what the message is does not change.

## Factories and Dependency Injection

Scenario 2 in the previous section revolved around the Factory design pattern and coding to the interface as opposed to the implementation, which is actually considered a flavor of Dependency Injection.

Using the Factory pattern offers a lot of advantages and features. Some of the features include the ability to apply services and constraints to an application. In this case, a factory may not necessarily return an object directly, but may return a proxy to an application, thus making a distributed application easier to design and maintain. A perfect example of this is .NET remoting architecture. Objects that are distributed can be declared in the application configuration file, and .NET will automatically utilize the declared distributed objects when the new keyword is used to create an object. This demonstrates how the configuration and management are abstracted from the calling application.

As great as software factories can be, they do have some pitfalls. One issue is that most implementations of the Factory pattern can be used only with the original application for which it was designed. In Listing 3-5, the Food class can return specific instances of the food interface, but those instances are probably defined specifically for this particular application. Being able to use the Food class, say, for cooking at home, would probably not be feasible (without having to modify the existing implementations and interfaces).

Other issues that can arise involve dependencies and maintenance. The dependency issue arises when an object that is created by the Factory pattern must be aware of the dependencies it will need at compile time. It would be better to define the dependencies of other resources at runtime; this way, the application would not need to be recompiled. Also, maintenance can be a nightmare, since it will be necessary to create interfaces for almost everything. Even though it is a good idea to use interfaces to decouple your implementations, overuse can become painful.

Thankfully, the Factory pattern is not the only way to implement the Dependency Injection pattern. You can use Visitor, Builder, and Assembly patterns as well.

## Containers and Dependency Injection

One of the important factors of Dependency Injection is that the creation of an object and handling the dependencies and services it needs are performed at runtime. Well, in scenario 2 (Listing 3-5), that is not completely the case, because the client still is aware of the Food, Beverage, and ContactCollection classes, and it also is sending a metadata string to determine which class to return. The problem here is that this metadata string is being specified at compile time.

The solution to the problem is to allow for the location, dependencies, and initialization instructions to be specified in some type of metadata file. A perfect example of this is to have an XML file contain the necessary references and dependencies to instantiate and initialize the objects that are returned. The Spring .NET application framework is a perfect example of how this is implemented. Listing 3-6 shows an example of a metadata file for the game-day scenario.

**Listing 3-6.** *Metadata File for Spring .NET*

```
<?xml version="1.0" encoding="utf-8" ?>
<objects xmlns="http://www.springframework.NET">
```

```
<object name="BeverageClass"
            singleton="false"
            type="GameDay.Beverage, GameDay">
            <constructor-arg name="beverageType " value="Frosty"/>
</object>
<object name="ContactCollectionClass"
            singleton="false"
            type=" GameDay.ContactCollection, GameDay ">
            <constructor-arg name="contactType " value="Friends"/>
</object>
<object name="FoodClass"
            singleton="false"
            type=" GameDay.Food, GameDay ">
            <constructor-arg name="foodType " value="Pizza"/>
</object>
</objects>
```

The code to use the gameday.xml file in Listing 3-6 would look like Listing 3-7.

**Listing 3-7.** *Using Spring .NET*

```
using Spring.Objects.Factory.Xml;
public class GameDayPrep
{
    private IFood m_Food;
    private IContactCollection m_Contacts;
    private IBeverage m_Beverage;

    public void DoGameDayPrep()
    {
        //Get container
        Stream stream = new FileStream( "gameday.xml", FileMode.Open,
            FileAccess.Read );
        XmlObjectFactory xmlObjectFactory = new XmlObjectFactory( stream );

        m_Food = (IFood) xmlObjectFactory.GetObject("FoodClass");
        m_Contacts = (IContactCollection)
            xmlObjectFactory.GetObject("ContactCollectionClass");
        m_Beverage = (IBeverage) xmlObjectFactory.GetObject("BeverageClass");

        //Load fridge with frosty beverage
        m_Beverage.Load(Fridge.Get());

        //Invite friends
        m_Contacts.Message = "Come watch the football game with me.    " +
            "I got pizza and frosty beverage. ";
        m_Contacts.SendInvite();
```

```
        //Order pizza
        m_Food.Order("Sausage ");


    }
}
```

In this example, the XML describes the classes to instantiate as well as the constructor arguments to be passed along. The actual GameDayPrep class simply creates and initializes the object via the XmlObjectFactory.GetObject() method. This kind of design, known as a *container*, allows someone to modify the type of beverage, contacts, or food required for game day, without the actual GameDayPrep logic changing.

Although the container solves the problems introduced by the Factory pattern, there is a cost associated with it. Usually, the cost is in the form of reduced performance.

# Dependency Injection Implementation

You can implement the Dependency Injection pattern in many ways. The most widely used methods of Dependency Injection are the constructor-based method and the setter-based method. Interface-based and field-based methods (also known as getter-based), although not as common as the constructor-based and setter-based methods, have gained popularity. In fact, interface-based Dependency Injection is actually implemented in the .NET Framework with the System.Component namespace.

With Enterprise Library for .NET Framework 2.0, a new way of implementing Dependency Injection was introduced, called *attribute-based Dependency Injection*.

## Constructor-Based and Setter-Based Dependency Injection

The constructor-based and setter-based methods of Dependency Injection use slightly different techniques to return the correct object and to ensure it is parameterized correctly. In Listings 3-6 and 3-7, which demonstrate using the Spring .NET framework, the Dependency Injection method used was the constructor. Although it is normally suggested that the setter be used over the constructor and interface types to simplify design and ease of maintenance, the constructor type was used because there was only one parameter. If there were multiple patterns, the constructor method would then become difficult to maintain, especially with languages that do not handle optional parameters well. Listing 3-8 is an example of what the XML file configuration might look like when using the setter method.

**Listing 3-8.** *XML Example for Setter Method*

```xml
<?xml version="1.0" encoding="utf-8" ?>
<objects xmlns="http://www.springframework.NET">
    <object name="BeverageClass"
                singleton="false"
                 type="GameDay.Beverage, GameDay">
                    <property name="beverageType " value="Frosty"/>
    </object>
    <object name="ContactCollectionClass"
                singleton="false"
```

```
              type=" GameDay.ContactCollection, GameDay ">
              <property name="contactType " value="Friends"/>
    </object>
    <object name="FoodClass"
              singleton="false"
              type=" GameDay.Food, GameDay ">
              <property name="foodType " value="Pizza"/>
    </object>
</objects>
```

## Attribute-Based Dependency Injection

Essentially, attribute-based Dependency Injection allows for the decoration of a particular
class, property, or field with an attribute that will define the necessary dependencies for that
particular class or member. Now the GameDayPrep class would look like Listing 3-9.

**Listing 3-9.** *Attribute-Based Dependency Injection Example*

```
public class GameDayPrep
{
    private IFood m_Food;
    private IContactCollection m_Contacts;
    private IBeverage m_Beverage;

    [Factory("FoodClass")]
    public IFood Food
    {
        set
        {
            m_Food = value;
        }
    }

    [Factory("ContactCollectionClass")]
    public IContactCollection ContactCollection
    {
        set
        {
            m_ContactCollection = value;
        }
    }

    [Factory("BeverageClass")]
    public IBeverage Beverage
    {
        set
        {
```

```
            m_Beverage = value;
        }
    }


    public void DoGameDayPrep()
    {
        //Build up
        Factory.BuildUp(typeof(GameDayPrep));

        //Load fridge with frosty beverage
        m_Beverage.Load(Fridge.Get());

        //Invite friends
        m_Contacts.Message = "Come watch the football game with me.  " +
            "I got pizza and frosty beverage. ";
        m_Contacts.SendInvite();

        //Order pizza
        m_Food.Order("Sausage");
    }
}
```

The example in Listing 3-9 uses attributes to define the Dependency Injections required for the Food, Beverage, and ContactCollection objects. In this scenario, a static method called BuildUp takes a System.Type parameter. This parameter is used to reflect the GameDayPrep class so that any dependencies that are discovered can be, well, injected.

# Patterns, Extensibility, and the Enterprise Library

The design patterns described in the previous sections are key to the overall infrastructure of Enterprise Library. The pattern utilization gives Enterprise Library its robust features and allows for simplified extensibility. Each application block uses one or more software design patterns. For instance, the Plug-in pattern is used for the various pluggable providers across the application blocks, such as trace listeners (also known as sinks) in the Logging Application Block and backing stores in the Caching Application Block. The ObjectBuilder and Composite UI Application Block use the Dependency Injection pattern extensively. You can find the Factory pattern in the Caching Application Block and the Data Access Application Block.

## Extending the Enterprise Library Application Blocks

With the creation of each software application are requirements that define its purpose. These requirements can range from simple business rules to complex security measures and protocols mandated by governing bodies. It would be impractical to try to make a one-size-fits-all solution to accommodate every possible scenario under the sun. If this were attempted, the outcome would be a big monolithic mess that would be nearly impossible to maintain and would probably not perform very well.

There are multiple ways to extend Enterprise Library. One of the most obvious ways is to modify its source code directly, which is easy to do because the source code is provided with the installation. However, even though the source code is provided with Enterprise Library, it is more meaningful as a learning tool, as opposed to a way to customize the application blocks. One reason you would not want to modify the source code directly is maintainability. It is generally easier to implement a specific interface and provide your own customized features for that interface. By doing this, you can simply test the customized code you have written. If you modify the actual source code, you will need to test the entire block to ensure that it functions correctly. This means you must learn and understand the internals of an application block. Although this is not a bad thing in itself, most people would prefer to learn the internals at leisure, as opposed to while being under the gun to get a particular application into production.

Another reason modifying the source code is not suggested is that other team members will have a higher learning curve to understand the changes that were made outside the standard Enterprise Library offering. By extending Enterprise Library through the interfaces it provides, team members only need to be concerned with new code when it directly affects their use of the new custom interface implementations.

Another method of extending Enterprise Library is by adding new providers to a specific application block. An example of this would be to write a new Database class for a specific data storage provider such as a MySQL database. Adding providers is considered a good way to give new functionality to Enterprise Library. By adding new providers, you can meet the specific needs for a particular software application based on the requirements of that application.

Finally, you can extend Enterprise Library by creating new application blocks. This method allows a specific need within an organization to be met. For instance, say that a money management organization has multiple requirements involving email:

- Sending email to specific users when the price of a particular security reaches a certain price

- Sending reports via email every morning to specific users that need to analyze those reports

- Sending application warning and error messages to the help desk staff members so they can react quickly to issues

If only the need to capture application error and warning messages were required, it might be easier to create a trace listener specifically for emailing error messages. However, since there are multiple emailing requirements throughout the application, it would be more feasible to create an Email Application Block that can encapsulate generic emailing requirements.

As with other aspects of designing an application, you need to take into account multiple variables when customizing Enterprise Library, such as time, maintenance, and requirements. In the end, you need to decide which is the right approach for your organization. Choose wisely.

## Extensibility Guidelines

When extending Enterprise Library, especially when creating a new custom application block, it is important to try to follow the guidelines set forth by the Microsoft patterns & practices group. These guidelines have been created by Microsoft and the industry as a whole to provide the best architectural guidance in developing software, including the application blocks themselves.

One of the foremost considerations in designing a new application block is extensibility, and one of the ways to ensure extensibility is by providing a public API to expose the application block's internal functionality. The easiest way to expose an application block is by using interfaces or base classes to define the different possible points that an application block can be extended. It is never a good idea to force an application developer to know the internals of an application (although that might be a good learning experience, it is probably more imperative for the developer to get the application coded and into production). By creating interfaces and base classes, and using the Factory pattern, the Dependency Injection pattern, the Plug-in pattern, or some combination of the three, you can allow developers to simply modify a particular extension point to meet their specific needs. Allowing this kind of extensibility is one of the main design goals of Enterprise Library and is considered a best practice throughout the software development industry.

Another important consideration is to ensure the implementation of the application block uses resources efficiently. It is always best to make software with the leanest profile possible. Here are just a few resource-efficiency recommendations for developing any software application:

- Never try to create instances of a class unnecessarily—if you don't need it, why use it?

- Try to let the .NET garbage collector do its job. Forcing the deallocation of resources can hinder the performance of an application or, in some cases, produce unexpected results.

- Ensure that your application meets the business requirements—no more, no less. Don't try to overdesign or design for the future. Ninety percent of the time, the extra added features won't meet the future requirements anyway, and they will usually just hinder performance.

Instrumentation is another concern. As with any application, when a component is developed, it may have a bug or potential performance issue accidentally introduced by the developer or by the environment in which the component is running. This is why it is important to have instrumentation capabilities within a component, including application blocks, to monitor the behavior and performance of a particular software component.

Finally, security is also another major consideration in developing any application component. It is important to ensure that a given caller has the appropriate rights to perform a certain function, and it is up to the application component performing the function to ensure those rights exist. Any highly trusted code that asserts a permission to perform some function must determine that the callers have adequate rights to perform that function.

---

**Note** You can find more about code access permissions and securing code in the MSDN documentation provided on the Web or with the .NET Framework 2.0 SDK download.

---

# Application Block Conceptual Architecture

The Enterprise Library for .NET Framework 2.0 design has undergone some changes since the earlier 1.1 version. As mentioned in Chapter 2, the Configuration Application Block no longer exists. That's not to say that these features have completely gone away; instead, they have been tweaked into the Common assembly, on which all the application block components rely. The main reasoning behind this change comes from the new enhancements made to the System.Configuration namespace in .NET Framework 2.0. These new features made many of the features provided in the Configuration Application Block obsolete. (You can find more information about the System.Configuration changes in .NET Framework 2.0 and how they affect configuration with Enterprise Library for .NET Framework 2.0 in Chapter 4.)

Although there are some mandated dependencies for some of the application blocks, there are also optional dependencies that might be required to use certain features available in Enterprise Library. A few examples of these optional dependencies are the Caching Application Block, which may use the Data Access Application Block to provide persistence of cached data to a database, or the Exception Handling Application Block, which may use the Logging Application Block if the logging handler is to be used for recording application exceptions. Figure 3-2 shows the required and optional dependencies of the application blocks.

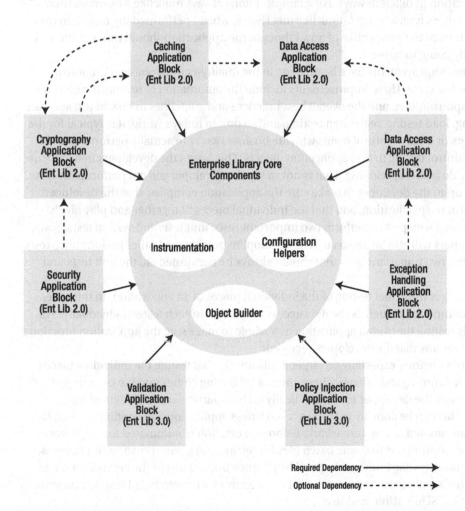

**Figure 3-2.** *Application block dependencies*

All the application blocks depend on the Instrumentation, Configuration, and ObjectBuilder classes, except for the Composite UI Application Block. The Composite UI Application Block depends only on the ObjectBuilder classes. Physically, the Composite UI Application Block contains a copy of the source code for the ObjectBuilder classes as part of its solution. The component still compiles as a separate assembly. The reason for this separately compiled ObjectBuilder assembly is that the Composite UI Application Block was released separately from the core application blocks provided in Enterprise Library.

# Unit Testing

Testing an application is key to the success of any project. The initial days of software development testing involved manual, labor-intensive work. What made matters worse was that testing was done by a human, typically the developer. Although it was good that the application was getting tested, people can make mistakes, such as skipping tests accidentally. In larger software applications, where there might be thousands of test cases, chances were that tests would be missed. The other issue, especially if a developer were performing the test, was subjective reasoning. The developer and actual user of the application are typically going to use an application in different ways. For example, I don't always think like a business user, and business users typically don't think like me. Hence, when I performed my testing manually, I tested it from the perspective of how I thought the application should run, not the way it was actually going to be used.

Over time, improvements have been made in the quality-control phase of the software development life cycle. These improvements include the automation of testing, the division of testing responsibilities, and the overall best practices and guidelines in how to test software (stress testing, load testing, regression testing, and so on). In today's world, it is typical for the business users or quality-control teams who are business savvy to actually perform most of the quality-control testing to find application defects. This leaves the developers free to focus on what they do best—developing. That is not to say the developer will not perform any testing. It is still up to the developer to make sure the application compiles, that the developed pieces perform to specification, and that the individual pieces fit together and play nicely.

This leaves developers to perform two important tests: unit tests and system tests. Sometimes, developers will also be involved in integration, regression, and other performance tests, but overall, the two important ones that should always be performed are the unit tests and system tests.

Unit testing is the actual testing of the individual pieces of an application. In this case, the specific components, such as the data access methods, are each tested individually. System testing is testing the overall application as a whole to make sure the application functions to the specifications that the developers received.

It becomes obvious, especially on larger applications, that testing the individual pieces can become a daunting task. This is where automated testing comes into the picture. Automated tests allow the developer to systematically retest a particular component of an application. This can be done by creating a test harness application and running a batch file, or using an automated testing framework. Before the creation of automated testing frameworks, the only option was to create batch files for testing and create a custom test harness. Today, automated testing frameworks provide a framework to assist in the creation and running of unit tests, and, in some cases, system tests. Examples of automated testing frameworks include NUnit, CSUnit, JUnit, and so on.

A new addition to the automated testing frameworks comes from Microsoft. This new tool comes with Visual Studio 2005 Team System, and much like NUnit, it provides a mechanism for performing automated tests, along with other features.

The Microsoft patterns & practices team, in keeping with its best practices and guidance suggestions, created unit tests for Enterprise Library. In fact, the group created two sets of unit tests: one that utilizes NUnit and the other that utilizes Visual Studio 2005 Team System. This gives you the option to use either testing framework to perform your unit tests.

---

■**Note** The Enterprise Library unit tests provided for NUnit will work only with version 2.2 and later.

---

Having these unit tests provides many features and benefits. Some of them include the following:

- The ability to test the application blocks to ensure they function as they were originally designed

- The ability to test any changes that might be made to the application blocks to ensure the original functionality still works

- A guideline in how to create tests and what should be tested when creating new custom application block components

As custom providers or application blocks are created, it would be very beneficial to create new unit tests to ensure they work as intended. Although this may seem like a time-consuming task up front, over the long haul, the time to test an application will typically be reduced. Essentially, the initial time you put in will be gained in the end, as you will spend far less time bug fixing, testing, and so on.

# Migrating from Earlier Enterprise Library Versions

Migrating from earlier versions of the Enterprise Library to Enterprise Library for .NET Framework 2.0 or 3.0 is not as easy as "upgrade and go." One reason is that the Configuration Application Block has been removed. Additionally, some of the public interfaces have changes from the prior versions.

There is light at the end of the tunnel, though. Most of the public APIs have not been modified (unless a particular feature was made obsolete by .NET Framework 2.0). Also, Enterprise Library can run alongside prior versions. This means an application can utilize both version 1.1 and version 2.0 at the same time. Also, Enterprise Library for .NET Framework 1.1 will work with .NET Framework 2.0, thus allowing migration of Enterprise Library for .NET Framework 2.0 or 3.0 at a later time.

---

**Note** Although Enterprise Library for .NET Framework 1.1 (June 2005 release) will work with .NET Framework 2.0, it does not use all the best practices and features offered by .NET Framework 2.0. Hence, performance might not be as good as using Enterprise Library for .NET Framework 2.0.

---

# Migrating Version 1.1 to 2.0 or 3.0

You can run different versions of Enterprise Library side by side in a number of ways. One way is to strong name the application block components and add them to the global assembly cache (GAC). This allows an application to reference a specific version of a component.

Another way for side-by-side execution is to have each application deployed with a specific version of Enterprise Library. It is important to note that different versions of Enterprise Library cannot reside within the same folder. So, a version 1.1 Data Access Application Block could not be located in the same folder as a version 2.0 Exception Handling Application Block, for example.

When migrating an application, you do not need to migrate the entire thing. Each assembly may reference a different version of Enterprise Library. So, it would be possible to have an application using version 1.1 and decide to migrate just the data access assembly to version 2.0. This way, you can migrate pieces of your application when it makes sense to do so. This technique is referred to as *partial migration*, and although it is supported, it is difficult to implement and typically not recommended.

## Migrating Configuration Data

If an environment has side-by-side execution of different versions of Enterprise Library, or more important, if an application is using a partial migration strategy to slowly migrate to a new version of Enterprise Library, two versions of the configuration data must be maintained by the specific version of the Enterprise Library configuration console for that version of Enterprise Library. This is because not only is the data stored in different locations for version 2.0 and version 1.1, but the schema of the configuration data is also different. The configuration console for Enterprise Library for .NET Framework 1.1 can be used only to configure Enterprise Library for .NET Framework 1.1 application blocks.

Generally speaking, the easiest way to migrate configuration data from version 1.1 to version 2.0 is to reenter the version 1.1 configuration data into the version 2.0 configuration console. It is possible to manually convert the configuration data by hand, but this technique is somewhat difficult and error-prone; hence, it is not recommended. Currently, a tool does not exist to perform this transformation.

## Migrating to Version 3.0

Migrating to Enterprise Library for .NET Framework 3.0 has some of the same challenges and strategies as migrating to version 2.0. However, it is not necessary to have .NET Framework 3.0 installed on the user's desktop to use Enterprise Library for .NET Framework 3.0, since the 2.0 version was developed before Windows Communication Foundation (WCF) was provided with .NET Framework 3.0 (unless you plan on utilizing .NET Framework 3.0–specific features such as WCF).

With that said, it would be beneficial to utilize the new features provided by Enterprise Library for .NET Framework 3.0, even if your current environment is still .NET Framework 2.0.

## Migrating from Version 2.0 to 3.0

The good news in the migration story is that migrating from Enterprise Library for .NET Framework 2.0 to 3.0 is actually very simple. In fact, it may be the easiest migration ever, assuming you used Enterprise Library for .NET Framework 2.0 as is out of the box.

The process of migrating is really just compiling Enterprise Library for .NET Framework 3.0 and changing the references from the 2.0 assemblies to the 3.0 version. Then modify the application configuration file and change the version number from 2.0.0.0 to 3.0.0.0. Everything should then work as normal.

# Setting Up the ACME POS Application

In this book, we'll set up an application called ACME POS and use it to demonstrate the Enterprise Library application blocks. To get started, you need to install some components and create the Service solution, which will contain the web service's layer, business logic, and data access logic.

## Installing the Components

To create the ACME POS application, you need to download and install a series of software components to the development workstation. The following list shows the software components and software factories required for this sample application. It is important to install the software in the following order. It is also helpful to opt to compile Enterprise Library during the installation process when prompted to do so.

- NUnit 2.2 or Visual Studio Team System

- Guidance Automation Extensions

- Enterprise Library for .NET Framework 3.0 (April 2007)

- Web Service Software Factory (December 2006)

---

**Note** The installation of NUnit is optional if you have Visual Studio Team System. If you decide not to install NUnit, it might be necessary to remove NUnit-specific testing projects from the solutions of Enterprise Library.

---

## Creating the ACME Service Solution

To create the ACME POS Service solution, start Visual Studio 2005 and select to create a new project. In the list of available project types, you will see a new item called Guidance Packages. Under Guidance Packages are two nodes: Smart Client Development and Web Service Software Factory (ASMX). Select Web Service Software Factory (ASMX), and then click the ASMX Service icon in the list of templates. Name the solution ACME.POS.Service, as shown in Figure 3-3.

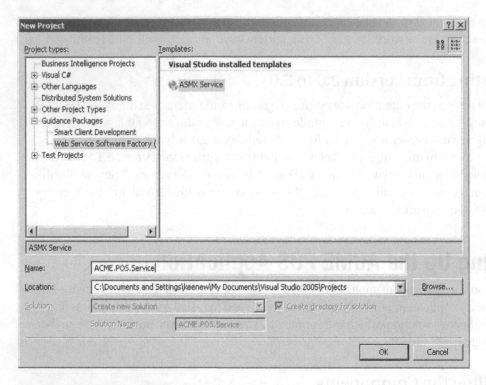

**Figure 3-3.** *Creating the ACME POS Service solution*

---

**Caution** The Microsoft Guidance Automation Extensions have a 260-character limitation on the total length of a file path. A workaround is to use a shorter folder structure such as C:\Guided Solutions\ as opposed to the default Visual Studio 2005\Projects directory.

---

A series of projects will be created for you, as shown in Figure 3-4.

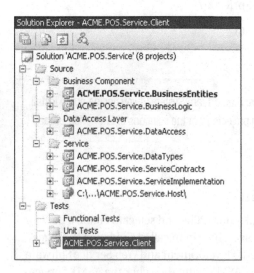

**Figure 3-4.** *The ACME POS Service solution in the Solution Explorer*

Also added to the solution is a set of recipes and templates that can be used for creating the components of the ACME POS Service solution. You can find these recipes and templates in the Guidance Package Manager, available from the Tools menu, as shown in Figure 3-5.

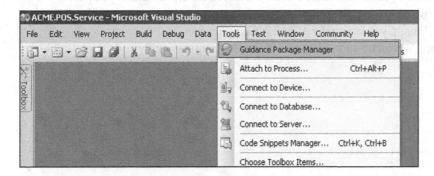

**Figure 3-5.** *Guidance Package Manager item on the Tools menu*

Choose Tools ➤ Guidance Package Manager to see the dialog box shown in Figure 3-6. The recipes provide functionality for performing specific tasks such as creating a database connection string. The templates define the different projects that make up the solution.

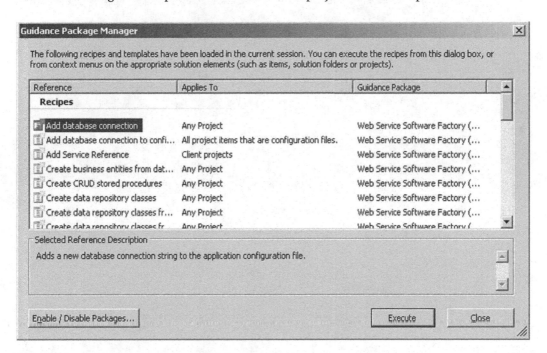

**Figure 3-6.** *Guidance Package Manager dialog box*

We'll work with the ACME POS application in the next chapters. For now, close the Guidance Package Manager dialog box and ACME POS Service solution.

# Summary

This chapter focused on the overall design of Enterprise Library and the types of industry best practices implemented by the application blocks. It covered Enterprise Library patterns, extensibility, conceptual architecture, unit testing, and migrating from earlier versions of Enterprise Library. Finally, you set up the ACME POS application.

The next chapter will focus on the features of the Common assembly and ObjectBuilder.

■■■

# CHAPTER 4

# The Common Assembly and ObjectBuilder Components

**A**s with any application or system framework, certain services and common functionality are required to support the features of that framework. Enterprise Library is no exception to this requirement. In Enterprise Library, the common services required by all application blocks include the handling of configuration data, instrumentation, and object creation and management.

The Microsoft patterns & practices group implemented these common services through two assemblies. One is called the Common assembly, which handles the configuration and instrumentation services required by Enterprise Library. The other assembly is called ObjectBuilder, which handles the creation and management of objects used within Enterprise Library.

---

**Note** While this book focuses on Enterprise Library 3.0 - April 2007 (and 3.1 - May 2007), the current version has not had any significant breaking or design changes from the prior 2.0 release. Hence, everything in this chapter will apply to Enterprise Library for .NET Framework 2.0 - January 2006, as well.

---

## Common Assembly Configuration Support

The Common assembly supports two major functions for the Enterprise Library application blocks. First, it provides a series of helper classes to assist in the management of configuration data. Second, it provides support for instrumentation for the various Enterprise Library application blocks. Here, we'll look at the configuration features. The instrumentation features are covered later in the chapter.

As noted in earlier chapters, a major change from Enterprise Library for .NET Framework 1.1 is the removal of the Configuration Application Block. The main reason for the removal of this application block is that the new configuration features inside .NET Framework 2.0 and 3.0 allow for many of the features that were provided by the Configuration Application Block. The new Enterprise Library configuration features rely on the new ConfigurationSection class in the .NET Framework 2.0 and 3.0 System.Configuration namespace. The ConfigurationSection class provides methods and properties that represent a custom configuration section within a configuration file.

## How the Configuration Features Work

To completely understand how Enterprise Library uses these new .NET Framework configuration features, it is important to understand the features themselves. Listings 4-1 through 4-4 demonstrate how to define a custom configuration section within an XML file (whether it is the application configuration or a stand-alone file), how to implement the code to serialize and deserialize XML data into inherited instances of the ConfigurationSection class, and how to utilize that custom configuration data within a simple console application.

Listing 4-1 shows what a custom configuration section might look like within a configuration file.

**Listing 4-1.** *Sample Configuration File: myCustom.config*

```
<?xml version="1.0" encoding="utf-8"?>
<configuration>
<configSections>
<section name="myCustomSection" type="Samples.MyCustomSection, Samples,
    Version=1.0.0.0, Culture=neutral, PublicKeyToken=null"
    allowDefinition="Everywhere" allowExeDefinition="MachineToApplication"
    restartOnExternalChanges="true" />
</configSections>
<myCustomSection myFirstSetting="1" mySecondSetting="A" />
</configuration>
```

With the configuration file created, the next step is to be able to deserialize this information into something useful within an application. Listing 4-2 demonstrates how to inherit from the ConfigurationSection class to utilize the custom configuration section in Listing 4-1 using the programmatic model.

**Listing 4-2.** *Inherited ConfigurationSection Class Using the Programmatic Model*

```
using System.Configuration;
public sealed class MyCustomSection : ConfigurationSection
{
    // The collection (property bag) that contains the section properties.
    private static ConfigurationPropertyCollection m_Properties;

    // The myFirstSetting property.
    private static readonly ConfigurationProperty m_MyFirstSetting =
        new ConfigurationProperty("myFirstSetting",
        typeof(long), (long) 1,
        ConfigurationPropertyOptions.IsRequired);

    // The mySecondSetting property.
    private static readonly ConfigurationProperty m_MySecondSetting =
        new ConfigurationProperty("mySecondSetting",
        typeof(string), "A",
        ConfigurationPropertyOptions.IsRequired);

    // CustomSection constructor.
```

```csharp
public MyCustomSection()
{
    // Property initialization
    m_Properties =
        new ConfigurationPropertyCollection();

    m_Properties.Add(m_MyFirstSetting);
    m_Properties.Add(m_MySecondSetting);
}


// This is a key customization.
// It returns the initialized property bag.
protected override ConfigurationPropertyCollection Properties
{
    get
    {
        return m_Properties;
    }
}

[LongValidator(MinValue = 1, MaxValue = 10000,
    ExcludeRange = false)]
public long MyFirstSetting
{
    get
    {
        return (long)this["myFirstSetting"];
    }
    set
    {
        this["myFirstSetting"] = value;
    }
}

[StringValidator(InvalidCharacters = " ~!@#$%^&*()[]{}/;'\"|\\",
    MinLength = 1, MaxLength = 60)]
public string MySecondSetting
{
    get
    {
        return (string)this["mySecondSetting"];
    }
    set
    {
        this["mySecondSetting "] = value;
    }
}
}
```

Although the code in Listing 4-2 will get the job done, in most cases, there is an easier way to do this using the declarative model. Listing 4-3 demonstrates the use of the declarative model for defining the custom configuration section. Using the declarative model typically allows for reduced coding and an overall cleaner approach to creating customized ConfigurationSection classes.

**Listing 4-3.** *Using the Declarative Model to Define the Custom Configuration Section*

```
using System.Configuration;
public sealed class MyCustomSection : ConfigurationSection
{

    // CustomSection constructor.
    public MyCustomSection()
    { }

    [ConfigurationProperty("myFirstSetting", DefaultValue = (long) 1,
        IsRequired = true)]
    [LongValidator(MinValue = 1, MaxValue = 10000, ExcludeRange = false)]
    public long MyFirstSetting
    {
        get
        {
            return (long)this["myFirstSetting"];
        }
        set
        {
            this["myFirstSetting"] = value;
        }
    }

    [ConfigurationProperty("mySecondSetting", DefaultValue = "A",
        IsRequired = true)]
    [StringValidator(InvalidCharacters = " ~!@#$%^&*()[]{}/;'\"|\\",
        MinLength = 1, MaxLength = 60)]
    public string MySecondSetting
    {
        get
        {
            return (string)this["mySecondSetting"];
        }
        set
        {
            this["mySecondSetting "] = value;
        }
    }
}
```

Now that the MyCustomSection class has been implemented, it is time to actually do something with it. Listing 4-4 demonstrates how to use the custom configuration file and the newly created MyCustomSection class to read the custom configuration data defined in Listing 4-1.

**Listing 4-4.** *Display Configuration Settings in Console Window*

```
using System;
using System.Configuration;

namespace Sample
{
    public class MyApp
    {
        static public void Main(string[] args)
        {
            ExeConfigurationFileMap fileMap = new ExeConfigurationFileMap();
            fileMap.ExeConfigFilename = @"C:\test\myCustom.config";

            Configuration config = ConfigurationManager.OpenMappedExeConfiguration(
                fileMap, ConfigurationUserLevel.None);

            //Load my section from config
            MyCustomSection section = config.Sections["myCustomSection"]
                as MyCustomSection;

            if (section != null)
            {
                //Section found
                Console.WriteLine("My First Setting : {0}", section.MyFirstSetting);
                Console.WriteLine("My Second Setting : {0}",
                    section.MySecondSetting);
            }
        }
    }
}
```

In Listing 4-4, the OpenMappedExeConfiguration method of the ConfigurationManager class accepts a parameter of type ExeConfigurationFileMap. An instance of ExeConfigurationFileMap allows the developer to define the location of the configuration file to use to create an instance of the Configuration class. This allows developers to point to other files beyond the *app_name*.exe.config for configuration data. This is basically how the FileConfigurationSource class in Enterprise Library is implemented.

## Interfaces for Handling Configuration

As with the application blocks of Enterprise Library, the Common assembly used interfaces extensively to abstract the implementation of a component from its actual contract. This allows for different implementations of configuration components to be inserted with minimal effort. The two main interfaces provided by Enterprise Library for handling configuration are `IConfigurationSource` and `IConfigurationParameter`. By creating your own implementations for these two interfaces, you can define custom ways of storing configuration data.

The `IConfigurationSource` interface is the heart of the configuration features in Enterprise Library. It provides a series of contracts that all the application blocks use to retrieve and store application configuration data at runtime. It contains five methods that allow for retrieving, removing, and saving the configuration section data, as well as methods for adding and removing handlers that can monitor the configuration data for changes. Currently, Enterprise Library 3.0 - April 2007 (or 3.1 - May 2007) release contains two concrete implementations of the interface: the `FileConfigurationSource` class, which contains the implementation to allow configuration data to be stored and retrieved from any user-defined XML file, and the `SystemConfigurationSource` class, which provides the ability to retrieve data from the application configuration file (`app.config`/`web.config`). The Enterprise Library 3.0 - April 2007 (or 3.1 - May 2007) release installation also contains a QuickStart example of a SQL Server–based configuration source implementation.

The `IConfigurationParameter` interface presents a placeholder for possible future methods or properties that should be inherited from it. Any concrete class that inherits from `IConfigurationParameter` is typically used for providing parameter data used to store the configuration data. For example, in the current Enterprise Library 3.x offerings, the `FileConfigurationSource` class needs a filename parameter to define where the configuration data should be stored. The `FileNameConfigurationSaveParameter` class that inherits from `IConfigurationParameter` provides a property to store the filename to be used by the `FileConfigurationSource` class.

`ICustomProviderData` and `IHelperAssistedCustomConfigurationData`, which inherits from `ICustomProviderData`, provide interfaces for defining configuration objects for custom providers that are used throughout Enterprise Library. Typically, these are internal resources and would never be used directly from within your code, unless you are modifying the Enterprise Library behavior and features for handling configuration.

The Common assembly also contains `IObjectWithName` and `IObjectWithNameAndType` interfaces. The `IObjectWithName` interface, which contains a string property called `Name`, is imple- mented by the `NameConfigurationElement` class. The `IObjectWithNameAndType` interface inherits from `IObjectWithName` and adds a property called `Type`. The `IObjectWithNameAndType` interface is implemented by the `NameTypeConfigurationElement` class. Both the `NameTypeConfigurationElement` and `NameConfigurationElement` classes provide the base implementations for defining the different custom sections used by the application blocks. When defining custom application blocks requiring new configuration sections, you should inherit from either the `NameTypeConfigurationElement` class or the `NameConfigurationElement` class.

The overall interaction of the Enterprise Library configuration namespace components is pretty straightforward. The application blocks, as well as any application code, use the `IConfigurationSource` interface and the appropriate concrete class to retrieve and/or save the configuration data.

## File Watcher Feature

The configuration source implementations will cache the configuration data in memory for subsequent calls to the configuration sections. This creates a problem if the configuration file changes while an application is executing. To solve this, Enterprise Library has a file watcher feature that monitors the configuration files for changes. If a change does occur, it can refresh the configuration section objects to reflect the recent changes to keep the in-memory cached data as up-to-date as possible.

# Using the System Configuration Source

Using the system configuration source is probably the easiest and simplest way to use the configuration features—at least from a coding standpoint. One of the big reasons for this simplicity is that the storage of the configuration data is the actual application configuration file for the application (app.config/web.config). However, you do need to be careful to make sure the configuration data is still manageable. The more configuration data that is stored, the harder it can become to manage. Although it is possible to create components for the Enterprise Library Configuration Console to help manage your configuration data, it may not always be practical to do so. (Chapter 5 discusses the Configuration Console and how to create your own design-time classes to manage configuration data.)

In Listing 4-2, a simple class called MyCustomSection was created to store two configuration settings that were shown in the configuration file in Listing 4-1. Listing 4-4 then displayed the configuration data to a console window. Listing 4-5 demonstrates how this is done using the SystemConfigurationSource class.

**Listing 4-5.** *Display Configuration Settings in Console Window Using the SystemConfigurationSource Class*

```
using System;
using System.Configuration;
using Microsoft.Practices.EnterpriseLibrary.Common.Configuration;
public class MyApp
{
    static public void Main(string[] args)
    {
        IConfigurationSource myConfigurationSource = new
            SystemConfigurationSource();

        //Load my section from config
        MyCustomSection section = myConfigurationSource.GetSection
            ("myCustomSection") as MyCustomSection;

        //Code to display configuration data to console
    }
}
```

By using the `IConfigurationSource` interface, other concrete `IConfigurationSource` implementations such as the `FileConfigurationSource` or `SqlConfigurationSource` class can be implemented with little effort. Listing 4-6 shows how the `FileConfigurationSource` class would be implemented to read the configuration in Listing 4-1 as an external file.

**Listing 4-6.** *Display Configuration Settings in Console Window Using the FileConfigurationSource Class*

```
using System;
using System.Configuration;
using Microsoft.Practices.EnterpriseLibrary.Common.Configuration;
public class MyApp
{
    static public void Main(string[] args)
    {
        IConfigurationSource myConfigurationSource = new
            FileConfigurationSource(@"c:\myCustom.config");

        //Load my section from config
        MyCustomSection section = myConfigurationSource.GetSection
            ("myCustomSection") as MyCustomSection;

        //Code to display configuration data to console

    }
}
```

As you can see, the system configuration source is relatively easy to use. Maybe it's not as easy as `AppSettings`, which allows only for name/value relationships, but that is the small price to pay for the extensibility you get with custom configuration sections. In the prior examples, all the configuration data was stored in the application's configuration file. Although this may work out beautifully for applications requiring only a few configuration settings, for enterprise applications that host multiple modules, you may need a better method of storing configuration data. One way is to use external configuration files.

## Using External Configuration Files

Enterprise Library provides a way to have the application configuration file reference another file that stores all your configuration settings. The external file can be used by Enterprise Library or by custom components within your application. Although this is on the right track, it still forces the developer to incorporate all Enterprise Library configuration data into one file, so it still can create maintenance issues with applications requiring large amounts of configuration data.

Using an external configuration file is pretty straightforward. Listing 4-7 shows the necessary changes to the application configuration. Notice the new configuration section with the name `enterpriseLibrary.ConfigurationSource`, which defines the section required to allow for referencing external configuration files. The new Enterprise Library section contains an element called sources, which allows you to add multiple external sources as noted by the add elements. The enterpriseLibrary.ConfigurationSource element also contains a selectedSource attribute. This attribute must be specified; otherwise, you will receive an exception that the "system configuration source is not defined in the configuration file." Also make sure it is a valid source; otherwise, you will receive an exception stating that the "configuration source section is not found in the application configuration file." The selectedSource attribute defines which source is used by default. In this case, the myExternalConfigurationSource source is used by default.

---

**Note** The configuration sections in the examples use the Enterprise Library for .NET Framework 3.0 assemblies via the Version parameter in the type attribute. If you are using Enterprise Library for .NET Framework 2.0, you will want to change the parameter to 2.0.0.0.

---

**Listing 4-7.** *Application Configuration File for External File*

```
<?xml version="1.0" encoding="utf-8"?>
<configuration>
  <configSections>
    <section name="enterpriseLibrary.ConfigurationSource"
        type="Microsoft.Practices.EnterpriseLibrary.Common.Configuration.➥
            ConfigurationSourceSection, Microsoft.Practices.EnterpriseLibrary.➥
            Common, Version=3.0.0.0, Culture=neutral, PublicKeyToken=null" />
  </configSections>
  <enterpriseLibrary.ConfigurationSource
    selectedSource="myExternalConfigurationSource">
    <sources>
      <add name="myExternalConfigurationSource"
        type="Microsoft.Practices.EnterpriseLibrary.Common.Configuration.➥
            FileConfigurationSource, Microsoft.Practices.EnterpriseLibrary.➥
            Common, Version=3.0.0.0, Culture=neutral, PublicKeyToken=null"
        filePath="external.config" />
    </sources>
  </enterpriseLibrary.ConfigurationSource>
</configuration>
```

---

**Note** The external configuration file for this example looks identical to the configuration file in Listing 4-1.

---

By default, the Enterprise Library application blocks are designed to use the configuration source as defined by the selectedSource attribute, even though there is a static method in the ConfigurationSourceFactory class that is responsible for returning the correct configuration source, which allows for a configuration source to be defined by name. Each application block calls the Create() method of the ConfigurationSourceFactory. The Create() method determines whether a ConfigurationSource section is present; if it is, the configuration source will be determined and returned.

## Using Multiple Configuration Sources

In most enterprise applications, it is necessary to have configuration data that is not only defined by the environment (production, testing, development, and so on), but also by geographic region, line-of-business, and so on. Well, there is more good news: Enterprise Library allows you to define configuration sources manually within your application code. It does this by using the FileConfigurationSource class.

To use the FileConfigurationSource class with an application block, you must create an instance of the particular application block factory by passing the FileConfigurationSource instance into the constructor. Listing 4-8 demonstrates how the Data Access Application Block uses the static Create() method of the DatabaseFactory class to create a Database class instance. Compare that with Listing 4-9, which creates a FileConfigurationSource object and creates an instance of the DatabaseProviderFactory to create a Database class instance.

**Listing 4-8.** *How the Data Access Application Block Creates a Database Instance*

```
using System;
using System.Collections.Generic;

using System.Text;
using Microsoft.Practices.EnterpriseLibrary.Data;
using Microsoft.Practices.EnterpriseLibrary.Common.Configuration;

namespace Sample
{
    public class MyDataApp
    {
        static void Main(string[] args)
        {
            //Get Database instance from Database Factory class
            Database db = DatabaseFactory.CreateDatabase("myDataConnection");
            db.ExecuteNonQuery("usp_myStoredProcedure");
        }
    }
}
```

**Listing 4-9.** *Using the FileConfigurationSource Class*

```
using System;
using System.Collections.Generic;
using System.Text;
```

```
using Microsoft.Practices.EnterpriseLibrary.Data;
using Microsoft.Practices.EnterpriseLibrary.Common.Configuration;

namespace Sample
{
    public class MyDataApp
    {
        public static void Main(string[] args)
        {
            FileConfigurationSource myConfigSource =
                new FileConfigurationSource("myConnections.config");

            //Create instance of Database Provider Factory and create
            //Database instance
            DatabaseProviderFactory dbFactory =
                new DatabaseProviderFactory(myConfigSource);
            Database db = dbFactory.Create("myConnection");

             //Execute stored procedure
             db.ExecuteNonQuery("usp_myStoredProcedure");
        }
    }
}
```

Listing 4-9, although requiring a bit more code, allows for the developer to specifically define the configuration file to create the Database class instance. Although this allows for configuration data to be in multiple configuration files, the filename in this instance must be defined within the code. It is possible to use AppSettings to define a configuration key-value pair, or a custom configuration section could be created to define the configuration filename to use. The downside to this is that some identifier or key must still be coded into the application.

## Saving and Removing Configuration Data

Although the current implementation of Enterprise Library application blocks does not actually save or remove configuration data, the code has been implemented to support the read and write needs of the Enterprise Library Configuration Console. The IConfigurationSource interface specifies Add and Remove methods that allow you to add and remove configuration sections from a configuration source. It is possible to use the implemented methods of FileConfigurationSource and SystemConfigurationSource to add and remove configuration data.

---

**Note** The Enterprise Library Configuration Console uses the configuration runtime for its ability to read and write data to the configuration file.

---

To add data to the configuration file, you must call the Add method of the configuration source. The Add method accepts three parameters: addParameter, sectionName, and configurationSection. addParameter is of type IConfigurationParameter; it is used to determine any specific parameters needed to save the configuration data for a particular configuration source. Both FileConfigurationSource and SystemConfigurationSource require the FileConfigurationSaveParameter class to be passed into the addParameter parameter; otherwise, an exception would be thrown.

---

■**Note** When it comes to the SystemConfigurationSource, it would seem that the implementation could be changed so the IConfigurationParameter could be ignored and the configuration filename could be determined internally. However, in this case, it was not implemented in that manner because of the support of the polymorphic configuration features described later in this chapter.

---

Listing 4-10 demonstrates how configuration data can be added and then removed from the configuration file defined in Listing 4-1.

**Listing 4-10.** *Adding and Removing Configuration Data from Any Configuration Source*

```
using System;
using System.Collections.Generic;
using System.Text;
using Microsoft.Practices.EnterpriseLibrary.Data;
using Microsoft.Practices.EnterpriseLibrary.Common.Configuration;

namespace Sample
{
    public class ManipulateConfigData
    {
        public static void Main(string[] args)
        {
            string configFileName = @"c:\myCustom.config";
            string sectionName = "myCustomSection";

            IConfigurationSource myConfigurationSource = new
            FileConfigurationSource(configFileName);

            //Load my section from config
            MyCustomSection section = myConfigurationSource.GetSection
                (sectionName) as MyCustomSection;

            //Output current config settings to console
            WriteConfigData(section);

            //If section was not there its null, so create a new instance
```

```
    if (section == null)
    {
        section = new MyCustomSection();
    }

    //Set new config values
    section.MyFirstSetting = 2;
    section.MySecondSetting = "B";

    //Create and set IConfigurationParameter
    FileConfigurationParameter configParameter =
        new FileConfigurationParameter(configFileName);

    //Add configuration data
    myConfigurationSource.Add(configParameter, sectionName);

    //Get configuration section again
    section = myConfigurationSource.GetSection(sectionName) as
        MyCustomSection;

    //Output current config settings to console
    WriteConfigData(section);

    //Remove configuration data
    myConfigurationSource.Remove(configParameter, sectionName, section);

    //Get configuration section for the last time
    section = myConfigurationSource.GetSection(sectionName)
        as MyCustomSection;

    //Output current config settings to console
    WriteConfigData(section);

}

private static void WriteConfigData(MyCustomSection customSection)
{
    if (customSection!= null)
    {
        //Section found
        Console.WriteLine("The Existing settings are as follows");
        Console.WriteLine("My First Setting : {0}",
            customSection.MyFirstSetting);
        Console.WriteLine("My Second Setting : {0}",
            customSection.MySecondSetting);
        Console.WriteLine();
    }
```

```
        else
        {
            Console.WriteLine("Configuration section not found");
        }
      }
    }
}
```

After running the code in Listing 4-10, the configuration file should no longer contain the configuration section named MyCustomSection.

You should note the following about how the FileConfigurationSource and SystemConfigurationSource classes behave when adding and removing configuration sections:

- The Add method will replace an existing configuration section if it has the same name as the one being added to it.

- Both the FileConfigurationSource and SystemConfigurationSource classes implement caching functionality. While the code in Listing 4-10 was saving the changes to the configuration file, the changes were also being pushed to cache.

- The FileConfigurationSource and SystemConfigurationSource classes can sense changes to their configuration data and will refresh their caches according.

- The FileConfigurationSource updates all the configuration sections when it senses a change; however, the SystemConfigurationSource class uses the .NET Framework's ConfigurationManager class to update the modified sections.

## Using the SQL Server Configuration Source

Enterprise Library contains a number of QuickStart sample applications to help developers get acquainted with some of the most commonly used features. One of these is actually a SQL Server implementation of IConfigurationSource. This implementation allows for the storage of configuration settings to be kept in a SQL Server database. In some environments, storing configuration data in a SQL Server database can prove useful. A few reasons are as follows:

- Changes can be made within a transaction.

- Configuration data could be normalized in some fashion and then rebuilt or disassembled within a stored procedure.

- Data can be fault-tolerant with the use of clustering and other failover technologies.

- Data can be replicated to other servers.

- Data can be securely stored.

- Configuration changes can be logged and archived easily.

These are just a few reasons why an organization might want to use SQL Server as its configuration storage repository. Although a lot of these features can be implemented with minimal effort using the normal file system and operating system features of a server, some may argue that it is easier to use SQL Server 2000 or newer because it provides all these features out of the box.

To use the SQL Configuration QuickStart as provided in with Enterprise Library, you need to have Visual Studio 2005 installed, along with SQL Server Express and the Northwind database. Then run the Create SQL Configuration Database command, which is found in the Enterprise Library Start menu folder.

Although using the Northwind database is fine for the QuickStart example, you might want to use a different database in your own environment. It might also be necessary to modify the names of stored procedures, triggers, and tables to meet your organization standards. For example, some organizations like to prefix their stored procedure with usp_ to signify that a user-defined stored procedure is not a system stored procedure. In the SqlConfiguration folder, the SqlConfiguration.SQL file is responsible for setting up the necessary tables, stored procedures, and triggers to run the SQL Configuration QuickStart. You can use this file as a template to create the necessary stored procedure, triggers, and tables that will be required within your environment.

Once the SQL Server database is set up, the next task is to configure the application configuration file to use the SqlConfigurationSource. The NUnit example that comes with the Enterprise Library QuickStart demonstrates the ConfigurationSource technique where the SqlConfigurationSource is defined in the application configuration file. Listing 4-11 shows what a typical application configuration file may look like when implementing SqlConfigurationSource in this way.

**Listing 4-11.** *ConfigurationSource Method of Specifying SqlConfigurationSource*

```xml
<?xml version="1.0" encoding="utf-8"?>
<configuration>
  <configSections>
    <section name="enterpriseLibrary.ConfigurationSource"
        type="Microsoft.Practices.EnterpriseLibrary.Common.Configuration.➡
        ConfigurationSourceSection, Microsoft.Practices.EnterpriseLibrary.➡
        Common, Version=3.0.0.0, Culture=neutral, PublicKeyToken=null" />
  </configSections>
  <enterpriseLibrary.ConfigurationSource
    selectedSource="myExternalConfigurationSource">
    <sources>
      <add name="myExternalConfigurationSource"
        type="Microsoft.Practices.EnterpriseLibrary.SqlConfigurationSource.➡
          SqlConfigurationSource, Microsoft.Practices.EnterpriseLibrary. ➡
          SqlConfigurationSource"
        connectionString="server=(local)\SQLExpress;➡
        database=Northwind;Integrated Security=true"
        getStoredProcedure="EntLib_GetConfig"
        setStoredProcedure="EntLib_SetConfig"
        refreshStoredProcedure="UpdateSectionDate"
        removeStoredProcedure="EntLib_RemoveSection" />
    </sources>
  </enterpriseLibrary.ConfigurationSource>
</configuration>
```

As for using the SqlConfigurationSource directly within application code, the technique is pretty much identical to using FileConfigurationSource or SystemConfigurationSource. The only difference is that the connection string and stored procedure names must be specified. Listing 4-12 shows an example of this technique.

**Listing 4-12.** *Using the SqlConfigurationSource Directly Within an Application*

```
using System;
using System.Configuration;
using Microsoft.Practices.EnterpriseLibrary.Common.Configuration;
using Microsoft.Practices.EnterpriseLibrary.SqlConfigurationSource;
namespace Sample
{
    public class MyApp
    {
        static public void Main(string[] args)
        {
            IConfigurationSource myConfigurationSource = new
                SqlConfigurationSource(
                    @"server=(local)\SQLExpress;database=Northwind;"
                    + "Integrated Security=true",
                    "EntLib_GetConfig",
                    "EntLib_SetConfig",
                    "UpdateSectionDate",
                    "EntLib_RemoveSection");

            string sectionName = "myCustomSection";

            //Load my section from config
            MyCustomSection section = myConfigurationSource.GetSection(sectionName)
                as MyCustomSection;

            //Perform other actions.
        }
    }
}
```

Saving data is also identical to the method used to store FileConfigurationSource and SystemConfigurationSource, except that instead of using an instance of the FileConfigurationSaveParameter class, an instance of SqlConfigurationParameter is used. Listing 4-13 demonstrates how to save configuration data using SqlConfigurationSource.

**Listing 4-13.** *Adding and Removing Configuration Data from Any Configuration Source*

```
using System;
using System.Collections.Generic;
using System.Text;
using Microsoft.Practices.EnterpriseLibrary.Data;
```

```csharp
using Microsoft.Practices.EnterpriseLibrary.Common.Configuration;
using Microsoft.Practices.EnterpriseLibrary.SqlConfigurationSource;
using Microsoft.Practices.EnterpriseLibrary.SqlConfigurationSource.Configuration;

namespace Sample
{
    public class ManipulateSqlConfigData
    {
        public static void Main(string[] args)
        {
            string connectionString =
                @"server=(local)\SQLExpress;database=Northwind;"
                + "Integrated Security=true";
            string getStoredProc = "EntLib_GetConfig";
            string setStoredProc = "EntLib_SetConfig";
            string refreshStoredProc = "UpdateSectionDate";
            string removeStoredProc = "EntLib_RemoveSection";

            string sectionName = "myCustomSection";

            IConfigurationSource myConfigurationSource = new
                SqlConfigurationSource(
                    connectionString,
                    getStoredProc,
                    setStoredProc,
                    refreshStoredProc,
                    removeStoredProc);

            //Load my section from config
            MyCustomSection section = myConfigurationSource.
                GetSection(sectionName) as MyCustomSection;

            //If section was not there its null, so create a new instance
            if (section == null)
            {
                section = new MyCustomSection();
            }

            //Set new config values
            section.MyFirstSetting = 2;
            section.MySecondSetting = "B";

            //Create and set SqlConfigurationParameter
            SqlConfigurationParameter configParameter = new
                SqlConfigurationParameter(
                    connectionString,
```

```
                    getStoredProc,
                    setStoredProc,
                    refreshStoredProc,
                    removeStoredProc);

            //Add configuration data
            myConfigurationSource.Add(configParameter, sectionName, section);
        }
    }
}
```

---

**■Note**  SqlConfigurationSource has a known bug that does not allow it to work with the Data Access Application Block. If this particular issue is a concern in your environment, you can use the Enterprise Library 3.0 (April 2007) release or greater, as it will work with both .NET Framework 2.0 and 3.0.

---

## Migrating from Version 1.1 to 2.0 or 3.0

With both the Configuration and Instrumentation features in Enterprise Library 3.x and the prior 2.0 version, migrating from the 1.1 version is not straightforward. In fact, for the most part, it will require a complete rewrite from prior versions. The best suggestion is to open the Configuration Console for version 1.1 and note the specific settings used. Then transfer those settings to the new .NET Framework 2.0 or 3.0 applications.

# Common Assembly Instrumentation Support

The Common assembly contains another namespace called Instrumentation (Microsoft.Practices.EnterpriseLibrary.Common.Instrumentation). This namespace provides all the functionality needed by Enterprise Library to instrument the application blocks. This includes event log events, performance counters, and Windows Management Instrumentation (WMI) events. By default, all instrumentation is disabled; however, you can easily turn it on by specifying the correct configuration settings. It is also possible to use these instrumentation features directly from your application.

## How the Instrumentation Features Work

The Instrumentation namespace employs an event-based architecture that separates the code that calls the event from the code that actually performs the action. Instrumentation uses the following three attributes to support this model:

- [InstrumentationListener] defines which listener class to instantiate.

- [InstrumentationConsumer] determines which methods will respond to events.

- [InstrumentationProvider] determines which consumer method in the listener class to execute.

The InstrumentationProvider attribute determines which method to call by matching the name given in the corresponding InstrumentationConsumer. Listing 4-14 demonstrates a simple implementation of this.

**Listing 4-14.** *Simple Instrumentation Example*

```
using System;
using System.Collections.Generic;
using System.Text;
using Microsoft.Practices.EnterpriseLibrary.Common.Instrumentation;

namespace Sample.SimpleInstrumentationSample
{
    public class SomeListener
    {
        [InstrumentationConsumer("StartMe")]
        public void Started(object sender, EventArgs e)
        {
            //perform some action
        }
    }

    [InstrumentationListener(typeof (SomeListener))]
    public class SomeProvider
    {
        [InstrumentationProvider("StartMe")]
        public event EventHandler<EventArgs> OnStart;

    }
}
```

In Listing 4-14, when SomeProvider is instantiated by ObjectBuilder, it will examine the class type provided in the InstrumentationListener attribute. (ObjectBuilder is detailed later in this chapter.) If the class is found, it will instantiate that class. Then all of the events with the InstrumentationProvider attribute are associated with their respective counterparts in the SomeListener class. In this case, the OnStart event in the SomeProvider class is associated with the Started method in the SomeListener class.

A typical application consists of many components. This can include web services, data access logic, business logic, user interface components, and so on—the list can go on forever. It is usually considered better for these components themselves, rather than the application, to call their respective instrumentation providers. The Instrumentation namespace provides an interface called IInstrumentationEventProvider to allow a component to delegate the instrumentation to another component. To invoke this feature, ObjectBuilder must be used with the InstrumentationStrategy during the creation phase of an object. By default, Enterprise Library uses InstrumentationStrategy during the object creation and initialization process via ObjectBuilder. Listing 4-15 shows the use of the IInstrumentationEventProvider

interface within a class. When the `InstrumentationStrategy` sees the
`IInstrumentationEventProvider` interface, it will call the `GetInstrumentationEventProvider`
method to return the object responsible for being the `InstrumentationProvider`.

**Listing 4-15.** *Use of the IInstrumentationEventProvider Interface*

```
using System;
using System.Collections.Generic;
using System.Text;
using Microsoft.Practices.EnterpriseLibrary.Common.Instrumentation;

namespace Sample.SimpleInstrumentationSample
{
    public class MyComponent : IInstrumentationEventProvider
    {
        private SomeProvider myProvider = new SomeProvider();

        public object GetInstrumentationEventProvider()
        {
            return myProvider;
        }
    }
}
```

## Installing Instrumentation

To use the instrumentation features within Enterprise Library, the listener components must
be installed on the target computer. These include the performance counter and event log
features. Enterprise Library uses a component called `ReflectionInstaller`, along with the
attributes listed here, to assist the .NET `InstallUtil.exe` file in locating these components for
installation:

- `[HasInstallableResource]` signals that the listener has installable resources.

- `[EventLogDefinition]` defines an event log category to be added.

- `[PerformanceCountersDefinition]` defines a performance counter category to be
  added.

`InstallUtil.exe` looks for the `HasInstallableResource` attribute, and then installs the
corresponding event log and/or performance counter categories. Listing 4-16 takes the
`SomeListener` class in Listing 4-14 and adds the appropriate attributes so it can log to the
event log.

**Listing 4-16.** *Adding Event Log Features to Listener Class*

```
using System;
using System.Collections.Generic;
using System.Diagnostics;
```

```
using System.Text;
using Microsoft.Practices.EnterpriseLibrary.Common.Instrumentation;

namespace Sample.SimpleInstrumentationSample
{
    [HasInstallableResourcesAttribute]
    [EventLogDefinition("Application", "My Component")]
    public class SomeListener
    {
        [InstrumentationConsumer("StartMe")]
        public void Started(object sender, EventArgs e)
        {
            EventLog.WriteEntry("My Component",
                "Component Started", EventLogEntryType.Information);
        }
    }
}
```

As noted earlier, Enterprise Library has all the instrumentation turned off by default. So if you do not want to use instrumentation, you don't need to install the listener components. Therefore, you can make simple Xcopy deployments.

# ObjectBuilder

ObjectBuilder is a new subsystem that was introduced in the Enterprise Library for .NET Framework 2.0 offering. This new subsystem, which is sometimes called a *smart factory*, takes on the responsibility of creating, configuring, initializing, and disposing of objects. ObjectBuilder manages the process of object creation through what the Microsoft patterns & practices team calls a *pipeline*. This pipeline allows multiple operations to be performed on objects as they are created and initialized for use. ObjectBuilder also can manage the disposal of an object by performing the stages in reverse order.

ObjectBuilder provides the following features and services:

- Creating specific concrete class instances, even if the original request was for an abstract type

- Determining whether to return an existing object instance or create a new one

- Selecting the appropriate constructor, if more than one exists

- Watching for attributes that are declared on properties and methods, and taking appropriate actions as necessary during the creation of new objects

- Using configuration data to determine the objects to be created

- Initializing properties and call methods as predefined by policies

- Making objects that implement the IBuilderAware interface aware of an object's completed creation

## How ObjectBuilder Works

ObjectBuilder works differently for the core Enterprise Library application blocks than it does for other application blocks like the Composite UI Application Block. ObjectBuilder itself is just a framework; the customized factory class determines what creation, initialization, and teardown features, known as *strategies*, are used.

Using ObjectBuilder with Enterprise Library required two major design requirements. First, there had to be a way to determine which type of object to create without explicitly stating it within code. Second, the creation process of an object had to be driven by configuration data. To keep ObjectBuilder extremely flexible, neither of these two requirements was specifically created within ObjectBuilder. Instead, the Enterprise Library team created a series of strategies to address these requirements. The use of these pluggable strategies allow for code to be as simple as this:

```
Database db = DatabaseFactory.CreateDatabase();
```

This single line of code will create an instance or return a singleton instance that was already created of the Database class with any necessary instrumentation features attached. To get a better idea of how this works, it is necessary to take a look at what the static CreateDatabase() method does.

The CreateDatabase() method determines the appropriate configuration source to use, via the ConfigurationSourceFactory, and then creates a DatabaseProviderFactory instance. The DatabaseProviderFactory class inherits from the NameTypeFactoryBase class found in the ObjectBuilder namespace. It also specifies that it will create instances of Database, which is the abstract class used in the Data Access Application Block that is implemented by the SqlDatabase and OracleDatabase classes.

The CreateDatabase() method of the DatabaseFactory class calls the inherited CreateDefault() method of the DatabaseFactoryProvider class. The CreateDefault() method then calls the BuildUp() method of the EnterpriseLibraryFactory class. The BuildUp() method is the heart and soul of the objection creation process:

```
EnterpriseLibraryFactory.BuildUp<T>(configurationSource);
```

EnterpriseLibraryFactory is a static class and hence a singleton. It has a private constructor that creates an instance of BuilderBase. It then adds four strategies to the new BuilderBase instance:

- ConfigurationNameMappingStrategy

- SingletonStrategy

- ConfiguredObjectStrategy

- InstrumentationStrategy

The BuildUp method has seven overloads. In the end, they call a method called GetObjectBuilder(), which returns an instance of BuilderBase. The BuildUp<T> method of the BuilderBase instance is called with an instance of the PolicyList class.

The PolicyList class contains transient policies, which can override the existing permanent policies that are contained within the BuilderBase class. Transient polices are derived from strategies or by using reflection to examine the members of a class. The policies help define how the object will be created. For instance, `ConfigurationObjectPolicy` allows a strategy to look at a configuration source to determine how to create itself.

Finally, the `BuilderBase.BuildUp<T>` method creates and initializes the object based on the strategies and policies defined.

Each strategy that is registered with ObjectBuilder can gather information and context at runtime, when it is invoked, by querying any one of several policy instances that can be associated with a particular strategy. You can use this to use the same strategy for several purposes and inform the strategy about the details of its purpose using a policy at runtime.

The strategies are associated with the ObjectBuilder pipeline stages: PreCreation, Creation, Initialization, and PostInitialization. These are detailed in the following sections.

## PreCreation Stage

The PreCreation stage is where all the initial steps take place to determine what will be created. The PreCreation stage consists of the following strategies:

- `ConfigurationNameMappingStrategy`

- `SingletonStrategy`

- `ConfiguredObjectStrategy`

- `TypeMappingStrategy`

- `ConstructorReflectorStrategy`

- `PropertyReflectionStrategy`

- `MethodReflectionStrategy`

### ConfigurationNameMappingStrategy Class

The `ConfigurationNameMappingStrategy` class is responsible for converting an empty instance name to a default instance name as defined by a configuration source. It does this by looking for an attribute called `ConfigurationNameMapperAttribute`, which describes a helper class used to parse a configuration source for the default instance name to use. This helper class, which inherits from `IConfigurationNameMapper`, will have a method called `MapName` that accepts a string and has an `IConfigurationSource` parameter. The `MapName` method returns the default instance name that is then used to configure the object being created. The `ConfigurationNameMappingStrategy` class uses this technique because each configuration section schema can vary from component to component.

### SingletonStrategy Class

The `SingletonStrategy` class determines whether a particular object should be created only one time within the lifetime of an application domain. If multiple requests are made, the same original instance would be returned in each case. An example of this is the `CacheManager` class used by the Caching Application Block. This class needs to have only one instance so it can keep the in-memory data and on-disk data in sync.

The method used by ObjectBuilder to determine whether an object should be treated as a singleton is through *locators* and *lifetime containers*. The `LifetimeContainer` class manages

the lifetime instance of an object. It essentially keeps an object alive until the
LifetimeContainer is disposed of. This way, your application can no longer reference an
object, and because the LifetimeContainer is still holding a reference to that particular
instance, the garbage collector will not try to remove the object from memory.

The Locator essentially cross-references instance names to an object. This way, an
instance name can look up a particular object. This is done to allow components to create a
singleton instance for their own use within an application domain; otherwise, using a static
class would force a singleton instance to be used by all components.

Using the SingletonStrategy class is pretty simple, because most of the work is
done for you. You just need to have the instance-based factories inherit from
LocatorNameTypeFactoryBase<T>, as in the example in Listing 4-17.

**Listing 4-17.** *Using SingletonStrategy*

```
using System;
using System.Collections.Generic;
using System.Text;
using Microsoft.Practices.EnterpriseLibrary.Common.Configuration;
using Microsoft.Practices.EnterpriseLibrary.Common.Configuration.ObjectBuilder;

namespace Sample.SingletonSample
{
    public class MyClassFactory : LocatorNameTypeFactoryBase<MyClass>
    {
        public MyClassFactory(IConfigurationSource configurationSource)
            : base(configurationSource)
            { }

        ///The rest of the class code.
    }
}
```

When an instance of MyClass already exists as defined by the instance name,
SingletonStrategy will short-circuit the creation process and return the existing instance.

### ConfiguredObjectStrategy Class

The ConfiguredObjectStrategy class determines the object type that needs to be created,
determines the appropriate factory class to accomplish this task, and calls the CreateObject
method of the factory class to create the object. It does this through the use of attributes, as
shown in Listing 4-18.

**Listing 4-18.** *Using ConfiguredObjectStrategy*

```
[CustomFactory(typeof(CacheManagerCustomFactory))]
public class CacheManager : IDisposable
{

}
```

### TypeMappingStrategy Class

The TypeMappingStrategy class allows for a concrete instance of a class to be returned when only a generic type and ID are presented. The mapping is performed by TypeMappingPolicy policies. An example of this would be class MyFoo inherits from interface IFoo. When IFoo is requested to be built, a concrete class of MyFoo is returned. This would be determined through a TypeMappingPolicy policy that maps the MyFoo type to IFoo and some identifier.

### Reflection Strategy Classes

The ConstructorReflectionStrategy, PropertyReflectionStrategy, and MethodReflection➥ Strategy classes use the Dependency Injection model for injecting values. These three strategies are used extensively within the Composite UI Application Block. They provide a mechanism to determine whether any action should be taken on the constructor, property, or method during the Creation or Initialization stages. The constructor actions take place during the Creation stage, and the property and method actions take place during the Initialization stage. These three strategies use the [Dependency] and [CreateNew] attributes to define how they will behave.

When the ConstructorReflectionStrategy class is used, it searches the class that is to be instantiated for a constructor that is decorated with the [InjectionConstructor] attribute. If none is found, then it will determine whether only one constructor exists and will use that constructor. However, if multiple constructors exist and none of them has the [InjectionConstructor] attribute, or the [InjectionConstructor] attribute is defined on multiple constructors, an exception will be raised. Listing 4-19 demonstrates the use of the ConstructorReflectionStrategy class with the [InjectionConstructor] attribute.

**Listing 4-19.** *Using ConstructorReflectionStrategy*

```
using System;
using Microsoft.Practices.ObjectBuilder;
namespace ObjectBuilderExample
{
    public class MyClass
    {
        [InjectionConstructor()]
        public MyClass()
        {
            //construct
        }
    }
}
```

### Creation Stage

The Creation stage is where the object typically gets created. Currently, ObjectBuilder has one strategy for this stage called CreationStrategy. The CreationStrategy looks for policies intended for this interface type and applies those strategies to define how the object is created. If no policies exist, the CreationStrategy will use the first constructor returned by reflection and then populate any necessary parameters required by the constructor.

Currently, the CreationStrategy uses two policies:

- ConstructorPolicy determines the appropriate constructor to use by looking at the parameters. If no parameters are present, then the default constructor will be used.

- DefaultCreationPolicy selects the first public constructor of an object and passes any necessary parameters to it in order to create the object.

## Initialization Stage

The Initialization stage occurs after creation of the object. This stage has three strategies. Two strategies are used to set properties or execute methods that ObjectBuilder was made aware of during the PreCreation stage via the MethodReflectionStrategy and PropertyReflectionStrategy. The third strategy is used to add instrumentation to an object. The two strategies used for executing methods and setting property values are called PropertySetterStrategy and MethodExecutionStrategy.

### PropertySetterStrategy Class

The PropertySetterStrategy class is used to set public property values based on the policies defined in the PolicyList passed into the BuildUp method. By decorating a public property with the Dependency attribute, the property will be populated with the type specified in the Dependency attribute call. Listing 4-20 shows an example of what this may look like.

**Listing 4-20.** *Property Setter Attributes Example*

```
using System;
using Microsoft.Practices.ObjectBuilder;
namespace ObjectBuilderExample
{
   public class MyClass
   {
      private Foo m_MyFoo;

      [InjectionConstructor()]
      public MyClass()
      {
         //construct
      }

      [Dependency(SearchMode = SearchMode.Local, CreateType = typeOf(Foo), ➦
         NotPresentBehavior = NotPresentBehavior.CreateNew)]
      public Foo myFoo
      {
         set
         {
            this.m_MyFoo = value;
         }
      }
   }
}
```

The Dependency attribute contains a series of properties that can be set to determine what and how a particular property or parameter will be created. In Listing 4-20, three properties were set:

- SearchMode determines how the object will be located. This determines whether the object is already instantiated. The Local enumerator will search only the local context; the Up enumerator will search up the hierarchy for the object.

- CreateType determines the type of object to build depending on whether it is not found during the search.

- NotPresentBehavior determines what ObjectBuilder should do if the object does not already exist. The available values are as follows:

  - CreateNew creates a new instance.

  - ReturnNull returns null.

  - Throw throws a DependencyMissingException.

### MethodExecutionStrategy Class

The MethodExecutionStrategy class is used to execute public methods based on the policies defined in the PolicyList passed into the BuildUp method. When a method is decorated with the InjectionMethod attribute, it will execute the method. In Listing 4-21, a method called DoSomething is used to demonstrate the use of the InjectionMethod attribute, as well as to show how the Dependency attribute can be used to specify the parameters for the DoSomething method.

**Listing 4-21.** *Method Execution Attributes Example*

```
using System;
using Microsoft.Practices.ObjectBuilder;
namespace ObjectBuilderExample
{
   public class MyClass
   {
      private Foo m_MyFoo;

      [InjectionConstructor()]
      public MyClass()
      {
         //construct
      }

      [Dependency(SearchMode = SearchMode.Local, CreateType = typeOf(Foo), ➡
         NotPresentBehavior = NotPresentBehavior.CreateNew)]
      public Foo myFoo
      {
         set
```

```
        {
            this.m_MyFoo = value;
        }
    }

    [InjectionMethod()]
    Public void DoSomething([Dependency(SearchMode = SearchMode.Local, ➥
        CreateType = typeOf(Foo),
        NotPresentBehavior = NotPresentBehavior.CreateNew)] ➥
        Foo paramFoo)
    {
        //Do Something with Foo;
    }
    }
}
```

**InstrumentationAttachmentStrategy Class**

Enterprise Library also includes a third Initialization stage strategy called the
InstrumentationAttachmentStrategy. This strategy attaches instrumentation events to
the creating instance of the listener object. If the performance counters, event logging,
and WMI are all disabled, then the attachment of instrumentation is short-circuited.
Otherwise, the Instrumentation provider is bound to the Instrumentation consumer
using the CreateBinder method of the InstrumentationAttacherFactory class.

## PostInitialization Stage

The final stage of the BuildUp method of ObjectBuilder is PostInitialization. The only strategy
that exists in this phase is the BuilderAwareStrategy, which will notify an object of when the
BuildUp method is completed. This is useful if an object needs to execute some code immediately after being created, such as a TCP listener.

The BuilderAwareStrategy checks an object as it is moving through the BuildUp
method. If that object implements the IBuilderAware event, it will execute the
IBuilderAware.OnBuiltUp method after the Initialization stage, and then call the
IBuilderAware.OnTearingDown method at the beginning of the object's teardown process.

The BuilderAwareStrategy uses "substrategies" in the Composite UI Application Block.
These substrategies are used for hooking commands and event brokers, notifying objects
when an object is fully built, and assisting the application to properly initialize the root object
known as a *work item* when it is created.

**Note** You can find more information about the Composite UI Application Block's event brokers,
commands, and work items in Chapter 15.

## Composite UI Application Block Strategies

The Composite UI Application Block uses different strategies than those used for the core
Enterprise Library application blocks. The only strategy that both the core Enterprise Library
application blocks and the Composite UI Application Block share is the SingletonStrategy.
The strategies that the CAB uses are as follows:

- TypeMappingStrategy

- SingletonStrategy

- ConstructorReflectionStrategy

- PropertyReflectionStrategy

- MethodReflectionStrategy

- CreationStrategy

- PropertySetterStrategy

- MethodExecutionStrategy

- BuilderAwareStrategy

# Using ObjectBuilder

To use the ObjectBuilder class to create an object, you should create a "builder" factory class.
This builder class will be responsible for creating the context, determining the strategies to
use, and defining the policies.

To handle the context of constructing objects, ObjectBuilder provides a simple implementation of IBuilderContext called BuilderContext. The BuilderContext class provides the
context in which all of the operations for building up and tearing down objects operate. This
class will contain all the meat and potatoes necessary to manage the policies and lifetime of
the objects that are created. This also gives you the flexibility of creating your implementation
for defining policies and managing objects through their life cycles.

Listing 4-22 shows an implementation of the BuilderContext class called MyContext and a
factory called MyFactory, which sets the strategies and policies to create objects like the one in
Listing 4-21.

**Listing 4-22.** *MyContext and MyFactory Classes for Creating New Objects*

```
using System;
using System.Collections.Generic;
using System.Text;
using Microsoft.Practices.ObjectBuilder;

namespace ObjectBuilderExample
{
    public class MyFactory<T> where T : class
    {
```

```
        public static T BuildObject( string name )
        {
            MyContext context = new MyContext();

            context.MyStrategyChain.Add(new CreationStrategy());

            context.MyStrategyChain.Add(new MethodReflectionStrategy());
            context.MyStrategyChain.Add(new MethodExecutionStrategy());

            context.MyStrategyChain.Add(new PropertyReflectionStrategy());
            context.MyStrategyChain.Add(new PropertySetterStrategy());

            context.MyPolicies.SetDefault<ICreationPolicy>(new
                DefaultCreationPolicy());

            return context.HeadOfChain.BuildUp(context, typeof(T), null, name)
                as T;
        }
    }

    public class MyContext : BuilderContext
    {
        private IReadWriteLocator m_MyLocator;
        private PolicyList m_MyPolicies = new PolicyList();
        private LifetimeContainer m_MyLifetimeContainer = new LifetimeContainer();
        private BuilderStrategyChain m_MyStrategyChain =
            new BuilderStrategyChain();

        public BuilderStrategyChain MyStrategyChain
        {
            get { return m_MyStrategyChain; }
        }

        public PolicyList MyPolicies
        {
            get { return m_MyPolicies; }
        }

        public LifetimeContainer MyLifetimeContainer
        {
            get { return m_MyLifetimeContainer; }
        }

        public IReadWriteLocator MyLocator
        {
            get { return m_MyLocator; }
        }
```

```
public MyContext() : this(new Locator()) { }

public MyContext(IReadWriteLocator locator)
{
    m_MyLocator = locator;
    SetLocator(m_MyLocator);
    StrategyChain = m_MyStrategyChain;
    SetPolicies(m_MyPolicies);
    if (!Locator.Contains(typeof(ILifetimeContainer)))
        Locator.Add(typeof(ILifetimeContainer), m_MyLifetimeContainer);
}
}
}
```

Finally, the last step is to create a new object. To do so, simply call the BuildObject method of the MyFactory class, as shown here:

```
MyClass myClass = MyFactory<MyClass>.BuildObject( "MyClass" );
```

# Adding Custom Configuration Settings for the ACME POS Application

The ACME Cosmetics Company has been using a web application for many years so its sales consultants can manage clients, sales orders, and other business-related tasks. One of the major issues brought up by the on-road sales team is that they must be connected to the Internet in order to use the application.

ACME Cosmetics has decided to create a new smart client application that will allow the sales team to work both online and offline. A Windows smart client interface will utilize web services to communicate with the ACME back-end systems. These web services will require a URL to be configured for the smart client application. Also, in the interest of disaster recovery, failover protection, and load balancing, there will be three web server hosting locations across the country: East Coast, Midwest, and West Coast. This will require configurable URLs for the smart client application.

## Defining the Configuration Data

The application will need to know the URL of each web server location, as well being able to determine which URL is the default web server host. Instead of creating an application block, you will create a simple independent runtime component that can be consumed by the smart client application. The configuration data in the XML configuration file should look similar to Listing 4-23.

**Listing 4-23.** *Smart Client Web Service Configuration*

```
<configuration>
  <configSections>
    <section name="webServiceSettingsConfiguration" ➡
        type="ACME.POS. UserInterface.Configuration.WebServiceSettings, ➡
          ACME.POS. UserInterface.Configuration" />
  </configSections>
  <webServiceSettingsConfiguration defaultWebServiceURL="MidWest">
    <webServiceURLs>
      <add url="http://services.midwest-acme.com"
        name="MidWest" />
      <add url="http://services.eastcoast-acme.com"
        name="EastCoast" />
      <add url="http://services.westcoast-acme.com"
        name="WestCoast" />
    </webServiceURLs>
  </webServiceSettingsConfiguration>
</configuration>
```

Beneath the webServicesURLs element, Listing 4-23 has three add elements that define the different web service URLs that are available to the application. More services could be added easily and just as easily removed.

The default web service is defined in the webServiceSettingsConfiguration element by the defaultWebServiceURL attribute. This attribute points to the proper webServicesURL/add element that should be used as the default web service.

## Creating the Configuration Runtime Component

Now that the configuration requirements have been determined, there must be a way to get and set the configuration data. This is where the configuration runtime comes into play. This will require the creation of two classes: one to handle the web service URLs themselves and one as the parent class that will contain the child web service URLs and define the default URL to use.

First, you will create the WebServiceURL class. This class will define the web service URL and the name to reference the URL. Since the web service name and URL are a key-value pair, it makes sense to use the NamedConfigurationElement class from the Microsoft.Practices.EnterpriseLibrary.Common.Configuration namespace. This class already contains the Name property that is required. All you need to do is to create the URL property and create a new constructor that will set the name and URL properties. When creating the URL property, it will be necessary to mark it with the .NET Framework ConfigurationProperty attribute. Listing 4-24 shows the WebServiceURL class.

**Listing 4-24.** *WebServiceURL Configuration Class*

```
using System.Configuration;
using Microsoft.Practices.EnterpriseLibrary.Common.Configuration;

namespace ACME.POS. UserInterface.Configuration
```

```
{
    public class WebServiceURL : NamedConfigurationElement
    {
        private const string m_Url = string.Empty;

        public WebServiceURL()
        {}

        public WebServiceURL(string name, string url)
            : base(name)
        {
            this.URL = url;
        }

        [ConfigurationProperty(url, IsRequired = true)]
        public string URL
        {
            get { return (string)base[url]; }
            set { base[url] = value; }
        }
    }
}
```

The second class to complete the configuration runtime component is the WebServiceSettings class. This class will define the child WebServiceURL nodes, as well as the default web service URL to use. The WebServiceSettings class will inherit from the SerializableConfigurationSection class, which is a serializable version of System.Configuration.ConfigurationSection. As with the WebServiceURL class, it is necessary to mark up the configuration properties so that new .NET Framework 2.0 configuration features can properly handle the saving and reading of configuration data. Listing 4-25 shows the WebServiceSettings class.

**Listing 4-25.** *WebServiceSettings Configuration Class*

```
using System.Configuration;
using Microsoft.Practices.EnterpriseLibrary.Common.Configuration;

namespace ACME.POS.UserInterface.Configuration
{
    public class WebServiceSettings : SerializableConfigurationSection
    {
        public const string SectionName = "webServiceSettingsConfiguration";

        private const string defaultWebServiceURL = "defaultWebServiceURL";
        private const string webServiceURLs = "webServiceURLs";
```

```csharp
[ConfigurationProperty(defaultWebServiceURL, IsRequired = true)]
public string DefaultWebServiceURL
{
    get { return (string)base[defaultWebServiceURL]; }
    set { base[defaultWebServiceURL] = value; }
}

[ConfigurationProperty(webServiceURLs, IsRequired = true)]
public NamedElementCollection<WebServiceURL> WebServiceURLs
{
    get
    {
        return (NamedElementCollection<WebServiceURL>)base[webServiceURLs];
    }
}
}
}
```

**Note** Although the exercise of creating the configuration runtime is useful in understanding how it works, the Application Block Software Factory might be a better choice for creating this code for you. See Chapter 14 for details on the Application Block Software Factory.

# Summary

Understanding the core components found in the Common assembly and ObjectBuilder that are used by all the application blocks is key to understanding how each application block can be used. Also, this understanding can assist when debugging is required.

You may want to use some of the Common assembly configuration features in your own applications. In the case of configuration management, it allows for extensibility in how you store the application configuration data. In a development environment, you can use a simple external XML file, and yet for security purposes the SQL configuration source can be implemented with only a simple configuration change.

The next chapter will go into the details of the Configuration Console, used for creating and managing configuration data at design time.

# CHAPTER 5

■ ■ ■

# The Enterprise Library Configuration Console

**C**hapter 4 discussed the internals of how the application blocks use and interact with configuration data. You learned how to set up configuration files and even how to create your own configuration runtime component. This chapter describes how to manage that configuration data.

## The Configuration Dilemma

While it is great that the Enterprise Library application block components are highly configurable, it also can produce a maintenance nightmare. Imagine trying to manage a configuration file for an application that contains multiple database connections and configuration details for logging, caching, and security. Attempting to manage all of this data can quickly result in a large and unwieldy configuration file. Although one way to handle this is to separate the configuration data into separate files for each application block (a strategy discussed in Chapter 4), a configuration file for data access could still look something like Listing 5-1.

**Listing 5-1.** *Database Access Configuration Example*

```
<configuration>
  <configSections>
    <section name="dataConfiguration"
      type="Microsoft.Practices.EnterpriseLibrary.Data.
        Configuration.DatabaseSettings,
        Microsoft.Practices.EnterpriseLibrary.Data,
        Version=3.0.0.0, Culture=neutral, PublicKeyToken-null" />
  </configSections>
  <dataConfiguration defaultDatabase="ApplicationDB" />
  <connectionStrings>
    <add name="ClientDB" connectionString="Database=ClientDB;
      Server=MyDBServer;Integrated Security=SSPI;"
      providerName="System.Data.SqlClient" />
```

```
    <add name="AccountingDB"
        connectionString="Database=AccountingDB;
            Server=MyDBServer;Integrated Security=SSPI;"
        providerName="System.Data.SqlClient" />
    <add name="ApplicationDB"
        connectionString="Database=ApplicationDB;
            Server=MyDBServer;Integrated Security=SSPI;"
        providerName="System.Data.SqlClient" />
    <add name="WarehouseDB"
        connectionString="Database=Database;
            Server=MyDBServer;Integrated Security=SSPI;"
        providerName="System.Data.SqlClient" />
    <add name="SalesDB" connectionString="Database=SalesDB;
            Server=MyDBServer;Integrated Security=SSPI;"
        providerName="System.Data.SqlClient" />
    <add name="ReportingDB"
        connectionString="Database=ReportingDB;
            Server=MyDBServer;Integrated Security=SSPI;"
        providerName="System.Data.SqlClient" />
  </connectionStrings>
</configuration>
```

As features and resources are added to an application, a configuration file could end up with many entries, as in the example in Listing 5-1. Although you can edit a configuration file with Visual Studio, Notepad, or some other XML/text-editing tool, there is always the chance that some type of error could be introduced into an application. And the error may not be a simple typo—it could be bad data, such as an out-of-range value or an invalid URL.

To assist in the entry and maintenance of configuration data, the Microsoft patterns & practices team introduced the Configuration Console with Enterprise Library. With the release of Enterprise Library for .NET Framework 3.0, the Microsoft patterns & practices team added a variant of the Configuration Console that is integrated within Visual Studio 2005, called the Configuration Editor.

# How the Configuration Console and Configuration Editor Work

The Configuration Console and Configuration Editor allow you to manipulate configuration data relatively easily via a graphical user interface (GUI). These tools work in conjunction with the application block components to allow each application block to have its configuration data represented differently. The Configuration Console and Configuration Editor both provide validation features, and they can even be used to edit configuration sections that are not related to the application blocks, with the help of some open source projects.

The differences between the Configuration Console and Configuration Editor are minor, as you will learn in the "Using the Configuration Editor within Visual Studio 2005" section later in this chapter. In this section, I'll refer to just the Configuration Console, but the discussion of how the components work together also applies to the Configuration Editor.

# Design of the Configuration Console and Editor

Three main components work together to manage configuration:

- The Configuration Console and Configuration Editor provide the GUI.

- The design-time configuration components provide the glue between the GUI and the runtime configuration components.

- The runtime configuration components provide the read and write functionality.

These three pieces provide for customized configuration manipulation on a per-application block basis. This is necessary because each application block has its own configuration data structure and hierarchy that best suits the needs of that application block. For example, compare the configuration of the Exception Handling Application Block shown in Listing 5-2 with that of the Data Access Application Block shown earlier in Listing 5-1.

**Listing 5-2.** *Exception Handling Configuration Example*

```
<configuration>
    <configSections>
        <section name="exceptionHandling"
            type="Microsoft.Practices.EnterpriseLibrary.
                ExceptionHandling.Configuration.
                ExceptionHandlingSettings,
                Microsoft.Practices.EnterpriseLibrary.ExceptionHandling,
                Version=3.0.0.0, Culture=neutral, PublicKeyToken=null" />
    </configSections>
    <exceptionHandling>
        <exceptionPolicies>
            <add name="Exception Policy">
                <exceptionTypes>
                    <add type="System.Exception, mscorlib,
                        Version=3.0.0.0, Culture=neutral,
                        PublicKeyToken=b77a5c561934e089"
                    postHandlingAction="NotifyRethrow" name="Exception">
                    <exceptionHandlers>
                        <add exceptionMessage="Application Error Occurred"
                            replaceExceptionType="
                                System.ApplicationException, mscorlib,
                                Version=3.0.0.0, Culture-neutral,
                                PublicKeyToken=b77a5c561934e089"
                                type="Microsoft.Practices.EnterpriseLibrary.
                                ExceptionHandling.ReplaceHandler,
                                Microsoft.Practices.EnterpriseLibrary.
                                ExceptionHandling, Version=3.0.0.0,
                                Culture=neutral, PublicKeyToken=null"
                            name="Replace Handler" />
                    </exceptionHandlers>
                </add>
```

```
            </exceptionTypes>
         </add>
      </exceptionPolicies>
   </exceptionHandling>
</configuration>
```

As you can see, the configuration data structures and hierarchy for the two application blocks are drastically different. Such differences require customized handling of the configuration data for each application block.

Figure 5-1 shows the Configuration Console UI. On the surface, it may appear that the Configuration Console has the ability to manipulate each application block. Actually, the Configuration Console is loosely coupled with each application block. It uses the design-time components to determine how to interact with the configuration settings for each application block. The design-time components act as the intermediary between the Configuration Console and the configuration runtime components. They describe how to display the configuration data and how the displayed data should be mapped to the runtime components.

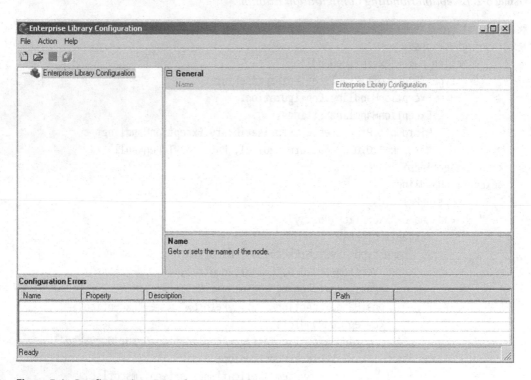

**Figure 5-1.** *Configuration Console user interface*

## Differences from Earlier Versions

Although the UI looks the same as that of the Configuration Console in earlier versions, some changes have been made underneath the hood. The changes revolve around how the versions implement the architecture. For instance, in Enterprise Library 1.1, the design-time component for the Data Access Application Block implemented a Save method that contained the implementation for saving the configuration data to the appropriate configuration source.

Now the design-time component uses a base class called `ConfigurationDesignManager`, which contains an implementation of the `Save` method that can be used by all of the application blocks for saving configuration data.

These design changes were implemented to resolve the complexity and amount of work involved in creating design-time components. This should make it easier to create new design-time components for custom application blocks.

---

**Note**  The only application block that modifies the `ConfigurationDesignManager` implementation is the Cryptography Application Block. The Cryptography Application Block also performs extra steps during the save routine in order to save protected keys to a file.

---

The Configuration Console provided with Enterprise Library 3.0 adds the ability to edit some configuration sections that are not related to application blocks, such as `AppSetting`. A few open source initiatives support this ability for Enterprise Library 2.0. One such project is the .NET Configuration Manager, developed by Olaf Conjin. The .NET Configuration Manager contains configuration design-time components that assist in the management of the `System.Web` and `AppSetting` configuration nodes, so that they may be managed within the Configuration Console. This effectively gives development projects that still use Enterprise Library 2.0 the ability to manage environmental overrides and application settings. The .NET Configuration Manager also allows the management of the `System.Web` configuration settings, which at the time of writing this book, Enterprise Library 3.0 does not allow. However, chances are someone in the .NET community will get this ported, hopefully in the not-to-distant future. I'll show you how to use the .NET Configuration Manager in Chapter 15.

## Configuration Console Initialization

During the initialization of the Configuration Console, it looks for assemblies that are marked with the `ConfigurationDesignManagerAttribute` attribute. This attribute tells the Configuration Console that the assembly contains an implementation of the abstract class `ConfigurationDesignManager`. The attribute takes a parameter of `System.Type`. The `System.Type` determines the appropriate class type that will be used by the Configuration Console to display and manipulate the configuration data in the UI. Listing 5-3 shows an example of what the Data Access Application Block design-time assembly `ConfigurationDesignManagerAttribute` attribute looks like in the `AssemblyInfo.cs` file.

**Listing 5-3.** *Data Access Application Block ConfigurationDesignManagerAttribute*

```
[assembly: ConfigurationDesignManager(typeof(DataConfigurationDesignManager))]
[assembly: ConfigurationDesignManager(
    typeof(ConnectionStringsConfigurationDesignManager),
    typeof(DataConfigurationDesignManager))]
[assembly: ConfigurationDesignManager(
    typeof(OracleConnectionConfigurationDesignManager),
    typeof(ConnectionStringsConfigurationDesignManager))]
```

The first line in Listing 5-3 denotes that the DataConfigurationDesignManager is the main ConfigurationDesignManager instance. The second and third lines show dependencies on other ConfigurationDesignManagers. In this case, the ConnectionStringsConfigurationDesignManager has a dependency on the DataConfigurationManager, and the OracleConnectionConfigurationDesignManager has a dependency on the ConnectionStringsConfigurationDesignManager. This hierarchical dependency ensures that the configuration data is persisted properly when the Save event is fired.

When the Configuration Console looks up assemblies, it simply looks for all files in its executing folder with the .dll extension. As a Visual Studio add-in, the Configuration Editor will look up assemblies in a folder specified by a registry setting. To simplify maintenance and reduce the chances of unexpected behavior, it is a good idea to put only design-time and runtime .dll assemblies in the folder searched by the Configuration Console or Configuration Editor.

---

**Note** The design-time assemblies must reside in the executing folder in order for the Configuration Console to pick them up. This means that design-time assemblies that are in the GAC will not be picked up either; a physical version would need to reside in the Configuration Console's executing folder.

---

Now that the Configuration Console has loaded the configuration design-time components, it knows which application blocks are available. When a configuration file is opened, it will be able to display the appropriate application blocks within the menu.

The design-time component is the brain of the Configuration Console. The design-time component defines how the configuration runtime will map visually to the UI. It is responsible for any customized UI elements such as wizards. The configuration design-time components also will help the Configuration Console to display the proper hierarchy of the configuration data, validate data entered, and save the configuration data.

## Type Selection

The Configuration Console contains a special dialog element called the TypeSelectorUI to assist the application block design-time components in allowing users to properly configure them. The TypeSelectorUI is passed in certain parameters from a configuration design-time component. The Type Selector dialog box then displays the appropriate types, as shown in the example in Figure 5-2. The TypeSelectorUI also allows you to specify an assembly and use an appropriate type found in that assembly.

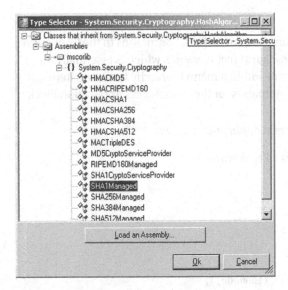

**Figure 5-2.** *Type Selector dialog box*

## Configuration Nodes

During the initialization of the design-time component, a method called Register is called. This method performs two critical functions: it tells the Configuration Console which nodes to display and how to display them, and it tells the Configuration Console which command items to display in the context menus.

The registration of a design-time component is typically handled by an implementation of the CommandRegistrar class. The CommandRegistrar class contains methods for creating menu items and adding, removing, moving, and validating configuration nodes, as listed in Table 5-1.

**Table 5-1.** *CommandRegistrar Class Methods*

| Method | Description |
| --- | --- |
| AddUICommand | Adds a command that performs some action when executed (like a menu item or toolbar button) |
| AddChildNodeCommand | Adds a command that allows for child nodes to be created |
| AddSingleChildNodeCommand | Adds a command that forces only one child node to be created |
| AddMultipleChildNodeCommand | Adds a command that allows for multiple child nodes to be created |
| AddRemoveCommand | Adds a command for removing a particular registered type |
| AddValidateCommand | Adds a command for validating a particular registered type |
| AddDefaultsCommand | Adds both a remove and validate command for a particular registered type |
| AddMoveUpCommand | Adds a command to move a particular registered type |
| AddMoveDownCommand | Adds a command to move a particular registered type |
| AddMoveUpDownCommand | Adds a command to move a particular registered type up or down |

## Adding Nodes

The AddUICommand is the core method for adding new menu item commands to the Configuration Console. It accepts an instance of the ConfigurationUICommand, which is essentially the menu item itself, and a type to determine where within a menu hierarchy the menu item will go. Listing 5-4 shows an example of adding commands for the Data Access Application Block.

**Listing 5-4.** *Adding Commands for the Data Access Application Block*

```
sealed class DataCommandRegistrar : CommandRegistrar
{
    //constructor...

    public override void Register()
    {
        AddDataCommand();
        AddDefaultCommands(typeof(DatabaseSectionNode));

        AddProviderMappingCommand();
        AddDefaultCommands(typeof(ProviderMappingNode));
    }

    private void AddDataCommand()
    {
        ConfigurationUICommand item =
            ConfigurationUICommand.CreateSingleUICommand(ServiceProvider,
                Resources.DataUICommandText,
                Resources.DataUICommandLongText,
                new AddDatabaseSectionNodeCommand(ServiceProvider),
                typeof(DatabaseSectionNode));

        AddUICommand(item, typeof(ConfigurationApplicationNode));
    }

    private void AddProviderMappingCommand()
    {
        AddMultipleChildNodeCommand(
            Resources.ProviderMappingUICommandText,
            Resources.ProviderMappingUICommandLongText,
            typeof(ProviderMappingNode),
            typeof(ProviderMappingsNode));
    }
}
```

In Listing 5-4, the Register method in the DataCommandRegistrar class calls three methods to build the Data Access Application Block's Add New, Remove, and Validate command menu items, and also builds the provider-mapping command menu items.

The first method that is called from the Register method is AddDataCommand. This method uses a static method of the ConfigurationUICommand class to create a UICommand (menu item) that can exist only once within the menu hierarchy. This particular method takes five parameters: a service provider, a text caption for the menu item, a text description that will be displayed in the status bar, a node command to execute, and the type of node that should be created.

The node command is an important class for defining any special tasks that should be performed when adding this particular node. In this case, it performs any tasks by calling the OnExecuted method of the AddDatabaseSectionNodeCommand class. This class inherits from an AddChildNodeCommand class, and is intended to add a child node to the existing executing node. In this case, when the New ➤ Data Access Application Block menu item is selected, it will try to determine the default database connection and add a new configuration node instance of the ProviderMappingsNode class as a child node of itself.

Before the node command is executed, the Configuration Console looks through the available command menu items and determines which ones should be added to the existing node. In the case of adding the Data Access Application Block, the ConnectionStringsSettingsNode object is added. This is determined by the parent System.Type of which the ConnectionStringsSettingsNode object said it should be a child. In this case, the parent System.Type is the DatabaseSectionNode. Now whenever a DatabaseSectionNode object is created, a child ConnectionStringSettingsNode object is created along with it. Then the OnExecuted method of the AddDatabaseSectionNodeCommand class will set the DefaultDatabase property to the correct connection string node and also add the custom provider-mappings node (ProviderMappingsNode class).

In the DataCommandRegistrar class, the AddProviderMappingCommand method calls the base class's (CommandRegistrar's) AddMultipleChildNodeCommand method. The AddMultipleChildNodeCommand is one of three methods to simplify the process of adding new command menu items. The other two methods are AddChildNodeCommand and AddSingleChildNodeCommand. These methods allow the developer to add child nodes to the menu hierarchy without needing to create redundant code. Typically, only the AddSingleChildNodeCommand method and the AddMultipleChildNodeCommand method would be called, as the AddChildNodeCommand is simply a helper method for simplifying the creation of the single-instance or multiple-instance child nodes.

## Removing and Validating Nodes

The AddRemoveCommand method simply adds a command menu item to allow the removal of the current selected configuration node and its child nodes. The AddValidateCommand method adds a command menu item that performs validation on the currently selected node and its child nodes. Both the AddValidateCommand and the AddRemoveCommand methods have one parameter that takes a System.Type, which determines the type to which to apply the menu items. Since these two commands are typically desired, calling the AddDefaultCommands method will automatically set up the Remove and Validate menu items for the specified System.Type.

## Moving Nodes

The AddMoveUpCommand and AddMoveDownCommand methods allow for the creation of menu items used for repositioning the current node in respect to other sibling nodes. Both of these methods take a System.Type parameter that determines to which node type to apply the menu items.

As with the remove and validate menu items, you can use a single method to add both of these move menu items: AddMoveUpDownCommands.

## Displaying Icons

Each node has a default icon associated with it in the tree list, as shown in Figure 5-3. However, it is possible to customize that image by using the ImageAttribute class. The ImageAttribute's "grandparent" class is ToolboxBitmapAttribute.

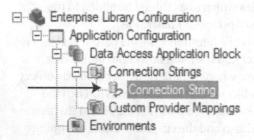

**Figure 5-3.** *Configuration Console tree node icons*

The ImageAttribute class has two constructors: one takes a parameter of just System.Type, and the other takes a parameter of System.Type and System.String. The constructor with the single parameter of System.Type uses the System.Type to determine the assembly in which that image is located. It then looks for a resource named *namespace*. *classname*.bmp. The *namespace* and *classname* are defined by the System.Type parameter passed in.

The constructor with the System.Type and System.String parameters works a little differently. In this instance, the System.Type determines in which assembly to look and the namespace it will use to find the resource. However, the System.String will determine the specific resource within the namespace to find the image.

---

■**Note**  For more information about the ToolboxBitmapAttribute, see the Visual Studio 2005 help documentation or MSDN online (http://msdn.microsoft.com).

---

Using the ImageAttribute is easy. Just add the appropriate 16-by-16 bitmap to the solution within one of your projects, create a custom implementation of the ConfigurationNode class, and then mark up the custom ConfigurationNode class with the ImageAttribute. Listing 5-5 shows an example.

**Listing 5-5.** *Icon Markup for Database Section Node*

```
[Image(typeof(DatabaseSectionNode))]
public sealed class DatabaseSectionNode : ConfigurationNode
{
   //Class Code
}
```

# Configuration Files

Once the configuration design-time components are loaded and the UI has been presented, the Configuration Console gives you the option of opening an existing configuration file or creating a new configuration file.

## Creating and Opening Configuration Files

When creating a new configuration file, the Configuration Console creates an instance of the AddConfigurationApplicationNodeCommand class, which inherits from ConfigurationNodeCommand. After the instance of the AddConfigurationApplicationNode➡ Command is created, the Execute method is called. This method handles calling the OnExecuting method, which in turn raises the Executing event. Once the OnExecute method has been called, any errors displayed in the user interface are cleared via the ClearErrorDisplay method of the ConfigurationNodeCommand's UIService property, the ExecuteCore method is called, the Executed event is raised via the OnExecute method call, and finally, any log error cleanup they may need takes place.

The key method that performs the actual command function that must be overridden is the ExecuteCore method. In the case of the AddConfigurationApplicationNodeCommand class, the overridden ExecuteCore method creates an instance of the ConfigurationApplicationNode class, as well as an instance of the ConfigurationUIHierarchy class. Finally, the ConfigurationApplicationNode is loaded into the proper location of the TreeListView control in the UI by calling the Load method of the ConfigurationUIHierarchy instance.

When opening a configuration file, an instance of OpenConfigurationApplication➡ NodeCommand is created instead of the AddConfigurationApplicationNodeCommand class. The OpenConfigurationApplicationNodeCommand class performs almost the same steps as the AddConfigurationApplicationNodeCommand class, except that it displays an Open File dialog box, and instead of creating a blank ConfigurationApplicationNode instance, it will create an instance of ConfigurationApplicationNode that contains the configuration data found in the file that was selected through the Open File dialog box. Also, the Open method of the ConfigurationUIHierarchy instance, as opposed to the Load method, is called.

In both the opening and new creation of an application configuration file, an instance of the ConfigurationApplicationNode is created. The ConfigurationApplicationNode is the root node for the application block configuration node. It essentially contains only one property that determines the location of the configuration file. An example of this is shown in Figure 5-4.

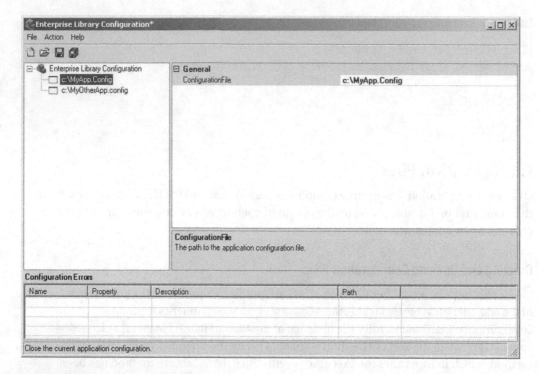

**Figure 5-4.** *Configuration application node*

In Figure 5-4, notice that there are two application configuration file nodes that have a parent node. This parent node is called the SolutionConfigurationNode, and it allows for multiple child nodes of application configuration files (ConfigurationApplicationNode). This effectively will allow the manipulation of multiple configuration files at one time through a single UI.

## Saving Configuration Files

When the Save button or the Save menu item is selected, the Configuration Console creates an instance of a class called SaveConfigurationApplicationNodeCommand. This class is responsible for calling the appropriate components and services in order to save the configuration data. This class also inherits from the ConfigurationNodeCommand class and has a specific implementation of the ExecuteCore method.

In the case of the SaveConfigurationApplicationNodeCommand class, the ExecuteCore method first validates the configuration data via the ValidateNodeCommand class, and then creates a configuration file, if necessary. It checks for any errors, and if they are found, the method is halted and the errors are displayed. Finally, the configuration data is saved by calling the Save method of the ConfigurationUIHierarchy class.

The ConfigurationUIHierarchy class' Save method calls the Save method on the configDomain property, which is an instance of the ConfigurationDesignDomainManager. Ultimately, the Save method of the ConfigurationDesignManager is called to perform the actual work of saving the configuration data to disk.

## Editing Configuration Files

While it is great being able to open and save configuration files, it would not be very useful to do so without being able to manipulate the configuration data inside them. This is where the ConfigurationNode class comes in. Each application block contains specific custom implementations of this class. For example, the Data Access Application Block requires a default database property. The custom ConfigurationNode implementation called DatabaseSectionNode contains a property to display available databases to select from to satisfy this property value. An example of this property is shown in Listing 5-6.

**Listing 5-6.** *DefaultDatabase Property Example*

```
[Editor(typeof(ReferenceEditor), typeof(UITypeEditor))]
[ReferenceType(typeof(ConnectionStringSettingsNode))]
[SRCategory("CategoryGeneral", typeof(Resources))]
[SRDescription("DefaultDatabaseDescription", typeof(Resources))]
public ConnectionStringSettingsNode DefaultDatabase
{
    get
    {
        return connectionStringSettingNode;
    }

    set
    {
        connectionStringSettingsNode = LinkNodeHelper.CreateReference
            <ConnectionStringSettingsNode>
            (connectionStringSettingsNode,
            value,
            connectionStringNodeRemovedHandler,
            null);
    }
}
```

However, even though each application block has specific requirements for configuration data, some common features—such as removing nodes, adding nodes, and moving nodes—are required by all configuration nodes. These common functions are found within the ConfigurationNode class. All design-time nodes will inherit from the ConfigurationNode class.

In Listing 5-6, notice the three attributes that make up the DefaultDatabase property:

EditorAttribute: This is a .NET Framework attribute that describes the editor to be used for modifying the property value. Currently, only one type of editor is provided by the .NET Framework: the UITypeEditor. The UITypeEditor allows for three types of editing methods: direct text editing, a modal pop-up dialog box, or a drop-down list. It is possible to create a custom implementation of the UITypeEditor to handle special needs while editing a property value.

ReferenceTypeAttribute: This attribute helps the Configuration Console to determine the System.Type that the configuration node references. This is used by the Configuration Console to help determine the type to display in the ReferenceEditorUI control. In this case, the available ConnectionStringSettingsNode objects would be displayed in the drop-down list for the default database connection string, as shown in Figure 5-5.

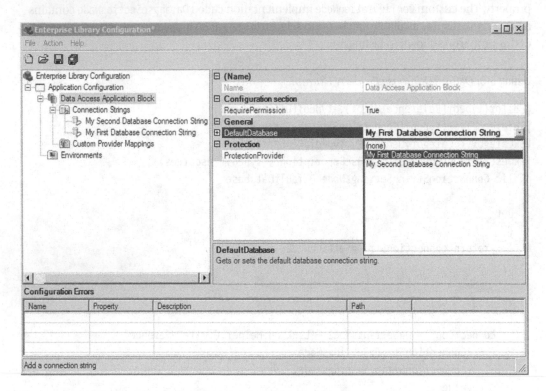

**Figure 5-5.** *Reference type window showing available connections*

SRCategory and SRDescription: These attributes define localized versions of the CategoryAttribute and DescriptionAttribute classes. They both use the System.Type and string that are passed in to determine the specific string value for the properties category and description via the ResourceStringLoader class. The ResourceStringLoader class uses the System.Type to determine the assembly from which to pull the resource string. If the assembly is not found, it will attempt to look for the resource string in the current execut-ing assembly. If the resource still cannot be found or if the value is not present, an empty string is returned.

The LinkNodeHelper class is very important, especially regarding the default instances for an application block. For example, the Database Access Application Block's DefaultDatabase property is essentially one of the connection strings defined for the application block. If two connections strings exist for an application and one of them is selected as the default string, and then that connection string is removed, the default database setting should return to null. Well, that function does not happen on its own; it needs the assistance of the LinkNodeHelper class. This class will set a reference to the connection strings (ConnectionStringSettingsNode), as well as a special event handler that will be fired in the event a ConnectionStringsSettingsNode is removed from the configuration file via the Configuration Console's UI. Now when a connection string is removed, it is checked to see whether the connection string is the DefaultDatabase property value. If it is, the DefaultDatabase property value is set to null.

## Validating Configuration Data

Now that the configuration data can be opened, edited, and saved, the data should be validated to ensure each setting makes sense. For instance, if a property requires a value to describe how many connections were allowed to connect to a particular service, that value must be numeric. Trying to insert grandma's homemade chocolate-chip cookie recipe into that property probably would not give the desired results.

The solution to the problem is to provide the ability to validate the configuration data before saving the changes. This is performed by a combination of the ValidateNodeCommand and the validation attributes.

The validation attributes allow for the markup of properties to determine which validation rules should apply to a particular property. All of the attributes inherit from the ValidationAttribute class, which provides some common services and features required by all ValidationAttribute implementations. The following validation attributes are available:

Required: This attribute requires that a value be present for that particular property. To require a property to contain a value, simply mark the property with the Required attribute.

```
[Required]
public string MyRequiredProperty...
```

AssertRange: This attribute specifies that a property will have a specific value in between a range of values. Its constructor takes four parameters: lower bound, lower range boundary, higher bound, and higher range boundary. The lower and higher bound inclusive parameters (RangeBoundaryType enum) determine whether the respective higher or lower bound property value should be included in the acceptable range of values. Here is an example of using AssertRange to require a positive integer between 0 and 100:

```
[AssertRange(130, RangeBoundaryType.Inclusive, 200,
    RangeBoundaryType.Inclusive)]
public int MyIQ...
```

DenyRange: This is the opposite of the AssertRange attribute. To pass validation, the values must be outside the lower and higher bound parameters. If DenyRange were used instead of AssertRange in the previous example, to pass validation, the property value would need to be any integer that is less than 0 or more than 100.

MaximumLength and MinimumLength: These attributes require that a string value be no more or no less than the specified length values. The constructors for these attributes take one parameter value that determines the maximum or minimum length to require. These attributes work only with strings; if the property value is not of a type System.String, the validation rule is simply passed over. Here is an example of the MaximumLength and MinimumLength attributes used to require the string value to be a minimum of 10 characters and a maximum of 100 characters:

```
[MinimumLength(10)]
[MaximumLength(100)]
public string MyName...
```

Regex: This attribute allows for validation rules that validate a property based on a regular expression. A good example of this is requiring that a property value of a web service URL be in a proper format before saving. The Regex attribute has two constructors: one accepts a string as the pattern to validate against, and the other takes a pattern string and also the System.Text.RegularExpressions.RegexOptions enumerator. Here is an example of using the Regex attribute to validate an email address:

```
[Regex("^[\w-\.]+@([\w-]+\.)+[\w-]{2,4}$")]
public string MyEmailaddress...
```

**Note** With the Regex attribute, the property must be able to be cast into a string. Otherwise, an exception will be thrown.

UniqueName: This attribute requires that all configuration nodes (ConfigurationNode) of a specific System.Type be uniquely named. The constructor contains two parameters: the first parameter determines the System.Type of the configuration node that should be unique, and the second parameter specifies the root node's System.Type to determine which parent configuration node it should search to ensure unique child nodes. Here is an example of using UniqueName:

```
[UniqueName(typeof(CacheStorageNode),
        typeof(CacheManagerSettingsNode))]
public string Name
```

**Note** The UniqueName attribute can be used on only the Name property of the ConfigurationNode class. Also, at the time of this writing, its second parameter can be left null, as it is not used to determine the parent or root node. Instead, all nodes of a specific System.Type are validated to ensure a name's uniqueness, regardless of where it is located within the hierarchy.

TypeValidation: This attribute takes the property value and determines if it is of a valid System.Type. You use this attribute in the same way as the Required attribute, except that it is [TypeValidation], rather than [Required].

CustomAttributesValidation: This attribute allows the Configuration Console to validate custom key-value pairs. It ensures that each item has a key, and that the key contains a value. This attribute should be used only on properties or fields that are of System.Collections.Generic.List<T>; otherwise, the validation routine will simply be passed over. You use this attribute in the same way as the Required and TypeValidation attributes, except [CustomAttributesValidation] is used.

Now that the ConfigurationNodes are properly marked up with the validation attributes, some mechanism needs to be in place to take the appropriate action to validate them during the save process. This is where the ValidateNodeCommand class comes into play. This class performs validation on the current configuration node, as well as any child configuration nodes found.

There are three instances when the configuration node can be validated:

- When the Save toolbar button or menu item is selected. In this case, all of the configuration nodes within the application configuration node will be validated before saving.

- When the Validate menu item is selected from the context menu.

- When a value is changed and the focus of the property is lost, such as in the example shown in Figure 5-6. When the connection property is set to blank, and the property loses focus, the property is then validated and an error message is displayed.

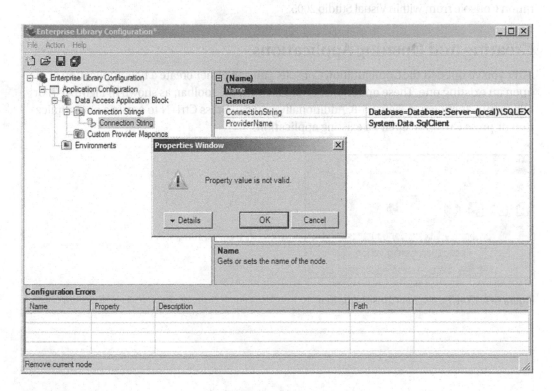

**Figure 5-6.** *Validating a connection string Name value*

When the `ValidationNodeCommand` is instantiated and the `Execute` method is called, the `ValidationNodeCommand` instance will first attempt to validate its properties using the validation attributes. Secondly, it will look for any child nodes and attempt to validate them. Finally, it calls the configuration node's `Validate` method. The `Validate` method is there so that each configuration node can have its own customized validation routine. One example of this is to ensure the sum of two property values is not outside a given range.

### Mapping Runtime Components to Design-Time Components

While the Configuration Console uses the `ConfigurationUIHierarchy` for opening and saving configuration files, there is still one problem. The `ConfigurationUIHierarchy` has no idea how to map the configuration runtime components to the design-time components. This is where the builder classes come in.

There are two types of builder classes: one for creating the UI and the other for saving the configuration data. The builder class that is used for creating the UI will inherit the `NodeBuilder` base class. This class is called by the `OpenCore` method of the implemented instance of the `ConfigurationDesignManager`. You will see an example of the builder classes in the "Defining Builders" section later in this chapter.

# Using the Configuration Console

When you install Enterprise Library, a shortcut is created in the Programs menu. You can also start the Configuration Console from the root installation folder of Enterprise Library. Or since the source code is provided, you can open the Enterprise Library solution and start the Configuration Console from within Visual Studio 2005.

## Creating and Opening Applications

After you've opened the Configuration Console, you can either create a new application or open an existing one. These options are available from the toolbar, as shown in Figure 5-7, or File menu, as shown in Figure 5-8. Additionally, you can press Ctrl+N to create a new application or press Ctrl+O to open an existing application.

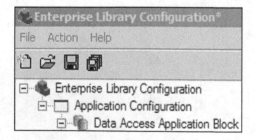

**Figure 5-7.** *Configuration Console toolbar*

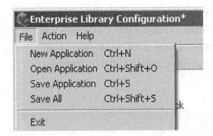

**Figure 5-8.** *Configuration Console File menu*

When you create a new application, the tree view on the left will add a node underneath the Enterprise Library Configuration root node called Application Configuration, and a new property called ConfigurationFile will appear in the properties grid on the right, as shown in Figure 5-9.

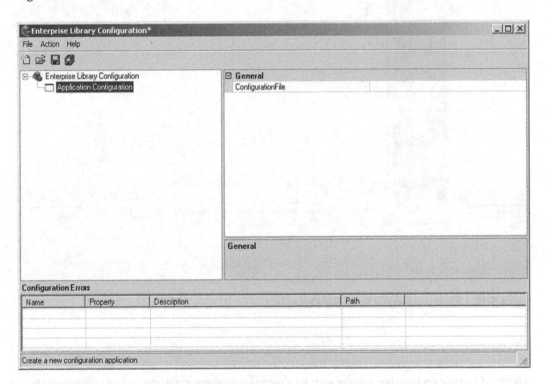

**Figure 5-9.** *Adding a new application to the Configuration Console*

The ConfigurationFile property determines where the core configuration data will reside. All of the configuration data will reside in this file, unless a file or SQL configuration source is created, as described in the next section. If a file or SQL configuration source is selected, the only configuration data that will be saved in the configuration file is that necessary to point to the corresponding external configuration file or SQL Server database.

To select the main application configuration file for the application, click the ConfigurationFile value field, and then click the ellipse button. A Save File dialog box will appear, as shown in Figure 5-10. Select the appropriate filename and click Save. Note that the file will not be created yet; that will only happen when the Save menu item or toolbar button is selected.

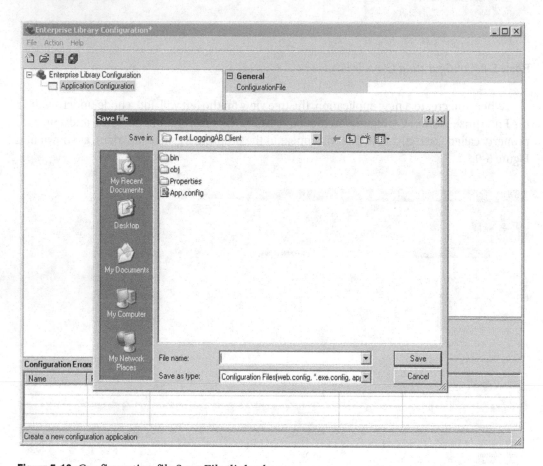

**Figure 5-10.** *Configuration file Save File dialog box*

---

■**Note** If multiple configuration sources exist for a particular application, only the first one will be used to save and read configuration data.

---

When you choose to open an application, you are prompted to select the existing file. The Configuration Console will check the application's main configuration file and determine if there are any external configuration sources, such as an external file or SQL Server database. If any are found, it attempts to incorporate that configuration data. Otherwise, the configuration data is pulled from the selected application configuration file.

## Setting the Configuration Source

As mentioned, an application can have its configuration data hosted in some other location besides the application configuration file, such as in an external XML file or a SQL Server database.

To set a configuration source, right-click the Application Configuration node and select New ➤ Configuration Source from the context menu. A System Configuration Source node will be created automatically, as shown in Figure 5-11.

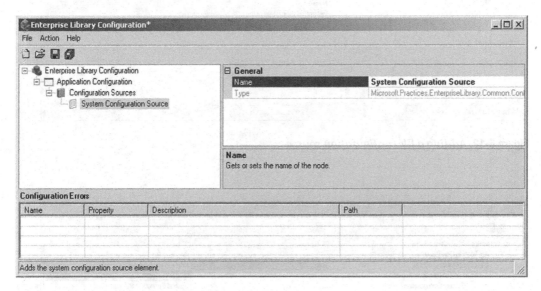

**Figure 5-11.** *Adding a system configuration source*

### Setting a File Configuration Source

If you want to set a file configuration source, right-click the Configuration Sources node and select New ➤ File Configuration Source from the context menu. A new File Configuration Source node will be added, as shown in Figure 5-12. Click the File property, click the ellipse button, and select the appropriate file to save the configuration data to, or you can manually enter the filename for the File property. Then set the Configuration Sources node's SelectedSource property to the proper configuration source, as shown in Figure 5-13.

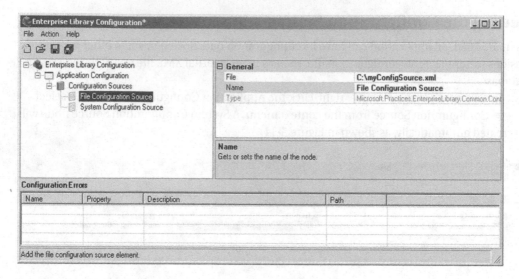

**Figure 5-12.** *Adding a file configuration source*

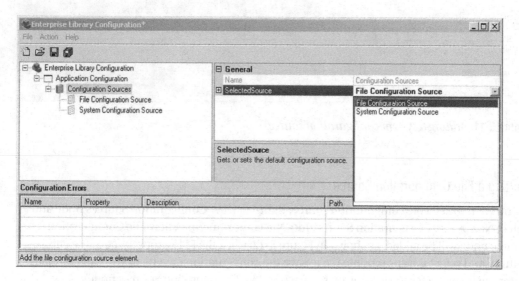

**Figure 5-13.** *Selecting a file configuration source*

## Setting a Manageable Configuration Source

New to Enterprise Library 3.0, the manageable configuration source allows for the use of a Group Policy or Windows Management Instrumentation (WMI). This way, configuration overrides can be defined in the registry, and they will apply to the application.

To use a manageable configuration source, select the Manageable Configuration Source menu item when adding a new configuration source. Then specify the filename to use as the source. Next, select the appropriate values for either WMI or Group Policy. Finally, specify the application name.

## Adding a SQL Configuration Source

You may have noticed that SQL configuration source is not an option on the Configuration Sources context menu. This is because the SQL configuration source is not part of the core Enterprise Library offering, but instead is included as a QuickStart. To make it a selectable configuration source, follow these steps:

1. Open the SQL Configuration Source QuickStart, which can be found in the QuickStart folder where you installed the Enterprise Library source code (typically, C:\EntLib3Src for version 3.0, and under the default installation directory for version 2.0).

2. Compile the SQL Configuration Source QuickStart solution.

---

**Caution**  It may be necessary to build the SQL Configuration Source QuickStart object with the Data Access binaries from the strongly named assemblies in the bin folder of the Enterprise Library installation directory in order for them to behave properly with the Configuration Console.

---

3. Copy the compiled binaries out of the SQL Configuration Source QuickStart bin folder and into the Configuration Console's bin folder. The binary names are as follows:

   - Microsoft.Practices.EnterpriseLibrary.SqlConfigurationSource.dll

   - Microsoft.Practices.EnterpriseLibrary.SqlConfigurationSource.Design.dll

4. Start the Configuration Console. The Sql Configuration Source option will now appear on the Configuration Source node's context menu, as shown in Figure 5-14.

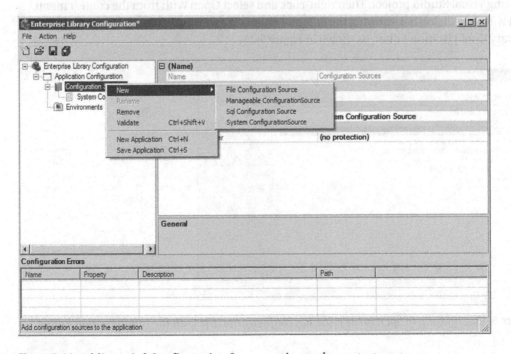

**Figure 5-14.** *Adding a Sql Configuration Source option to the context menu*

## Saving Configuration Files

You can either save a single application configuration file or save all open application configuration files at once. To save a single application configuration file, select the Save option from the toolbar or File menu, or press Ctrl+S. To save all configuration files at once, select Save All from the toolbar or File menu, or press Ctrl+Shift+S.

If the file has any validations, the Configuration Console will run them before saving. If any errors occur, they will be listed at the bottom of the Configuration Console. Everything must pass validation before the configuration data can be saved. If the Application Configuration node's ConfigurationFile property has not been set, you will be prompted to select a filename. Finally, the Configuration Console will navigate the configuration node hierarchy and save the data.

---

**■Note** The advanced configuration features provided with Enterprise Library 3.x are covered in Chapter 15. These features include environmental overrides, AppSettings management, protection providers, and partial trust support.

---

# Using the Configuration Editor within Visual Studio 2005

The Configuration Editor is an add-in for Visual Studio 2005. It works just like the Configuration Console, except for how you open application configuration files.

To use the Configuration Editor, simply add an application configuration file to your existing Visual Studio project. Then right-click and select Open With from the context menu. You will see a dialog box showing the different editors that are available. Choose Enterprise Library Configuration Editor, as shown in Figure 5-15.

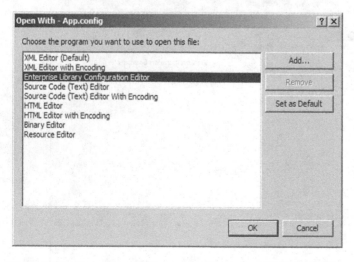

**Figure 5-15.** *Choosing to open an application configuration file with the Configuration Editor*

If you want to make the Configuration Editor the default tool to open configuration files, click the Set as Default button in the Open With dialog box. After you click OK, the Configuration Editor will open, as shown in Figure 5-16.

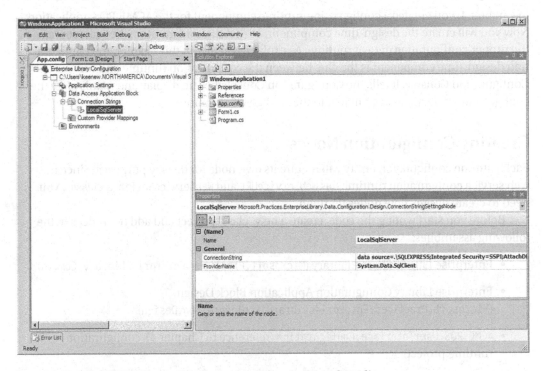

**Figure 5-16.** *Enterprise Library Configuration Editor in Visual Studio*

Just like the Configuration Console, the Configuration Editor shows a tree view on the left and a properties grid on the right. In the example in Figure 5-16, the LocalSqlServer connection string node is selected, and the ConnectionString and ProviderName properties are shown in the properties grid on the lower-right side.

Beyond the GUI layout, all the functionality is basically the same as that in the Configuration Console.

---

**Note**  While the Configuration Console looks inside the executing folder to determine the available configuration design-time assemblies, the Configuration Editor does not. This is because the executing folder of a Visual Studio add-in is the executing folder of the Visual Studio application. To get around this, the Microsoft patterns & practices team created a registry setting for determining the location of these assemblies, which is set to [*Enterprise Library Installation Folder*]\bin by default.

---

# Creating the ACME POS Configuration Design-Time Components

In Chapter 4, you created a configuration runtime component for the ACME POS application. Now you will create the design-time component, so that the configuration files can contain the proper configuration data at runtime. As explained earlier in this chapter, the configuration design-time component is the glue between the configuration runtime and the Configuration Console. It tells the Configuration Console how to display and manipulate the configuration data and how to map it to the configuration runtime.

## Creating Configuration Nodes

Each runtime configuration entity will require its own node for display purposes. Since the web service configuration runtime has WebServiceURL and WebServiceSettings classes, you need to create design-time nodes for them.

Before you start writing the code, create a new "class" project and add references to the following assemblies:

- Enterprise Library Shared Library (Microsoft.Practices.EnterpriseLibrary.Common)

- Enterprise Library Configuration Application Block Design (Microsoft.Practices.EnterpriseLibrary.Configuration.Design)

- ACME.POS.UserInterface.Configuration (reference to Chapter 4's configuration runtime project)

- System.Drawing (System.Drawing.dll)

- System.Drawing.Design (System.Drawing.Design.dll)

- System.Configuration (System.Configuration.dll)

**Note** Even though the Enterprise Library configuration design assembly was strong named as Enterprise Library Configuration Application Block Design, it is still not considered an application block (at least at the time of writing this book).

Once the references have been added to the project, the next task is to create a resource file and add the three string resources listed in Table 5-2.

**Table 5-2.** *Resource Strings for the Configuration Nodes*

| Resource Name | Resource Value |
| --- | --- |
| CategoryGeneral | General |
| DefaultWebServiceSettingsNodeName | Default Web Service |
| URLDescription | Web Service URL |

Listing 5-7 shows the WebServiceURLNode and WebServiceURLCollectionNode classes. The WebServiceURLNode class will simply define the web service URL via the URL property. It uses the Required attribute to require a value to be present before saving, and sets the appropriate property description and category. The WebServiceURLCollectionNode provides the necessary "spacer" to show a node in the tree view. It has no other functionality

**Listing 5-7.** *WebServiceURLCollectionNode and WebServiceURLNode Classes*

```
using System;
using System.ComponentModel;
using System.Diagnostics;
using Microsoft.Practices.EnterpriseLibrary.Configuration.Design;
using Microsoft.Practices.EnterpriseLibrary.Configuration.
    Design.Validation;
using Microsoft.Practices.EnterpriseLibrary.Common.Configuration;
using System.Configuration;
using ACME.POS.UserInterface.Configuration.Design.Properties;

namespace ACME.POS.UserInterface.Configuration.Design
{
    public class WebServiceURLNode : ConfigurationNode
    {
        private string url;

        public WebServiceURLNode()
            : this(new WebServiceURL(
                "Default URL", "HTTP://someURL.com"))
        {

        }

        public WebServiceURLNode(WebServiceURL webServiceURL)
            : base((webServiceURL == null) ? "" :
                webServiceURL.Name)
        {
            if (webServiceURL == null) { throw new
                ArgumentNullException("webServiceURL"); }

            this.url = webServiceURL.URL;
        }

        [Required]
        [SRDescription("URLDescription", typeof(Resources))]
        [SRCategory("CategoryGeneral", typeof(Resources))]
        public string URL
        {
            get { return url; }
            set { url = value; }
        }
    }
```

```
    }

    public class WebServiceURLCollectionNode : ConfigurationNode
    {
        public WebServiceURLCollectionNode()
            : base("Web Service URL's")
        {
        }

        [ReadOnly(true)]
        public override string Name
        {
            get { return base.Name; }
        }
    }
}
```

The WebServiceSettingsNode class, shown in Listing 5-8, is a bit more complex. It will define the default web service for the application via the DefaultWebServiceURL. As with the URL property, it will have Required, Category, and Description attributes, but it will also require the Editor and ReferenceType attributes. As mentioned earlier in the chapter, these two attributes define how the properties grid will allow the manipulation of the property. WebServiceSettingsNode also has code for setting the default web service URL to null in the event the default WebServiceURLNode is removed. Those features are provided by the CreateReference method of the LinkNodeHelper class and the OnWebServiceSettingNodeRemoved method. Other features include a protective feature that allows only one WebServiceSettingsNode to be created in the configuration file, and the Dispose method is overridden to properly remove the WebServiceSettingNodeRemovedHandler from the WebServiceURLNode.

**Listing 5-8.** *WebServiceSettingsNode Class*

```
using System;
using System.ComponentModel;
using System.Diagnostics;
using Microsoft.Practices.EnterpriseLibrary.Configuration.Design;
using Microsoft.Practices.EnterpriseLibrary.Configuration.
    Design.Validation;
using Microsoft.Practices.EnterpriseLibrary.Common.Configuration;
using ACME.POS.UserInterface.Configuration.Design.Properties;
using System.Drawing.Design;

namespace ACME.POS.UserInterface.Configuration.Design
{
    /// <summary>
    /// Represents the root configuration for the ACME POS Web Service Settings.
    /// </summary>
```

```
public class WebServiceSettingsNode : ConfigurationNode
{
  private WebServiceURLNode webServiceURLNode;
  private EventHandler
        <ConfigurationNodeChangedEventArgs>
        WebServiceSettingNodeRemovedHandler;


  public WebServiceSettingsNode()
    : base(Resources.DefaultWebServiceSettingsNodeName)
  {
    this.WebServiceSettingNodeRemovedHandler =
        new EventHandler
        <ConfigurationNodeChangedEventArgs>
          (OnWebServiceSettingNodeRemoved);
  }

  protected override void Dispose(bool disposing)
  {
    try
    {
      if (disposing)
      {
        if (null != webServiceURLNode)
        {
          webServiceURLNode.Removed -=
              WebServiceSettingNodeRemovedHandler;
        }
      }
    }
    finally
    {
      base.Dispose(disposing);
    }
  }

  [ReadOnly(true)]
  public override string Name
  {
    get { return base.Name; }
  }

  [Required]
  [SRDescription("DefaultWebServiceSettingDescription",
    typeof(Resources))]
  [Editor(typeof(ReferenceEditor), typeof(UITypeEditor))]
  [ReferenceType(typeof(WebServiceURLNode))]
```

```
    [SRCategory("CategoryGeneral", typeof(Resources))]
    public WebServiceURLNode DefaultWebServiceURLSetting
    {
        get { return webServiceURLNode; }
        set
        {
            webServiceURLNode = LinkNodeHelper.CreateReference
                <WebServiceURLNode>(webServiceURLNode, value,
                WebServiceSettingNodeRemovedHandler, null);
        }
    }


    protected override void OnChildAdded
        (ConfigurationNodeChangedEventArgs e)
    {
        base.OnChildAdded(e);

        if (Nodes.Count > 1 && e.Node.GetType() ==
            typeof(WebServiceURLCollectionNode))
        {
            throw new InvalidOperationException
                ("Oops you can only have one");
        }
    }

    private void OnWebServiceSettingNodeRemoved(object sender,
        ConfigurationNodeChangedEventArgs e)
    {
        this.webServiceURLNode = null;
    }
  }
}
```

## Creating the Command Registrar and Command Nodes

The next task in creating the design-time component is setting up commands to allow the proper menu commands to be present based on the current state and selection in the Configuration Console. This requires an add node command to create the necessary commands and a command registrar that will register them.

In Listing 5-9, the AddWebServiceSettingsNodeCommand and AddWebServiceURLNodeCommand are defined. The AddWebServiceSettingsNodeCommand is where the rubber meets the road when it comes to adding the command functionality. When the OnExecuted method is overridden, the necessary steps to display a configuration node are executed. In this case, a new WebServiceURLCollectionNode is created and added as a child node of the current node, which would be the WebServiceSettingsNode. The AddWebServiceURLNodeCommand provides the necessary placeholder to allow multiple web service URLs to be defined.

**Listing 5-9.** *AddWebServiceSettingsNodeCommand and AddWebServiceURLNodeCommand Classes*

```
using System;
using System.Collections.Generic;
using System.Text;
using Microsoft.Practices.EnterpriseLibrary.Configuration.Design;

namespace ACME.POS.UserInterface.Configuration.Design
{
    /// <summary>
    /// Represents a command for adding the ACME POS Web Service
    /// configuration section to the current application.
    /// </summary>
    public class AddWebServiceSettingsNodeCommand :
        AddChildNodeCommand
    {
        public AddWebServiceSettingsNodeCommand(IServiceProvider
            serviceProvider)
            : base(serviceProvider, typeof(WebServiceSettingsNode))
        {}

        protected override void OnExecuted(EventArgs e)
        {
            base.OnExecuted(e);
            WebServiceSettingsNode node = ChildNode as
                WebServiceSettingsNode;

            WebServiceURLCollectionNode webServiceURLCollectionNode =
                new WebServiceURLCollectionNode();
            node.AddNode(webServiceURLCollectionNode);
        }
    }

    public class AddWebServiceURLNodeCommand : AddChildNodeCommand
    {
        public AddWebServiceURLNodeCommand(IServiceProvider
            serviceProvider)
            : base(serviceProvider, typeof(WebServiceURLNode))
        { }
    }
}
```

Listing 5-10 shows the definition of the WebServiceCommandRegistrar class. This class registers the AddWebServiceSettingsNodeCommand and AddWebServiceURLNodeCommand classes so that they may be used in the Configuration Console. The WebServiceCommandRegistrar class

provides the necessary plumbing to create the appropriate menu item and toolbar commands
via the Register method. In this case, the Register method first creates a new UI command
with the ConfigurationUICommand class to allow the WebServiceSettingsNode to be added
to the Configuration Console UI, and then it adds the WebServiceURLNodeCommand to the
WebServiceURLNode nodes. It is important to note that the WebServiceSettingsNode is allowed
to be created only once via the CreateSingleUICommand method, and WebServiceURLNode may
be added multiple times via the CreateMultipleUICommand method.

**Listing 5-10.** *WebServiceCommandRegistrar Class*

```
using System;
using System.Collections.Generic;
using System.Text;
using Microsoft.Practices.EnterpriseLibrary.Configuration.Design;

namespace ACME.POS.UserInterface.Configuration.Design
{
    public class WebServiceCommandRegistrar : CommandRegistrar
    {
        public WebServiceCommandRegistrar(IServiceProvider
            serviceProvider)
            : base(serviceProvider)
        {}

        public override void Register()
        {
        ConfigurationUICommand cmd =
            ConfigurationUICommand.CreateSingleUICommand(
            ServiceProvider,
            "ACME POS WebService Settings",
            "Add ACME POS WebService Settings",
            new AddWebServiceSettingsNodeCommand(ServiceProvider),
            typeof(WebServiceSettingsNode));
            AddUICommand(cmd,
                typeof(ConfigurationApplicationNode));
            AddDefaultCommands(typeof(WebServiceSettingsNode));

        ConfigurationUICommand item =
            ConfigurationUICommand.CreateMultipleUICommand(
            ServiceProvider,
            "Web Service URL",
            "Add Web Service URL",
            new AddWebServiceURLNodeCommand(ServiceProvider),
            typeof(WebServiceURLNode));
            AddUICommand(item, typeof(WebServiceURLCollectionNode));
            AddDefaultCommands(typeof(WebServiceURLNode));
        }
    }
}
```

## Defining Builders

The next step is to provide the configuration runtime mappings to and from the Configuration Console. This requires two builders:

- The WebServiceSettingsNodeBuilder class will allow the visual representation of the WebServiceSettings configuration section of a configuration file.

- The WebServiceSettingsBuilder will then take a visual representation of the web service configuration and map it to the configuration runtime so that it may be saved.

Listing 5-11 defines the WebServiceSettingsNodeBuilder class, and Listing 5-12 defines the WebServiceSettingsBuilder class.

**Listing 5-11.** *WebServiceSettingsNodeBuilder Class*

```
using System;
using System.Collections.Generic;
using System.Text;
using Microsoft.Practices.EnterpriseLibrary.Configuration.Design;

namespace ACME.POS.UserInterface.Configuration.Design
{
    class WebServiceSettingsNodeBuilder : NodeBuilder
    {
        private WebServiceSettings webServiceSettings;
        private WebServiceURLNode defaultNode;

        public WebServiceSettingsNodeBuilder(IServiceProvider
            serviceProvider, WebServiceSettings webServiceSettings)
            : base(serviceProvider)
        {
            this.webServiceSettings = webServiceSettings;
        }

        public WebServiceSettingsNode Build()
        {
            WebServiceSettingsNode rootNode = new
                WebServiceSettingsNode();
            WebServiceURLCollectionNode node = new
                WebServiceURLCollectionNode();
            WebServiceURLNode webServiceURLNode;
            foreach (WebServiceURL data in
                webServiceSettings.WebServiceURLs)
            {
                webServiceURLNode = new WebServiceURLNode(data);
                node.AddNode(webServiceURLNode);
                if (webServiceURLNode.Name ==
                    webServiceSettings.DefaultWebServiceURL)
```

```
                    defaultNode = webServiceURLNode;
            }

        rootNode.AddNode(node);
        rootNode.DefaultWebServiceURLSetting = defaultNode;
        return rootNode;
        }
    }
}
```

**Listing 5-12.** *WebServiceSettingsBuilder Class*

```
using System;
using System.Collections.Generic;
using System.Text;
using Microsoft.Practices.EnterpriseLibrary.Configuration.Design;
using Microsoft.Practices.EnterpriseLibrary.Common.Configuration;
using Microsoft.Practices.EnterpriseLibrary.Configuration.
   Design.Properties;
using ACME.POS.UserInterface.Configuration;

namespace ACME.POS.UserInterface.Configuration.Design
{
    class WebServiceSettingsBuilder
    {
        private WebServiceSettingsNode webServiceSettingsNode;
        private IConfigurationUIHierarchy hierarchy;
        private WebServiceSettings webServiceSettings;

        public WebServiceSettingsBuilder(IServiceProvider
            serviceProvider, WebServiceSettingsNode
            webServiceSettingsNode)
        {
            this.webServiceSettingsNode = webServiceSettingsNode;
            hierarchy = ServiceHelper.GetCurrentHierarchy(
                serviceProvider);
            webServiceSettings = new WebServiceSettings();
        }

        public WebServiceSettings Build()
        {
            webServiceSettings.DefaultWebServiceURL =
                webServiceSettingsNode.DefaultWebServiceURLSetting.
                Name;

            foreach (WebServiceURLNode webServiceURLNode in
                hierarchy.FindNodesByType(webServiceSettingsNode,
```

```
            typeof(WebServiceURLNode)))
        {
            webServiceSettings.WebServiceURLs.Add(new
            WebServiceURL(webServiceURLNode.Name,
            webServiceURLNode.URL));
        }

        return webServiceSettings;
    }
  }
}
```

## Putting It All Together

The final steps are to create the `WebServiceConfigurationDesignManager` class and add the necessary attributes to the `Assembly.cs` file.

The `WebServiceConfigurationDesignManager` class gets the ball rolling, so to speak. This class is used by the Configuration Console to register the correct registrar classes. In the case of the `WebServiceConfigurationDesignManager` class, only the `WebServiceCommandRegistrar` class is registered. In more complex application blocks, many more classes could be registered. As shown in Listing 5-13, the `Register` method is overridden, an instance of the `WebServiceCommandRegistrar` class is created, and the `Register` method on that instance is called.

**Listing 5-13.** *WebServiceConfigurationDesignManager Class*

```csharp
using System;
using System.Collections.Generic;
using System.Configuration;
using System.Text;
using Microsoft.Practices.EnterpriseLibrary.Configuration.Design;

namespace ACME.POS.UserInterface.Configuration.Design
{
    public class WebServiceConfigurationDesignManager :
        ConfigurationDesignManager
    {
        public override void Register(IServiceProvider
            serviceProvider)
        {
            WebServiceCommandRegistrar webServiceCommandRegistrar =
                new WebServiceCommandRegistrar(serviceProvider);
            webServiceCommandRegistrar.Register();
        }

        protected override void OpenCore(IServiceProvider
            serviceProvider, ConfigurationApplicationNode rootNode,
```

```
        ConfigurationSection section)
    {
        if (null != section)
        {
            WebServiceSettingsNodeBuilder builder = new
                WebServiceSettingsNodeBuilder(serviceProvider,
                (WebServiceSettings)section);
            rootNode.AddNode(builder.Build());
        }
    }

    protected override ConfigurationSectionInfo
        GetConfigurationSectionInfo(IServiceProvider
        serviceProvider)
    {
        ConfigurationNode rootNode =
            ServiceHelper.GetCurrentRootNode(serviceProvider);
        WebServiceSettingsNode node = null;
        if (rootNode != null)
            node = (WebServiceSettingsNode)rootNode.
                Hierarchy.FindNodeByType(rootNode,
                typeof(WebServiceSettingsNode));

        WebServiceSettings webServiceSection = null;
        if (node == null)
        {
            webServiceSection = null;
        }
        else
        {
            WebServiceSettingsBuilder builder = new
                WebServiceSettingsBuilder(serviceProvider, node);
            webServiceSection = builder.Build();
        }

        return new ConfigurationSectionInfo(node,
            webServiceSection, WebServiceSettings.SectionName);
    }
  }
}
```

The last task is to add the `ConfigurationDesignerManager` attribute to the `Assembly.cs` file. This helps the Configuration Console to determine if this assembly contains a configuration design manager and of what `System.Type` it is. Here is an example of this `assembly` attribute and the necessary `using` statement:

```
using Microsoft.Practices.EnterpriseLibrary.Configuration.Design;
using ACME.POS.Client.Configuration.Design;

//Other assembly information

[assembly: ConfigurationDesignManager(typeof(
    WebServiceConfigurationDesignManager))]
```

After compiling the code and copying the configuration components to the executing folder of the Configuration Console, you should be able to choose a new ACME POS Web Service Settings configuration node, as shown in Figure 5-17.

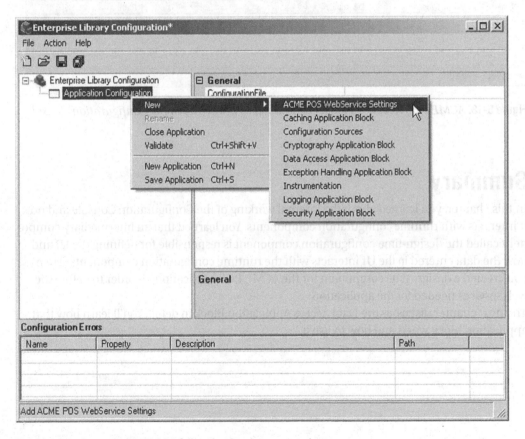

**Figure 5-17.** *New ACME POS Web Service Settings menu item*

Figure 5-18 shows the entire Web Service Settings configuration tree and the properties grid.

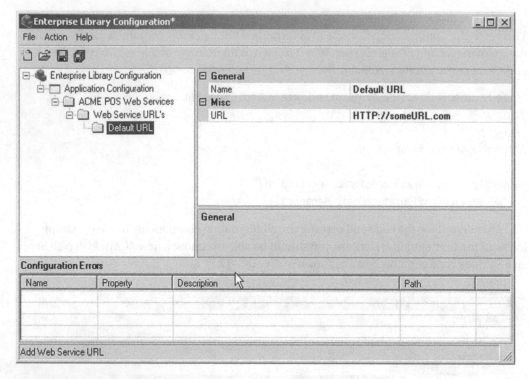

**Figure 5-18.** *ACME POS Web Service Settings nodes and properties in the Configuration Console*

# Summary

In this chapter, you learned about the internal working of the Configuration Console and how it interacts with runtime configuration components. You learned that an intermediary component called the design-time configuration component is responsible for defining the UI and how the data entered in the UI interacts with the runtime configuration components. Then you created a design-time component for the ACME POS application, in order to define the web services needed for the application.

The next chapter discusses the Data Access Application Block in detail. You'll learn how that application block works and how to use it.

# CHAPTER 6

■■■

# The Data Access Application Block

For almost every software application in existence, the storage of data is critical. Business software, consumer software, video games, and even operating systems have a way to store data. The storage needs for software may differ among applications. Some may require volatile storage solutions, others might need nonvolatile storage, and some may require a little of both.

As mentioned in Chapter 1, the data access layer is the most common location where an application will perform data-manipulation functions against some sort of data store. This could be a file system, a database (file-based or a relational database management application), or even a service application like a web service.

This chapter will focus on one type of data access: database access using the Enterprise Library 3.0 Data Access Application Block. This application block has gone through four evolutions, each adding new features to improve its usefulness and functionality.

## Evolution of the Data Access Application Block

The Data Access Application Block was first released as one of the original application blocks back when Visual Studio .NET was first released. This version, called Data Access Application Block version 1.0, worked only with SQL Server databases and basically provided only helper classes to make database calls. One of the biggest complaints about this application block was that it did not support the filling of typed datasets. This is where the second evolution came in. It added the ability to pass in a typed dataset, which then could be filled based on the SQL commands and SQL parameters provided. Overall, both of these versions were liked by most of the development community, and in many organizations, they are still used to this day.

Then came along Enterprise Library for .NET Framework 1.1, released in January 2005. This version of Enterprise Library contained multiple application blocks that were designed to work together to complete the Enterprise Framework picture. In this version, the prior functionality was fundamentally the same, with some new features added. These new features included the ability to store connection string information in a configuration file and support for Oracle and DB2 databases.

Next came the Data Access Application Block, which is part of Enterprise Library 2.0 (January 2006 release). This version retained the same overall features of the previous version, but was designed to work more efficiently with the System.Data namespace in .NET Framework 2.0. These changes included no longer using the Configuration Application Block for connection string management; instead, the new .NET Framework 2.0 connection string configuration features were harnessed by the Data Access Application Block. Also, the DbCommandWrapper was replaced with the .NET Framework's DbCommand class.

The latest iterations of the Data Access Application Block in Enterprise Library 3.0 (April 2007) and Enterprise Library 3.1 (May 2007) do not add any groundbreaking features. In fact, the only new features are the ability to specify a batch size when performing updates using the UpdateDataSet method and the addition of a SQL Server Compact Edition data access provider.

# Data Access in an Application

In order to understand how the Data Access Application Block can assist in the development of a data access layer component, it is necessary to look at what typical data access layer components do. These components usually provide the ability to exchange data between an application and some data store. They also manage the information necessary for accessing the data store, such as the connection string (including the username and password, for instance) or a file path to some file-based data storage.

Listing 6-1 presents a simple data access layer class that handles the connection and execution of a database query, and returns a DataTable as a result of the query. The class constructor handles the creation of the connection object, which will be used to point to the correct database instance. The MyQuery method would then be called by some domain layer (business layer) component to set up the command object, execute the query, and finally return the dataset.

**Listing 6-1.** *Data Access Layer Example*

```
using System;
using System.Data;
using System.Data.SqlClient;

public class MyDataAccessLayer
{

    private SqlConnection myConnection;

    public MyDataAccessLayer()
    {
        string connStr = @"(local)\SQLEXPRESS;Initial Catalog=MyDatabase;" +
            "integrated security=SSPI;Asynchronous Processing=True";

        myConnection = new SqlConnection(connStr);
    }
    public DataTable MyQuery()
    {
```

```
    string getAllCustomers = "Select FirstName, LastName from Customers";

    SqlCommand cmd = new SqlCommand(
        getAllCustomers,
        myConnection);

    SqlDataAdapter adapter = new SqlDataAdapter(cmd);

    DataTable dtCustomers = new DataTable("Customers");

    adapter.Fill(dtCustomers);

    return dtCustomers;
    }
}
```

While Listing 6-1 works great at returning the first name and last name of each customer in the Customers table from the SQL Server Express database named MyDatabase, writing the data access layer like this presents a couple limitations:

- It is data provider-specific. If an Oracle database were to be used instead of the SQL Server Express database, the SqlClient classes used here would need to be swapped out with the OracleClient classes.

- The database connection string is hard-coded. Most organizations will want to be able to easily point an application to different database servers, particularly during the development of the application.

The solution to the first problem would be to make the data access layer code database-independent. To resolve the second problem, the ability to store multiple connection strings in a configuration file would make it easy to switch between different environments. ADO.NET 2.0 has taken great strides in providing database-independence and the management of connection strings.

# New Features in ADO.NET 2.0

The .NET Framework 2.0 improved existing features of ADO.NET, as well as added new features. The new ADO.NET features improve the performance of DataSets and DataTables. They include the new TableAdapter class, which takes the DataAdapter class and allows for simplified data manipulation. Also, the DataTable can now live on its own without a DataSet and contains many of the features of the DataSet, such as XML serialization. Even the DataView has a new method that allows it to take the current view and create a DataTable from it.

Here, we'll focus on two important new features introduced in ADO.NET 2.0: the ability to store database connection strings in the application configuration file and support for independent database provider classes.

## Connection Strings in the Application Configuration File

The application configuration file now allows for a dedicated location to store the connection strings for an application. This simplifies the development of an application because developers no longer need to deal with building a custom configuration handler for their applications. And, of course, since the database connection string is located in a configuration file, changes to the connection string can be made on a per-environment basis. Listing 6-2 shows an example of a connection string entry in a configuration file.

**Listing 6-2.** *Sample Connection String Settings*

```
<configuration>
 <connectionStrings>
   <add name="MyDatabase"
     connectionString="(local)\SQLEXPRESS;Initial Catalog=MyDatabase;
                       integrated security=SSPI;Asynchronous Processing=True" />
 </connectionStrings>
</configuration>
```

Listing 6-3 demonstrates how to retrieve the connection string within a .NET class.

**Listing 6-3.** *Retrieving a Connection String*

```
public DbConnection GetInitializedConnectionBaseClass()
{
    ConnectionStringSettings connSetting =
        ConfigurationManager.ConnectionStrings["MyDatabase"];

    SqlConnection conn = new SqlConnection();

    conn.ConnectionString = connSetting.ConnectionString;

    return conn;
}
```

## Support for Independent Database Providers

When .NET Framework 1.0 was introduced, it brought with it the first native database provider (SQL Server). Later, new database providers started to show up for databases such as Oracle, DB2, and MySQL. While these native providers allow for better performance and the utilization of provider-specific features, they don't support database-independent code.

Some readers might suggest simply using OLEDB or ODBC, which provide the ability to write application code that is relatively database-independent. However, OLEDB and ODBC generally do not perform as well as native providers do.

Most databases have the same kind of functionality to select and manipulate data. Typically, almost all databases use some flavor of ANSI SQL to accomplish these tasks. This gives the developer the ability to create data access layers that can perform most of the necessary functions of manipulating or selecting data from a database, without needing to change the SQL command statements, for the most part.

In .NET Framework 1.0 and 1.1, ADO.NET provided the following interfaces to help facilitate creating database provider-independent application code:

- IDbConnection: Represents the necessary members for connecting to a relational database from the .NET Framework.

- IDbCommand: Specifies the necessary members for accessing data from a relational database from the .NET Framework.

- IDbDataAdapter: Specifies the properties for specifying the IDbCommand objects for performing select, insert, update, and delete functions to and from a DataSet or DataTable.

- IDbDataParameter: Represents the necessary members for specifying parameters that can be used with retrieving, saving, and deleting data from a relational database.

- IDbDataParameterCollection: Represents the members required to support a collection of IDbParameter objects.

- IDataReader: Represents the members required to read records from a database in a read-only forward fashion.

- IDataRecord: Provides the necessary members for retrieving the specific column values from a row of data.

- IDbTransaction: Specifies the necessary members to support and manage a database transaction while performing read, save, and delete operations.

In most organizations requiring database provider-independent code, the application developer would create some sort of static method that would implement a factory pattern. This method would typically look into some configuration file to determine which database provider implementation to instantiate and return to the application. An example of this kind of method is shown in Listing 6-4.

**Listing 6-4.** *Using a Software Factory to Determine Database Connection Type*

```
public static IDbConnection GetConnectionImplementation()
{
    string prov =
        ConfigurationManager.AppSettings["dbProvider"];
    IDbConnection conn = null;

    switch (prov) {
        case "sqlserver":
            conn = new SqlConnection();
            break;
        case "oracle":
            conn = new OracleConnection();
            break;
        default:
```

```
        throw new ConfigurationException("Database provider
            not found in Configuration File");
        break;
    }
    return conn;
}
```

While the technique in Listing 6-4 would work, it would also require code changes if new database providers were to be added. Another concern with the use of the database provider-independent interfaces is that they are immutable. This creates a major problem when a new base feature needs to be added to a database provider via the base interface.

A perfect example of this was a new public property called HasRows, which was added to the IDataReader interface. The purpose of this property was to let the developer know when a DataReader contained rows. The issue was that it required all implementations of the interface to be modified in order to implement the new addition to the interface. In reality, this kind of feature was probably common in design and could have been simply implemented in a base class one time. If the other database provider inherited from this base class, then it would have automatically consumed the HasRows property.

## ADO.Net 2.0 Database Provider Base Classes

In ADO.NET 2.0, a series of new base classes were created to essentially replace the existing IDb* interfaces. In the case of the HasRows property in the IDbDataReader interface, this property has now been included in the new ADO.NET 2.0 DbDataReader class. This new class is one of many new database provider-independent classes that allow common functionality to be centralized into a base that inherited classes can override or use as is to implement the code necessary to perform that function.

As an example, suppose that the HasRows property implementation in the DbDataReader class could throw a NotImplementedException when called. (This is hypothetical, as the actual HasRows method in the DbDataReader class does not throw the NotImplementedException.) Then the inherited classes, like the SqlDataReader class, could override that method and provide the necessary code to determine the HasRows return value. This way, the other providers that also inherit from the DbDataReader class could be left alone, until it was necessary to actually implement that functionality—assuming the HasRows property makes sense to implement for a particular database provider class. If the HasRows method were called in one of the other classes that did not override the HasRows property, then the NotImplementedException would be thrown.

These new base classes, found in the System.Data.Common namespace, make the earlier interfaces obsolete (although those interfaces are included in ADO.NET 2.0 for backward compatibility). Table 6-1 lists these ADO.NET 2.0 base classes.

**Table 6-1.** *ADO.NET 2.0 Base Classes in System.Data.Common*

| Class | Description |
|---|---|
| DbConnection | Inherits from IDbConnection and provides a base class for connecting to a relational database from the .NET Framework |
| DbCommand | Inherits from IDbCommand and provides a base class for accessing data from a relational database from the .NET Framework |
| DbDataReader | Inherits from IDataReader and provides the base class for performing forward read-only reading of a resultset from a database |
| DbParameter | Inherits from IDbParameter and provides the base implementation to set parameters used in a database command such as a stored procedure |
| DbParameterCollection | Inherits from IDbParameterCollection and provides the base class for managing a collection of DbParameter objects |
| DbDataAdapter | Inherits from IDbDataAdapter and provides a base implementation for performing select, insert, update, and delete functions between a relational database and a Dataset, DataTable, or DataRow array |
| DbTransaction | Inherits from IDbTransaction and provides the base implementation for managing transactions while multiple commands are being performed against a relational database |
| DbDataSourceEnumerator | Provides the base functionality for enumerating SQL Server databases on a network |
| DBDataPermission | Enables the provider to ensure that a user has adequate permissions to access a relational database |
| DbCommandBuilder | Generates single-table commands for inserting, updating, and deleting data in a relational database based on changes made to a DataSet (it typically does this by analyzing the SelectCommand property of the DataAdapter that is specified in the DbCommandBuilder's DataAdapter property) |
| DbConnectionStringBuilder | Provides the base implementation for building and parsing syntactically correct connection strings |

■**Note** The DbDataAdapter and DBDataPermission classes did exist in ADO.NET 1.0.

While these base classes help resolve some of the issues involved in using interfaces, using them by themselves would not resolve the issue found in Listing 6-4, where the switch statement was required to determine which connection object to instantiate. This is where the new ADO.NET 2.0 DbProviderFactory factory class comes in to fill that gap.

## ADO.NET 2.0 Provider Factories

The DbProviderFactory class can create all the concrete classes necessary for a specific provider. Table 6-2 lists the methods used to create concrete classes for specific providers.

**Table 6-2.** *DbProviderFactory Methods*

| Method | Description |
| --- | --- |
| CreateConnection | Creates and returns a new provider-specific DbConnection object |
| CreateCommand | Creates and returns a new provider-specific DbCommand object |
| CreateCommandBuilder | Creates and returns a new provider-specific DbCommandBuilder object |
| CreateConnectionStringBuilder | Creates and returns a provider-specific DbConnectionStringBuilder object |
| CreateDataAdapter | Creates and returns a new provider-specific DbDataAdapter object |
| CreateDataSourceEnumerator | Creates and returns a new provider-specific DbDataSourceEnumerator object |
| CreateParameter | Creates and returns a new provider-specific DbParameter object |
| CreatePermission | Creates and returns a new provider-specific CodeAccessPermission object |

These methods are self-explanatory. The CreateConnection method will create and return a connection object specific to a database provider, the CreateCommand method will create and return a command object specific to a database provider, and so on. Each database provider has its own specific implementation of the DbProviderFactory class to support its functionality.

The DbProviderFactories class is responsible for creating the correct concrete instance of the DBProviderFactory class. It contains the three methods described in Table 6-3.

**Table 6-3.** *DbProviderFactories Methods*

| Method | Description |
| --- | --- |
| GetFactoryClasses() | Returns a DataTable of provider information specified in the machine configuration or application configuration file |
| GetFactory(DataRow) | Returns a DbProviderFactory instance based on the DataRow from the DataTable produced by GetFactoryClasses |
| GetFactory(string) | Returns a DbProviderFactory instance based on the provider-invariant name string that identifies the provider |

In order for the DbProviderFactories class to function properly, it is necessary for the proper configuration data to be inserted into the machine.config or application file. Listing 6-5 shows the entries in a sample configuration file.

**Listing 6-5.** *DbProviderFactories Configuration Data*

```
<system.data>
  <DbProviderFactories>
    <add name="SqlClient Data Provider"
      invariant="System.Data.SqlClient"
      support="FF"
      description=".Net Framework Data Provider for SqlServer"
      type="System.Data.SqlClient.SqlClientFactory, System.Data,
        Version=2.0.3600.0, Culture=neutral, PublicKeyToken=b77a5c561934e089" />
  </DbProviderFactories>
</system.data>
```

Listing 6-5 contains three critical attributes that define the factory specifics:

- The invariant attribute, which can be used by the GetFactory(string) method to return the specific DbProviderFactory concrete implementation. In Listing 6-5, calling the GetFactory method using System.Data.SqlClient would return the instance of SqlClientFactory.

- The support attribute, which is responsible for determining the types that the DbProviderFactory's Create methods can create.

- The type attribute, which defines the actual DbProviderFactory concrete implementation that should be instantiated.

Now with the use of the connection string settings, database provider base classes, and provider factory classes, it is possible to create a connection object without specifying its type within the code of an application. Listing 6-6 shows the application code used to create the connection object, and Listing 6-7 shows the use of the providerName attribute to define the correct factory provider class to instantiate.

**Listing 6-6.** *Sample Provider Factory*

```
public DbConnection GetConnection ()
{
  ConnectionStringSettings connSetting =
    ConfigurationManager.ConnectionStrings["MyDataBase"];

  DbProviderFactory factory =
    DbProviderFactories.GetFactory(connSetting.ProviderName)

  DbConnection connection = null;

  connection = factory.CreateConnection();
  connection.ConnectionString = connSetting.ConnectionString;


  return connection;
}
```

**Listing 6-7.** *Sample Configuration for Provider Factory*

```
<configuration>
  <connectionStrings>
  <add name="MyDatabase"
      connectionString="(local)\SQLEXPRESS;Initial Catalog=MyDatabase;
                        integrated security=SSPI;Asynchronous Processing=True"
      providerName="System.Data.SqlClient" />
  </connectionStrings>
  <system.data>
    <DbProviderFactories>
      <add name="SqlClient Data Provider"
          invariant="System.Data.SqlClient"
          support="FF"
          description=".Net Framework Data Provider for SqlServer"
          type="System.Data.SqlClient.SqlClientFactory, System.Data,
              Version=2.0.3600.0, Culture=neutral, PublicKeyToken=b77a5c561934e089"
          />
    </DbProviderFactories>
  </system.data>
</configuration>
```

Now it is possible to write code that is generic and be able to use any provider that implements the database provider base classes. Typically, developers would then use the DbProviderFactory class to create the necessary DbCommand objects, DbDataAdapter objects, DbDataReader objects, and so on to complete their data access layer implementation.

With all these new features provided in ADO.NET 2.0, you may wonder what more the Data Access Application Block can actually provide. I'll answer that in the next section.

# Features of the Data Access Application Block

While the database provider base classes have allowed for database provider-independent code, they do not cover all situations. There maybe instances where it would be necessary to modify the data access layer to handle database provider-specific features. An example is handling packages in the OracleClient database provider. If you were to use the OracleCommand object directly, you would need to specify the package and procedure together, something like this:

```
MyDbCommand.CommandText = "MyPackage.MyProcedure";
```

This would work fine if the application communicated with only an Oracle database, but would probably require modification if you needed to use it with some other database provider, such as the SQL Server database provider.

Along with the ability to configure an application's data access needs through the Enterprise Library Configuration Console, as described in the previous chapter, the Data Access Application Block offers the following benefits:

- It helps make the data access layer more provider-independent by providing greater degrees of encapsulation than what is available in ADO.NET 2.0.

- It wraps the most commonly used commands to simplify the amount of code required for performing data queries and manipulation from a data store.

- The parameter cache can cache database parameters, so that they may be reused, thus reducing the amount of code execution overhead needed to create new parameter objects every time a database SQL command is performed.

The Database Access Application Block includes the Database and DbProviderFactory classes for handling data access.

## Understanding the Database Class

The Database class is the heart of the Data Access Application Block. This is an abstract class that has the following four concrete implementations:

- GenericDatabase: Typically used when provider-specific features are not required or the database type is not known.

- SqlDatabase: Contains SQL Server provider-specific functionality. This class may be used with all versions of SQL Server except SQL Server 2005 Compact Edition.

- SqlCeDatabase: Provides the necessary implementation to use the SQL Server 2005 Compact Edition database engine. This class is new to Enterprise Library for 3.0 (April 2007).

- OracleDatabase: Provides specific Oracle database functionality such as the handling of Oracle packages.

The Database class holds an instance of a DbProviderFactory class inside itself. It manages all the data parameters for SQL commands, DbCommand objects, DbConnection objects, and DbDataAdapter objects necessary to execute the appropriate database SQL commands and return the expected results. Figure 6-1 shows the public methods and return types for the Database class.

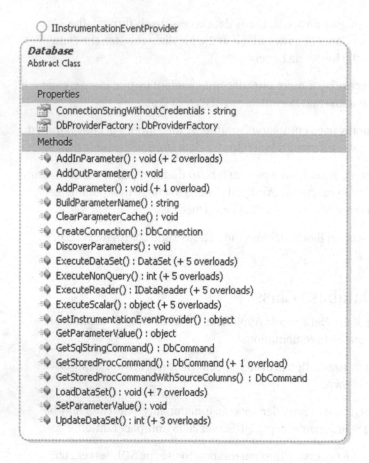

○ IInstrumentationEventProvider

**Database**
Abstract Class

**Properties**
- 🔐 ConnectionStringWithoutCredentials : string
- 🔐 DbProviderFactory : DbProviderFactory

**Methods**
- ⬤ AddInParameter() : void (+ 2 overloads)
- ⬤ AddOutParameter() : void
- ⬤ AddParameter() : void (+ 1 overload)
- ⬤ BuildParameterName() : string
- ⬤ ClearParameterCache() : void
- ⬤ CreateConnection() : DbConnection
- ⬤ DiscoverParameters() : void
- ⬤ ExecuteDataSet() : DataSet (+ 5 overloads)
- ⬤ ExecuteNonQuery() : int (+ 5 overloads)
- ⬤ ExecuteReader() : IDataReader (+ 5 overloads)
- ⬤ ExecuteScalar() : object (+ 5 overloads)
- ⬤ GetInstrumentationEventProvider() : object
- ⬤ GetParameterValue() : object
- ⬤ GetSqlStringCommand() : DbCommand
- ⬤ GetStoredProcCommand() : DbCommand (+ 1 overload)
- ⬤ GetStoredProcCommandWithSourceColumns() : DbCommand
- ⬤ LoadDataSet() : void (+ 7 overloads)
- ⬤ SetParameterValue() : void
- ⬤ UpdateDataSet() : int (+ 3 overloads)

**Figure 6-1.** *Database class public methods and properties*

## Executing Commands Against the Database

The Database class contains the methods necessary for executing commands against a database. Like the DbCommand class, Database has ExecuteScalar, ExecuteNonQuery, and ExecuteReader methods. The Database class also adds three more methods—ExecuteDataSet, LoadDataSet, and UpdateDataSet—which are used for retrieving untyped and typed DataSets, as well as updating data from a DataSet to a database.

The ExecuteScalar, ExecuteNonQuery, ExecuteReader, and ExecuteDataSet methods contain six common method signatures for executing database commands. These execution methods are described in Table 6-4, and their common signatures are listed in Table 6-5.

**Table 6-4.** *Database Class Execute Methods*

| Method | Description |
|---|---|
| ExecuteScalar | Returns the first column of the first row from the executed command |
| ExecuteNonQuery | Does not return a resultset (it is possible to return output parameters) |
| ExecuteReader | Returns the resultset as a DataReader based on the results of the command executed |
| ExecuteDataSet | Returns the resultset as a DataTable within a DataSet based on the results of the command executed |

**Table 6-5.** *Database Class Execute Method Signatures*

| Method Signature | Description |
|---|---|
| DbCommand | Executes the command text specified in the DbCommand class's CommandText property along with any necessary predetermined parameters. It returns the expected resultset for the method executed. |
| CommandType, string | By specifying the command type and the command text (string), a DbCommand object will be created and executed along with any necessary predetermined parameters. It returns the expected resultset for the method executed. |
| string, object[]* | By specifying the stored procedure name (string), a DbCommand object will be created and executed along with any specified parameters with their values (object[]). It returns the expected resultset for the method executed. |
| DbCommand, DbTransaction | Executes the command text specified in the DbCommand along with any necessary predetermined parameters within the context of a database transaction (DbTransaction). It returns the expected resultset for the method executed. |
| DbTransaction, CommandType, string | By specifying the command type and the command text (string), a DbCommand object will be created and executed along with any necessary predetermined parameters within the context of a database transaction (DbTransaction). It returns the expected resultset for the method executed. |
| DbTransaction, string, object[]* | By specifying the stored procedure name (string) a DbCommand object will be created and executed along with any specified parameters with their values (object[]) within the context of a database transaction (DbTransaction). It returns the expected resultset for the method executed. |

\*    *The order of the values contained within the object array must match the order of the parameters as they are defined in the stored procedure.*

The two Database class methods specifically for filling typed or untyped DataSets and updating DataSets are LoadDataSet and UpdateDataSet. These methods are described in Table 6-6, and their signatures are listed in Tables 6-7 and 6-8, respectively.

**Table 6-6.** *Database Class Methods for Filling and Updating DataSets*

| Method | Description |
|---|---|
| LoadDataSet | Used for filling a typed or untyped dataset. It also can be used for adding a DataTable to an existing DataSet. This can be useful when you need to load data from multiple data store providers, such as to create one DataSet with DataTables filled with data from an Oracle database and a DB2 database. |
| UpdateDataSet | Takes the data from a DataSet and calls the necessary update, insert, and delete commands to make the appropriate changes to the database, based on the data changes in the dataset. |

**Table 6-7.** *LoadDataSet Signatures*

| Method Signature | Description |
|---|---|
| DbCommand, DataSet, string | Executes the database command specified by the DbCommand object, and adds a new table named by the string parameter to the specified DataSet. |
| DbCommand, DataSet, string[] | Executes the database command specified by the DbCommand object. Then it fills the specified DataSet's DataTables based on the table name mapping provided by the string[] parameter. |
| CommandType, string, DataSet, string[] | Creates and executes a DbCommand object based on the CommandType and command text (string) parameters. Then it fills the specified DataSet's DataTables based on the table name mapping provided by the string[] parameter. |
| DbCommand, DataSet, string, DbTransaction | Executes the database command specified by the DbCommand object, and adds a new table named by the string parameter to the specified DataSet within the context of a database transaction (DbTransaction). |
| DbCommand, DataSet, string[], DbTransaction | Executes the database command specified by the DbCommand object. Then it fills the specified DataSet's DataTables based on the table name mapping provided by the string[] parameter within the context of a database transaction (DbTransaction). |
| string, DataSet, string[], object[] | Creates and executes a DbCommand object based on the stored procedure parameter (string) and values based on the object array parameter. Then it fills the specified DataSet's DataTables based on the table name mapping provided by the string[] parameter. |
| DbTransaction, CommandType, string, DataSet, string[] | Creates and executes a DbCommand object based on the command type (CommandType) and command text (string) parameters. Then it fills the specified DataSet's DataTables based on the table name mapping provided by the string[] parameter within the context of a database transaction (DbTransaction). |
| DbTransaction, string, DataSet, string[], object[] | Creates and executes a DbCommand object based on the stored procedure parameter (string) and values based on the object array parameter (object[]). Then it fills the specified DataSet's DataTables based on the table name mapping provided by the string[] parameter within the context of a database transaction (DbTransaction). |

**Table 6-8.** *UpdateDataSet Signatures*

| Method Signature | Description |
| --- | --- |
| DataSet, string, DbCommand [insert], DbCommand [update], DbCommand [delete], DbTransaction | Creates the necessary data adapter with the three specified DbCommand objects. Then it takes the DataTable specified by the string and DataSet parameter and executes the appropriate insert, update, and/or delete DbCommand based on whether a specific row was changed. All this takes place within the context of a database transaction (DbTransaction). |
| DataSet, string, DbCommand [insert], DbCommand [update], DbCommand [delete], DbTransaction, UpdateBatchSize* | Same as the first method, except that it also allows an UpdateBatchSize parameter to be passed in. UpdateBatchSize tells ADO.NET to send updates in batches of the specified size to the database. This reduces the number of round-trips and improves performance. |
| DataSet, string, DbCommand [insert], DbCommand [update], DbCommand [delete], UpdateBehavior** | Creates the necessary data adapter with the three specified DbCommand objects. Then it takes the DataTable specified by the string and DataSet parameter and executes the appropriate insert, update, and/or delete DbCommand based on whether a specific row was changed. The execution of the DbCommand takes place based on the UpdateBehavior parameter's value. |
| DataSet, string, DbCommand [insert], DbCommand [update], DbCommand [delete], UpdateBehavior, UpdateBatchSize* | This method is the same as the previous one, except that it also allows a UpdateBatchSize parameter to be passed in. |

\*    *The* UpdateBatchSize *property is not directly supported in Enterprise Library 2.0 (January 2006).*

\*\*   *The* UpdateBehavior *enumerator specifies whether the* DataAdapter *should continue if errors occur, stop when an error occurs but commit the successful rows, or execute within a transaction where all rows will be rolled back if an error occurs.*

## Specifying Parameters for a Database Command Object

The handling of parameters is done through the Database object. You can either add parameters explicitly to a DbCommand object or let the parameters be determined by discovering them via the DiscoverParameters method.

### Explicitly Adding Parameters

Parameters can be added to the DbCommand object directly via the DbCommand.Parameter.Add method. However, while this may seem like the easiest approach, it actually may not be the best practice. Each database provider has its own way of marking up a parameter name. For instance, preceding each parameter name, SQL Server adds an at sign (@), Oracle adds a colon (:), and OLEDB and ODBC add a question mark (?). The Data Access Application Block Database class handles each prefix for you. This way, it is easier to switch from one database provider to another with very little, if any, code changes.

You can add parameters to the DbCommand object through the AddParameter method, the AddInParameter method, or the AddOutParameter method. Typically, it is easier to use the AddInParameter or AddOutParameter method. Listing 6-8 demonstrates adding parameters using the Database class.

**Listing 6-8.** *Adding Database Command Parameters via the Database Class*

```
public string MyDataQuery(int myFirstValue, string mySecondValue)
{
    Database db = DatabaseFactory.CreateDatabase();

    string sqlCommand = "MyStoredProc";
    DbCommand dbCommand = db.GetStoredProcCommand(sqlCommand);

    db.AddInParameter(dbCommand, "MyFirstValue", DbType.Int32, myFirstValue);
    db.AddInParameter(dbCommand, "MySecondValue", DbType.String);
    db.AddOutParameter(dbCommand, "MyReturnValue", DbType.String, 30);

    db.SetParameterValue(dbCommand, "MySecondValue", mySecondValue);

    db.ExecuteNonQuery(dbCommand);

    return (string)db.GetParameterValue(dbCommand, "MyReturnValue");
}
```

In Listing 6-8, the parameter names were not marked up with the database provider-specific formatting. This way, the database provider can be easily swapped out without having to modify the data access layer code.

### Understanding Parameter Discovery

Another method for defining database parameters is the "derived" method. Essentially, it uses the database provider to ask the database what the parameters are for a given database command. Assuming the stored procedure in Listing 6-8 had only the three parameters defined for it, you could call the Database object's DiscoverParameters method to discover the parameters necessary to execute the stored procedure. The one drawback to using this method is that the first call to the DiscoverParameters method requires a database round-trip to do the discovery. For batch processing, this may become a time-consuming burden. The Data Access Application Block solves this by caching the parameters discovered from the first call for later use. This way, subsequent calls to the DiscoverParameters method to request parameters for the MyStoredProc stored procedure will actually have its parameters cloned from an internal cache. Listing 6-9 shows how it would be used with the derived method.

**Listing 6-9.** *Adding Database Command Parameters via the Derived Method*

```
public string MyDataQuery(int myFirstValue, string mySecondValue)
{
    Database db = DatabaseFactory.CreateDatabase();

    string sqlCommand = "MyStoredProc";
    DbCommand
    dbCommand = db.GetStoredProcCommand(sqlCommand);

    db.DiscoverParameters(dbCommand);

    db.SetParameterValue(dbCommand, "MyFirstValue", myFirstValue);
    db.SetParameterValue(dbCommand, "MySecondValue",
        mySecondValue);

    db.ExecuteNonQuery(dbCommand);

    return (string)db.GetParameterValue(dbCommand, "MyReturnValue");
}
```

## Using the SQL Server-Specific Database Class Implementation

The SqlDatabase class, which implements the Database class, adds another Execute method called ExecuteXmlReader. This method can return an XmlReader based on the command executed. This is a SQL Server-specific feature that requires the For XML clause in the SQL statement. The ExecuteXmlReader has two method signatures. Both require a DbCommand object as a parameter, and one method signature adds the DbTransaction object as a parameter as well. Listing 6-10 shows how to use the ExecuteXmlReader method.

**Listing 6-10.** *Using the ExecuteXmlReader Method*

```
public XmlReader GetAllCustomersXml()
{
    SqlDatabase dbSQL = DatabaseFactory.CreateDatabase("MyDatabase") as SqlDatabase;
    string sqlCommand = "usp_GetAllCustomersXml";
    DbCommand dbCommand = dbSQL.GetStoredProcCommand(sqlCommand);
    XmlReader customersReader = null;

    try
    {
        customersReader = dbSQL.ExecuteXmlReader(dbCommand);
    }
    catch
    {}

    return customersReader;
}
```

## Using the SQL Server 2005 CE Database Provider Class Implementation

The SqlCeDatabase class provides the functionality needed to consume the SQL Server 2005 Compact Edition database with the Data Access Application Block. Like the rest of the database providers, this class also consumes the Database class; however, most of the public members of the Database class used for accessing and manipulating data are not implemented. In fact, if the following methods are used, an exception will be thrown:

- ExecuteDataSet(string storedProcedureName, params object[] parameterValues)

- ExecuteNonQuery(string storedProcedureName, params object[] parameterValues)

- ExecuteScalar(string storedProcedureName, params object[] parameterValues)

- LoadDataSet(string storedProcedureName, DataSet dataSet, string[] tableNames, params object[] parameterValues)

- GetStoredProcCommand(string storedProcedureName, params object[] parameterValues)

- GetStoredProcCommand(string storedProcedureName)

These six methods are not supported because they are intended to be used with stored procedures. Since SQL Server CE does not support stored procedures, it does not make sense to implement these methods.

The SqlCeDatabase class does add a series of new methods that support the specific needs of SQL Server 2005 Compact Edition, as listed in Table 6-9.

**Table 6-9.** *SqlCeDatabase Class Extension Methods*

| Method | Description |
|---|---|
| CreateFile | Creates a new database file based on the connection string provided. |
| CreateParameter | Creates a parameter with a specified name, data type, size, and value. |
| ExecuteDataSetSql | Executes a SQL command string with or without parameters and returns a DataSet. |
| ExecuteNonQuerySql | Executes a SQL command string with or without parameters and returns an integer specifying the number of rows affected. An overload of this method can also return the value of an identity column through an output parameter called lastAddedId of the method. |
| ExecuteReaderSql | Executes a SQL command string with or without parameters and returns an instance of IDataReader. |
| ExecuteResultSet | Returns the new SqlCeResultSet object provided with SQL Server CE. This method contains four different overloads that allow for specific resultset types and whether to use a transaction. It is very important to remember to close the connection that is associated with the command object, since the close behavior is not implemented within these methods. |
| ExecuteScalarSql | Executes a SQL command string with or without parameters and the first column of the first row. |
| TableExists | Determines if a table exists within the specified database specified by the connection string. |

---

■**Note** The SQL Server 2005 Compact Edition database provider is not provided in Enterprise Library 2.0 (January 2006) or prior versions.

---

### Using the Oracle Database Class Implementation

The OracleDatabase class also contains its own unique feature: the constructor can take not only a connection object, but also adds a method constructor that can take IList of IOraclePackage. The IOraclePackage is implemented by the OraclePackageData class. It contains two properties for defining the name of a package and a prefix: Name and Prefix, respectively.

## Understanding the Database Factory Class

A Database object can be created by using a factory via the DatabaseFactory class or by directly constructing one. The DatabaseFactory class uses configuration information to determine the connection string, ADO.NET data provider, and appropriate Data Access Application Block Database class implementation to instantiate.

The DatabaseFactory class uses the static method CreateDatabase to create the specific Database subtype. The CreateDatabase method has two signatures, as shown in Table 6-10. Listings 6-9 and 6-10, presented earlier, show examples of implementing both of these methods.

**Table 6-10.** *CreateDatabase Method Signatures*

| Method Signature | Description |
|---|---|
| CreateDatabase() : Database | Does not take any parameters and creates the default database instance defined in the application's configuration file |
| CreateDatabase(stringname) : Database | Takes a string parameter that allows the developer to determine by name which instance should be returned |

The DatabaseFactory class uses the connections defined in the connectionStrings node of the application configuration file. If no provider is specified in the specific named instance of a connection string, a SqlDatabase instance is presumed.

By default, the DatabaseFactory class creates Database objects of the following types:

- SqlDatabase for data providers specified as System.Data.SqlClient

- SqlCeDatabase for data providers specified as System.Data.SqlServerCe

- OracleDatabase for data providers specified as System.Data.OracleClient

- GenericDatabase for all other data provider types

An instance of the GenericDatabase class can be used with any .NET managed provider, including the ODBC and OLEDB providers that are included in .NET Framework 2.0 and 3.0.

> ■ **Note** The GenericDatabase class supports only basic database provider functionality provided by ADO.NET. Thus, the data access overloads that support parameter discovery will not work.

## Instrumenting the Data Access Calls

For the Data Access Application Block, you can set up the following instrumentation features:

- *Performance counters*: The performance counters included in the Data Access Application Block are Commands Executed Per Second, Commands Failed Per Second, Connections Opened per Second, and Connections Failed Per Second.

- *Event logging*: The event logging includes a ConnectionFailed event when attempting to open a connection in the Database object, and a configuration error when trying to create a Database object.

- *WMI*: The WMI events include Command Failed, Connection Failed, and Configuration Error events.

To turn on these features, you must specify the instrumentationConfiguration section in the application configuration file, and set the appropriate event logging, performance counter, and WMI attributes to true. See Chapters 4 and 5 for details on how instrumentation works and how to turn it on via the application configuration file.

# Configuring the Data Access Application Block

Using the Data Access Application Block is as simple as installing, writing the data access layer, setting up the application configuration file, and deploying the application. OK, it may not always be that simple, but the tasks are straightforward.

To paraphrase a famous playwright, "To GAC or not to GAC, that is the question." When it comes to installing the Data Access Application Block assemblies, they can be put in the GAC by strong naming them, or they can be placed in the executing directory of the application. If strong naming is desired, Enterprise Library 3.0 (April 2007) contains precompiled assemblies; however, prior versions of Enterprise Library will require the necessary steps to be performed for strong naming assemblies.

Configuring the Data Access Application Block can be done either manually through a text editor or via the Configuration Console. The benefit of using the Configuration Console is that it will validate the configuration data entered, thus ensuring that that data is set up properly. Therefore, although it is possible to modify the configuration data manually, it is generally suggested that the Configuration Console be used whenever possible.

# Editing Configuration Data Manually

In the configuration file, there are two configuration sections used by the Data Access Application Block:

- DatabaseSettings: This configuration section defines the default database and any custom data mappings that maybe required.

- OracleConnectionSettings: This configuration section handles the unique configuration data needed by the OracleDatabase class.

To add the configuration settings, you need to add the appropriate section handlers to the configSections element of the application configuration file, as shown in Listing 6-11. However, if you use the Enterprise Library Configuration Console, that task will be done for you.

**Listing 6-11.** *Data Access Application Block Section Handlers*

```
<configSections>
    <section name="dataConfiguration"
    type="Microsoft.Practices.EnterpriseLibrary.Data.Configuration.DatabaseSettings,
    Microsoft.Practices.EnterpriseLibrary.Data, Version=3.0.0.0, Culture=neutral,
    PublicKeyToken=null" />

    <section name="oracleConnectionSettings"
    type="Microsoft.Practices.EnterpriseLibrary.Data.Oracle.Configuration.
    OracleConnectionSettings,
    Microsoft.Practices.EnterpriseLibrary.Data, Version=3.0.0.0, Culture=neutral,
    PublicKeyToken=null" />
</configSections>
```

---

**Note** In Listing 6-11, the type attributes should be all on one line, with only one space after each comma. It was necessary to use multiple lines here to fit the code on the page. In the sample application source code, it is formatted properly.

---

The connectionStrings, dataConfiguration, and oracleConnectionSettings elements are the core elements used to configure the Database Access Application Block.

## connectionStrings Element

The connectionStrings elements are actually configuration settings included in .NET Framework 2.0 and 3.0 for ADO.NET. Hence, it is not necessary to define a configSection handler for them, as it was defined in the machine.config file during the installation of .NET Framework 2.0 and/or 3.0.

> **Tip**  If certain section handlers are to be used throughout many applications within a particular computer, it may prove worthwhile to simply add those configuration section handlers to the `machine.config` file.

The `connectionStrings` element uses the `add`, `clear`, and `remove` elements found in the `AppSettings` elements. The `add` element allows for a `name` attribute, which defines a unique name of the `connectionString`; a `providerName`, which is used to define the database provider associated with the connection string; and a `connectionString`.

The `remove` and `clear` elements are responsible for removing and clearing inherited connection strings. In other words, by specifying the `clear` element in an application's configuration file, all connection strings defined in the `machine.config` file will be ignored. The `remove` element will remove inherited connection strings that contain the same `name` value as the `remove`'s element `name` attribute. This way, a connection string can be defined in the `machine.config` file, and an application configuration can remove it, and then add a new connection string with the same name, essentially like overriding a base class's method. Listing 6-12 shows what an application's connection settings may look like in the configuration file.

**Listing 6-12.** *Application File Connection Strings*

```
<connectionStrings>
   <clear />
   <add
      name="MyDatabase"
      connectionString="data source=(local);Integrated  Security=SSPI;
         Database=MyDatabase"
      providerName="System.Data.SqlClient"
   />
   <add
      name="YourDatabase "
      connectionString="data source=(local);Integrated  Security=SSPI;
         Database=YourDatabase "
      providerName="System.Data.SqlClient"
   />
   <add
      name="LocalSqlServer "
      connectionString="data source=.\SQLEXPRESS;Integrated  Security=SSPI;
         AttachDBFilename=|DataDirectory|CustomAspDb.mdf;User Instance=true"
      providerName="System.Data.SqlClient"
   />
</connectionStrings>
```

Listing 6-12 uses the `clear` method to override the existing `LocalSqlServer` connection string setting that is defined in the `machine.config` file. This way, the application can use a different `.mdf` file named `CustomAspDb.mdf`, as opposed to the default `aspnetdb.mdf` database file. The `remove` element with the `name` attribute set to `LocalSqlServer` could have also been used in place of the `clear` element, as follows.

```
<remove name="LocalSqlServer " />
```

## dataConfiguration Element

The dataConfiguration element defines the default connectionString to use when no instance is specified. It contains an attribute called defaultDatabase, which specifies the default connection string to use. It can also have child elements called dataMappings, which define custom provider mappings that are required if database-derived classes are used instead of the default GenericDatabase class. It contains two attributes: databaseType, which defines the type that derives from the Database class; and name, which defines the appropriate ADO.NET database provider to use. The following is an example of a dataConfiguration element.

```
<dataConfiguration defaultDatabase="MyDatabase" />
```

It is important that the defaultDatabase attribute value matches one of the connectionString's add element's name attributes; otherwise, an exception will be thrown when attempting to create a Database object.

> **Note** It is not necessary to specify data mappings for the SqlDatabase and OracleDatabase classes, as this is already done in the Data Access Application Block by default.

## oracleConnectionSettings Element

The oracleConnectionSettings element defines the prefixes necessary when Oracle packages are to be used by an application. The oracleConnectionSettings element can contain many add elements that have an attribute called name. The add element's name attribute will correspond to a specific connection string. The add elements will then have child elements called packages.

The packages element will again contain one to many child add elements. Each one of the packages add elements contains two attributes: name, which defines the name of the Oracle package; and prefix, which defines the prefix of the Oracle package. Listing 6-13 shows how the oracleConnectionSettings element may be used in an application.

**Listing 6-13.** *Application File Oracle Connection Strings*

```
<configuration>
  <connectionStrings>
    <add
      name="MyOracleDb"
      connectionString="data source=192.168.0.100;Integrated  Security=SSPI;
        Database=MyDatabase"
      providerName="System.Data.OracleClient"
    />
  </connectionStrings />

  <dataConfiguration defaultDatabase="MyOracleDb" />
```

```
<oracleConnectionSettings>
   <add>
      <packages>
         <add name="MyFirstPackage" prefix="first" />
         <add name="MySecondPackage" prefix="second" />
      <packages>
   </add>
</oracleConnectionSettings>
</configuration>
```

## Editing Configuration Data via the Configuration Console

Using the Configuration Console to configure the Data Access Application Block can both simplify the task and reduce the chances of human error.

To get started, open the Configuration Console and select the Enterprise Library Configuration node in the tree list. Then choose to add a new application (either through the node's context menu or the main menu bar). Next, add the Data Access Application Block to the newly created application (again through the context menu or main menu). The end result should look something like Figure 6-2.

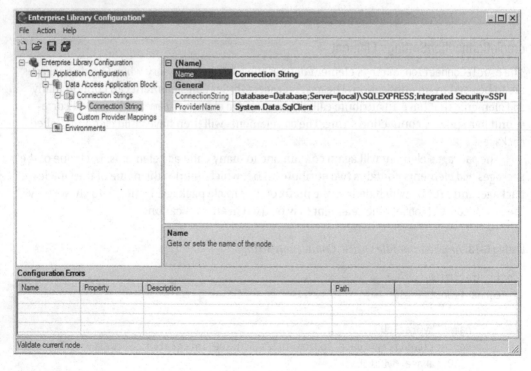

**Figure 6-2.** *Creating a new connection string*

As you can see, the machine.config's LocalSqlServer entry, which was named Connection String by default, has been added automatically. This is expected behavior because of the way the System.Configuration components behave in .NET. If you remove the LocalSqlServer connectionString entry in the machine.config file, it will no longer appear in the Configuration Console.

## Setting Up SQL Server Connection Strings

To set up your connection strings, right-click the Connection Strings node and select New ➤ Connection String from the context menu. A new connection string node, named Connection String 1, is added. As an example, we'll go through the steps to set up a connection string for SQL Server Express. Modify the Name attribute in the properties grid to change the name to MyConnection, as shown in Figure 6-3.

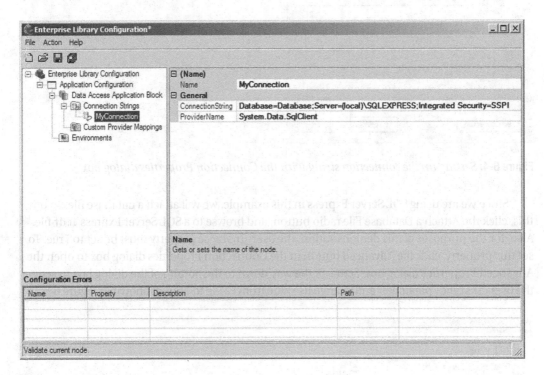

**Figure 6-3.** *Changing the connection string name*

Next, click the ConnectionString attribute value, and an ellipse button will appear to the right of that value. Click that button, and you will see the Connection Properties dialog box, as shown in Figure 6-4. Notice that the Server Name field is already selected, and the database name is set to Database.

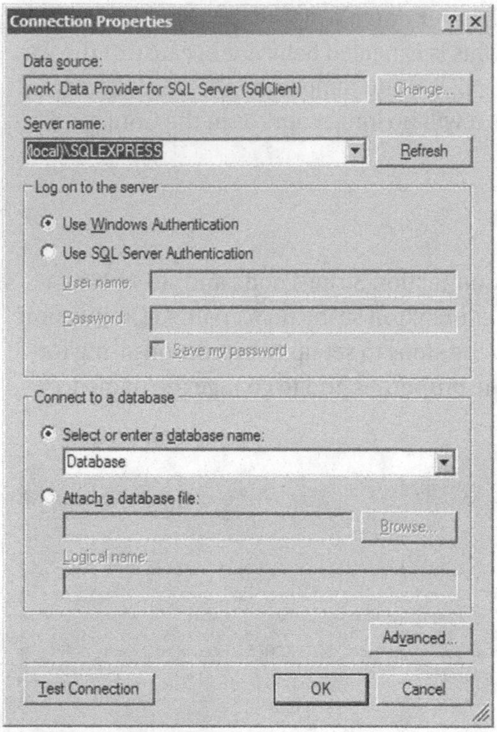

**Figure 6-4.** *Setting up the connection string with the Connection Properties dialog box*

Since we are using SQL Server Express in this example, we will attach a database file. To do this, click the Attach a Database File radio button, and browse to a SQL Server Express .mdf file. Also, for the purposes of this demonstration, the User Instance property must be set to True. To set this property, click the Advanced button in the Connection Properties dialog box to open the Advanced Properties dialog box. Scroll all the way down to the bottom of the dialog box to see the User Instance parameter and change its value from False to True, as shown in Figure 6-5.

**Figure 6-5.** *Advanced Properties dialog box*

## Setting Oracle-Specific Connection Settings

Creating the Oracle packages for an Oracle connection is pretty simple. First, create a new Connection String node, as described in the previous section, and name it MyOracleDatabase. Change the ProviderName property to System.Data.OracleClient. Next, click the ConnectionString attribute value, and then click the ellipse button to its right to open the Connection Properties dialog box (see Figure 6-4). Use this dialog box to set the specifics of the connection.

---

■**Note**  You may get an error message stating the database parameter is not valid when trying to open the Connection Properties dialog box when you first create the connection. To work around this, remove the existing connection string value, and then open the Connection Properties dialog box.

---

Next, right-click the MyOracleDatabase node and select New ➤ Oracle Packages from the context menu. A new node called Oracle Packages will appear under the MyOracleDatabase node. Right-click the Oracle Packages node and select New ➤ Oracle Package. A new node called Oracle Package will appear, as shown in Figure 6-6. The properties grid lists Name and Prefix properties. Set the Name property to MyFirstPackage and the Prefix value to First. This completes the configuration of the Oracle-specific connection settings.

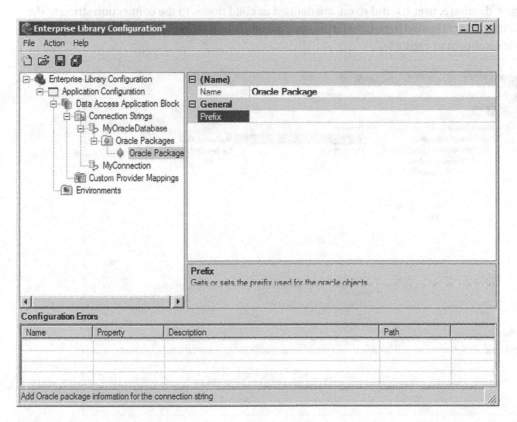

**Figure 6-6.** *Adding an Oracle Package*

## Specifying the Default Database Instance

Now that the connection strings for the application are set, you need to set the DefaultDatabase property for the entire application. The DefaultDatabase property is associated with the Database Application Block node, so select that node, and the DefaultDatabase property will appear in the properties grid. For the DefaultDatabase property, select MyConnection. Now the default database instance to be used is defined by the connection settings found in the MyConnection node.

## Adding Data Mappings

When using custom build or third-party implementations of the Database class, you will need to add an entry to the Custom Provider Mappings node. This way, the Data Access Application Block knows which database provider to tie to a specific subtype of the Database class.

Right-click the Custom Provider Mappings node and select New ➤ Provider Mapping. A new Provider Mapping node will appear under the Custom Provider Mappings node, with two properties: Name and TypeName. The Name property defines the database provider implementation, such as System.Data.SqlClient. The TypeName property specifies the specific implementation of the Database class that will be associated with the database provider.

## Connection Strings and Enterprise Library 2.0

Enterprise Library 2.0 handles the creation of connection strings differently than described in the previous sections. In Enterprise Library 2.0, the parameters of a connection string. such as server, database, user ID, and so on, are defined as child nodes to the connection string node, and then concatenated together to produce the connection string. An example of these child nodes is shown in Figure 6-7.

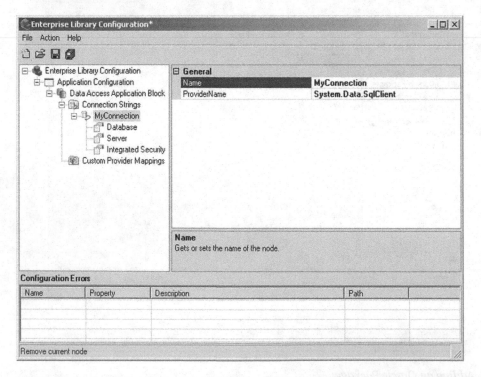

**Figure 6-7.** *Connection string parameter nodes in the Enterprise Library 2.0 Configuration Console*

# ACME POS Application Data Access

Since the particular vertical slice of the sample ACME POS application presented in this book revolves around customer information, the data access layer will focus on retrieving and storing customer data. Setting up this data access involves four tasks:

- Create the Customers database.

- Define the Customers business entity.

- Create the Customers data access layer.

- Update the Customers web service web.config file with the proper configuration settings.

This section assumes that you have installed SQL Server Express with Visual Studio or SQL Server 2005 on your workstation.

## Creating the Customers Database

The first step is to create a new SQL Server database. Open the ACME POS solution in Visual Studio and add a new database project to it. Specify the correct instance of SQL Server. In the Database Selection field, type ACMECustomers. Select Yes when you are asked if you want to create a new database called ACMECustomers.

The script in Listing 6-14 contains a simplified, table-only version of the full table creation script (available on the Apress website). The full script will create the tables, foreign key relationships, and stored procedures necessary for querying and manipulating the tables. This simplified version should be used for reference only.

**Listing 6-14.** *ACMECustomers Database Table Creation Script*

```
CREATE TABLE [dbo].[Customer](
   [CustomerId] [int] IDENTITY(1,1) NOT NULL,
   [FirstName] [varchar](50)
      COLLATE SQL_Latin1_General_CP1_CI_AS NOT NULL,
   [LastName] [varchar](50) COLLATE SQL_Latin1_General_CP1_CI_AS
      NOT NULL,
   [BirthDate] [datetime] NOT NULL,
   [MemberSince] [datetime] NOT NULL,
   [IsActive] [bit] NULL,

   CONSTRAINT [PK_Customer] PRIMARY KEY CLUSTERED
   (
      [CustomerId] ASC
   )WITH (IGNORE_DUP_KEY = OFF) ON [PRIMARY]
) ON [PRIMARY]

GO

CREATE TABLE [dbo].[Address](
```

```
    [AddressId] [int] IDENTITY(1,1) NOT NULL,
    [Address] [varchar](50)
        COLLATE SQL_Latin1_General_CP1_CI_AS NOT NULL,
    [City] [varchar](50)
        COLLATE SQL_Latin1_General_CP1_CI_AS NOT NULL,
    [State] [varchar](2)
        COLLATE SQL_Latin1_General_CP1_CI_AS NOT NULL,
    [ZipCode] [varchar](20)
        COLLATE SQL_Latin1_General_CP1_CI_AS NOT NULL,
    [IsPrimaryShipping] [bit] NOT NULL,
    [CustomerId] [int] NOT NULL,
    [IsActive] [bit] NOT NULL,

CONSTRAINT [PK_Address] PRIMARY KEY CLUSTERED
(
    [AddressId] ASC
)WITH (IGNORE_DUP_KEY = OFF) ON [PRIMARY]
) ON [PRIMARY]

GO

CREATE TABLE [dbo].[PaymentMethod](
    [PaymentMethodId] [int] NOT NULL,
    [Name] [varchar](50)
        COLLATE SQL_Latin1_General_CP1_CI_AS NOT NULL,
 CONSTRAINT [PK_PaymentMethod] PRIMARY KEY CLUSTERED
(
    [PaymentMethodId] ASC
)WITH (IGNORE_DUP_KEY = OFF) ON [PRIMARY]
) ON [PRIMARY]

GO

CREATE TABLE [dbo].[BillingMethod](
    [BillingMethodId] [int] IDENTITY(1,1) NOT NULL,
    [PaymentMethodId] [int] NOT NULL,
    [CreditCardNumber] [varchar](20)
        COLLATE SQL_Latin1_General_CP1_CI_AS NULL,
    [CreditCardExpiration] [datetime] NULL,
    [CreditCardBillingAddressId] [int] NULL,
    [CustomerId] [int] NOT NULL,
    [NetTermDays] [int] NULL,
    [IsActive] [bit] NOT NULL,
 CONSTRAINT [PK_BillingMethod] PRIMARY KEY CLUSTERED
(
    [BillingMethodId] ASC
)WITH (IGNORE_DUP_KEY = OFF) ON [PRIMARY]
```

```
) ON [PRIMARY]

GO
```

This script creates four tables:

- The Customer table is for defining the customer's first name, last name, member since date, and birth date.

- The Address table defines one or more addresses a customer may use for shipping and/or billing purposes.

- The PaymentMethod table defines the different forms of payment ACME will accept. In this case, the available payment methods are credit card, net term, and cash.

- The BillingMethod table defines the different payment types and can store the appropriate data for those types.

## Creating the Customer Business Entity

Listing 6-15 shows the EntityBase class and Customer class. The Address and BillingMethod classes are located in the source code for the reference implementation. The Customer class contains a property for each column in the Customer table, plus an address list and billing method list. Also, the Customer class inherits from EntityBase, so it will automatically contain an IsModified property.

**Listing 6-15.** *EntityBase and Customer Classes*

```
using System;
using System.Collections.Generic;
using System.Text;

namespace ACME.POS.Domain.Entity
{
    public class EntityBase
    {
        private bool m_IsModified;

        public bool IsModified
        {
            get { return m_IsModified; }
            set { m_IsModified = value; }
        }

    }

    public class Customer : EntityBase
    {
        private int m_CustomerId;
```

```csharp
private string m_FirstName;
private string m_LastName;
private DateTime m_MemberSince;
private DateTime m_BirthDate;
private AddressList m_Addresses;
private BillingMethodList m_BillingMethods;

public int CustomerId
{
    get { return m_CustomerId; }
    set { m_CustomerId = value; }
}

public string FirstName
{
    get { return m_FirstName; }
    set { m_FirstName = value; }
}

public string LastName
{
    get { return m_LastName; }
    set { m_LastName = value; }
}

public DateTime MemberSince
{
    get { return m_MemberSince; }
    set { m_MemberSince = value; }
}

public DateTime BirthDate
{
    get { return m_BirthDate; }
    set { m_BirthDate = value; }
}

public AddressList Addresses
{
    get { return m_Addresses; }
    set { m_Addresses = value; }
}
```

```
    public BillingMethodList BillingMethods
    {
        get { return m_BillingMethods; }
        set { m_BillingMethods = value; }
    }
}

public class CustomerList : IList<Customer>
{

}
}
```

## Creating the Customer Data Access Layer

With the database and business entity classes created, it is now possible to create the data access layer for the ACME POS application. Create a new class project devoted solely to the data access layer, named ACMECustomerDAL. In the project, set assembly references to Microsoft.Practices.EnterpriseLibrary.Data and Microsoft.Practices.EnterpriseLibrary.Common. Then add a project reference to the Domain.Entity project (which can be found in the reference implementation's source code).

Next, rename the class to CustomerDAL. Edit the class to add using statements for Microsoft.Practices.EnterpriseLibrary.Data and ACME.POS.Domain.Entity. Stub out two methods: GetAllCustomers (for gathering the customer data) and SaveCustomers (for saving customer data to the database). Listing 6-16 shows the class at this point.

**Listing 6-16.** *Stubbed Out CustomerDAL Class*

```
using System;
using System.Collections.Generic;
using System.Data;
using System.Data.Common;
using System.Text;
using Microsoft.Practices.EnterpriseLibrary.Data;
using ACME.POS.Domain.Entity;

namespace ACME.POS.Domain.DAL
{
    public class CustomerDAL
    {
        public CustomerDAL()
        {

        }
```

```
    public CustomerList GetAllCustomers()
    {

    }

    public void SaveCustomers(CustomerList customers)
    {

    }
  }
}
```

Now that the CustomerDAL class has been stubbed out, add a private member called m_CustomerDb, and call the CreateDatabase method of the DatabaseFactory class and assign its return value to the m_CustomerDb in the CustomerDAL constructor. This will use the default database instance specified in the application configuration file to create the appropriate Database subtype. In this case, the SqlDatabase class will be created and assigned to m_CustomerDb.

## Retrieving Data from the Database

The GetAllCustomers method will be responsible for getting a list of all active customers. It will use the ExecuteReader method of the Database class to create a DbDataReader object. The DbDataReader object will be read and the values saved into the CustomerList object. Listing 6-17 shows the implementation of the GetAllCustomers method.

**Listing 6-17.** *Implementing the GetAllCustomers Method*

```
public class CustomerDAL
{
   Database m_CustomerDb;

   public CustomerDAL()
   {
      m_CustomerDb = DatabaseFactory.CreateDatabase();
   }

   public CustomerList GetAllCustomers()
   {
      CustomerList customers = new CustomerList();

      DbCommand command =
        m_CustomerDb.GetStoredProcCommand("usp_Customer_List");

      using(IDataReader reader = m_CustomerDb.ExecuteReader(command))
      {
```

```
        Customer customer;
        while (reader.Read())
        {
            customer = new Customer();
            customer.CustomerId = (int)reader["CustomerId"];
            customer.FirstName = (string)reader["FirstName"];
            customer.LastName = (string)reader["LastName"];
            customer.BirthDate = (DateTime)reader["BirthDate"];
            customer.MemberSince= (DateTime)reader["MemberSince"];
            customer.IsActive = true;

            customers.Add(customer);
        }
    }

    return customers;
    }
}
```

In the GetAllCustomers method, a new instance of CustomersList is created. This is where the customer data will be placed. Next, a DbCommand instance called command is created, by calling the GetStoredProcCommand with the specified stored procedure name (usp_Customer_List). Then the m_CustomerDb's ExecuteReader command is executed to return a DbDataReader class. Once the DbDataReader is returned, the data rows are iterated through and new Customer class is instantiated and added to the customers object via the Add method. Finally, the customers object is returned.

## Saving Data to the Database

Saving changes to the database will be done through the m_CustomerDb's ExecuteNonQuery method. It works as follows:

- The SaveCustomers method will create a DbCommand object based on the stored procedure by calling the GetStoredProcCommand of the m_CustomerDb object.

- All the necessary parameters will be added to that command object.

- Each customer object in customers will be iterated through. If the IsModified flag is set to true, its values will be added to their respective parameters and the usp_Customer_Save stored procedure will be called via the ExecuteNonQuery method. If the CustomerId is less than one, which means that a new customer is being added to the database, then the newly created customer id value will be inserted back into the appropriate customer object.

- Finally, the IsModified flag will be set to false.

Listing 6-18 shows the implementation of the SaveCustomers method.

**Listing 6-18.** *Implementing the SaveCustomers Method*

```
public void SaveCustomers(CustomerList customers)
{
    DbCommand command = m_CustomerDb.GetStoredProcCommand("usp_Customer_Save");

    m_CustomerDb.AddInParameter(command, "FirstName", DbType.String);
    m_CustomerDb.AddInParameter(command, "LastName", DbType.String);
    m_CustomerDb.AddInParameter(command, "BirthDate", DbType.String);
    m_CustomerDb.AddInParameter(command, "MemberSince", DbType.String);
    m_CustomerDb.AddInParameter(command, "IsActive", DbType.String);
    m_CustomerDb.AddOutParameter(command, "CustomerId", DbType.Int32, 4);

    foreach (Customer customer in customers)
    {
        if (customer.IsModified)
        {
            m_CustomerDb.SetParameterValue(command,
                "FirstName", customer.FirstName);
            m_CustomerDb.SetParameterValue(command,
                "LastName", customer.lastName);
            m_CustomerDb.SetParameterValue(command,
                "BirthDate", customer.BirthDate);
            m_CustomerDb.SetParameterValue(command,
                "MemberSince", customer.MemberSince);
            m_CustomerDb.SetParameterValue(command,
                "IsActive", customer.IsActive);
            m_CustomerDb.SetParameterValue(command,
                "CustomerId", customer.CustomerId);

            m_CustomerDb.ExecuteNonQuery(command;

            if (customer.CustomerId < 1)
                customer.CustomerId = (int)m_CustomerDb.GetParameterValue(command,
                    "CustomerId");

            customer.IsModified == false;
        }
    }
}
```

## Setting Up the Application's Configuration File

For the reference implementation, creating the configuration data will be pretty easy. In the Configuration Console, open the appropriate web.config file for the ACME POS web service. Then add a new connection called ACMECustomer. Set the necessary connection string parameters, which may vary among database providers. Then set the DefaultDatabase instance property to the ACMECustomer node.

# Summary

The Data Access Application Block provides a lot of functionality for making database calls from a data access component. It can save coding time, reduce code, and support database provider independence. It is important to note that while a lot of features are provided in the Data Access Application Block, there may be times when it's necessary to use only certain features, or possibly none at all. However, for the most part, it should meet most, if not all, of your data access needs.

The next chapter will focus on the Caching Application Block. As the ACME POS application is an offline smart client application, it needs to cache data on client computers, so the sales team members can perform their work while on the road or at a customer's site.

# CHAPTER 7

■ ■ ■

# The Caching Application Block

In the previous chapter, you discovered how the Data Access Application Block can aid in accessing a back-end data store. Almost all applications require some sort of ability to store and retrieve data. However, the nonvolatile, persisted storage of data comes with a cost. While it is good to have data that will not disappear when a computer is shut off, the actual task of storing data can hinder performance. The most expensive performance costs typically involve the reading and writing of data to disk, as well as passing data around on a network.

The need for storing data to disk will remain, at least for the near future. The use of storage area networks (SANs) alleviates a lot of disk I/O performance issues because they typically employ an in-memory cache that will buffer the data as it is being read or written to the physical disk. Usually, SANs are reserved for only larger enterprise environments, as their cost can be quite steep.

In the future, there will probably be faster storage mediums, such as the use of RAM. A few companies are starting to build cards that take regular computer memory chips and create a "RAM" disk drive with them. While this technology is still in its infancy, it does show promise. Currently, some of these devices can store about 4GB of data, and they use a battery to maintain the data while the computer is without power. In time, these devices should mature to the point of being able to hold 8GB to 16GB of data. Then this technology could become very useful for the workstation PC.

But how do you get the benefits of an application that is scaled among multiple physical tiers and still have it perform as well as a single-tiered application? In this chapter, you will look at how you can help increase the performance of an application by giving it a means of storing nonvolatile data in a cache that can be accessed more readily than a back-end data store.

## Deciding When to Use Caching

Knowing when to cache data and when not to cache data is a critical factor in the success of an application. While caching of data may seem like the immediate answer to a performance problem, it can quickly become a problem from a functional standpoint.

Caching can offer the following benefits:

- *Performance:* When using a local cache of relatively static data, an application no longer needs to deal with the overhead of making a call to a data store to retrieve the data.

- *Scalability:* Caching allows for increased scalability of an application. The resources that are required to retrieve the data stay constant as an application environment is scaled out horizontally. If you don't use a cache, the resources against the data store that would have contained the cached data are strained as more servers are added to the environment.

- *Offline availability:* Caching can be very useful in offline smart client applications, such as the sample ACME POS application in this book.

However, there are some downsides to using caching, and these downsides must be balanced with the upsides to see if caching is truly a good choice for the application you are building.

## Business and System Requirements

First and foremost, you need to understand the business requirements for the application. Knowing what the application is supposed to do will give you a good understanding of what kind of functionality it needs. For example, suppose a business requirement is for the user to enter contact information, including the contact's state of residence. Because the 50 states in the United States are very static, the state of residence is an ideal item to cache, so you don't need to retrieve the data from a data store each time it is required.

The system requirements and restrictions are also important. When using in-memory caching, RAM will naturally be used up to support the immediate access of the data. It is important to understand how much memory can be used with the application; otherwise, you may bring the computer to its knees.

In the end, you should know how much data will be cached and how much RAM will be available for your application. If you find that your application cannot support all the cached items that you desire, you could then prioritize the cached items based on expected data size and how frequently they will be used. This way, you can determine which items to store in the cache to get the most bang for your buck.

## Cache Invalidation

Another consideration with applications using a cache is the actual validation of the data itself. Cached items are typically not connected to the original data source, so if the original data source changes, then the cached data would reflect old data. Thus, it is important to have some kind of event that will allow an application to know when the data in the cache has been invalidated or expired. Typically, these events are as simple as the passage of time, called time-based events. Other types of events can be system events or application events.

### Time-Based Events

Time-based events come in two common flavors:

- *Absolute time:* This method waits for a specific point in time and then invalidates the data. The point in time can be achieved by counting down; for instance, stating that the cache will refresh itself every 5 minutes. Alternatively, it can be achieved by specifying a point in time; for example, configuring the cache to refresh itself at 10 p.m. every day. The absolute time method can also be designed for more advanced cache expiration methods, such as expiring a cache on every Tuesday at 10 p.m.

- *Sliding method*: This method invalidates the data based on a specified elapsed time after the last access of the cached data. A common example of this would be the ASP.NET session time-out. The default setting for the ASP.NET session time-out is 20. Every time a user accesses an ASP.NET application, the session timer is reset to 20 minutes. After the user has been inactive for those 20 minutes, the objects stored in the user's Session object are removed.

Time-based events are probably the most common way to invalidate cached data. For example, consider the requirements of a capital market organization that processes security data at the close of a securities market, such as the New York Stock Exchange. Since the security prices would stay static until the market opens again on the next business data, it could be beneficial to keep the prices of actively held securities in memory for end-of-day processing, as opposed to storing them in a database where the data would have to be constantly retrieved. Of course, there would still need to be persisted storage of this data in the event of a system outage, but the end-of-day processing could be greatly improved by the use of an in-memory cache.

### Application-Based Events

An application-based event is created by the application itself, as opposed to by the system. Examples of application-based events are changes in a database, changes in the state of an application, and changes made by the user in the UI of the application. The key point to remember is that application-based events are created within the context of the application.

### System-Based Events

System-based events differ from application-based events in that they do not come from the context of an application. Instead, system-based events are raised by the operating system environment itself. Examples of system-based events include file creation, modification, and deletion and operating system state changes, such as starting up and shutting down.

## When to Use the Caching Application Block

Knowing what your caching needs are and understanding the features, design goals, and limitations of the Caching Application Block will help you determine if it is the right fit for the solution you are trying to build or enhance. We'll look at its limitations in the next section. Here, we'll discuss the Caching Application Block's features and design goals:

- Consistent form of caching
- Configurable configuration settings
- Persistent and configurable backing store
- Several expiration types

If an application needs one or more of these features, then the Caching Application Block could be the right choice for you.

## Consistent Form of Caching

With any application, as components are added to it by different application developers, redundant functionality will eventually be developed. Even worse, this functionality can be implemented in many different ways. The Caching Application Block provides an organization with the ability to use one implementation to support a required application feature. In this case, that application feature is caching.

Having a consistent method of implementing a caching feature allows an organization to have its developers implement caching in a consistent, repeatable manner that requires only the code to actually hook up the Caching Application Block to the application itself. This is not only handy when developing a single application, but it can also be used within multiple types of applications, such as ASP.NET applications, smart client applications, and Windows services. Now all the developers can have a consistent manner to implement caching without having to reinvent the wheel over and over again.

## Configurable Configuration Settings

Having a configurable caching solution brings even more value to an application. The Caching Application Block's features are configured through the Configuration Console. The deployment and application management become greatly simplified, since there is only one UI to handle the management of the Caching Application Block. The maintenance and configuration of the caching settings can be handled by network support staff, as opposed to developers.

## Persistent and Configurable Backing Store

Many applications not only need to be able to cache data in-memory, but also to provide a way to allow the cache to be persisted to disk. Out of the box, the Caching Application Block provides an isolated storage (file-based) and a database backing store solution.

With the flexibility of the Caching Application Block, if the isolated storage or database does not meet the needs of an application, a developer could create a custom backing store solution that can plug into the Caching Application Block. This is easy to do because of the configurable nature of the Caching Application Block. In this situation, developers or administrators can just specify the specific implementation of the backing store they would like to use—whether it's one of the out-of-box solutions or a custom solution.

Another feature of the backing store functionality provided in the Caching Application Block is the ability to persist the data in an encrypted form. This gives an organization a way to prevent sensitive data from being viewed by prying eyes.

### Expiration Types

As discussed earlier, almost every cache must have some way of expiring itself. The Caching Application Block provides the following methods for expiring cached data:

- *Absolute time:* Caches expire at a specified time of day.

- *Extended time format:* Extends the absolute time, and allows an application to not only expire at a specific time, but also on a specific day of the week or month.

- *Sliding time:* Allows a cache to expire after a specified amount of time has passed since the last time the cache was accessed.

- *File dependency:* Expires when a file is modified.

- *No expiration:* Lasts for as long as the application is running.

## Limitations of the Caching Application Block

While the Caching Application Block can provide an application with the most common features required by a caching solution, it does not provide every solution under the sun. Two limitations that stand out are in-memory encryption and cross-application domain synchronization.

While the Caching Application Block does have the ability to encrypt data that is persisted to a file or database, it cannot encrypt cached data that is in memory. It is critical to make sure that you understand the sensitivity of the data your application will be handling or could be handling in a future enhancement, because it will help determine whether the Caching Application Block will be a viable option for you in its out-of-the-box implementation.

Another limitation of the Caching Application Block is that it cannot synchronize across application domains. The application blocks are designed to assist the development of an application and to live within the context of a single application domain. In order to support cache synchronization between application domains, it would be necessary to create some sort of service that can manage the synchronization of the caching. This synchronization application would be out of the scope of what the Microsoft patterns & practices team has focused on in delivering Enterprise Library. However, since the source code is provided with Enterprise Library, it is possible for consumers of Enterprise Library to create their own implementations for managing the synchronization of cached data across application domains.

## What About the ASP.NET Cache?

.NET Framework 2.0 contains a caching mechanism called the ASP.NET Cache. The ASP.NET Cache is tuned for ASP.NET applications. However, it is possible to use the ASP.NET Cache outside an ASP.NET application, such as with smart client or even Windows service applications.

This then leads to the ultimate question: When should you use the Caching Application Block as opposed to the ASP.NET Cache? Well, the answer is not a simple one. Your answers to the following questions will help you decide:

- For a non-ASP.NET application, would the deployment of the System.Web assembly be undesirable?

- Do you need multiple configurable caching policies? ASP.NET caching allows for only one caching policy to be defined.

- Will it be necessary to use the Policy Injection Application Block to provide injected caching functionality?

- Will you need a backing store to persist the data in the event of an application shutdown?

- Will you need more than one time expiration rule, such as both an absolute time-based and sliding time-based expiration rule?

- Do you need extended time formats, such as being able to specify an expiration on the third day of a month or the third day of the second week of a month?

If you answered yes to one or more of these questions, chances are that the Caching Application Block will be a good choice for you. And, in general, if you are creating a non-ASP.NET application, it is probably better to use the Caching Application Block, not only to keep the deployment of the application simpler, but also because the ASP.NET Cache is intended and tuned more for ASP.NET applications.

Now it is time to look underneath the hood of the Caching Application Block and understand what it is doing for you.

# Getting Underneath the Hood

The Caching Application Block is composed of a series of core classes and interfaces that provide the caching functionality. The architecture of this application block also allows for great extensibility, such as providing new backing stores, expiration policies, cache refresh actions, and backing store data encryption. The following are the core classes and interfaces of the Caching Application Block:

- CacheManager class

- CacheFactory class

- BackgroundScheduler class

- IBackingStore interface

- ICacheItemExpiration interface

- ICacheItemRefreshAction interface

- IStorageEncryptionProvider interface

## Understanding the CacheManager and CacheFactory Classes

The CacheManager class is the "public-facing" core of the Caching Application Block. It is the class that you will interact with most in your application. The CacheManager is a singleton object per named instance. It uses the CacheFactory class to create a single instance for each unique name as defined in the configuration file. This means that if you had two cache managers named CustomersCache and OrdersCache, you could not have more than one instance of CustomersCache or OrdersCache within the application domain.

The CacheFactory class not only makes sure that there is only one named instance for an application domain, but it also handles the plumbing to create a CacheManager instance by using a private instance of the CacheManagerFactory class, and it provides exception handling in the event that you attempt to instantiate a named instance that has not been defined in the configuration file. A class diagram of the CacheFactory class is shown in Figure 7-1.

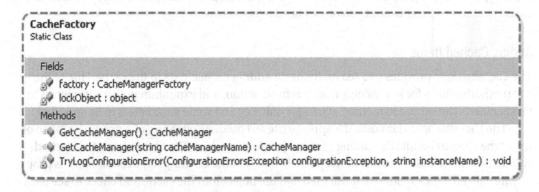

**Figure 7-1.** *CacheFactory class diagram*

■**Note** The GetCacheManager method of the CacheFactory class returns the default CacheManager instance as defined in the configuration file.

Once the CacheManager instance has been created, you can start creating and removing cached items. Figure 7-2 shows the public interfaces that the CacheManager class provides to support adding and removing cached objects.

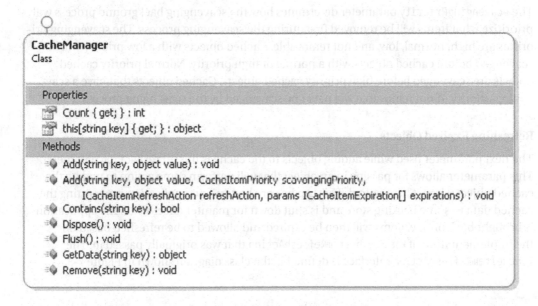

**Figure 7-2.** *CacheManager class diagram showing public members*

The CacheManager class is the public-facing workhorse of the Caching Application Block, but the Cache class is actually doing the bulk of the work. In other words, the Cache class is the meat and potatoes, and is the central gateway that manages adding, retrieving, removing, expiring, and scavenging cached objects. From the developer's standpoint, however, the Cache class is behind the scenes, and you do not need to interact with it.

## Adding Cached Items

The CacheManager provides two Add methods for adding cached data to the cache. One of the Add methods allows for key, value, priority, refresh action, and expiration policy parameters to be specified. The other Add method allows for only key and value parameters to be specified.

The CacheManager class calls the appropriate Add method signature of a private instance of the Cache class to handle the adding of the object to be cached. The Cache class's Add method will then validate that a key has been specified and that the Caching Application Block is properly initialized. Once validated, it will then add the object into the cache and check to see if any scavenging should be performed on existing cached objects

### Using Key and Value Parameters

The Add method that only allows the key and value parameters to be specified will force the cached object to never expire and set the scavenging priority (discussed next) to normal.

The key and value parameters are relatively straightforward in terms of purpose and use. The value parameter is the actual object that you want to cache, and the key parameter is the identifier that will be used to retrieve a cached object. If you call the Add method with a key value that already exists within the named CacheManager instance, the CacheManager class will first remove the existing item, and then add the new one that was specified.

### Determining Scavenging Prioritization

The scavengingPriority parameter determines how the scavenging background process will prioritize what items will be removed first during the scavenging process. The scavenging priorities are high, normal, low, and not removable. Cached objects with a low priority will be scavenged before cached objects with a normal or high priority. Normal priority cached objects are scavenged before high priority cached objects. Cached objects that have a scavenging priority of not removable will never be scavenged by the scavenging process.

### Refreshing Expired Objects

The next parameter used while adding objects to the cache is the refreshAction parameter. This parameter allows for passing in an object that will perform some action to update the cached object when it has expired. This can be very handy if an application is persisting the cached data to some backing store and is shut down for maintenance. When the application is brought back online, items will then be expired and allowed to be refreshed based on the implementation of the ICacheItemRefreshAction that was originally passed in. The ICacheItemRefreshAction interface is defined in the class diagram shown in Figure 7-3.

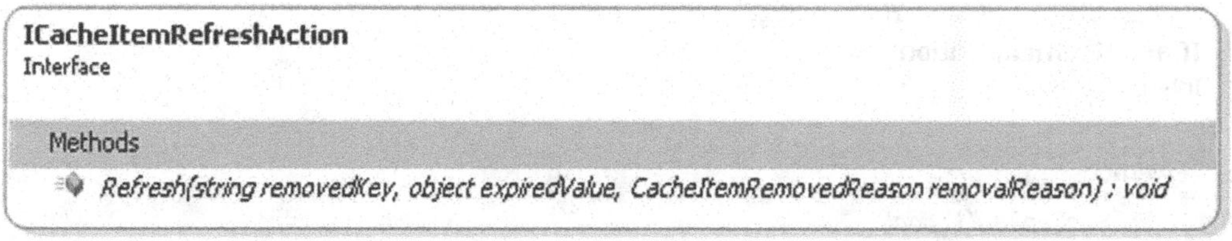

**ICacheItemRefreshAction**
Interface

Methods

　　🔘　*Refresh(string removedKey, object expiredValue, CacheItemRemovedReason removalReason) : void*

**Figure 7-3.** *ICacheItemRefreshAction class diagram*

The ICacheItemRefreshAction interface contains only one method, called Refresh, which must be implemented. The method will have three parameters passed to it from the Cache object via the RefreshActionData and RefreshActionInvoker classes:

- removedKey: The key that was removed.

- expiredValue: The value that was removed.

- removalReason: Why the key and value were removed.

The Refresh call occurs under two events in the Cache object, either during the retrieval of cached data or during the removal of cached data.

---

**Note**  The refresh action is not intended to refresh the cached object to which it is related. When the refresh action is called, the cached object has already been removed from the cache and requires the cached object to be re-created and inserted back into the cache. Thus, a user should pull a newly created cached object from the cache, as opposed to waiting for it to be created.

---

### Using Expiration Policy Parameters

The expiration policy parameters are rules that determine when a cached item should be expired from the cache. Since the params keyword is used, it is possible to specify more than one expiration policy per cached object.

The expiration policies are classes that implement the ICacheItemExpiration interface, as shown in Figure 7-4.

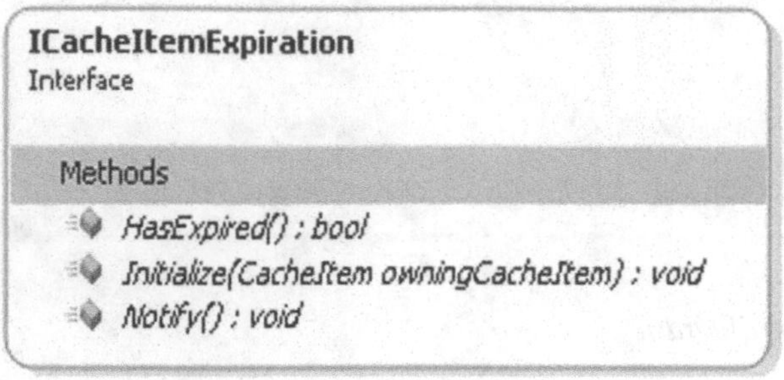

**Figure 7-4.** *ICacheItemExpiration class diagram*

The ICacheItemExpiration interface contains three methods that must be implemented by any expiration policy class:

- HasExpired: Determines if the cached object has expired.

- Initialize: Allows the expiration policy to initialize itself based on information on the cached object.

- Notify: Used by the CacheManager class to notify the expiration policy object that the cached object has been touched by the user.

The Caching Application Block contains five implementations of the ICacheItemExpiration interface. These five implementations correspond to the five types of expiration policies that the Caching Application Block provides:

- AbsoluteTime class: Expires cached data after a preset amount of time from when it was last created.

- ExtendedFormatTime class: Allows the expiration of a cached object based on an extended time format.

- SlidingTime class: Expires cached data after a preset amount of time from when it was last accessed.

- FileDependency class: This expiration policy will expire a cached object anytime a specified file has been changed.

- NeverExpired class: Never allows a cached object to expire.

## Retrieving Cached Items

The CacheManager class provides two mechanisms for retrieving cached objects. The first is using the GetData method, where you pass in a key. The other is by using the indexer of the CacheManager class.

When a cached object is requested from the cache, the CacheManager class will make a call to the Cache class's GetData method. This applies when either the GetData method or

CacheManager's indexer is used to get a cached object. The Cache class's GetData method will determine if the requested cached object has expired. If the cached object has expired, GetData will begin the removal process to remove the cached object and returns null. If the cached object has not expired, GetData returns the cached object, and then resets the date and time when the cached object was last touched.

The CacheManager class's Contains method can be used to determine whether the item actually expired or was never loaded into the cache manager. This can be a better technique for determining the proper course of action to refresh a cached object as opposed to testing for a null value. For instance, if a cache object was determined to never have been added to the cache, it might be useful to retrieve multiple objects that need to be cached. A typical scenario of where this may be applied is during application initialization.

### Removing Cached Items

Two methods can be use for removing cached objects from the Caching Application Block, depending on what you are trying to accomplish. One method is via the Remove method, which allows you to remove a single cached object based on the key that is passed in. The other is the Flush method, which will remove all cached objects from the CacheManager instance.

## Understanding the BackgroundScheduler Class

The BackgroundScheduler class manages the life of cached objects in a background thread of the application domain. This includes expiring cached objects based on the expiration policies and scavenging stale cached objects that have not been accessed for an extended amount of time. Figure 7-5 shows the class diagram of the BackgroundScheduler class.

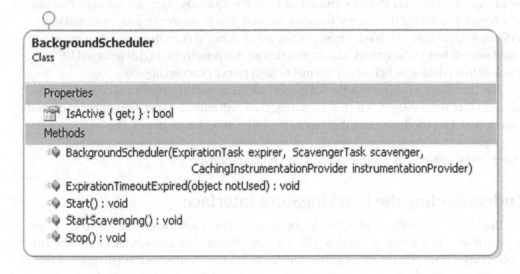

**Figure 7-5.** *BackgroundScheduler class diagram showing public members*

The BackgroundScheduler class contains a built-in queuing mechanism that processes items on a first-in, first-out basis. The queuing process is part of the *marking* and *sweeping* mechanism, which is used to make sure an item that is marked to be removed is not currently in use by the application. When an item is marked for removal during the marking process and is in use by the application, the sweeping process will see that the object is in use and will not remove it. On the next pass of the queuing process, the item that was not removed will be reassessed to see if it is eligible and able to be removed from the cache.

## ExpirationTask Class

The ExpirationTask class essentially runs the expiration policies to determine if a particular cached item is eligible for removal from the cache. If an item is deemed removable, it is removed using the marking and sweeping process. Expirations are checked based on the polling frequency set in the configuration file.

The ExpirationTask class will iterate through each cached object and determine if any of the expiration policies state the cached object as being expired. If a policy does state an item has expired, the ExpirationTask class will stop checking any other expiration policies, and then mark the item for removal.

## ScavengerTask Class

One of the main reasons for caching data is to increase the performance of an application. However, it is possible to cache too much data, to the point where it starts to degrade the performance of the application. This is where the ScavengerTask class of the Caching Application Block comes into play. This class is responsible for cleaning up cached objects that have not been used for an extended period of time. This cleanup process will help keep the overall amount of data in memory in check and ensure a healthy application.

When a new object is added to the CacheManager instance, the CacheManager instance calls the BackgroundScheduler instance and asks it to queue up a ScavengerTask instance that will be processed by calling the StartScavenging method. The ScavengerTask instance will then perform a major sort on the scavenger priority and a minor sort on the age of the cached object since it was last accessed. This means that all low priority cached objects will be removed from the cache before any normal or high priority cached objects.

The CacheManager object tells the ScavengerTask the maximum amount of cached objects allowed. Once the threshold is met, the ScavengerTask will remove a specific number of cached objects, based on another setting that comes from the CacheManager object. The CacheManager object gets both of these values from the MaximumElementsInCacheBeforeScavenging and NumberToRemoveWhenScavenging settings in the configuration file.

# Understanding the IBackingStore Interface

The IBackingStore interface provides the interface that the Cache object will use to store the cached objects in a persisted location. This way, cached data can be reloaded easily when an application is started in the event it was shut down. Figure 7-6 shows a class diagram of the IBackingStore interface.

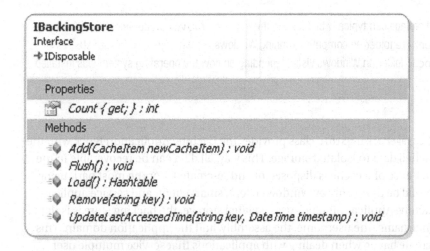

**Figure 7-6.** *IBackingStore class diagram*

As you can see, IBackingStore has Add, Flush, Load, Remove, and UpdateLastAccessedTime methods. What you don't see is a GetData method. This is because when an application requests objects from the cache, they are retrieved from memory.

The backing store's purpose is to provide a nonvolatile mechanism to keep the cached objects in the event the application domain is shut down. This is where the Load event comes into play. When an application is started, it will look into the persisted caches and load them—assuming the cached data has not expired.

## The NullBackingStore Class

With the NullBackingStore class, the cached data is never persisted. This class is essentially just an empty placeholder so that the CacheManager class can think a caching store does exist. However, when the Add, Load, Flush, and Remove methods are called, nothing happens. Use this backing store when cached data does not need to be persisted. Using this backing store is useful when you only want to use cache data in memory that needs to expire after a certain time period or event. This is the default backing store used when creating a new named instance of a cache through the Enterprise Library Configuration Console.

## IsolatedStorageBackingStore Class

*Isolated storage* is a mechanism where data can be persisted to disk and isolated from other applications. The data is stored on a per user and application basis, and can even be stored on a user, an application, and an application domain basis. Isolated storage provides a safe mechanism for reading and writing application-specific data, such as cached data, or possibly a storage location for offline disconnected data.

> **Note** The isolated storage can typically be found in the `<System Drive>`\Documents and Settings\ `<user>`\ApplicationData folder on computers running Windows XP and `<System Drive>`\Users\ `<user>`\AppData\Local folder on Windows Vista, depending on how the operating system was installed on the computer.

The IsolatedStorageBackingStore class provides the Caching Application Block with the ability to persist cached data to isolated storage. This way, all data can be recoverable in the event the named instance of a cache is disposed of and re-created. For the most part, using isolated storage should be done only by Windows client, smart client, and service applications. When the Caching Application Block uses isolated storage, the backing store is isolated by the cache instance name, the username, the assembly, and the application domain. This could potentially create havoc when dealing with applications that service multiple user requests and/or that are within a server farm.

## DataBackingStore Class

The DataBackingStore class provides the ability to persist data to a database. This can be very useful, especially with applications that service multiple clients such as web and web service applications, as well applications that reside on a server farm. The DataBackingStore class uses the Database Access Application Block to read and write data to and from the database. This allows the application to use any database that has a Data Access Application Block database provider. Out of the box, the Caching Application Block gives you the Oracle and SQL Server database options.

As with the IsolatedStorageBackingStore, some care must be taken when using the DataBackingStore class with multiple application domains on a server farm. The DataBackingStore class uses a combination of the cached instance name, application name, and partition name to persist the cached data into the database. The partition name allows multiple instances of an application to either share a common storage cache or have a separate cache for each instance.

> **Note** If multiple application domains of the same application are to share one partition name, it is important to ensure that you use only one instance that writes the data, and the other instances are read-only. Otherwise, cached data can become inconsistent between application domains.

# Understanding the IStorageEncryptionProvider Interface

While having cached data is great, it must be used properly. One consideration is the protection of sensitive data, such as personal data or financial data. This is where the IStorageEncryptionProvider interface comes into play. It allows the data that is persisted to a backing store to be encrypted, thus preventing prying eyes from viewing that data. However, it is important to note that the cached data in memory is not encrypted. Figure 7-7 shows the IStorageEncryptionProvider class diagram.

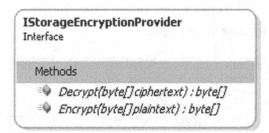

**Figure 7-7.** *IStorageEncryptionProvider class diagram*

The Caching Application Block provides a symmetric cryptography provider that allows the use of the Cryptography Application Block to determine how to encrypt and decrypt data. It is possible to provide your own encryption solution by implementing the IStorageEncryptionProvider interface and supplying the necessary configuration support.

# Using the Caching Application Block

Using the Caching Application Block within your application involves writing the code to support the reading and writing of cached data, and configuring the backing store and encryption providers as needed. This section provides a walk-through of creating a simple application that uses the Caching Application Block.

## Setting Up the Application

In order to see the application block in action, you will need to create a simple Windows application for the sample provided in this book. Follow these steps:

1. Create a C# Windows application called CachingSampleApp.

2. Add a reference to the following Enterprise Library 3.0 assemblies:

   - Microsoft.Practices.EnterpriseLibrary.Caching.dll

   - Microsoft.Practices.EnterpriseLibrary.Common.dll

   - Microsoft.Practices.ObjectBuilder.dll

3. Create a Windows form class named CacheSampleForm.

4. Add the following Windows controls to the form:

   - Two Label controls with the text Cached Message and Message To Cache

   - Two Textbox controls named cachedMessageTextBox and messageToCacheTextBox

   - Four Button controls: one named getCachedDataButton with the text Get Cached Data, one named writeCachedDataButton with the text Write Cached Data, one named removeCachedItemButton with the text Remove Cached Item, and one named flushCacheButton with the text Flush Cache

**5.** Add an application configuration file to the project.

Figure 7-8 shows the completed Windows form for this example.

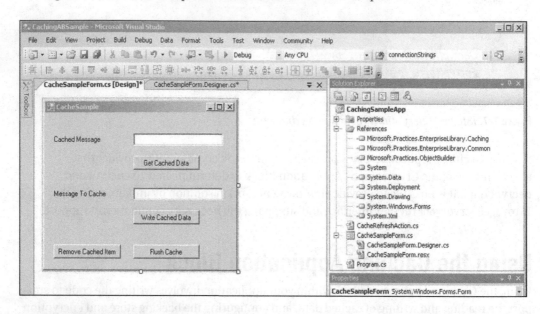

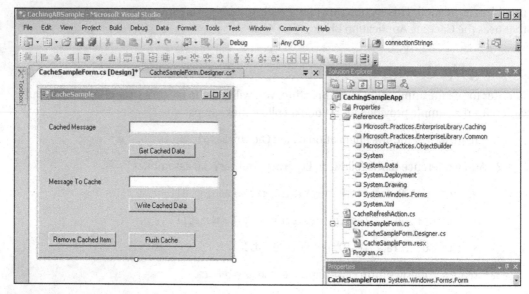

**Figure 7-8.** *Sample Windows application for demonstrating the Caching Application Block*

To keep this application as simple as possible, the cached data will simply be a string passed back and forth. To create this string, you will create a class called Domain, which will essentially pass in the string value.

Create a new class in the CachingSampleApp project and add a new method called GetData. With the GetData method, add the code shown in Listing 7-1.

**Listing 7-1.** *Creating the Domain Layer*

```
[Serializable]
public class Domain
{
    public string GetData()
    {
        return "Data was retrieved on " +
            DateTime.Now.ToShortDateString() + " at " +
            DateTime.Now.ToShortTimeString();
    }
}
```

As you can see, the GetData method will return a simple text message with the current date and time.

The next step is to create an instance of this class in the Windows form class. First, create a private member called domain, and then instantiate the domain member in the CacheSampleForm class's constructor. Listing 7-2 shows the code in the CacheSampleForm class.

**Listing 7-2.** *Instantiating the Domain Class*

```
public partial class CacheSampleForm : Form
{
    Domain domain;

    public CacheSampleForm()
    {
        InitializeComponent();
        domain = new Domain();
    }
}
```

## Configuring the Caching Application Block

Configuring the Caching Application Block is pretty easy, especially with the Enterprise Library Configuration Console. The caching configuration design-time components allow multiple caching named instances to be created. Each instance can have a backing store specified. Both the isolated backing store and database backing store allow for data encryption via the Cryptography Application Block. The database backing store also allows for specifying the database connection via the Database Application Block. As noted earlier, the null backing store is assumed if the isolated or database backing store is specified. Figure 7-9 shows an example of the Caching Application Block in the Configuration Console.

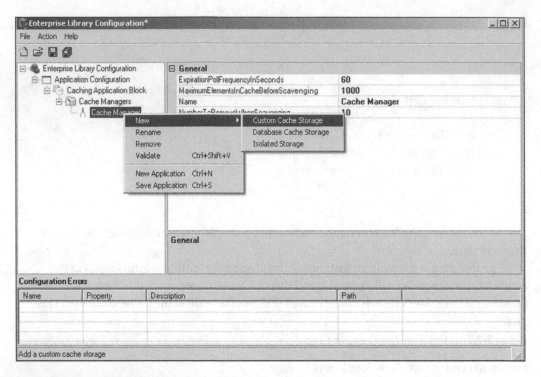

**Figure 7-9.** *Sample Caching Application Block configuration*

You can specify a default instance of the cache manager by setting the default instance property. For this example, configure a default instance of the cache manager that uses isolated storage as a backing store, as follows:

1. Open the CacheSampleForm application configuration file in the Configuration Console.

2. Right-click Application Configuration and select New ➤ Caching Application Block, as shown in Figure 7-10. A default cache manager is created for you automatically. Also notice that the DefaultCacheManager property of the Caching Application Block node is automatically set to the cache manager instance as well.

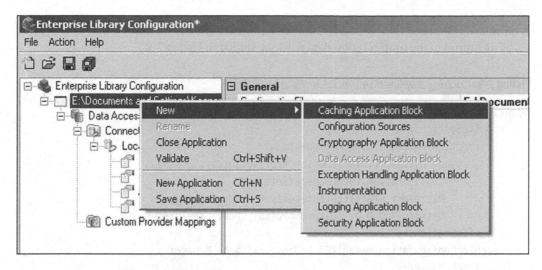

**Figure 7-10.** *Adding a new Caching Application Block*

3. To create a backing store, right-click the Cache Manager node and select New ➤ Isolated Storage.

4. Select the PartitionName property and name it MyCachingSample, as shown in Figure 7-11.

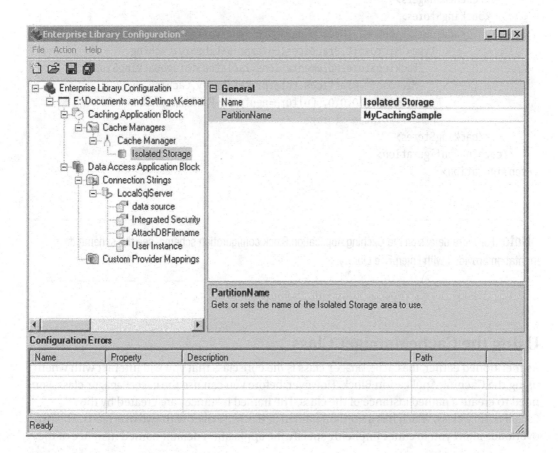

**Figure 7-11.** *Configuring isolated storage*

**5.** Save the configuration changes.

The output of the configuration data will look similar to Listing 7-3.

**Listing 7-3.** *Caching Application Block Configuration Data*

```
<configuration>
    <configSections>
        <section name="cachingConfiguration"
            type="Microsoft.Practices.EnterpriseLibrary.Caching.
                Configuration.CacheManagerSettings,
                Microsoft.Practices.EnterpriseLibrary.Caching,
                Version=2.0.0.0, Culture=neutral, PublicKeyToken=null" />
    </configSections>
    <cachingConfiguration defaultCacheManager="Cache Manager">
        <cacheManagers>
            <add expirationPollFrequencyInSeconds="60"
                maximumElementsInCacheBeforeScavenging="1000"
                numberToRemoveWhenScavenging="10"
                backingStoreName="Isolated Storage"
                name="Cache Manager" />
        </cacheManagers>
        <backingStores>
            <add partitionName="MyCachingSample" encryptionProviderName=""
                type="Microsoft.Practices.EnterpriseLibrary.Caching.
                    BackingStoreImplementations.IsolatedStorageBackingStore,
                    Microsoft.Practices.EnterpriseLibrary.Caching,
                    Version=2.0.0.0, Culture=neutral, PublicKeyToken=null"
                name="Isolated Storage" />
        </backingStores>
    </cachingConfiguration>
</configuration>
```

**■Note** For more details on the Caching Application Block configuration schema, see the schema documentation provided with Enterprise Library.

## Using the CacheManager Class

As mentioned earlier, the CacheManager class is the core class that you will interact with when using the Caching Application Block. However, before you can use the CacheManager class, you need to create a named instance of the class. The named instances are created by the CacheFactory class, which has a method named GetCacheManager with two overloads. The two overloads allow you to either implicitly specify the application default named instance of the

cache or explicitly specify a named instance. Listing 7-4 shows the code added to the
CacheSampleForm class to create the default named instance of the CacheManager class.

**Listing 7-4.** *Creating a Named Instance of the CacheManager Class*

```
using System.ComponentModel;
using System.Data;
using System.Drawing;
using System.Text;
using System.Windows.Forms;

using Microsoft.Practices.EnterpriseLibrary.Caching;
using Microsoft.Practices.EnterpriseLibrary.Caching.Expirations;

namespace CachingSampleApp
{
    public partial class CacheSampleForm : Form
    {
        Domain domain;
        CacheManager myCacheManager;

        public CacheSampleForm()
        {
            InitializeComponent();
            domain = new Domain();

            myCacheManager = CacheFactory.GetCacheManager();
        }
    }
}
```

As shown in Listing 7-4, the default instance of the application cache manager is retrieved
by using the GetCacheManager method overload without parameters.

If you need to have more than one named cache instance, then you must specify the
name of the cache by using the GetCacheManager method that contains the named instance
parameter, like this:

```
myCacheManager = CacheFactory.GetCacheManager("MyCache");
```

Note that if you try to create two cache managers with the same name, as in the following
example, both classes will be the same instance.

```
public void CreateCacheManagers()
{
    CacheManager myCacheManager1;
    CacheManager myCacheManager2;

    myCacheManager1 = CacheFactory.GetCacheManager("MyCache");
    myCacheManager2 = CacheFactory.GetCacheManager("MyCache");
}
```

Another way to look at it is, with the preceding example, the following statement would be true.

```
myCacheManager1 == myCacheManager2;
```

**Note** The named instances are defined in the configuration file of the application.

## Adding Objects to the Cache

Now that the `CacheManager` instance has been created, data can be added to the cache. This example will have two methods for adding values into the cache. The first will use just the key and value overload of the `CacheManager`'s Add method. The other will use the key, value, scavenging priority, cached item refresh action, and expiration policy overload.

### Key and Value Overload

Listing 7-5 shows the key and value overload used to initially add a value during the construction of the `CacheSampleForm` class.

**Listing 7-5.** *Using the Key and Value Add Method Overload*

```
public partial class CacheSampleForm : Form
{
    Domain domain;
    CacheManager myCacheManager;
    const string cacheKey = "MyString";

    public CacheSampleForm()
    {
        InitializeComponent();
        domain = new Domain();

        myCacheManager = CacheFactory.GetCacheManager();

        myCacheManager.Add(cacheKey, domain.GetData());
    }
}
```

### ICacheItemRefreshAction Instance

An instance of the `ICacheItemRefreshAction` interface is required to allow the cached data to be refreshed when it is expired. Otherwise, a null reference for the refresh action parameter can be passed into the key, value, scavenging priority, cached item refresh action, and expiration policy Add method overload of the `CacheManager` class, to have no action performed when the cached item is expired.

**Note**  The refresh action does not necessarily have to refresh the cached data when it expires. It is possible to perform whatever action is desired.

For this example, you will add a new class to the CacheSampleApp project. This new class will be called CacheRefreshAction and it will implement the Microsoft.Practices. EnterpriseLibrary.Caching.ICacheItemRefreshAction interface. This class will contain a private field of the Domain class instance, a public constructor with a Domain class parameter that will be set to the private field, and the required implementation of the ICacheItemRefreshAction.Refresh() method. Listing 7-6 shows the code to implement the CacheRefreshAction class.

**Note**  Each concrete class of the ICacheItemRefreshAction class should be specific to each cache item. This is especially true because the Refresh method does not contain a reference to a CacheManager instance, thus requiring the CacheManager to be explicitly specified.

**Listing 7-6.** *CacheRefreshAction Class*

```
using System;
using System.Collections.Generic;
using System.Text;

using Microsoft.Practices.EnterpriseLibrary.Caching;

namespace CachingSampleApp
{
    [Serializable]
    public class CacheRefreshAction : ICacheItemRefreshAction
    {
        Domain domain;

        public CacheRefreshAction(Domain domain)
        {
            this.domain = domain;
        }

        #region ICacheItemRefreshAction Members

        public void Refresh(string removedKey, object expiredValue,
            CacheItemRemovedReason removalReason)
        {
            CacheManager myCacheManager = CacheFactory.GetCacheManager();
```

```
        myCacheManager.Add(removedKey, domain.GetData());
    }

    #endregion
}
}
```

---

■**Caution**  All ICacheItemRefreshAction implementations must be serializable and be marked with the serializable attribute.

---

### Key, Value, Scavenging Priority, Refresh Action, and Expiration Policy Overload

The key, value, scavenging priority, cache item refresh action, and expiration policy overload allows the developer to specify how a cached item will be expired, scavenged, and refreshed. For the example, the click event of writeCachedDataButton will be implemented to add the cached data to the cache using the key, value, scavenging priority, cache item refresh action, and expiration policy overload. This is demonstrated in Listing 7-7.

**Listing 7-7.** *Implementing the WriteCacheDataButton Event*

```
public partial class CacheSampleForm : Form
{
    Domain domain;
    CacheManager myCacheManager;
    const string cacheKey = "MyString";

    public CacheSampleForm()...

    private void WriteCachedDataButton_Click(object sender, EventArgs e)
    {
        if(myCacheManager == null)
            myCacheManager = CacheFactory.GetCacheManager();

        myCacheManager.Add(cacheKey, messageToCacheTextBox.Text,
            CacheItemPriority.Normal, new CacheRefreshAction(domain),
            new SlidingTime(TimeSpan.FromSeconds(30)));
    }
}
```

You can create the WriteCachedDataButton_Click event by double-clicking the button on the form designer, adding the method name to the DoubleClick event in the event list of the Visual Studio properties grid, or adding the event in the constructor of the CacheSampleForm class by hand, as follows:

```
this.WriteCachedDataButton.Click +=
   new System.EventHandler(this.WriteCachedDataButton_Click);
```

**Multiple Expiration Policies**

The Caching Application Block has the ability to specify more than one expiration policy. To do this, you can either create an array of ICacheExpiration instances, as shown in Listing 7-8, or pass in multiple ICacheExpiration instances as parameters, as shown in Listing 7-9.

**Listing 7-8.** *Passing in an Array of Expiration Policies*

```
private void WriteCachedDataButton_Click(object sender, EventArgs e)
{
   if(myCacheManager == null)
      myCacheManager = CacheFactory.GetCacheManager();

   ICacheItemExpiration[] expirationPolicies = new ICacheItemExpiration[2];

   expirationPolicies[0] = new SlidingTime(TimeSpan.FromSeconds(30));
   expirationPolicies[1] = new AbsoluteTime(DateTime.Now.AddMinutes(5));

   myCacheManager.Add(cacheKey, MessageToCacheTextBox.Text,
      CacheItemPriority.Normal, new CacheRefreshAction(domain),
      expirationPolicies);
}
```

**Listing 7-9.** *Passing in Multiple Expiration Policies As Parameters*

```
private void WriteCachedDataButton_Click(object sender, EventArgs e)
{
   if(myCacheManager == null)
      myCacheManager = CacheFactory.GetCacheManager();

   myCacheManager.Add(cacheKey, MessageToCacheTextBox.Text,
      CacheItemPriority.Normal, new CacheRefreshAction(domain),
      new SlidingTime(TimeSpan.FromSeconds(30)),
      new AbsoluteTime(DateTime.Now.AddMinutes(5)));
}
```

## Retrieving Items from the Cache

Retrieving items from the CacheManager class is pretty simple. Just be aware that if the cached item has expired, it will return null. Listing 7-10 demonstrates retrieving a cached item and testing it to make sure it is not null via the GetCachedDataButton_Click event.

**Listing 7-10.** *Retrieving Cached Data*

```
public partial class CacheSampleForm : Form
{
    Domain domain;
    CacheManager myCacheManager;
    const string cacheKey = "MyString";

    public CacheSampleForm()…

    private void WriteCachedDataButton_Click(object sender, EventArgs e)…

    private void GetCachedDataButton_Click(object sender, EventArgs e)
    {
        if (myCacheManager != null)
        {
            if (myCacheManager.Contains(cacheKey))
            {
                string myValue = myCacheManager.GetData(cacheKey) as string;

                if (!string.IsNullOrEmpty(myValue))
                    cachedMessageTextBox.Text = myValue;
                else
                    cachedMessageTextBox.Text = string.Empty;
            }
            else
            {
                MessageBox.Show("Cached object is not present");
            }
        }
        else
        {
            MessageBox.Show("Cache manager is null");
        }
    }
}
```

It is also possible to use the indexer of the CacheManager to retrieve cached data, as follows:

```
string myValue = myCacheManager[cacheKey] as string;
```

---

**Note** The Contains method is used to check if the cached item was loaded into the CacheManager instance. This is because if a null reference is returned by the GetData method, it can mean either that the cached object has expired or the cached item was never loaded.

---

## Removing Items from the Cache

Removing items from the cache is straightforward. Just specify the cache object's key in the Remove method of the CacheManager class, and the cached object is removed. Listing 7-11 implements the removeCachedItemButton_Click event to remove the cached item.

**Listing 7-11.** *Removing Cached Items*

```
public partial class CacheSampleForm : Form
{
    Domain domain;
    CacheManager myCacheManager;
    const string cacheKey = "MyString";

    public CacheSampleForm()…

    private void WriteCachedDataButton_Click(object sender, EventArgs e)…

    private void GetCachedDataButton _Click(object sender, EventArgs e)…

    private void removeCachedItemButton_Click(object sender, EventArgs e)
    {
        if (myCacheManager != null)
        {
            myCacheManager.Remove(cacheKey);
            messageToCacheTextBox.Text = string.Empty;
        }
    }
}
```

## Flushing the Cache

Flushing the cache is like removing cache items, except instead of removing one named item, all items are removed from the CacheManager instance. Flushing is performed by the CacheManager's Flush method, as shown in Listing 7-12.

**Listing 7-12.** *Flushing Cached Items*

```
public partial class CacheSampleForm : Form
{
    Domain domain;
    CacheManager myCacheManager;
    const string cacheKey = "MyString";

    public CacheSampleForm()…

    private void WriteCachedDataButton_Click(object sender, EventArgs e)...
```

```
    private void GetCachedDataButton _Click(object sender, EventArgs e)...

    private void removedCachedItemButton _Click(object sender, EventArgs e)...

    private void flushCacheButton_Click(object sender, EventArgs e)
    {
       if (myCacheManager != null)
       {
          myCacheManager.Flush();
          messageToCacheTextBox.Text = string.Empty;
       }
    }
}
```

## Loading the Cache

To demonstrate the Caching Application Block's removing and flushing functionality, you will
need to modify the constructor to add a new cached item, and also to have the ability to display the count of cached items. Listing 7-13 shows the modifications necessary to support
these features.

**Listing 7-13.** *Adding a New Cached Object and Displaying Cached Item Counts*

```
public partial class CacheSampleForm : Form
{
   Domain domain;
   CacheManager myCacheManager;
   const string cacheKey = "MyString";
   const string cacheKey2 = "MyString2";

   public CacheSampleForm()
   {
      InitializeComponent();
      domain = new Domain();

      myCacheManager = CacheFactory.GetCacheManager();

      if(!myCacheManager.Contains(cacheKey))
            myCacheManager.Add(cacheKey, domain.GetData());

         if (!myCacheManager.Contains(cacheKey2))
            myCacheManager.Add(cacheKey2, "Some other data");

   }

   private void WriteCachedDataButton_Click(object sender, EventArgs e)…
```

```
private void GetCachedDataButton _Click(object sender, EventArgs e)…

private void removeCachedItemButton_Click(object sender, EventArgs e)
{
    if (myCacheManager != null)
    {
        myCacheManager.Remove(cacheKey);
        MessageToCacheTextBox.Text = string.Empty;
        cacheCountMessage();
    }
}

private void flushCacheButton_Click(object sender, EventArgs e)
{
    if (myCacheManager != null)
    {
        myCacheManager.Flush();
        MessageToCacheTextBox.Text = string.Empty
        cacheCountMessage();
    }
}

private void cacheCountMessage()
{
    if (myCacheManager != null)
    {
        MessageBox.Show("Current Cached item count is "
            + myCacheManager.Count.ToString());
    }
}
}
```

In Listing 7-13, the cacheCountMessage method was added to display the number of items currently in the cache, and the flushCacheButton_Click and removeCachedItemButton_Click methods were modified to call the cacheMessageMethod. The CacheSampleForm's constructor was also modified to add a second cached item, as well as check to see if cached items were loaded prior to trying to add them. This will demonstrate loading persisted data when a CacheManager instance is created, removing one cache item, and flushing the cache, which removes both cached items.

# Caching Static Data for the ACME POS Application

The ACME POS application will use the Caching Application Block in two ways: to cache static data, such as a list of states and payment methods, and to store customer data. For this chapter, we will concentrate on caching the static data for the ACME application. In Chapter 10, which covers the Cryptography Application Block, we will add caching capabilities for the customer data.

## Creating the ACME POS User Interface Project

To begin, add a new Windows Forms project to the ACME POS Solution. Name the project ACME.POS.UI.Forms. Next, rename the default class name Form1.cs to Main.cs and change the Form1 reference to Main in the Program.cs class file. Then add the application configuration file to the project.

The ACME.POS.UI.Forms project should have an application configuration file that was created when you created the new project. If it does not exist, you will want to create it now.

Open the ACME.POS.UI.Forms project application configuration file in the Configuration Console and add the Caching Application Block to it. Change the default name for the cache manager from Cache Manager to StaticData. Also make sure the DefaultCacheManager property of the Caching Application Block node is set to StaticData. For the new StaticData cache manager, create an isolated storage backing store. Figure 7-12 shows the Caching Application Block configured in the Configuration Console.

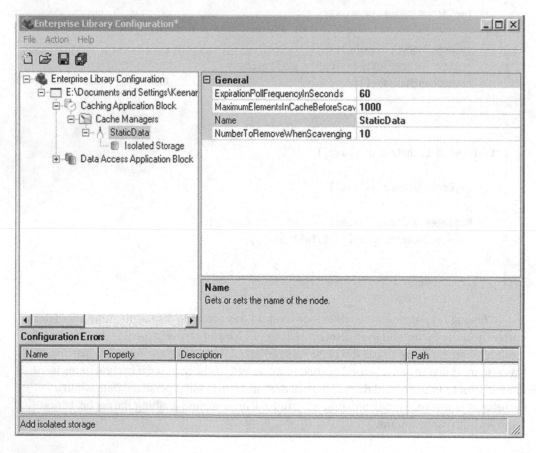

**Figure 7-12.** *StaticData cache manager configuration*

# Merging the Customer Data Access Code

In Chapter 6, you created the data access logic and domain entities for retrieving and saving customer data. Now you'll merge that code with the ACME.POS.Service solution and finalize it.

To merge the data access code, add the ACMECustomerDAL project you created in Chapter 6 to the ACME.POS.Service solution. If you created a separate project for the domain entities, you can also add that project to this solution; otherwise, you can simply add the code files to the ACME.POS.Service.BusinessEntities project.

## Adding the Connection String

First, you need to ensure you have the connection string data for the ACME Customer database added to the web.config file of the ACME.POS.Service.Host project. This connection string will be used by the Web Service Software Factory to determine the proper database with which to communicate.

You can either copy the data access configuration data from Chapter 6 into the web.config file or use the Web Service Software Factory to create it for you. To create a connection string with the Web Service Software Factory, right-click the web.config file and select Service Factory (Data Access) ➤ Add Database Connection to Configuration File. You're able to specify the name of the connection string and the connection string itself. You can click the ellipse in the Connection String field to have the connection string built for you. To make following along with this example easier, name the connection string ACMECustomer.

## Creating the Address, PaymentMethod, and BillingMethod Entities

The next step is to create the Address, PaymentMethod, and BillingMethod domain (business) entities. For this example, you'll use the Web Service Software Factory to create these business entities, as follows:

1. Right-click the ACME.POS.Service.BusinessEntities project and select Service Factory (Data Access) ➤ Create Business Entities from Database. You will see the dialog box shown in Figure 7-13.

2. Specify the service host project that contains the web.config file. Typically, this is preselected for you. Then select the connection name that points to the ACME database. Click Next to continue.

3. Specify the tables from which you want to create the domain (business) entities. Select the Address, BillingMethod, and PaymentMethod tables, but not the Customer table. Click Next.

4. You will see the Address, BillingMethod, and PaymentMethod entities listed with each property that should correspond with the fields of the Address, BillingMethod, and PaymentMethod tables. In this dialog box, you can customize the data types for the fields, however that won't be necessary for this example. Just click the Finish button.

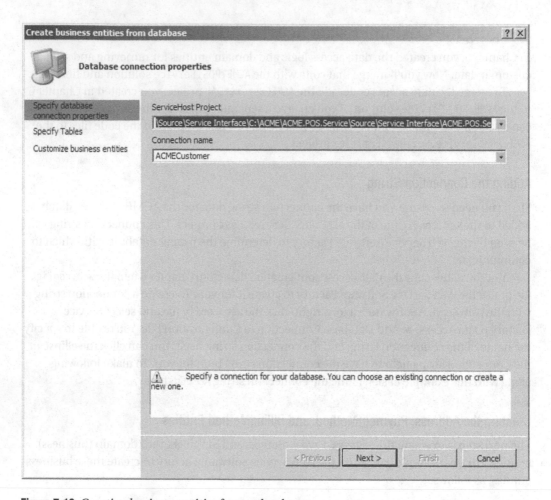

**Figure 7-13.** *Creating business entities from a database*

The last task is to create a List<> collection for each of the three entities that were just created. Add a new code file called EntityCollection.cs to the ACME.POS.Service. BusinessEntities project and add the code shown in Listing 7-14.

**Listing 7-14.** *Creating List<> Collections for Address, PaymentMethod, and BillingMethod*

```
using System;
using System.Collections.Generic;
using System.Text;

namespace ACME.POS.Service.BusinessEntities
{
    public class AddressList : List<Address>
    {
    }

    public class BillingMethodList : List<BillingMethod>
    {
```

```
    }

    public class PaymentMethodList : List<PaymentMethod>
    {
    }
}
```

---

■**Caution** The address field name cannot be the same as the `Address` class name in the `Address.cs` file that was created by the Web Service Software Factory. So you may want to change the field name to `StreetAddress`.

---

## Creating the State Entity

The state entity will be a `Dictionary<string, string>` collection. You can simply create a new code file called `State.cs` in the `ACME.POS.Service.BusinessEntities` project with the code shown in Listing 7-15.

**Listing 7-15.** *State Entity*

```
using System;
using System.Collections.Generic;
using System.Text;

namespace ACME.POS.Domain.Entity
{
    public class StateList : Dictionary<string, string>
    {
    }
}
```

## Creating the Stored Procedures

Now with the domain (business) entities created, the next task is to create the stored procedure for saving and retrieving customer data using the Web Service Software Factory, as follows:

1. Right-click the `ACME.POS.Service.DataAccess` project and select Service Factory (Data Access) ➤ Create CRUD Stored Procedures.

2. You will see a dialog box requesting the location of the configuration file and the connection name to use. Select the appropriate configuration file and connection name, and then select Next.

3. Just as when you created the business entities, you will be asked for which table you would like to create the stored procedures. Select just the Customer table, as shown in Figure 7-14. Click Next to continue.

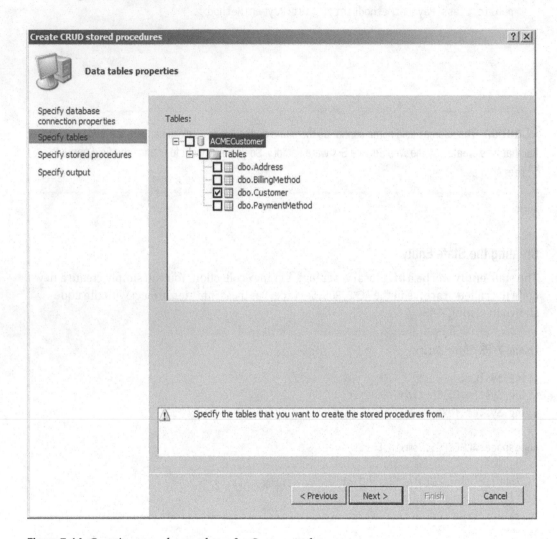

**Figure 7-14.** *Creating stored procedures for Customer data*

4. You will be presented with a series of stored procedures that will be created for the Customer table. Uncheck the Create Delete Stored Procedure option and the Create Get By PK Procedure option. You can leave the stored procedure names that the Web Service Software Factory provides or use the ones I used in Figure 7-15. Click Next.

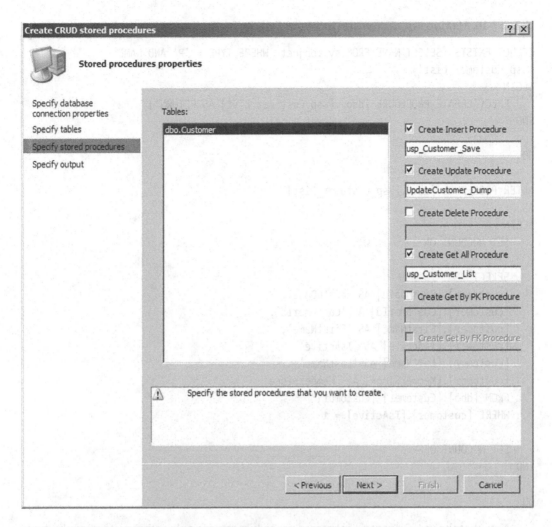

**Figure 7-15.** *Creating save and get all stored procedures for Customer data*

5. The last dialog box will request the name of the file in which to store the code. Enter the filename that is the same name as the Create Insert Procedure name. As shown in Figure 7-15, the stored procedure code filename in this example is usp_Customer_Save.sql. Click the Finish button.

Now you have a few cleanup tasks to do. If you remember, there is only one Save method for saving customer data, so this means the usp_Customer_Save stored procedure must handle the inserts, updates, and deletes. First, create a new file called usp_Customer_List.sql in the data access project and cut and paste the usp_Customer_List stored procedure code from the usp_Customer_Save stored procedure into it. Once it's copied, you will want to modify the stored procedure so that it will return only customers that have an IsActive value set to 1. Listing 7-16 shows an example.

**Listing 7-16.** *Making usp_Customer_List Return Only Active Customers*

```
IF NOT EXISTS (SELECT NAME FROM sys.objects WHERE TYPE = 'P' AND NAME =
'usp_Customer_List')
BEGIN
    EXEC('CREATE PROCEDURE [dbo].[usp_Customer_List] AS RETURN')
END

GO

ALTER PROCEDURE [dbo].[usp_Customer_List]
AS
BEGIN
    SET NOCOUNT ON

    SELECT
    [customer].[BirthDate] AS 'BirthDate',
    [customer].[CustomerId] AS 'CustomerId',
    [customer].[FirstName] AS 'FirstName',
    [customer].[IsActive] AS 'IsActive',
    [customer].[LastName] AS 'LastName',
    [customer].[MemberSince] AS 'MemberSince'
    FROM [dbo].[Customer] [customer]
    WHERE [customer].[IsActive] = 1

    SET NOCOUNT OFF
END

GO
```

Now that the usp_Customer_List stored procedure returns only active customers, the next task is to have the usp_Customer_Save stored procedure perform both an insert and an update. The decision to perform an update or insert will be based on whether the customer id presented in the stored procedure already exists. If it does exist, then an update will occur; otherwise, an insert occurs. Copy the update syntax in the UpdateCustomer_Dump stored procedure and paste it into the usp_Customer_Save stored procedure, and then add the logic to determine if the customer exists, as shown in Listing 7-17.

**Listing 7-17.** *Performing Both Update and Insert Functions in the usp_Customer_Save Stored Procedure*

```
IF NOT EXISTS (SELECT NAME FROM sys.objects WHERE TYPE = 'P' AND NAME =
'usp_Customer_Save')
BEGIN
    EXEC('CREATE PROCEDURE [dbo].[usp_Customer_Save] AS RETURN')
END

GO
```

```
ALTER PROCEDURE [dbo].[usp_Customer_Save]
    @birthDate datetime,
    @customerId int OUT,
    @firstName varchar(50),
    @isActive bit = 1,
    @lastName varchar(50),
    @memberSince datetime
AS
BEGIN
    SET NOCOUNT ON

    BEGIN TRY

    IF(EXISTS(SELECT * FROM [dbo].[Customer]
            WHERE [CustomerId]=@customerId))
    BEGIN
        UPDATE [dbo].[Customer]
        SET [BirthDate] = @birthDate, [FirstName] = @firstName,
                        [IsActive] = @isActive, [LastName] = @lastName,
                        [MemberSince] = @memberSince
        WHERE [CustomerId]=@customerId

        IF @@ROWCOUNT = 0
        BEGIN
            RAISERROR('Concurrent update error. Updated aborted.',
              16, 2)
        END
    END
    ELSE
    BEGIN
        INSERT INTO [dbo].[Customer] ([BirthDate], [FirstName],
                        [IsActive], [LastName], [MemberSince])
        VALUES (@birthDate, @firstName, @isActive, @lastName,
        @memberSince)
        SET @customerId = SCOPE_IDENTITY()
    END

    END TRY

    BEGIN CATCH
        EXEC RethrowError;
    END CATCH

    SET NOCOUNT OFF
END
GO
```

---

**■Note** The ACME POS application will never truly delete any data. Instead, it will set a customer to inactive by setting IsActive to 0.

---

Finally, you can run the stored procedure code in the usp_Customer_Save.sql and usp_Customer_List.sql files on the ACME database.

### Checking the Project Build

Add the following using statement to the Customer.cs class file in the ACME.POS.Service. BusinessEntities project and the CustomerDAL.cs class file in the data access project:

using ACME.POS.Service.BusinessEntities

Then build the ACME.POS.Service.BusinessEntities project. If you have any issues, just compare the code with the Chapter 7\Checkpoint folder in the source code for this book, available from the Apress website.

## Creating the GetStates Web Service

You'll create the GetStates web service in three steps: create the State data type, create a service contract interface, and finally, create the service contract implementation class. The state values will be hard-coded in the service contract implementation class.

### Creating the State Data Type

Create the State data type as follows:

1, Right-click the ACME.POS.Service.DataTypes project and select Service Factory (ASMX) ➤ Create Data Type.

2. You will see a dialog box that requests a name for the data type and the namespace. You can leave the namespace value as is, but specify State for the name value. Then click Next.

3. Specify the data members and the data types associated with the data members. The first data member should be called Abbrv with a data type of System.String. The second data member should be called Name with a data type of System.String. Click the Finish button to complete the State data type.

### Creating the Service Contract

Now it's time to create the service contract for retrieving states.

1. Right-click the ACME.POS.Service.ServiceContracts project and select Service Factory (ASMX) ➤ Create Service Contract.

2. You will see a dialog box requesting a service contract name and namespace. The namespace can be left as is, but change the service contract name to GetStates. Click Next to continue.

3. Define the methods. This service contract will contain only one method called GetStates. It will not have a request type, but the return type will be ACME.POS.Service.DataTypes.State[]. Set the Parameter Style option to Data Type. Figure 7-16 shows the defined operations. Click the Next button to continue.

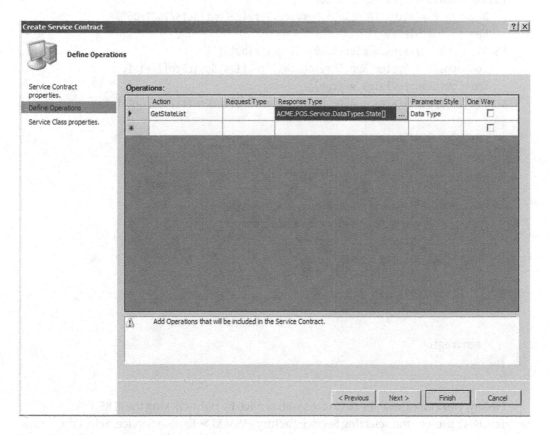

**Figure 7-16.** *Creating the service contract*

4. Check the Generate Service Contract Implementation check box. Three fields will appear. Now select the data types project and the service implementation project. The Service Class Name field can be left as is. Click the Finish button. The Web Service Software Factory will create the interface and implementation class for you.

## Implementing and Exposing the GetStates Web Service

Now you need to create the implementation code to retrieve the list of states. Listing 7-18 shows the implementation code for building and then returning an array of state values.

**Listing 7-18.** *Implementing StateCacheRefreshAction*

```
using System;
using System.Collections.Generic;
using System.Text;

namespace ACME.POS.Service.ServiceImplementation
{
    [System.Web.Services.WebService(
        Namespace ="http://ACME.POS.Service.ServiceContracts/2007/06",
        Name = "GetStates")]
    [System.Web.Services.WebServiceBindingAttribute(
        ConformsTo = System.Web.Services.WsiProfiles.BasicProfile1_1,
        EmitConformanceClaims = true)]
    public class GetStates : ACME.POS.Service.ServiceContracts.IGetStates
    {
        #region IGetStates Members

        public ACME.POS.Service.DataTypes.State[] GetStateList()
        {
            ACME.POS.Service.DataTypes.State[] states
                = new ACME.POS.Service.DataTypes.State[50];

            //Set all the state values

            return states;
        }

        #endregion
    }
}
```

Finally, you can expose the GetStates web service by right-clicking the ACME.POS. Service.Host project and selecting Service Factory (ASMX) ➤ Expose Service. Select the service you just implemented, and the Web Service Software Factory will create the GetStates.asmx file to expose the service.

## Adding the Model Class

The ACME POS client will use a Model-View-Presenter pattern. This software design pattern uses three components:

- The model contains the domain data.

- The view is typically the UI itself (the windows forms and controls). Since we're using a web service, it will perform the necessary proxy actions to get to the domain data.

- The presenter is the coordinator of the application. It provides the necessary plumbing to get the view and model to interact with each other.

The model class, which will be called ACMEModel, will manage the web service proxies. The service website was created in Chapter 3 using the Web Service Software Factory. Here, we will consume some of the web service and cache the static data.

The Web Service Software Factory created a Windows forms project called ACME.POS. Service.Client. You will use this project to provide the client UI.

First, create a new service reference by right-clicking the ACME.POS.Service.Client project and selecting Service Factory (ASMX) ➤ Add Service Reference. Then select the ACME.POS. Service.Host web service and call it ACMEStateWebService.

Add a new class to the ACME.POS.Service.Client project called StateCacheRefreshAction. This class will be responsible for getting a list of states from the ACMEStateWebService web service proxy.

Next, add a reference to the ACME.POS.Service.Client project to the Caching Application Block assembly. The StateCacheRefreshAction should be decorated with the [Serializable] attribute and implement the ICacheItemRefreshAction interface of the Caching Application Block. The Refresh method will then be responsible for retrieving the list of states from the web proxy. Listing 7-19 shows the implementation.

**Listing 7-19.** *Implementing StateCacheRefreshAction*

```
using System;
using System.Collections.Generic;
using System.Text;
using Microsoft.Practices.EnterpriseLibrary.Caching;
using Microsoft.Practices.EnterpriseLibrary.Caching.Expirations;

namespace ACME.POS.UI.Model
{
    [Serializable]
    public class StateCacheRefreshAction : ICacheItemRefreshAction
    {
        #region ICacheItemRefreshAction Members

        public void Refresh(string removedKey, object expiredValue,
            CacheItemRemovedReason removalReason)
        {
            ACMEWebService webService = new ACMEWebService();
            StatesList states = webService.GetStates();

            CacheManager staticData =
                CacheFactory.GetCacheManager("StaticData");
            staticData.Add("STATES", states, CacheItemPriority.NotRemovable,
                new StateCacheRefreshAction(),
                new AbsoluteTime(DateTime.Now.AddDays(1)));
        }

        #endregion
    }
}
```

The next task is to add the ACMEModel class to the ACME.POS.Service.Client project. Then add the cache manager to the ACMEModel class and instantiate it, as shown in Listing 7-20.

**Listing 7-20.** *Adding a Cache Manager to the ACMEModel Class*

```
using System;
using System.Collections.Generic;
using System.Text;
using Microsoft.Practices.EnterpriseLibrary.Caching;
using Microsoft.Practices.EnterpriseLibrary.Data;


namespace ACME.POS.UI.Model
{
    public class ACMEModel
    {
        CacheManager m_StaticDataCache;

        public ACMEModel ()
        {
            staticDataCache = CacheFactory.GetCacheManager("StaticData");
        }
    }
}
```

Finally, you need to retrieve the cached items in the UI. In the ACMEModel class in the ACME.POS.UI.Forms project, add the GetStates method, as shown in Listing 7-21.

**Listing 7-21.** *Adding the GetStates Method*

```
public State[] GetStates()
{
    if (m_StaticDataCache == null)
        throw new ApplicationException("Static Data Cache is Null") ;

    State[] stateList = m_StaticDataCache["STATES"] as State[];

    if(stateList == null)
    {
     //Attempt to retrieve the data from the web service and reset the cache
     //using the StateCacheRefreshAction class
     StateCacheRefreshAction refreshAction =
         new StateCacheRefreshAction();
     refreshAction.Refresh("STATES", null,
         CacheItemRemovedReason.Unknown);
     stateList = m_StaticDataCache["STATES"] as State[];
    }

    return stateList;
}
```

## Configuring the Caching Application Block

The last step for this chapter's exercise is to configure a named instance of the Caching Application Block. To do this, just open the application configuration file for the ACME.POS.Service. Client project and add the Caching Application Block to it. Immediately, a default named instance called Cache Manager is created for you. Change the Name property to StaticData, as shown in Figure 7-17. Then save the application configuration file.

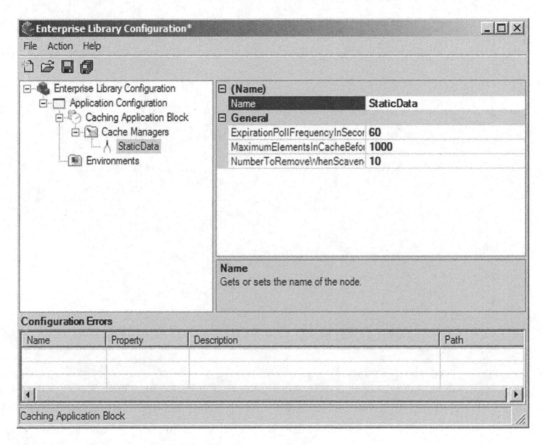

Figure 7-17. *Configuring the Caching Application Block*

# Summary

The Caching Application Block is a very powerful tool in the developer's tool chest. It can help improve the functionality and overall usability of an application. The flexibility of this application block gives developers multiple options for handling caching scenarios. The Caching Application Block can even be used outside the normal caching scenarios, as you will see in Chapter 12. However, as explained in this chapter, for ASP.NET applications, developers should evaluate the ASP.NET caching functionality as a possible solution.

Now that data access and caching have been handled in the ACME POS application, it is time to tackle another common area of pain for developers: exception handling. Yes, I know we all like to believe that our code is flawless, but once in a blue moon, the code goblins get in there and wreak havoc. The next chapter covers the Exception Handling Application Block, which will help manage those little code goblins.

# CHAPTER 8

■ ■ ■

# The Exception Handling Application Block

**N**o matter your level of programming experience, the introduction of programming errors and other unexpected behavior is a matter of course. Thankfully, most languages support the ability to identify these issues, report on them, and potentially even recover from them. How this is accomplished using the Exception Handling Application Block is the subject of this chapter.

## Introducing Exception Handling

Exceptions are detected and managed through a process known as *exception handling*. While exception handling comes at the cost of writing additional code, the ability to gracefully respond to and potentially recover from such unforeseen issues is the ideal alternative to simply ending the application and presenting the user with something like the dialog box shown in Figure 8-1.

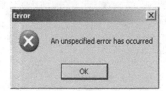

**Figure 8-1.** *Unspecified error message*

Typically, exception handling involves three tasks: capturing the exception, logging the exception for later analysis, and, if necessary, presenting the application user with an understandable error message.

### Capturing the Exception

Capturing an exception is the first and most essential step in the exception-handling process. Unfortunately, Visual Basic 6's process for capturing exceptions had some problems. A good friend of mine described Visual Basic's handling of errors as like "allowing a car without brakes to roll downhill into a town." Generally speaking, not being able to stop if necessary is a really bad thing if you are a car or if you are an application throwing exceptions. The On Error Resume Next statement presents the potential for such a disaster, as shown in Listing 8-1.

**Listing 8-1.** *On Error Resume Next Example*

```
Private Sub Form_Load()
   On Error Resume Next
   'Do something here
   If Err <> 0 Then
      'Do some error handling
      On Error Resume Next 'clears error
   End If

   'Do another thing
   If Err <> 0 Then
      'Do some error handling
      On Error Resume Next 'clears error
   End If
End Sub
```

Each condition you want to test requires an ensuing test to determine whether an error occurred.

Fortunately, this process is much improved in the .NET environment due to the introduction of the try-catch-finally block, which greatly simplifies the task of capturing exceptions as they occur. Listing 8-2 shows a C#-specific example involving the try-catch-finally block.

**Listing 8-2.** *Try-Catch-Finally Example*

```
private void MyMethod()
{
   try
   {
      // Potential exception-causing code
   }
   catch(ApplicationException apEx)
   {
      //Handle an application exception
   }
   catch(Exception ex)
   {
      //Handle a general exception
   }
   finally
   {
      // Execute cleanup code regardless of whether
      // there was an exception or not
   }
}
```

In Listing 8-2, it is not possible to have multiple lines of code within the `try` block without having to test each line. Also, the `catch` block allows the handling of different types of exceptions. In the case of Listing 8-2, a `System.ApplicationException` and a `System.Exception` could each be handled differently. Finally, the `finally` block executes code regardless of whether what occurred in the `try` block produced an exception or ran as expected. The `finally` block is where you would clean up the resources used in the `try` block, such as file handlers.

## Logging the Exception

Once the exception has been captured, information about the event should be handled and recovered from if possible, and logged in order to later diagnose and resolve the problem. But what should be logged? There are many schools of thought on this issue. I believe in recording as much information as possible, including a description of what I was trying to do, an exception type, message, stack traces, and important local variables and properties. While some may consider this to be a bit excessive, exceptions should generally be an uncommon occurrence and therefore staying fully informed of such matters shouldn't consume too many resources overall. After all, if exceptions are a regular occurrence, then the application should be reviewed to either properly handle the exceptions or prevent them from occurring in the first place.

The following are some options for logging exception data:

- Using a text file (plain text, XML, CSV, and so on)

- Saving to a database such as SQL Server

- Using the Windows event log

- Sending to a message queue

- Sending via email

- Using the Windows Management Interface/Enterprise Instrumentation Framework (WMI/EIF)

- Using some hybrid combination of the preceding options

In order to determine the best method for logging, it is important to understand how it will be consumed. For example, if it is a critical application yet has a small user base, sending error messages via email might be the best approach. On the other hand, applications with a large deployment base may be best served by the use of message queues or a database. This way, exception data can be centrally located and queried against.

More extensive planning would be in order for applications such as smart clients, which can be disconnected from the network for extended periods, and for applications having a large user base. In both cases, you may need to devise a hybrid approach. This is one of the advantages to using the Exception Handling Application Block, as you can delay the decisions on how to deliver the exceptions independently of the application design and development. You can even decide to change the delivery mechanism during the application's life, without needing to make changes to the application code itself.

## Presenting User-Friendly Messages

Not all exceptions can result in graceful recovery. Sometimes the only alternative is to notify the user that an exception has occurred and explain how that exception will impact what the user was trying to do. For instance, in a case where a user is trying to purchase a plane ticket, but the online ticketing website is down for maintenance, the exception message could tell the user what action she can take in order to complete the purchase, such as calling a toll-free number.

If you are reading this book, you probably are a fairly savvy computer user. But many people do not have that level of knowledge about computers. So it is important to make sure the user understands what has happened. For instance, if a user suddenly sees the message shown in Figure 8-2, it's likely he won't have a clue what just happened.

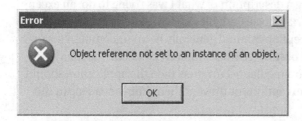

**Figure 8-2.** *Development environment exception message*

You should be sure to keep cryptic lingo hidden from the users, and they instead receive an exception message that they can understand. Figure 8-3 offers an ideal alternative to Figure 8-2.

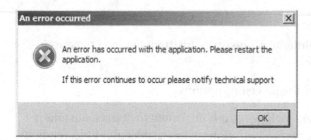

**Figure 8-3.** *User-friendly exception message*

Pop-up boxes are a common feature of many applications; however, you should still be cautious when using them to present messages pertinent to exception handling. For instance, a dialog box may not be appropriate in the following situations:

- When multiple exception messages should be displayed to the user

- When the application does not support a UI, such as a Windows service

- When a process with multiple transactions should continue even though one transaction produced an exception

For example, during unit testing of an application with an automated testing tool such as Visual Studio Team System or NUnit, it is best to supply multiple exception messages to the user.

When using a dialog box, you also need to make sure that the appropriate meaning is presented to the user. The MessageBox class in the System.Windows.Forms namespace allows for different icons to be associated with a dialog box, as well as different options for user interaction. It is essential that you don't confuse the user. For instance, suppose you need to notify a user that her data was not saved to the database server. It would be inappropriate to display a message box with a question mark icon and the Yes, No, and Cancel buttons, as shown in Figure 8-4.

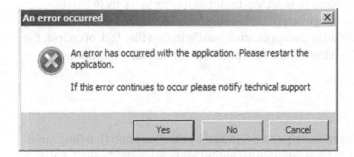

**Figure 8-4.** *Misleading exception message*

The message box shown in Figure 8-4 might give users the impression that they could click No or Cancel to prevent the exception, when the original intent was to notify the user that the exception had already occurred.

---

■**Caution**  Never display Windows forms or message boxes in server applications. Doing so may cause other exceptions to occur or the server application to stop working.

---

You should also consider the sensitivity of the data being displayed to the user or developer. This may require that an exception message be altered or thrown as another type of message to protect the data presented in the exception message from prying eyes. The following are some examples of sensitive information:

- Financial data (credit card numbers, bank account numbers, and so on)

- Personal data (first name, last name, address, passwords, and so on)

- Medical history data

- Legal data (criminal records, civil cases, and so on)

In these cases, it may be beneficial to mask the actual details of the error message, such as providing only the last four digits of a credit card number or bank account number. In other cases, it may be best to just throw another type of error. The best approach depends on the specific needs of the organization that will use the application you are building.

# Introducing the Exception Handling Application Block

The Exception Handling Application Block is designed to handle the most common exception-handling tasks. It allows developers to write less redundant code in trying to handle exceptions. It also lets developers change exception handling after the application is deployed, via exception policies that are defined in the application configuration file. And, of course, the Exception Handling Application Block offers the best practices for handling exceptions in .NET applications.

## Exception Policies

The policies define how certain exception types are handled by the Exception Handling Application Block. A particular policy can have multiple exception types associated with it. Each exception type within the policy can then have one or more exception handlers. The exception handlers supplied with Enterprise Library include those for logging, wrapping, and replacing exceptions, as discussed a little later in this chapter.

### ExceptionPolicy Class

The application code interacts with the Exception Handling Application Block via the static method HandleException, which is part of the ExceptionPolicy class. The HandleException method calls a private static method called GetExceptionPolicy. The GetExceptionPolicy method uses a Factory pattern implementation to create an instance of the ExceptionPolicyImpl class for the named policy that was passed in from the HandleException method. The HandleException method of the Exception class then executes the HandleException method of the ExceptionPolicyImpl class to handle the exception as defined by the policy. Figure 8-5 shows the complete signature for the HandleException method in the ExceptionPolicy class.

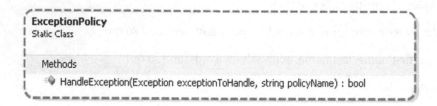

**Figure 8-5.** *ExceptionPolicy class diagram*

Once an exception has been handled (logged, wrapped, replaced, and so on), one of three exception posthandling actions may occur:

*None*: The None event means that nothing happens—do nothing after the exception handlers are processed. The exception will simply be absorbed, and the application will continue to process. If you use None, your application will not be able to throw a wrapped or replaced exception.

*Rethrow*: The HandleException method returns a Boolean value to determine whether the exception policy wants the caller to rethrow the exception. This allows the exception policy to determine if it is appropriate to rethrow the exception so it may be processed later on in the call stack. Determining whether to rethrow the exception is done by the exception policy for a specific exception type.

*Throw new exception*: The ThrowNewException method throws the resulting exception created by the exception handler chain. You must use ThrowNewException if you want to process a wrapped or replaced exception within your application, because a wrapped or replaced exception is essentially a brand-new exception. If you opted to rethrow the existing exception instead, the wrapped or replaced exception would never be processed by the Common Language Runtime (CLR).

## ExceptionPolicyImpl Class

The ExceptionPolicyImpl class provides the mechanism necessary to manage the named exception policies that are defined within the application configuration file. The ExceptionPolicyImpl object contains a dictionary collection of ExceptionPolicyEntry objects. When the class is first instantiated by the HandleException method of the ExceptionPolicy class, the ExceptionPolicyImpl constructor retrieves the various ExceptionPolicyEntry classes that were defined in the named policy. One ExceptionPolicyEntry object is created for each exception type that is specified by the named policy. Figure 8-6 shows ExceptionPolicyImpl's core methods for implementing a particular exception policy.

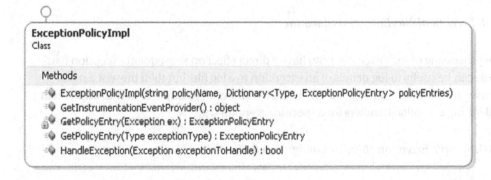

**Figure 8-6.** *ExceptionPolicyImpl class diagram*

The `ExceptionPolicyImpl` class also contains a method called `HandleException`. This method is called by the `ExceptionPolicy` class's `HandleException` method, and it is responsible for retrieving the appropriate `ExceptionPolicyEntry` object for the exception type that was passed in.

---

**Note** The Exception Handling Application Block will execute only the most specific exception type. For example, if you had a policy with exception types `SqlException` and `Exception`, only the handlers for the `SqlException` type will be executed.

---

## ExceptionPolicyEntry Class

The `ExceptionPolicyEntry` class will manage the handlers for each exception type of an exception policy. For each exception type, the `ExceptionPolicyEntry` object contains a collection of objects that implement the `IExceptionHandler` interface. This collection is determined by the exception handlers that were defined for this specific exception type in the named policy. The exception handlers are processed in the same order as they are presented in the application configuration file. Figure 8-7 shows the public methods of the `ExceptionPolicyEntry` class.

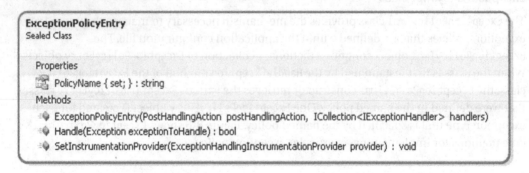

**Figure 8-7.** *ExceptionPolicyEntry class diagram*

The processing of each exception can have a direct effect on subsequent exception handlers. This can be useful to log details of an exception to a log file, but then present a more generic user-friendly message to the user. Listing 8-3 shows an example of how to implement this by defining exception handlers for a specific exception type.

**Listing 8-3.** *Sample Exception Handler Configuration File*

```
<configuration>
    <configSections>
        <section name="loggingConfiguration"
type="Microsoft.Practices.EnterpriseLibrary.
 Logging.Configuration.LoggingSettings,
 Microsoft.Practices.EnterpriseLibrary.Logging, Version=2.0.0.0, Culture=neutral,
PublicKeyToken=null" />
```

```
<configSections>
    <section name="loggingConfiguration"
        type="Microsoft.Practices.EnterpriseLibrary.
        Logging.Configuration.LoggingSettings,
        Microsoft.Practices.EnterpriseLibrary.Logging,
        Version=2.0.0.0, Culture=neutral,
        PublicKeyToken=null" />
    <section name="exceptionHandling"
        type="Microsoft.Practices.EnterpriseLibrary.
        ExceptionHandling.Configuration.
        ExceptionHandlingSettings,
        Microsoft.Practices.EnterpriseLibrary.
        ExceptionHandling,
        Version=2.0.0.0, Culture=neutral, PublicKeyToken=null" />
</configSections>
  <exceptionHandling>
    <exceptionPolicies>
      <add name="Exception Policy">
        <exceptionTypes>
          <add type="System.Exception, mscorlib, Version=2.0.0.0,
              Culture=neutral, PublicKeyToken=b77a5c561934e089"
              postHandlingAction="NotifyRethrow" name="Exception">
            <exceptionHandlers>
              <add logCategory="General" eventId="100"
                severity="Error"
                title="Enterprise Library Exception Handling"
                formatterType="Microsoft.Practices.
                EnterpriseLibrary.ExceptionHandling.
                TextExceptionFormatter,
                Microsoft.Practices.EnterpriseLibrary.
                ExceptionHandling,
                Version=2.0.0.0, Culture=neutral,
                PublicKeyToken=null"
                priority="0"
                        type="Microsoft.Practices.EnterpriseLibrary.
                        ExceptionHandling.Logging.
                        LoggingExceptionHandler, Microsoft.Practices.
                        EnterpriseLibrary.ExceptionHandling.
                        Logging, Version=2.0.0.0, Culture=neutral,
                        PublicKeyToken=null"
                        name="Logging Handler" />
              <add exceptionMessage="An error has occurred."
                        replaceExceptionType="System.ApplicationException,
                        mscorlib, Version=2.0.0.0, Culture=neutral,
                        PublicKeyToken=b77a5c561934e089"
                        type="Microsoft.Practices.EnterpriseLibrary.
                        ExceptionHandling. ReplaceHandler,Microsoft.Practices
                        EnterpriseLibrary.ExceptionHandling,
                        Version=2.0.0.0, Culture=neutral, PublicKeyToken=null"
```

```
                       name="Replace Handler" />
              </exceptionHandlers>
            </add>
         </exceptionTypes>
       </add>
     </exceptionPolicies>
   </exceptionHandling>
<loggingConfiguration name="Logging Application Block" tracingEnabled="true"
       defaultCategory="General" logWarningsWhenNoCategoriesMatch="true">
   <!-- Logging Configuration -->
   </loggingConfiguration>
</configuration>
```

In Listing 8-3, the logging exception handler is inserted before the replace exception handler, and this is the order in which the Exception Handler Application Block will process these exception handlers. Chapter 9 describes how to configure the Logging Application Block.

## Exception Handlers

The exception handlers are the components that actually handle the exception. Four exception handlers are provided with Enterprise Library:

- LoggingExceptionHandler: Logs an exception.

- ReplaceHandler: Replaces the existing exception with a new one.

- WrapperHandler: Wraps an existing exception within a new exception.

- FaultContractExceptionHandler: Converts an exception into a Windows Communication Foundation (WCF) Fault Contract (supported only in Enterprise Library 3.x).

You can also create your own exception handlers by implementing the IExceptionHandler interface.

Each exception handler must implement the IExceptionHandler interface in order for the Exception Handler Application Block to properly use it. The IExceptionHandler interface has one method called HandleException that must be implemented by an exception handler, as shown in the class diagram in Figure 8-8.

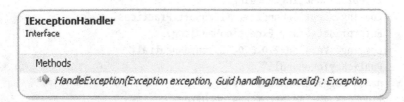

**Figure 8-8.** *IExceptionHandler class diagram*

The HandleException method contains two parameters:

- A parameter of type System.Exception called exception, which is the exception to be handled

- A GUID parameter named handlingInstanceId, which defines which instance the exception was logged for

The handlingInstanceId parameter is useful to be able to tie together an exception that may have been handled by multiple handlers. For example, an exception might be both logged to a file and sent out as an email. Using the handlingInstanceId parameter, the emailed message that contains the generic exception can be easily searched in the log file by the GUID.

The handling instance GUID is not automatically inserted into an exception message by the wrap or replace exception handlers. Instead, it is necessary to add the token {handlingInstanceId} to the wrapped or replaced message itself to have the handling instance GUID inserted into the message. The logging exception handler automatically adds the handling instance GUID. While this is not an issue if you use the logging exception handler to record an exception, you may want to include it in a dialog message to the user. This way, a help desk person can easily find the more detailed message within a log file.

## LoggingExceptionHandler Class

The LoggingExceptionHandler class is the most commonly used exception handler. This exception handler uses the Logging Application Block discussed in the next chapter. The LoggingExceptionHandler class will be responsible for logging a message to a text file, a queue, WMI, or any trace listener that is defined for the Logging Application Block.

The LoggingExceptionHandler class is actually part of the Logging Application Block's assembly. LoggingExceptionHandler takes the message and other details of the exception and records them in a plain text file or an XML file, depending on whether the TextExceptionFormatter or XmlExceptionFormatter was defined for the exception handler in the configuration file, as explained in the section about formatting exception messages, coming up shortly.

## ReplaceHandler Class

The ReplaceHandler class allows for exceptions to be replaced by another exception. This is a handy feature when an exception may cross some trust boundary or application domain and the original exception could possibly contain sensitive data. The ReplaceHandler class could provide a more generic exception to the calling process. The ReplaceHandler class could also be used for returning friendlier messages to a UI.

## WrapHandler Class

Unlike the ReplaceHandler class, the WrapHandler class does not replace the exception that occurred but instead wraps it inside another exception. This allows for specific exception types to be bubbled up so that they may be handled properly by other parts of an application. It's good practice to use the WrapperHandler class unless the exception contains sensitive data; in that case, the ReplaceHandler class is probably a better choice.

## FaultContractExceptionHandler Class

The FaultContractExceptionHandler class is introduced in Enterprise Library 3.0. It provides a mechanism for mapping exceptions that can occur within a WCF service boundary to a type of Fault Contract. Fault Contracts allow a WCF service and client application to agree on a contract of SOAP faults that could occur. This way, the client application can take appropriate action based on the type of SOAP fault or the metadata within the SOAP fault.

■**Note**  A SOAP fault is an exception message that is packaged into a SOAP message. For more information about SOAP faults, visit http://www.w3.org/TR/soap12-part1/#soapfault.

### Custom Handlers

Developers can define their own exception handler assembly that implements the IExceptionHandler interface, decorated with the ConfigurationElementType attribute with the CustomHandlerData type being passed in as a parameter. This ensures that the other built-in exception handlers that do implement the IExceptionHandler interface are not accidentally consumed through the custom handler, and it allows for configuration of the IExceptionHandler via key-value pairs.

## Exception Message Formatters

The exception formatter classes are responsible for properly formatting the exception message for logging purposes and inherit from the ExceptionFormatter abstract class. Figure 8-9 shows the class diagram.

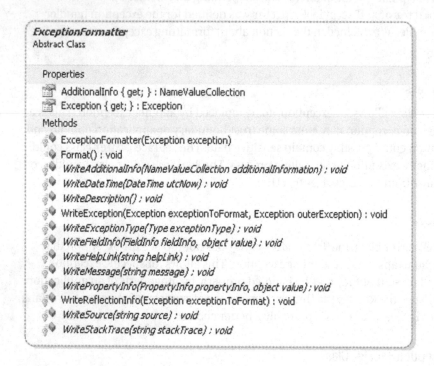

**Figure 8-9.** *ExceptionFormatter class diagram*

**Note** All of the protected methods that are italicized and have the key icon next to them in Figure 8-9, except for `WriteReflectionInfo` and `WriteException`, are abstract and must be implemented in an inherited class.

Two implementations of the `ExceptionFormatter` class come with Enterprise Library: `TextExceptionFormatter` and `XmlExceptionFormatter`. You can also design you own custom `ExceptionFormatter` simply by creating a subclass of `ExceptionFormatter` and provide your own formatting implementation.

## TextExceptionFormatter Class

The `TextExceptionFormatter` class allows the exception and the details about the exception to be written out as plain text to an instance of a `TextWriter` class. This can be useful for writing to log files that will be read by a support engineer. Figure 8-10 shows what a logged exception would look like in plain text format.

```
Event Type:      Error
Event Source:    Enterprise Library Logging
Event Category:  None
Event ID:        100
Date:            11/13/2006
Time:            9:12:57 AM
User:            N/A
Computer:        MyMachine
Description:
Timestamp: 11/13/2006 2:12:57 PM
Message: HandlingInstanceID: d46063f9-319f-4663-b16c-04924969e376
An exception of type 'System.Exception' occurred and was caught.
------------------------------------------------------------
11/13/2006 08:12:57
Type : System.Exception, mscorlib, Version=2.0.0.0, Culture=neutral,
PublicKeyToken=b77a5c561934e089
Message : Generated Exception
Source : ExceptionSample
Help link :
Data : System.Collections.ListDictionaryInternal
TargetSite : Void MyHandledMethod()
Stack Trace :    at DGMEL.Sample.Program.MyHandledMethod() in C:\Documents and
Settings\user\My Documents\Visual Studio
2005\Projects\ExceptionSample\ExceptionSample\Program.cs:line 22

Additional Info:

MachineName : MyMachine
TimeStamp : 11/13/2006 2:12:57 PM
FullName : Microsoft.Practices.EnterpriseLibrary.ExceptionHandling, Version=2.0.0.0,
Culture=neutral, PublicKeyToken=null□AppDomainName : ExceptionSample.vshost.exe
ThreadIdentity :
WindowsIdentity : domain\user
Category: General
Priority: 0
EventId: 100
Severity: Error
Title:Enterprise Library Exception Handling
Machine: MyMachine
Application Domain: ExceptionSample.vshost.exe
Process Id: 5968
Process Name: C:\Documents and Settings\user\My Documents\Visual Studio
2005\Projects\ExceptionSample\ExceptionSample\bin\Debug\ExceptionSample.vshost.exe
Win32 Thread Id: 5004
Thread Name:
Extended Properties:
```

**Figure 8-10.** *Exception message in plain text format*

## XmlExceptionFormatter

The XmlExceptionFormatter class takes the exception and writes it to an XmlWriter object. While it is possible to read XML, it is generally easier to use the TextExceptionFormatter, or the output of the XmlExceptionFormatter could be formatted as an HTML document by an XSLT document. Figure 8-11 shows what a logged exception would look like in the XML format.

```
Event Type:      Error
Event Source:    Enterprise Library Logging
Event Category: None
Event ID:        100
Date:            11/13/2006
Time:            9:23:50 AM
User:            N/A
Computer:        MyMachine
Description:
Timestamp: 11/13/2006 2:23:50 PM
Message: HandlingInstanceID: 719893e6-ff47-4389-a9ad-8fe4387d5dee
<Exception>
  <Description>An exception of type 'System.Exception' occurred and was caught.</Description>
  <DateTime>2006-11-13 08:23:50Z</DateTime>
  <ExceptionType>System.Exception, mscorlib, Version=2.0.0.0, Culture=neutral,
PublicKeyToken=b77a5c561934e089</ExceptionType>
  <Message>Generated Exception</Message>
  <Source>ExceptionSample</Source>
  <HelpLink />
  <Property name="Data">System.Collections.ListDictionaryInternal</Property>
  <Property name="TargetSite">Void MyHandledMethod()</Property>
  <StackTrace>    at DGMEL.Sample.Program.MyHandledMethod() in C:\Documents and
Settings\user\My Documents\Visual Studio
2005\Projects\ExceptionSample\ExceptionSample\Program.cs:line 22</StackTrace>
  <additionalInfo>
    <info name="MachineName" value="MyMachine" />
    <info name="TimeStamp" value="11/13/2006 2:23:50 PM" />
    <info name="FullName" value="Microsoft.Practices.EnterpriseLibrary.ExceptionHandling,
Version=2.0.0.0, Culture=neutral, PublicKeyToken=null" />
    <info name="AppDomainName" value="ExceptionSample.vshost.exe" />
    <info name="ThreadIdentity" value="" />
    <info name="WindowsIdentity" value="Domain\user" />
  </additionalInfo>
</Exception>
Category: General
Priority: 0
EventId: 100
Severity: Error
Title:Enterprise Library Exception Handling
Machine: MyMachine
Application Domain: ExceptionSample.vshost.exe
Process Id: 2672
Process Name: C:\Documents and Settings\user\My Documents\Visual Studio
2005\Projects\ExceptionSample\ExceptionSample\bin\Debug\ExceptionSample.vshost.exe
Win32 Thread Id: 4324
Thread Name:
Extended Properties: |
```

**Figure 8-11.** *Exception message in XML format (viewed in Event Viewer)*

In Figure 8-11, notice that the log entry contains a mixture of XML and plain text. This is because of the Logging Application Block's text formatter implementation, which is explained in Chapter 9. So you would need to parse out the XML entries so that they could be consumed by an XML parser.

# Using the Exception Handling Application Block

Using the Exception Handling Application Block within your application is a three-step process:

1. Reference the necessary Enterprise Library assemblies.

2. Create the necessary calls to process the exception policies.

3. Configure the exception policies in the application configuration file.

The first task is to create a new Windows console application and reference the correct assemblies in your project. At a minimum, you need to reference these three assemblies:

- `Microsoft.Practices.EnterpriseLibrary.Common.dll`: The shared Enterprise Library assembly

- `Microsoft.Practices.EnterpriseLibrary.ExceptionHandling.dll`: The core assembly for the Exception Handling Application Block

- `Microsoft.Practices.ObjectBuilder.dll`: The Enterprise Library Object Builder assembly for instantiating objects

If you intend on using the Logging Application Block to log exceptions as they occur, you will also need to add the following two assemblies to your project's references:

- `Microsoft.Practices.EnterpriseLibrary.Logging.dll`: The core Logging Application Block assembly.

- `Microsoft.Practices.EnterpriseLibrary.ExceptionHandling.Logging.dll`: Formats the exception and sends it to the Logging Application Block

The next task is to add the necessary code to handle the exceptions that may occur within your application.

## Catching and Handling Exceptions

As discussed at the beginning of the chapter, catching exceptions is pretty easy in the .NET environment with the use of the `try-catch-finally` block. Once the exception is captured, however, the next task is to figure out what to do with it. This is where the exception policies come in; they decide what the proper actions will be. As you learned earlier in the chapter, the handling of exceptions is performed by the `HandleException` static method of the `ExceptionPolicy` class. Listing 8-4 presents an example.

**Listing 8-4.** *Implementation of the HandleException Method*

```
using System;
using System.Collections.Generic;
using System.Text;
using Microsoft.Practices.EnterpriseLibrary.ExceptionHandling;

namespace DGMEL.Sample
{
    class Program
    {
        private const string MYPOLICY = "MyPolicy";

        static void Main(string[] args)
        {
            Program myProgram = new Program();
```

```
        myProgram.MyHandledMethod();
    }

    public void MyHandledMethod()
    {
        try
        {
            throw new Exception("Generated Exception");
        }
        catch(Exception ex)
        {
            ExceptionPolicy.HandleException(ex, MYPOLICY);
        }
    }
  }
}
```

The HandleException method takes the exception and named policy and uses that information to handle the exception.

To make the creation of the policies easier, take some time beforehand to think about what is required to handle the exception. Then you will be able to define only the policies required to meet your exception-handling needs.

Once your application has all of the necessary exception-handling code written, the next task is to actually configure the application. The configuration specifics depend on which exception handler you are implementing.

**Tip** Generally, it is advisable to have at least one catchall try-catch-finally block to handle all of the unhandled or unplanned exceptions that occur, so that they may be logged and a friendly message can be displayed to the user. This is especially important for Windows applications and web applications that will be used by nontechnical users.

# Configuring the Application to Log Exceptions

The logging exception handler is the most complex type to configure of the three exception handlers provided with the Exception Handling Application Block. The process of configuring this type of handler involves adding the Exception Handling Application Block to the configuration file, creating an exception policy, selecting an exception type, adding the logging handler, and finally configuring the logging handler.

## Adding the Exception Handling Application Block

First, create an application configuration file for your application and open it with the Enterprise Library Configuration Console. Then add the Exception Handling Application Block to it, as shown in Figure 8-12.

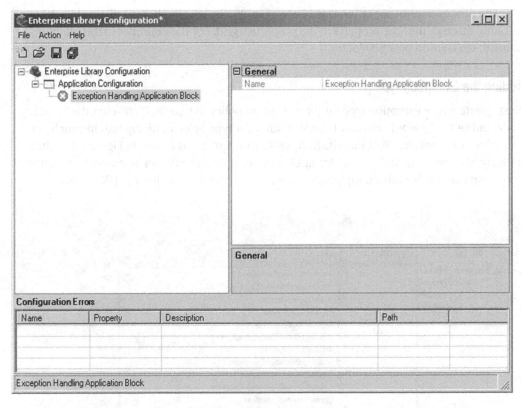

**Figure 8-12.** *Adding the Exception Handling Application Block to the Configuration Console*

You can see that a newly installed Exception Handling Application Block is quite bare due to the lack of implemented policies.

## Adding an Exception Policy

To create an exception policy, right-click the Exception Handling Application Block and select New ➤ Exception Policy, as shown in Figure 8-13.

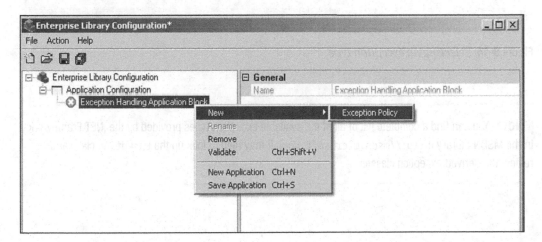

**Figure 8-13.** *Adding an exception policy*

The new exception policy is named Exception Policy by default. You will want to change its name through the Name property in the properties grid. For the examples in this chapter, name the exception policy MyPolicy.

## Adding the Exception Type

Next, create a new exception type for this exception policy to handle. Right-click the MyPolicy node and select New ➤ Exception Type. You will see a Type Selector dialog box, in which you can select a known class that inherits from System.Exception, as shown in Figure 8-14. Alternatively, you can click the Load an Assembly button to select a custom assembly that contains exception classes. For this example, select the Exception class and click the OK button.

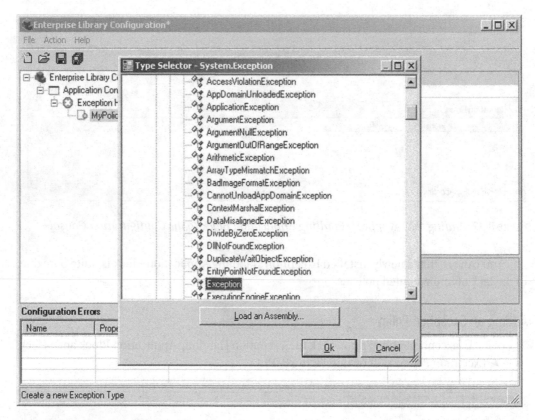

**Figure 8-14.** *Selecting an exception type*

**Note**  You can find a complete list of all of the available exception types provided by the .NET Framework in the MSDN Library (http://msdn.microsoft.com). It may help to look up the Exception class and review the derived exception classes.

## Adding the Logging Handler

Now that you've chosen the exception type, the next step is to add the logging handler to the exception type. Right-click the Exception node and select New ➤ Logging Handler. Figure 8-15 shows a logging handler added to the exception type.

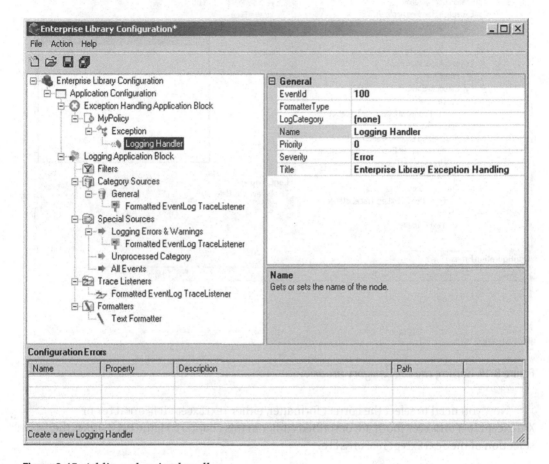

**Figure 8-15.** *Adding a logging handler*

As shown in Figure 8-15, a lot has happened in the Configuration Console. Notice that the Logging Application Block has been added to the configuration file. This is because the Exception Handling Application Block's logging handler utilizes the Logging Application Block to log exceptions. For right now, you don't need to change any settings of the Logging Application Block—that's covered in the next chapter.

## Configuring the Logging Handler

Your next step is to select the Logging Application Block category that will be used to log the exception, by setting the LogCategory property, as shown in Figure 8-16. You may want to change the category name from General to something more meaningful, especially if there will be many types of logging events within your application.

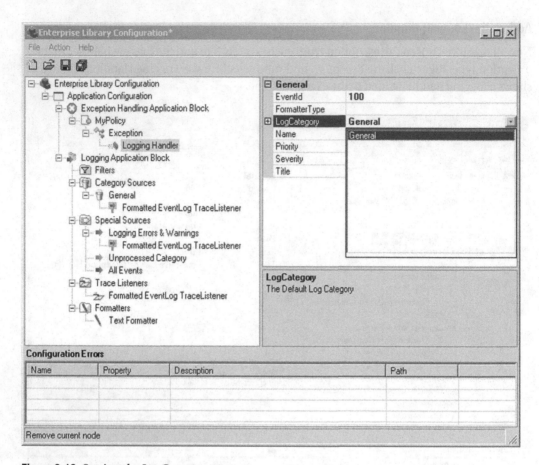

**Figure 8-16.** *Setting the LogCategory property*

Now you need to select the correct formatter, either TextExceptionFormatter or XmlExceptionFormatter (both are described earlier in this chapter). Figure 8-17 shows the selection of the TextExceptionFormatter.

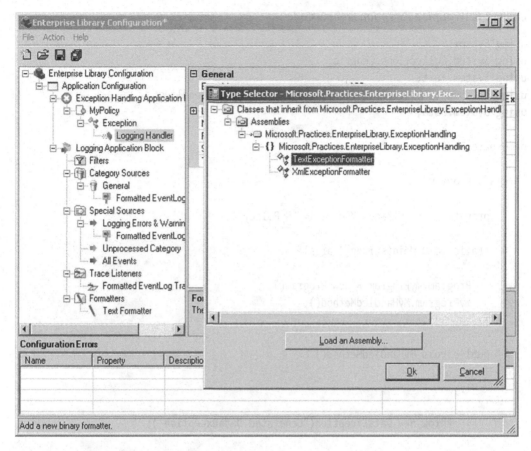

**Figure 8-17.** *Selecting an exception formatter*

The output of the TextExceptionFormatter will be simple name-value pairs of data (see Figure 8-10, earlier in the chapter). The output of the XmlExceptionformatter will contain XML data that will be placed in the message field of the log file (see Figure 8-11, earlier in the chapter).

## Wrapping Exceptions

In order to wrap an exception, you must need to choose an exception defined in the configuration policy and specify with which exception to wrap it. As an example, we will modify the sample code to throw a DataException, and then wrap it with an ApplicationException.

First, in the sample project, add a reference to the System.Data.dll assembly, if it is not already present. Next, add a using statement for the System.Data namespace, and then change the generated exception from Exception to DataException. Listing 8-5 shows the modified code.

**Listing 8-5.** *Wrapping Exception Sample Code*

```
using System;
using System.Collections.Generic;
using System.Text;
using Microsoft.Practices.EnterpriseLibrary.ExceptionHandling;
using System.Data;

namespace DGMEL.Sample
{
  class Program
  {
    private const string MYPOLICY = "MyPolicy";

    static void Main(string[] args)
    {
      Program myProgram = new Program();
      myProgram.MyHandledMethod();
    }

    public void MyHandledMethod()
    {
      try
      {
        throw new DataException("Generated DataException");
      }
      catch(Exception ex)
      {
        ExceptionPolicy.HandleException(ex, MYPOLICY);
      }
    }
  }
}
```

The next step is to configure a new exception type with new exception handlers for the MyPolicy exception policy. Open the Configuration Console, navigate down the tree until you get to the MyPolicy exception policy, right-click, and choose New ➤ Exception Type. Select DataException as the new exception type. This type is in the System.Data.dll assembly. If you don't see that assembly in the dialog box, click the Load Assembly button and navigate to the System.Data.dll assembly folder (System.Data.dll is typically located in C:\WINDOWS\Microsoft.NET\Framework\v2.0.50727 for .NET Framework 2.0 and 3.0). Then right-click the new DataException node and select Wrap Handler.

Three properties appear for the wrap handler: ExceptionMessage, Name, and WrapExceptionType. Fill in a text message for the ExceptionMessage property and select the exception type, which is System.ApplicationException in this example, as shown in Figure 8-18.

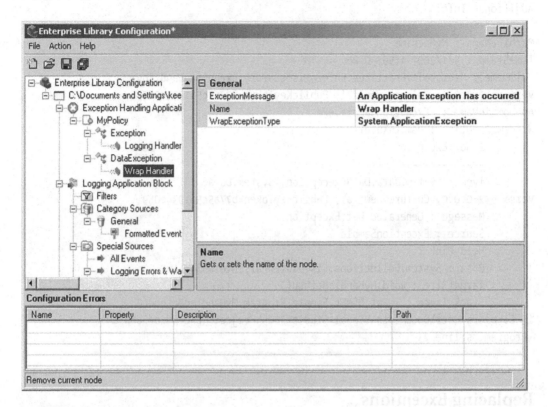

**Figure 8-18.** *Wrap handler properties*

Finally, add a log handler to the DataException node, as described in the previous section. This will allow you to see the output of the exception.

Now, run the sample application and look at the generated error message in the Event Viewer. You will see the wrapped exception as well as the inner exception, as in the following example.

```
5/1/2007 11:59:30
Type : System.ApplicationException, mscorlib, version=2.0.0.0,
Culture=neutral, PublicKeyToken=b77a5c561934e089
Message : An Application Exception has occurred
Source :
Help link :
```

```
Data : System.Collections.ListDictionaryInternal
TargetSite :
Stack Trace : The stack trace is unavailable.
Additional Info:

MachineName : MyMachine
TimeStamp : 5/1/2007 4:59:30 PM
FullName : Microsoft.Practices.EnterpriseLibrary.ExceptionHandling,
Version=2.0.0.0, Culture=neutral, PublicKeyToken=b77a5c561934e089
AppDomainName :  ExceptionSample.exe
WindowsIdentity : domain\user
        Inner Exception
        ----------------
        Type : System.Data.DataExecption, System.Data,
Version=2.0.0.0, Culture=neutral, PublicKeyToken=b77a5c561934e089
        Message : Generated DataException
        Source : ExceptionSample
        Help Link :
        Data : System.Collections.ListDictionaryInternal
        TargetSite : void MyHandleMethod()
        Stack Trace :    at DSMEL.Sample.Program.MyHandledMethod()
in C:\Users\user\Documents\Visual Studio 2005\Projects\ExceptionSample
\Program.cs:line 23
```

## Replacing Exceptions

Using the replace exception handler is similar to using the wrap exception handler. For this example, we will replace a NullReferenceException with an Exception type.

Open the application configuration file for the sample project you have been working with and add the NullReferenceException type to the MyPolicy exception policy. Next, add a replace handler for the policy and select the System.Exception type as the replacement exception. Put in a message associated with the exception, and then add a logging handler so that you may see the output in the Event Viewer. The configured replace exception handler should look something like Figure 8-19.

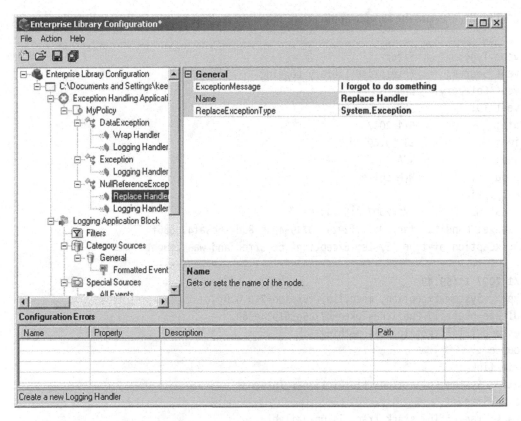

**Figure 8-19.** *Replace handler properties*

The next task is to modify the source code to throw the NullReferenceException. Listing 8-6 shows the necessary change.

**Listing 8-6.** *Changing MyHandleMethod to Throw NullReferenceException*

```
public void MyHandledMethod()
{
   try
   {
      throw new NullReference("Generated NullReferenceException");
   }
   catch(Exception ex)
   {
      ExceptionPolicy.HandleException(ex, MYPOLICY);
   }
}
```

Finally, execute the sample application. The output should look similar to the following.

```
Event Type:        Error
Event Source:      Enterprise Library Logging
Event Category:    None
Event ID:          100
Date:              5/1/2007
Time:              11:59:49 AM
User:              N/A
Computer:          MyMachine
Description:
TimeStamp:         5/1/2007 4:59:49 PM
Message: HandleInstandID: fff29295-0749-493b-8dd4-6b5af420686f
An exception of type 'System.Exception' occurred and was caught
--------------------------------------------------------------
5/1/2007 11:59:49
Type : System.Exception, mscorlib, version=2.0.0.0,
Culture=neutral, PublicKeyToken=b77a5c561934e089
Message : I forgot to do something
Source :
Help link :
Data : System.Collections.ListDictionaryInternal
TargetSite :
Stack Trace : The stack trace is unavailable.
Additional Info:

MachineName : MyMachine
TimeStamp : 5/1/2007 4:59:49 PM
FullName : Microsoft.Practices.EnterpriseLibrary.ExceptionHandling,
Version=2.0.0.0, Culture=neutral, PublicKeyToken=null
AppDomainName :  ExceptionSample.exe
WindowsIdentity : domain\user

Category: General
Priority: 0
EventId: 100
Severity: Error
Title:Enterprise Library Exception Handling
Machine: MyMachine
App Domain: ExceptionSample.exe
ProcessId: 4644
Process Name: C:\Users\user\Documents\Visual Studio 2005\Projects\
ExceptionSample\bin\Debug\ExceptionSample.exe
Thread Name:
Win32 ThreadId:3968
```

Notice that in the logged output there is no reference to the original NullReferenceException that was raised.

## Handling Exceptions in a WCF Service

Unexpected exceptions that are thrown inside a WCF service should be logged and properly handled by the client making the call to the WCF service. Implementing this process requires adding an ExceptionShielding attribute to the service implementation or contract, and configuring a Fault Contract exception handler.

The first step is to set the includeExceptionDetailsInFaults attribute to false in the WCF configuration <serviceDebug> node. This ensures that only the information you want to leave the WCF service boundary is allowed to do so. Next, add the FaultContract attribute to the service implementation or contract. Then add the Exception Handling Application Block's ExceptionShielding attribute to the service implementation and specify the exception policy that should be used. An example of what this might look like is shown in Listing 8-7.

**Listing 8-7.** *Using the ExceptionShielding Attribute*

```
Using Microsoft.Practices.EnterpriseLibrary.ExceptionHandling.WCF;

[ServiceContract]
public interface IMyService
{
    [OperationContract]
    [FaultContract(typeof(MyFaultContracts.UnavailableFault))]
    MyResponseType GetData(MyRequestType request);
}

[ExceptionShielding("MyWCFServicePolicy")]
public class MyService : IMyService
{
    public MyResponseType GetData(MyRequestType request)
    {
        // Implementation code here...
    }
}
```

Finally, configure the Fault Contract Exception Handler for the exception policy that is specified in the ExceptionShielding attribute. To do this, make sure that you have the exception policy created in the Configuration Console, select the exception type that you want to handle, and then select the Fault Contract Exception Handler.

Along with the ExceptionMessage property, the properties grid lists two other properties:

FaultContractType: The FaultContractType property needs to point to the Fault Contract that you want to use to pass the exception metadata to the calling client.

PropertyMappings: By default, the Fault Contract exception handler will try to map the properties of an exception to the properties of the Fault Contract. It does this by matching the property name and type. Alternatively, you can specify the mappings by clicking the PropertyMappings ellipse button and selecting the name of the Fault Contract property and the source name of the exception property. This also allows you to override the default exception property to Fault Contract property mappings. Additionally, you can prevent properties from being mapped by adding a Fault Contract property name and leaving the source empty.

---

**Note** The WCF features of the Exception Handling Application Block follow the Exception Shielding pattern. You can find more information about this pattern at http://msdn2.microsoft.com/en-us/library/aa480591.aspx.

---

## Configuring Exception Posthandling Events

For each exception type's PostHandlingAction property, you can configure one of three actions in the application's configuration file, as mentioned earlier in this chapter: NotifyRethrow, ThrowNewException, or None. By default, the NotifyRethrow value is selected for the PostHandlingAction property.

Implementing NotifyRethrow is pretty simple. Just add an if statement that conditionally throws the exception if the HandleException method of the ExceptionPolicy class returns true. An example of this is shown in Listing 8-8.

**Listing 8-8.** *Throwing Exceptions*

```
namespace DGMEL.Sample
{
    class Program
    {
        private const string MYPOLICY = "MyPolicy";

        static void Main(string[] args)
        {
            Program myProgram = new Program();
            myProgram.MyHandledMethod();
        }

        public void MyHandledMethod()
        {
            try
            {
                throw new NullReferenceException("Generated NullReferenceException");
            }
            catch(Exception ex)
            {
                If(ExceptionPolicy.HandleException(e, MYPOLICY)) throw;
            }
        }
    }
}
```

If you run the code in Listing 8-8, the console output will be as shown in Figure 8-20.

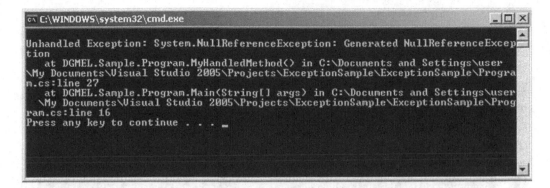

**Figure 8-20.** *NotifyRethrow throws the original exception to the console window*

However, if you change the `PostHandlingAction` property value to `ThrowNewException`, as shown in Figure 8-21, when you execute the sample application with the code from Listing 8-8, the output will be as shown in Figure 8-22. Since a replace handler is defined and the `PostHandlingAction` property is set to `ThrowNewException`, the exception defined in the replace handler will be thrown instead of the original exception.

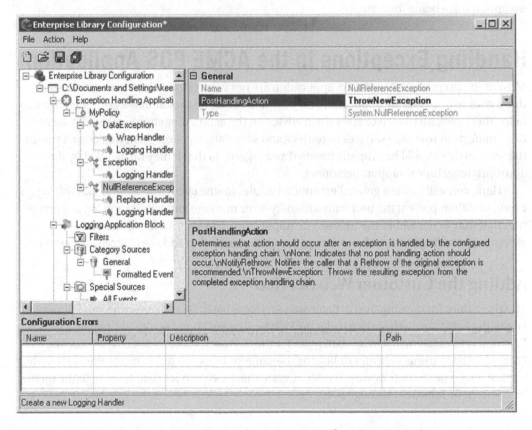

**Figure 8-21.** *Setting the PostingHandlingAction property to ThrowNewException*

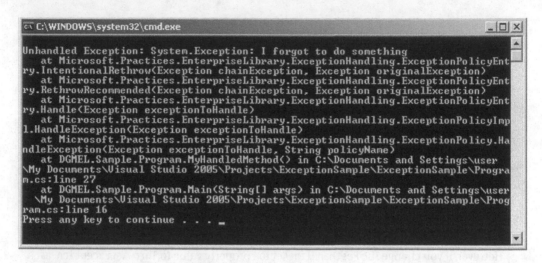

**Figure 8-22.** *Console output with ThrowNewException setting*

Selecting the value None for the PostHandlingAction property will just return a value of false to the ExceptionPolicy's HandleException method, which then can be used to prevent the exception from being thrown.

# Handling Exceptions in the ACME POS Application

Most of the users of the ACME POS application are not very technically oriented. So if something goes wrong with the application, they need to see an understandable error message that helps them seek assistance or gives them advice on the action they should take. Also, since this application uses web services to retrieve and save data, any exception that occurs within the web service should be properly handled and logged, so that it may be handled by the appropriate technical support personnel.

Here, you will create a general exception handler for the client application that will log an event, and then present the user with a friendly error message and handle and log any exception that may occur within the web service application. However, before you add the exception handling to the web service application, you need to add the Customer web service.

## Adding the Customer Web Service

The procedure for creating the Customer web service is basically the same one you followed to create the GetStates web service using the Web Service Software Factory in Chapter 7. The first step is to create web service data types for the Customer, Address, BillingMethod, and PaymentMethod business entities (following the same steps as you did to create the State web service data type in the previous chapter). Create these web service data types with the members shown in Tables 8-1 through 8-4.

**Table 8-1.** *Address Web Service Data Type Members*

| Member | Type |
| --- | --- |
| AddressId | System.Int32 |
| CustomerId | System.Int32 |
| StreetAddress | System.String |
| City | System.String |
| State | System.String |
| ZipCode | System.String |
| IsPrimaryShipping | System.Boolean |
| IsActive | System.Boolean |

**Table 8-2.** *PaymentMethod Web Service Data Type Members*

| Member | Type |
| --- | --- |
| PaymentMethodId | System.Int32 |
| Name | System.String |

**Table 8-3.** *BillingMethod Web Service Data Type Members*

| Member | Type |
| --- | --- |
| BillingMethodId | System.Int32 |
| CustomerId | System.Int32 |
| PaymentMethodId | System.Int32 |
| CreditCardNumber | System.String |
| CreditCardExpiration | System.DateTime |
| CreditCardBillingAddressId | System.Int32 |
| NetTermDays | System.Int32 |
| IsActive | System.Boolean |

**Table 8-4.** *Customer Web Service Data Type Members*

| Member | Type |
| --- | --- |
| CustomerId | System.Int32 |
| FirstName | System.String |
| LastName | System.String |
| MemberSince | System.DateTime |
| BirthDate | System.DateTime |
| Addresses | ACME.POS.Service.DataTypes.Address[] |
| BillingMethods | ACME.POS.Service.DataTypes.BillingMethod[] |
| IsModified | System.Boolean |
| IsActive | System.Boolean |

After you've created the Customer, Address, BillingMethod, and PaymentMethod web service data types, you need to create the service contract and the service contract translator classes. As you did in Chapter 7, create a service contract interface for the customer retrieve and save operations. Name this new service contract interface Customer and give it two actions (methods):

- GetCustomerList, with a response type of ACME.POS.Service.DataTypes.Customer[]

- SaveCustomer, with a request and response type of ACME.POS.Service.DataTypes. Customer

Also remember to check the Generate Service Contract Implementation check box in the last dialog box of the Service Contract Implementation wizard. The service contract implementation should look like Listing 8-9.

**Listing 8-9.** *Customer Service Contract Implementation*

```
using System;
using System.Collections.Generic;
using System.Text;

namespace ACME.POS.Service.ServiceImplementation
{
    [System.Web.Services.WebService(Namespace =
        "http://ACME.POS.Service.ServiceContracts/2007/06",
        Name = "Customer")]
    [System.Web.Services.WebServiceBindingAttribute(
        ConformsTo = System.Web.Services.WsiProfiles.BasicProfile1_1,
        EmitConformanceClaims = true)]
    public class Customer :
        ACME.POS.Service.ServiceContracts.ICustomer
    {

    #region ICustomer Members

    public ACME.POS.Service.DataTypes.Customer[] GetCustomerList()
    {
        throw new Exception("The method or operation
            is not implemented.");
    }

    public ACME.POS.Service.DataTypes.Customer
        SaveCustomer(ACME.POS.Service.DataTypes.Customer
        SaveCustomerRequest)
    {
        throw new Exception("The method or operation
            is not implemented.");
    }

    #endregion
    }
}
```

# Handling Web Service Exceptions

Both the GetCustomerList and SaveCustomer methods of the service implementation Customer class will have unimplemented exceptions created by the Web Service Software Factory. In these methods of the service implementation Customer class, add try-catch blocks and handle any exceptions that may occur with the Exception Handling Application Block. Here's the procedure:

1. For the ACME.POS.Service.ServiceImplementation project, add assembly references to the Exception Handling Application Block, the Exception Handling Application Block Logging Provider, and the Enterprise Library Common assembly.

2. Add a using statement for Microsoft.Practices.EnterpriseLibrary. ExceptionHandling to the Customer class.

3. Wrap the unimplemented exceptions with a try block, and then add a catch block and implement the ExceptionPolicy class's HandleException method for both the GetCustomerList and SaveCustomer methods. Name the exception policy ACMEServiceExceptionPolicy, and add a return statement. Listing 8-10 shows the modifications for the GetCustomerList method.

**Listing 8-10.** *Handling Exceptions for the GetCustomerList Method*

```
public ACME.POS.Service.DataTypes.Customer[] GetCustomerList()
{
    try
    {
        throw new Exception("The method or operation
            is not implemented.");
    }
    catch (Exception ex)
    {
        if(ExceptionPolicy.HandleException(
            ex, "ACMEServiceExceptionPolicy")) throw;
    }

    return null;
}
```

Now you must expose the Customer service implementation in the ACME.POS.Service.Host project, in the same way you exposed the GetStates service implementation in Chapter 7.

# Configuring the Exception Handling Application Block

The next task is to configure the Exception Handling Policy for the ACME POS web service, as follows:

1. Open the web.config file of the ACME.POS.Service.Host project, either via the Configuration Console or the Configuration Editor add-in for Visual Studio 2005.

2. Add the Exception Handling Application Block by right-clicking the Configuration File node and selecting New ➤ Exception Handling Application Block.

3. Right-click the Exception Handling Application Block node and select New ➤ Exception Policy.

4. Set the Name property of the exception policy to ACMEServiceExceptionPolicy.

5. Right-click ACMEServiceExceptionPolicy and select New ➤ Exception Type. Select Exception as the type. Note that the PostHandlingAction property defaults to NotifyRethrow, and you can leave this setting.

6. Right-click the Exception node and select New ➤ Logging Handler. A new Logging Handler node will be added, as well as the Logging Application Block. Leave the defaults for the Logging Application Block for now; you will modify them in the next chapter.

7. In the logging handler's properties grid, select the TextExceptionFormatter for the FormatterType property and the General category for the LogCategory property, as shown in Figure 8-23.

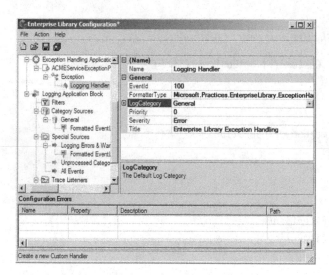

**Figure 8-23.** *Configuring exception handling for the ACME POS web service*

## Handling Client-Side Exceptions

Handling exceptions for the ACME POS client is very much like handling exceptions for the ACME POS web service. Here's the procedure:

1. For the ACME.POS.Client.Service project, add assembly references to the Exception Handling Application Block, the Exception Handling Application Block Logging Provider, and the Enterprise Library Common assembly.

2. Add the following using statement at the top of the Program class (Program.cs) of the ACME.POS.Client.Service project.

```
using Microsoft.Practices.EnterpriseLibrary.ExceptionHandling;
```

3. Add a try-catch block in the Main method of the Program class in the ACME.POS.Client.Service project and implement the UnHandledException method of the CurrentDomain object. Listing 8-11 shows the Program.cs file, with the added code in bold.

**Listing 8-11.** *Program.cs File*

```
using System;
using System.Collections.Generic;
using System.Windows.Forms;
using Microsoft.Practices.EnterpriseLibrary.ExceptionHandling;

namespace ACME.POS.Service.Client
{
    static class Program
    {
        /// <summary>
        /// The main entry point for the application.
        /// </summary>
        [STAThread]
        static void Main()
        {
            Application.EnableVisualStyles();
            Application.SetCompatibleTextRenderingDefault(false);
            AppDomain.CurrentDomain.UnhandledException += new
                UnhandledExceptionEventHandler(
                CurrentDomain_UnhandledException);

            try
            {
                Application.Run(new MainForm());
            }
            catch (Exception ex)
            {
                ExceptionPolicy.HandleException(ex,
                    "ACMEClientExceptionPolicy");

                DisplayExceptionMessage();
            }
            finally
            {
                Application.Exit();
            }
```

```
        }

        static void CurrentDomain_UnhandledException(object sender,
                UnhandledExceptionEventArgs e)
        {
            ExceptionPolicy.HandleException(
                (Exception)e.ExceptionObject,
                "ACMEClientExceptionPolicy");

            DisplayExceptionMessage();

            if(!e.IsTerminating)
                Application.Exit();
        }

        static void DisplayExceptionMessage()
        {
            MessageBox.Show("An unexpected problem has occurred "
                + "with the ACME POS application.\n "
                + "This application will now close down. "
                + "Any unsaved data may be lost."
                , "Unexpected Problem", MessageBoxButtons.OK,
                MessageBoxIcon.Error);
        }
    }
}
```

Finally, create the exception policy in the ACME.POS.Service.Client application configuration file. This exception policy will be just like the ACME POS web service ACMEServiceExceptionPolicy you created earlier, but with a different name.

1. Add the Exception Handling Block to the application file.

2. Add a new exception policy and name this policy ACMEClientExceptionPolicy.

3. Give it one exception type of System.Exception and one logging handler for the System.Exception type.

4. Set the exception formatter to TextExceptionFormatter and the logging category to General. You can use the default settings for everything else.

And that completes the creation of the exception handler for the Acme POS application.

# Summary

Exception handling can be one of the most critical components of an application. It is bad enough when something goes wrong within an application, but presenting the wrong information to the user and not logging the exception can make things worse. The next chapter will address logging information within an application. This applies to both logging tracing information and, as introduced in this chapter, logging exceptions.

# CHAPTER 9
■ ■ ■
# The Logging Application Block

**A**pplications generate logs to keep track of their health, to assist in debugging, and for auditing purposes. Logging makes applications more supportable by giving developers a standardized method for recording application information. The Logging Application Block is designed to support flexible and robust logging configurations.

The Logging Application Block originated as a stand-alone product. At that time, the original Exception Management Application block was tightly coupled to it. When it became part of the previous version of the Enterprise Library, the name was changed to the Logging and Instrumentation Application Block. In that incarnation, every effort was made to remove the dependencies between the application blocks where possible. In Enterprise Library 2.0, the application block's name changed once again, since instrumentation is now part of the core of the Enterprise Library. The Logging.Instrumentation namespace builds on the new core instrumentation components. The main difference is that the entire Logging Application Block no longer needs to be used in order for other blocks to be instrumented.

In this chapter, you'll learn about the design of the Logging Application Block and how to use it.

## Types of Logging

Instrumentation is logging that is performed for health tracking. This must be low impact, because the process of instrumentation alters the results of what it is measuring. If a logging call takes 3 milliseconds and it is measuring a process that takes only 5 milliseconds, the deviation of the final reading is approximately 38 percent. Another way to put this is that instead of measuring the true processing time of 5 milliseconds, you will measure 8 milliseconds. Of course, it will not significantly change the duration of a single transaction, but if the measurement is of the duration of 10,000 transactions, the logging then becomes part of the measurement. In this case, 30 seconds would be devoted to logging, while the actual transactions took 50 seconds.

Logging for tracing and debugging includes what was happening at a particular point in the application, and what was the state at the time. This type of logging can record any number of things, but most of them are less critical and provide more information than what goes into instrumentation. For example, records that have been rejected because they lack sufficient data to be processed may be logged to an external source, where they can be reviewed at a later time.

Many companies require audit logging, especially for applications that require history records (or audit trails) of operations performed on sensitive information. This type of logging tends to contain larger amounts of information. In some cases, it may include entire database records. If the auditing is for security purposes, it tends to capture previous and current state as well as who made the change.

The Logging Application Block can help you implement each of these types of logging.

# Understanding the Design of the Logging Application Block

Many considerations went into the design of the Logging Application Block. These included performance, making the routing of messages flexible, and making it easily configurable after an application has been compiled and delivered.

One of the main goals was to effectively use the System.Diagnostics namespace. The classes within this namespace provide access to the system processes, event logs, and performance counters. The Microsoft patterns & practices team wanted to ensure that the use of this namespace would be through a thin wrapper that would not impede performance.

The Logging Application Block has probably the greatest need to be configurable out of all the application blocks. When an issue arises with an application that is not replicable in a development environment, developers need to be able to turn on extra logging in a production environment without distributing new code.

As with all of the blocks, the Logging Application Block has the goals of reducing work for the developer, being extensible, and not impeding performance. This latter goal is especially important, because logging increases the amount of I/O that an application must perform.

The design has also been simplified by doing away with the distribution strategies that were used in the earlier version of the application block, which supported asynchronous logging by means of technologies such as Microsoft Message Queuing (MSMQ). This functionality is now supported by the MSMQ trace listener.

Figure 9-1 shows the class diagram for the Logging Application Block. The following sections describe each of its major components.

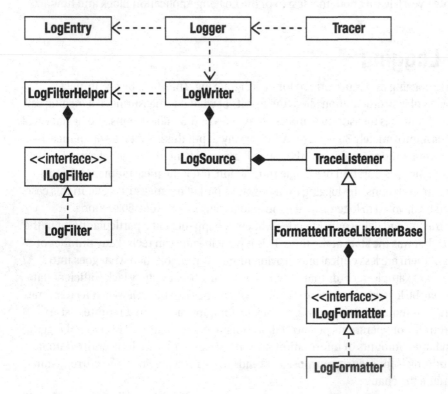

**Figure 9-1.** *Logging Application Block class diagram*

# Log Entries

The LogEntry class is the basic unit for logging information. While it is not necessary to use this class because of the overloads on the Write method of the Logger class, it is the preferred method for organizing logging data. This class inherits from the ICloneable interface so that it may clone itself. Figure 9-2 shows just the public methods. The public properties are described in Table 9-1 with a brief description of each property

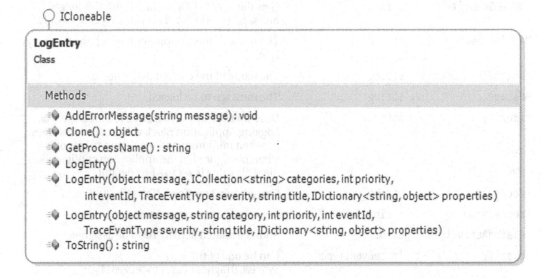

**Figure 9-2.** *LogEntry class public members*

**Table 9-1.** *LogEntry Properties*

| Property | Type | Description |
|---|---|---|
| ActivityId | Guid | Stores a trace activity ID. When this class is constructed and tracing is enabled, a tracing activity will be assigned to this property for you; otherwise, it will be an empty Guid. |
| ActivityIdString | string | A string representation of the ActivityId. This property is read-only. |
| AppDomainName | string | The name of the current AppDomain that is running. |
| Categories | ICollection<string> | A generic ICollection of categories that are used to route the message to one or more trace listeners. |
| CategoriesStrings | string[] | A string array of categories that are used to route the message to one or more trace listeners. This property is read-only. |
| ErrorMessages | string | Gets any error messages that were added to the LogEntry via the AddErrorMessage method. |
| EventId | int | Allows an event ID to be associated with the logged message. The default is 0. |

*Continued*

**Table 9-1.** *Continued*

| Property | Type | Description |
|---|---|---|
| ExtendedProperties | | A generic IDictionary collection of name-value pairs of extended information that is not predefined in the LogEntry class. Domain-specific information would be a prime candidate for this property. |
| LoggedSeverity | string | Gets the Severity associated with this logged message as a string. This property is read-only. |
| MachineName | string | The name of the computer on which the log entry is made. |
| ManagedThreadName | string | The name of the current .NET thread. |
| Message | string | The message to be logged. |
| Priority | int | Describes the importance of a log message. The Logging Application Block will process messages between minimum and maximum values only when configured in the application configuration file. This value is set to –1 by default. |
| ProcessId | string | Current Win32 process ID. |
| ProcessName | string | Name of the current process. |
| RelatedActivityId | Guid? | Allows a related activity ID to be assigned. |
| Severity | TraceEventType | Can be one of the System.Diagnostics.TraceEventType enumerators. The default for this value is Information. |
| TimeStamp | DateTime | Date and time of when the message was logged in UTC. The default is the current UTC date and time. |
| TimeStampString | string | A string representation TimeStamp property. This property is read-only. |
| Title | string | A title for the logged error message. This property can be used as an extra descriptor for the logged error message. |
| Win32ThreadId | string | The Win32 thread ID. |

A LogEntry instance has a number of properties that are set automatically by the Logging Application Block. These include the process ID, process name, and thread ID. Your application will then need to set properties for the message, title, priority, severity, and event ID. These properties can be set by using one of the constructors for the LogEntry class, as shown in Figure 9-2.

Additional information can be set on the log entry via the `ExtendedProperties` property. This is a set of key-value pairs implemented as an `IDictionary` generic class.

One of the main changes in the `LogEntry` class between versions 1.*x* and 2.*x* of the Logging Application Block is that it can now belong to multiple categories. This allows more flexibility in filtering and routing of the entry.

The following are three other implemented methods:

- `ToString`: This method is overridden and provides a string representation of the `LogEntry` class using the default `TextFormatter`.

- `AddErrorMessage`: This method allows error or warning messages to be added to the logged error message. The `AddErrorMessage` method can be called multiple times as the messages are concatenated and separated by a new line.

- `GetProcessName`: This static method is used to get the process name for the `LogEntry` class and typically shouldn't be used directly by the developer.

---

**Note**  To support XML, the Logging Application Block includes the `XmlLogEntry` class, which inherits from the `LogEntry` class and provides the necessary implementation to support the logging of XML messages.

---

## Logging Façade

The Logging Application Block has been simplified for the developer by using the Façade pattern. This is implemented in the `Logger` class, which hides the implementation class, `LogWriter`, required to perform all the heavy lifting.

The main method of the logging façade is the `Write` method, which has 19 overloads, as shown in Figure 9-3. These overrides allow you to create log entries in various ways, with as little as an object containing a message or as many as seven parameters, which supply most of the capabilities of the `LogEntry` class. Behind the scenes, the `Logger` class creates a new `LogEntry` instance from these parameters and uses that to call the hidden `LogWriter` instance. The only exception to this is that one of the overloaded methods takes a parameter of a `LogEntry` instance. In this case, the passed-in `LogEntry` instance is used.

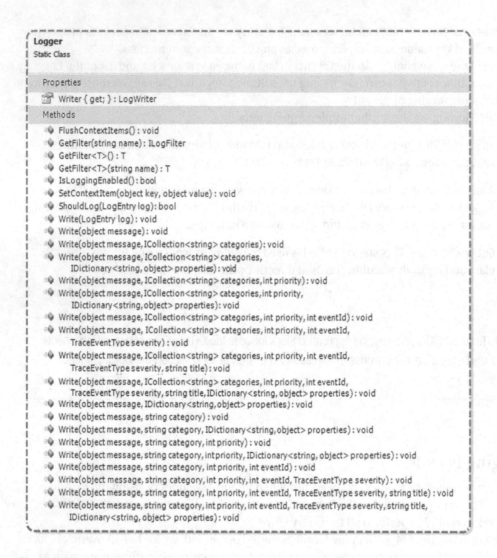

**Figure 9-3.** *Logger class public members*

Generally speaking, you should not need to use the `LogWriter` class directly, as the `Logger` class provides all the functionality for log messages.

A couple methods that are part of the `Logger` class are worth mentioning because they help simplify the logging of messages: `IsLoggingEnabled` indicates if logging is even enabled, and `ShouldLog` takes an instance of the `LogEntry` class and determines whether it should be logged based on the parameters set in the application configuration file.

## Logging Source

In order for the Logging Application Block to do its job, a method of routing logging requests is needed. This is handled by using the collection of listeners contained within the `LogSource` class. These are classes whose names map directly to categories and are held in a collection within the `LogWriter` class. That collection is defined from the source definition in the application configuration file.

Three standard LogSource objects are always contained within the collection: AllEventsLogSource, ErrorsLogSource, and NotProcessedLogSource. The order of precedence for these sources is that if the all events log source is configured, the log entry will be sent to this log source. If it has not been configured, then responsibility falls to the not processed log source, but only if none of the categories specified in the LogEntry have been configured. The trace listener defined for the errors log source category will be used only if none of the previously mentioned criteria are fulfilled, and the LogWarningsWhenNoCategoryMatch property of the Logging Application Block is set to true.

The property for the LogSource collection is marked as internal and therefore can be accessed directly only from within Logging Application Block.

## Trace Listeners

Trace listeners inherit from System.Diagnostics.TraceListener. They replace the event sinks that were used in earlier versions of the application block. The Logging Application Block listeners provide an implementation for this abstract base class, which uses formatters to write the LogEntry information. When a LogEntry instance is received by the LogSource instance, it sends the entry to each listener associated with that LogSource instance.

The trace listeners that ship with the Logging Application Block cover email, text files, database tables, event logs, WMI, and MSMQ as destinations. There is also an abstract CustomTraceListener for creating custom trace listeners.

Three of the listeners can use the same <system.diagnostics> configuration settings to build log entry information without receiving an actual LogEntry object: FormattedEventLogTraceListener, FlatFileTraceListener, and WmiTraceListener.

The configuration data for the Logging Application Block trace listeners is located in the <listeners> section of the configuration file. This is because many of the listeners need more information than what is provided in the <system.diagnostic> configuration section definition.

## Log Filters

The filters that are included with the block allow an application to ignore events based on their category before they are delivered to the trace listeners. The application block also allows for the creation of custom filters with more complex criteria.

A new feature of this application block is the ability to query filters from within an application's code. By doing so, you can determine if an event should be logged or ignored. This feature was added to help improve performance. The idea is that if it can be determined that an event will not be logged before it is created, the system can save the cycles of putting the message through the application block.

The CategoryFilter, PriorityFilter, and LogEnabledFilter classes are packaged as part of the application block. These three filters will handle 95 percent of situations requiring filters.

## Log Formatters

Log formatters are used by trace listeners that inherit from the FormattedTraceListenerBase class. When a LogEntry instance is passed to these listeners, they call the formatters to determine the way the message data is organized.

Two standard formatters ship as part of the code base:

- TextFormatter: This formatter uses a template built from tokens in order to determine what its output string should look like. It also allows for only certain properties of a LogEntry instance to be written to the log.

- BinaryLogFormatter: If a LogEntry instance is sent to the BinaryLogFormatter, it is serialized to a binary representation. This formatter is derived from the .NET Framework BinaryFormatter class.

## Tracers

The Tracer class, which has a design similar to that of the Logger class, is used for performance logging. It helps to track the entry and exit of a method, and its duration. No methods are called when using this class. What information is logged is determined by the lifetime of the object.

The log entries generated by the Tracer class belong to the operation and catchall categories. Therefore, these categories must contain listeners to log this entry type.

# Using the Logging Application Block

Now that you know about the basic components of the Logging Application Block, let's see how to use it within an application. We'll look at standard usage, configuration, and customization.

## Adding the Logging Application Block to an Application

For the upcoming examples, you need to create and configure an application that will use the Logging Application Block. Follow these steps:

1. Create a new C# Windows project for your application and add the following references to it:

   - System.Configuration

   - Microsoft.Practices.EnterpriseLibrary.Logging.dll

   - Microsoft.Practices.EnterpriseLibrary.Common.dll

   - Microsoft.Practices.EnterpriseLibrary.Logging.Database.dll (used for the FormattedDatabaseTraceListener)

2. In the default Form class, add the following using clauses:

   ```
   using Microsoft.Practices.EnterpriseLibrary.Common.Configuration;
   using Microsoft.Practices.EnterpriseLibrary.Logging;
   using Microsoft.Practices.EnterpriseLibrary.Logging.Filters;
   using System.Diagnostics;
   ```

3. Add an app.config file (right-click the project, select Add ➤ New Item, and then select Application Configuration File from the Add New Item dialog box).

4. Open the Enterprise Library Configuration Console and add the Logging Application Block (using the Action ➤ New menu item or the context menu of the app.config file in the Explorer pane). The application block should appear in the Configuration Console as shown in Figure 9-4.

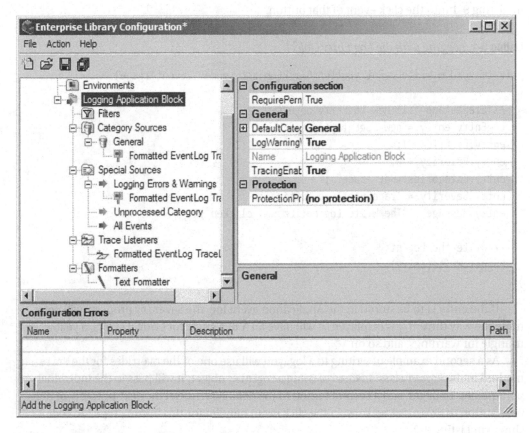

**Figure 9-4.** *Newly added Logging Application Block*

5. Execute the logging database script. This script is in the LoggingDatabase.sql file, located in the [src]Logging\TraceListeners\Database\Scripts directory of the Enterprise Library installation directory. To execute the script, run the CreateLoggingDb.cmd file. The script will create a database called Logging with three tables: Category, CategoryLog, and Log. It will also create four stored procedures. This database may not fit the needs of all applications, but it gives a starting point for development.

---

■**Note** If your SQL Server database instance is called something other than SQLEXPRESS, you will need to modify the command being executed within the CreateLoggingDb.cmd file and specify the proper SQL Server location and instance.

---

## Using the Logger Class

The Logger class is the main interface between your application and the Logging Application Block. As mentioned earlier in the chapter, the Write method has many overrides. Here, you'll use the LogEntry parameter and Write method that takes the event ID, priority, categories, and message as parameters.

The first demonstration will show how to populate a LogEntry object and write it. Add a button to the default form and set the Text property to Write Log Entry. Type the code shown in Listing 9-1 into the click event of that button.

**Listing 9-1.** *Logging with the Log Entry Object*

```
private void m_WriteLogEntryButton_Click(object sender, EventArgs e)
{
    // Create and fill new LogEntry object
    LogEntry entry = new LogEntry();
    entry.EventId = 1;
    entry.Priority = 0;
    entry.Categories.Add("Trace");
    entry.Severity = TraceEventType.Critical;
    entry.Message = "The Write Log button was clicked";

    // Write the LogEntry
    Logger.Write(entry);
}
```

If the entry is to be stored in the Application event log, the Severity property will determine the way the entry is displayed. It will have an *X* in a circle for critical errors, a yellow triangle for warnings, and so on.

As a second example of writing to a log, you will use one of the overrides for the Write method in the Logger class. Instead of using a LogEntry object, it will pass in the individual parameters. To begin, add a second button to the default form. Set the Text property of the new button to Write Parameters. In the click event handler for this button, type the code shown in Listing 9-2.

**Listing 9-2.** *Logging by Parameters*

```
private void m_WriteParametersButton_Click(object sender, EventArgs e)
{
    // Write to the log by specifying the EventId, Priority, Categories
    // and Message
    Logger.Write("The Write Parameters button was clicked", "Debug", -1, 2);
}
```

A third option gives an application the ability to add information beyond the standard properties. This is accomplished by using a property of the LogEntry class called ExtendedProperties. Here, you will populate the name value list of this property. Later in the chapter, you will see how to write these values using formatters. Add a CheckBox control to the Windows form and name it m_LogExtendedProp. Then modify the code in Listing 9-1, to check if the check box is checked, and if it is, add the extended property, as shown in Listing 9-3.

**Listing 9-3.** *Logging Using Extended Properties*

```
private void m_WriteLogEntryButton_Click(object sender, EventArgs e)
{
    // Create and fill new LogEntry object
    LogEntry entry = new LogEntry();
    entry.EventId = 1;
    entry.Priority = 0;
    entry.Categories.Add("Trace");
    entry.Severity = TraceEventType.Critical;
    entry.Message = "This is a test message";


    // Add extended properties to the LogEntry, if checked
    if (m_LogExtendedProp.Checked)
    {
        entry.ExtendedProperties.Add("AuditTrackingCode", 1000);
    }

    // Write the LogEntry
    Logger.Write(entry);
}
```

## Using the Tracer Class

The Tracer class has a simple usage model. By utilizing the using clause, trace information can be generated automatically for a series of operations. When executing a trace, the first parameter is a string identified as operation. This is actually the logging category.

Add a new button to the project form, set its Text property to Trace Click, and name it m_TraceButton. Write the code shown in Listing 9-4 into the click event handler for the button.

**Listing 9-4.** *Using Tracer*

```
private void m_TraceButton_Click(object sender, EventArgs e)
{
    using (new Tracer("TraceButton Trace Events"))
    {

        // Execute the button click event code

    }
}
```

The resulting output if the .NET Framework XmlWriterTraceListener is used would look like Listing 9-5.

**Listing 9-5.** *XmlWriterTraceListener Output*

```
<E2ETraceEvent xmlns="http://schemas.microsoft.com/2004/06/E2ETraceEvent">
  <System xmlns="http://schemas.microsoft.com/2004/06/windows/eventlog/system">
    <EventID>1</EventID>
    <Type>3</Type>
    <SubType Name="Start">0</SubType>
    <Level>255</Level>
    <TimeCreated SystemTime="2006-02-22T05:07:10.2302736Z" />
    <Source Name="ButtonClickTrace" />
    <Correlation ActivityID="{34f8df31-5858-486d-af01-02e173091fa7}" />
    <Execution ProcessName="LoggingDemo.vshost" ProcessID="5112" ThreadID="10" />
    <Channel/>
    <Computer>MyComputer</Computer>
  </System>
  <ApplicationData>
    <TraceData>
      <DataItem>Timestamp: 2/22/2006 5:07:10 AM&#xD;&#xA;Message:
Start Trace: Activity &apos;34f8df31-5858-486d-af01-02e173091fa7&apos;
in method &apos;traceButton_Click&apos; at 1458632339475 ticks&#xD;&#xA;
Category: ButtonClickTrace&#xD;&#xA;Priority: 5&#xD;&#xA;EventId: 1&#xD;&#xA;
Severity: Start&#xD;&#xA;Title:TracerEnter&#xD;&#xA;Machine: My Computer&#xD;&#xA;
App Domain: LoggingDemo.vshost.exe&#xD;&#xA; ProcessId: 5112&#xD;&#xA;
Process Name: C:\Vs2005Projects\LoggingDemo\LoggingDemo\bin\Debug\
LoggingDemo.vshost.exe&#xD;&#xA;Thread Name: &#xD;&#xA;Win32
ThreadId:4652&#xD;&#xA;Extended Properties: </DataItem>
    </TraceData>
  </ApplicationData>
</E2ETraceEvent>
<E2ETraceEvent xmlns="http://schemas.microsoft.com/2004/06/E2ETraceEvent">
  <System xmlns="http://schemas.microsoft.com/2004/06/windows/eventlog/system">
    <EventID>1</EventID>
    <Type>3</Type>
    <SubType Name="Stop">0</SubType>
    <Level>255</Level>
    <TimeCreated SystemTime="2006-02-22T05:07:10.2302736Z" />
    <Source Name="ButtonClickTrace" />
    <Correlation ActivityID="{34f8df31-5858-486d-af01-02e173091fa7}" />
    <Execution ProcessName="LoggingDemo.vshost" ProcessID="5112" ThreadID="10" />
    <Channel/>
    <Computer>MyComputer</Computer>
  </System>
  <ApplicationData>
    <TraceData>
      <DataItem>Timestamp: 2/22/2006 5:07:10 AM&#xD;&#xA;Message:
End Trace: Activity &apos;34f8df31-5858-486d-af01-02e173091fa7&apos;
in method &apos;traceButton_Click&apos; at 1458633023799 ticks
(elapsed time: 0.191 seconds)&#xD;&#xA;Category: ButtonClickTrace&#xD;&#xA;
```

```
Priority: 5&#xD;&#xA;EventId: 1&#xD;&#xA;Severity: Stop&#xD;&#xA;Title:
TracerExit&#xD;&#xA;Machine: My Computer&#xD;&#xA; App Domain:
LoggingDemo.vshost.exe&#xD;&#xA;ProcessId: 5112&#xD;&#xA; Process Name:
C:\Vs2005Projects\LoggingDemo\LoggingDemo\bin\Debug\LoggingDemo.vshost.exe
&#xD;&#xA;Thread Name: &#xD;&#xA;Win32 ThreadId:4652&#xD;&#xA;
Extended Properties: </DataItem>
    </TraceData>
  </ApplicationData>
</E2ETraceEvent>
```

■**Note** Notice that the `Correlation ActivityId` for both entries match. Also, the message title within the `DataItem` element identifies the entry as the start or end of the trace.

An alternative to this basic usage of the `Tracer` class is to supply all of the parameters that normally define a log entry. This approach uses the constructor that takes four parameters:

- As with the previous example, the first parameter is the category to which the trace message should be logged.

- The second parameter is the `activityId`, which accepts a `Guid` data type.

- The third parameter is an instance of a `LogWriter`, which is covered in the next section.

- The last parameter is defined as an instance of `IConfigurationSource`.

Add a new button to the project form, set its `Text` property to `Trace Parameters`, and name it `m_TraceParameters`. Write the code shown in Listing 9-6 into the click event handler for the button.

**Listing 9-6.** *Tracing the Parameters of a LogEntry Object*

```
private void m_TraceParameters_Click(object sender, EventArgs e)
{
    LogWriterFactory factory =
        new LogWriterFactory(ConfigurationSourceFactory.Create());

    LogWriter writer = factory.Create();

    using(new Tracer("Debug",Guid.NewGuid(),writer,new SystemConfigurationSource()))
    {
        // Execute the button click event code
    }
}
```

## Using the LogWriter Class

Using the LogWriter class directly is not recommended, since the Logger façade does such a good job of hiding its complexity. However, in order to better understand and better utilize the Logging Application Block, this example will demonstrate how the LogWriter class works.

Add a new button to your project form and name it m_WriteLogWriter. Then add the following using clause to the form:

```
using Microsoft.Practices.EnterpriseLibrary.Common.Configuration;
```

Write the code in Listing 9-7 in the click event handler of the new button.

**Listing 9-7.** *Using the LogWriter Class*

```
private void m_WriteLogWriter_Click(object sender, EventArgs e)
{
    // Create an entry to be logged
    LogEntry entry = new LogEntry();
    entry.EventId = 9;
    entry.Priority = 0;
    entry.Categories.Add("Debug");
    entry.Message = "Logged by LogWriter directly";

    LogWriterFactory factory = new
        LogWriterFactory(ConfigurationSourceFactory.Create());

    LogWriter writer = factory.Create();
    writer.Write(entry);
    MessageBox.Show("Done");
}
```

## Creating Custom Trace Listeners

A respectable number of trace listeners come with the Logging Application Block (see Table 9-2), but it's possible that none of them will fit your needs. If necessary, you can create custom trace listeners. To demonstrate, we'll walk through creating a simple custom trace listener named MessageBoxTraceListener. MessageBoxTraceListener will simply pop up a message box with the logged message whenever a message is passed in.

The MessageBoxTraceListener class must be derived from CustomTraceListener. This is a class that inherits from System.Diagnostics.TraceListener. The only members that it adds to the .NET Framework class are a protected constructor and a Formatter property.

Follow these steps to create the MessageBoxTraceListener custom trace listener:

1. Add a new public class to the LoggingDemoLibrary project named MessageBoxTraceListener.

2. Add the following using namespace directives to the code file:

```
using System.Diagnostics;
using System.Windows.Forms;
using Microsoft.Practices.EnterpriseLibrary.Common;
using Microsoft.Practices.EnterpriseLibrary.Logging;
using Microsoft.Practices.EnterpriseLibrary.Logging.Configuration;
using Microsoft.Practices.EnterpriseLibrary.Logging.TraceListeners;
using Microsoft.Practices.EnterpriseLibrary.Common.Configuration;
```

3. Inherit the class from CustomTraceListener.

4. Add a ConfigurationElementType attribute to the class so that the correct class will be used to load data for the trace listener from the configuration file.

5. Implement the Write and WriteLine methods.

6. Override the TraceData method. This is the method that will be called by the TraceData method of the LogSource class.

Listing 9-8 shows the MessageBoxTraceListener class.

**Listing 9-8.** *Custom MessageBoxTraceListener Class*

```
using System.Diagnostics;
using System.Windows.Forms;using Microsoft.Practices.EnterpriseLibrary.Common;
using Microsoft.Practices.EnterpriseLibrary.Logging;
using Microsoft.Practices.EnterpriseLibrary.Logging.Configuration;
using Microsoft.Practices.EnterpriseLibrary.Logging.TraceListeners;
using Microsoft.Practices.EnterpriseLibrary.Common.Configuration;

[ConfigurationElementType(typeof(CustomTraceListenerData))]
public class MessageBoxTraceListener : CustomTraceListener
{
    private string m_Title = "Message Box Trace Listener";

    public MessageBoxTraceListener(NameValueCollection attributes)
    {
        m_Title = attributes["title"];
    }

    public override void Write(string message)
    {
        MessageBox.Show(message, m_Title);
    }

    public override void WriteLine(string message)
    {
        Write(message);
    }
```

```
public override void TraceData(TraceEventCache eventCache, string source,
    TraceEventType eventType, int id, object data)
{
    if (data is LogEntry && this.Formatter != null)
    {
        this.WriteLine(this.Formatter.Format(data as LogEntry));
    }
    else
    {
        this.WriteLine(data.ToString());
    }
}
}
```

You can modify this implementation to suit your own needs.

## Configuring Trace Listeners

A number of default trace listeners are supplied with the Logging Application Block, as listed in Table 9-2.

**Table 9-2.** *Default Trace Listeners*

| Trace Listener | Description |
| --- | --- |
| Database | Writes the message to a database |
| Email | Sends the message via email |
| Flat file | Writes the message to a text file |
| Formatted event log | Writes the message to the event log |
| MSMQ | Writes the message to an MSMQ queue |
| Rolling flat file | Writes to a text file that can create new files based on either a specified time or file size |
| System.Diagnostics | Allows the message to be output to one of the System.Diagnostics trace listeners |
| WMI | Writes the message to a WMI event |
| XML | Writes messages to an XML file |

Common to almost all of the trace listeners are the Formatter and TraceOutputOptions properties. Behind the scenes, each listener has a specific listener implementation.

The TraceOutputOptions property is inherited from the System.Diagnostics namespace. This property is ignored by the event log trace listener because of the large number of entries sent to that log. Multiple options can be specified for one listener. This is accomplished by creating a comma-delimited list. The values for the TraceOutputOptions property are listed in Table 9-3.

**Table 9-3.** *TraceOutPutOptions Property Values*

| Value | Description |
| --- | --- |
| LogicalOperationStack | Writes the value of CorrelationManager.LogicalOperationStack |
| DateTime | Writes the current date and time |
| TimeStamp | Writes the value returned by System.Diagnostics.Stopwatch.GetTimeStamp |
| ProcessId | Writes the value of Process.Id |
| ThreadId | Writes the Thread.ManagedThreadId of the current thread |
| Callstack | Writes the value of Environment.StackTrace |

---

■**Caution**  The Configuration Console allows you to specify only one TraceOutputOption value. If you want to use multiple TraceOutputOption values, you must specify them manually in the application configuration file.

---

The Listener data type is automatically specified for all standard trace listeners. It identifies the class and assembly that will handle configuration setting data for the listener.

You can configure trace listeners through the Configuration Console or manually in the application configuration file. To add a trace listener through the Configuration Console, right-click the Trace Listeners node of the Logging Application Block, select New, and choose the type you want to use. Then click the new listener node and set its properties, as described in the following sections.

## Configuring the Formatted Event Log Trace Listener

The formatted event log trace listener writes entries to the Application event log. This is the most common destination for logging by application development teams.

The value entered for the source attribute determines the event source within the log to which the entry will be written. This value will show up in the Source column when the entries are viewed in the Event Viewer or the Events section of the Computer Management program. You can create a new event source, as described shortly.

A central server can be designated via the machineName attribute, rather than putting a log on each of the servers that runs an application. This has its own risks, since this creates a single point of failure.

Listing 9-9 shows an example of a formatted event log trace listener configuration in the app.config file.

**Listing 9-9.** *Formatted Event Log Trace Listener Configuration*

```
<listeners>
    <add source="LoggingDemo" formatter="Text Formatter"
            log="DemoLogs" machineName=""
            listenerDataType="Microsoft.Practices.EnterpriseLibrary.Logging.
```

```
            Configuration.FormattedEventLogTraceListenerData,
            Microsoft.Practices.EnterpriseLibrary.Logging, Version=3.0.0.0,
            Culture=neutral, PublicKeyToken=null"
        traceOutputOptions="Callstack"
            type="Microsoft.Practices.EnterpriseLibrary.Logging.TraceListeners.
            FormattedEventLogTraceListener,
            Microsoft.Practices.EnterpriseLibrary.Logging, Version=3.0.0.0,
            Culture=neutral, PublicKeyToken=null"
        name="Formatted EventLog TraceListener"
    />
</listeners>
```

Figure 9-5 shows the result in the Event Viewer of using the configuration in Listing 9-9 to log messages.

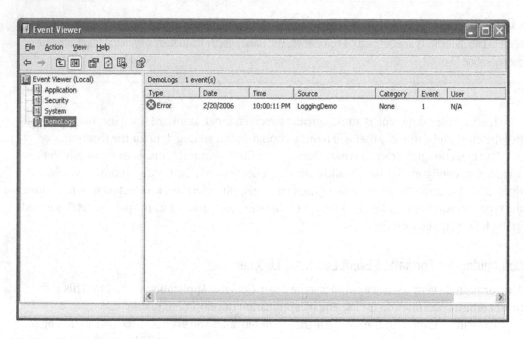

**Figure 9-5.** *Event Viewer with an entry made by a formatted event log trace listener*

You can create a new event source for logging. New event sources are normally created programmatically by creating an installer class. This class should use the CreateEventSource method of the LogEvent class to create the new event source. The steps to accomplish this are as follows:

1. Create a class that inherits from System.Configuration.Install.Installer.

2. Apply the RunInstallerAttribute attribute to the class with a parameter of true.

3. Implement the constructor of the class, creating an EventSourceCreationData instance and setting the Source and LogName parameters.

4. Pass the EventSourceCreationData instance to the CreateEventSource method.

Listing 9-10 shows an example of the code to create a new event source.

**Listing 9-10.** *Creating a New Event Source Installer*

```
[RunInstallerAttribute(true)]
public class LoggingDemoInstaller : Installer
{
    public LoggingDemoInstaller() :base()
    {
        System.Diagnostics.EventSourceCreationData creationData =
            new System.Diagnostics.EventSourceCreationData("LoggingDemo", "DemoLogs");
        EventLog.CreateEventSource(creationData);
    }
}
```

The installer is executed by running the command-line tool installutil.exe. This executable resides in the {windows}/Microsoft.NET/Framework/{framework_version} directory.

```
installutil.exe c:\LoggingDemo\LoggingDemoInstaller\LoggingDemoInstaller.dll
```

---

■**Note** When using installutil.exe, the assembly needs to be fully qualified with the directory in which it resides.

---

## Configuring the Flat File Trace Listener

When a flat file is the preferred logging destination, the flat file trace listener is the one for the job. A flat file is sometimes easier for a development team to access for debugging purposes. Administrators would much rather give application developers permissions to a file share than let them have administrative privileges on a server.

Since this is a listener with a flat file as a destination, you need to set a fileName attribute. If you set only a filename for the Filename property, the file will be generated in the executable directory. Alternatively, you can specify a full directory path.

The Header and Footer properties allow you to specify text that will make it easy to visually identify the beginning and ending points of a log entry. The default for this is a line of dashes.

Listing 9-11 shows an example of a flat file trace listener configuration in the app.config file, and Figure 9-6 shows it configured in the Configuration Console.

**Listing 9-11.** *Flat File Trace Listener Configuration*

```
<listeners>
   <add
      fileName="trace.log"
      header="---------------
Begin Trace ------------------------"
      footer="--------------
End Trace ------------------------"
      formatter="Text Formatter"
      listenerDataType="Microsoft.Practices.EnterpriseLibrary.Logging.
         Configuration.FlatFileTraceListenerData,
         Microsoft.Practices.EnterpriseLibrary.Logging,
         Version=3.0.0.0, Culture=neutral,
         PublicKeyToken=null" traceOutputOptions="DateTime, Callstack"
      type="Microsoft.Practices.EnterpriseLibrary.Logging.TraceListeners.
         FlatFileTraceListener,
         Microsoft.Practices.EnterpriseLibrary.Logging, Version=3.0.0.0,
         Culture=neutral, PublicKeyToken=null"
      name="FlatFile TraceListener"
   />
<listeners>
```

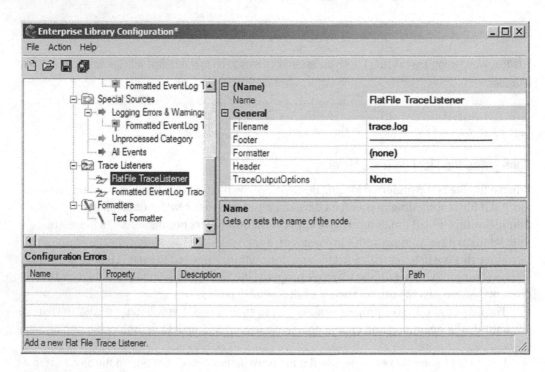

**Figure 9-6.** *Flat file trace listener configuration*

---

■**Caution** The application must have write access to the destination directory in order to create and write to the log file. In the case of an ASP.NET application, this means giving rights to the ASPNET user. Extra care should be taken when doing this in order to ensure that the system is not risking a security breach. It may be a good idea to give the ASPNET user write access to an isolated directory.

---

## Configuring the Email Trace Listener

Often, someone must be notified when there is a problem with an application. An efficient way to accomplish this is by sending an email to a distribution mailbox, using the email trace listener. The address for this mailbox would be specified in the ToAddress property of the EmailTraceListener class. There is also a FromAddress property to specify the sender of the message, which designates the application.

In order for the Logging Application Block to send an email, it needs to know how to talk to the server. This is the purpose of the SmtpServer and SmtpPort properties. They initially default to the localhost IP address and the standard SMTP port of 25.

The email trace listener contains a SubjectLineStarter property and a SubjectLineEnder property, which are similar to the Header and Footer properties of the flat file trace listener. The difference is that instead of being identifiers of the start and end of the log entry, they represent the prefix and suffix for the subject line of the email. Placed in between these two values is the LogEntry's severity.

Listing 9-12 shows an example of an email trace listener configuration in the app.config file, and Figure 9-7 shows the listener configured in the Configuration Console.

**Listing 9-12.** *Email Trace Listener Configuration*

```
<listeners>
  <add
    toAddress="to@example.com"
    fromAddress="from@example.com"
    subjectLineStarter=""
    subjectLineEnder=""
    smtpServer="127.0.0.1"
    smtpPort="25"
    formatter="Text Formatter"
    listenerDataType="Microsoft.Practices.EnterpriseLibrary.Logging.
      Configuration.EmailTraceListenerData,
      Microsoft.Practices.EnterpriseLibrary.Logging, Version=3.0.0.0,
      Culture=neutral, PublicKeyToken=null"
    traceOutputOptions="None"
    type="Microsoft.Practices.EnterpriseLibrary.Logging.TraceListeners.
      EmailTraceListener, Microsoft.Practices.EnterpriseLibrary.Logging,
      Version=3.0.0.0, Culture=neutral, PublicKeyToken=null"
    name="Email TraceListener"
  />
</listeners>
```

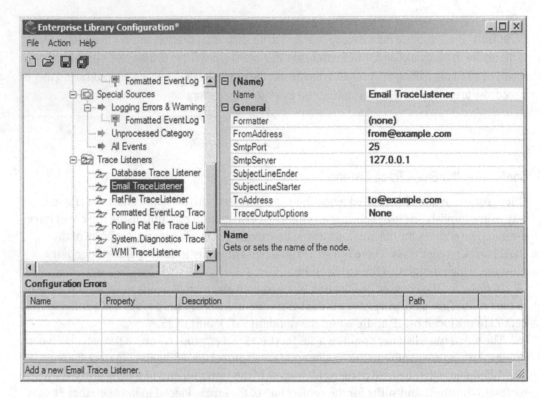

**Figure 9-7.** *Email trace listener configuration*

## Configuring the Database Trace Listener

For auditing purposes, the optimum log location is the database. This makes audit reporting much easier, since a query can be run against the database. The database trace listener provides a quick way of setting up a database logging scenario.

This listener has a `databaseInstanceName` attribute, which for this example should hold the connection string name for the database you created earlier in this chapter by running the `CreateLoggingDb.cmd` file.

Two properties for this trace listener specify stored procedures that must exist in the logging database: `AddCategoryStoredProcedure` and `WriteLogStoredProcedureName`. These default to `AddCategory` and `WriteLog`, respectively.

Listing 9-13 shows an example of a database trace listener configuration in the `app.config` file, and Figure 9-8 shows the configuration data in the Configuration Console.

**Listing 9-13.** *Database Trace Listener Configuration*

```
<listeners>
  <add
    databaseInstanceName="Connection String"
    writeLogStoredProcName="WriteLog"
    addCategoryStoredProcName="AddCategory"
    formatter="Text Formatter"
```

```
    listenerDataType="Microsoft.Practices.EnterpriseLibrary.Logging.Database.
       Configuration.FormattedDatabaseTraceListenerData,
       Microsoft.Practices.EnterpriseLibrary.Logging.Database, Version=3.0.0.0,
       Culture=neutral, PublicKeyToken=null"
    traceOutputOptions="None"
    type="Microsoft.Practices.EnterpriseLibrary.Logging.Database.
       FormattedDatabaseTraceListener,
       Microsoft.Practices.EnterpriseLibrary.Logging.Database,
       Version=3.0.0.0, Culture=neutral, PublicKeyToken=null"
    name="Database Trace Listener"
  />
</listeners>
```

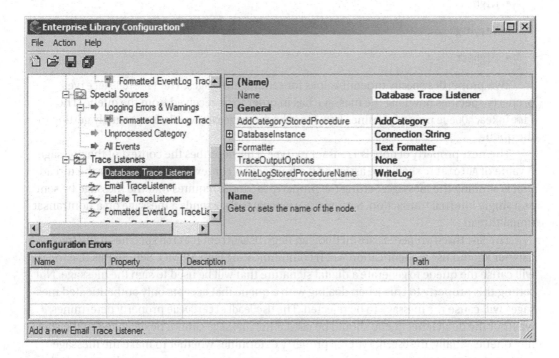

**Figure 9-8.** *Database trace listener configuration*

## Configuring the MSMQ Trace Listener

MSMQ enables logging in an asynchronous fashion. This asynchronous feature allows for a separate process to actually record the message, while the process that originally sent the message to the queue can continue to work on its main task. MSMQ also allows for a reliable way of ensuring messages are not lost. For instance, if an application uses a separate thread to store messages, and the application shuts down suddenly, some messages may not be logged properly. However, a queue will persist the message even if the computer loses power.

The MSMQ trace listener requires a destination. This is held in the `QueuePath` property and defaults to an imaginary value of `".\Private\myQueue$"`.

The message sent to the queue by the trace listener is assigned a priority. The priority actually belongs to the System.Messaging namespace and is defined in the MessagePriority enumeration. It is passed to the message queue within a Message object. The values for the priority are as follows:

- Lowest

- VeryLow

- Low

- Normal

- AboveNormal

- High

- VeryHigh

- Highest

Two properties specify timeout values for sending messages. The TimeToBeReceived property specifies how long the message has in order to be received from the queue. The TimeToReachQueue property defines how long the message can wait before actually getting to the queue.

The next property of note is TransactionType. This describes the context of the message. A value of Automatic should be assigned if a transaction context already exists for the thread that is sending the message. Setting the property to Single requires that the message be sent as a single internal transaction. Setting the property to None sends a message on a nontransactional thread.

The last three properties are all Boolean flags. UseAuthentication specifies if the trace listener should use authentication when communicating with MSMQ. Setting this flag to true will cause the queue to generate a digital signature that will be used to sign the message. Not setting this property to true when dealing with a queue that accepts only authenticated messages will cause the message to be rejected. The UseDeadLetterQueue property determines whether the dead letter queue should be used if the message cannot be delivered to the specified queue. Finally, the UseEncryption property determines whether to make the message private. A value of true will cause the message queuing system to automatically encrypt the body of the message.

Listing 9-14 shows an example of an MSMQ trace listener configuration in the app.config file.

**Listing 9-14.** *MSMQ Trace Listener Configuration*

```
<listeners>
  <add
    name="Msmq TraceListener"
    type="Microsoft.Practices.EnterpriseLibrary.Logging.TraceListeners.
      MsmqTraceListener,
    Microsoft.Practices.EnterpriseLibrary.Logging, Version=3.0.0.0,
      Culture=neutral, PublicKeyToken=null"
```

```
      listenerDataType="Microsoft.Practices.EnterpriseLibrary.Logging.
        Configuration.MsmqTraceListenerData,
      Microsoft.Practices.EnterpriseLibrary.Logging, Version=3.0.0.0,
        Culture=neutral, PublicKeyToken=null"
      traceOutputOptions="None"
      queuePath=".\Private$\myQueue"
      formatter="Text Formatter"
      messagePriority="Normal"
      timeToReachQueue="49710.06:28:15"
      timeToBeReceived="49710.06:28:15"
      recoverable="false"
      useAuthentication="false"
      useDeadLetterQueue="false"
      useEncryption="false"
      transactionType="None"
  />
</listeners>
```

## Configuring the System.Diagnostics Trace Listener

The System.Diagnostics trace listener comes in many flavors. The Type property determines which trace listener is actually employed. Since all of these trace listeners reside in the System.Diagnostics namespace, they are available even if an application is not using the Logging Application Block. The Type property can be set to the following values:

- ConsoleTraceListener: Writes messages to either Console.Out or Console.Error.

- DefaultTraceListener: Sends messages to the OutputDebugString and the Debug.Log method.

- DelimitedListTraceListener: Sends messages to a file stream using the specified delimiter.

- EventLogTraceListener: Sends messages to an event log.

- TextWriterTraceListener: Sends messages to a text writer or stream, such as Console.Out or FileStream.

- XmlWriterTraceListener: Sends XML-encoded messages to a text writer or stream, such as Console.Out or FileStream. The following XML elements are generated as part of the output:

  - CallStack

  - Computer

  - Correlation

  - DataItem

  - EventID

- Execution

- Level

- LogicalOperationStack

- Message

- Source

- SubType

- TimeCreated

- TimeStamp

- Type

The other property used by the System.Diagnostics trace listener is InitData, which provides the ability to supply data for the initialization of the trace listener.

Figure 9-9 shows the System Diagnostics trace listener configured with the Configuration Console.

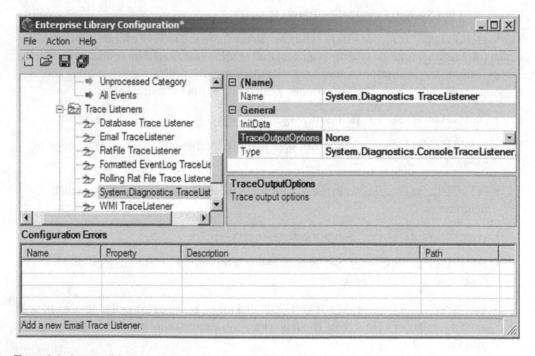

**Figure 9-9.** *System.Diagnostics trace listener configuration*

## Configuring the WMI Trace Listener

Most large companies have centralized monitoring of their systems. A number of tools can plug into WMI and give reports to the operations group.

You don't need to configure anything for the WMI trace listener aside from the standard TraceOutputOptions property. Listing 9-15 shows an example of the XML configuration data for a WMI trace listener.

**Listing 9-15.** *WMI Trace Listener Configuration*

```
<listeners>
   <add
      listenerDataType="Microsoft.Practices.EnterpriseLibrary.Logging.Configuration.
         WmiTraceListenerData, Microsoft.Practices.EnterpriseLibrary.Logging,
      Version=3.0.0.0, Culture=neutral, PublicKeyToken=null"
      traceOutputOptions="None"
      type="Microsoft.Practices.EnterpriseLibrary.Logging.TraceListeners.
         WmiTraceListener, Microsoft.Practices.EnterpriseLibrary.Logging,
         Version=3.0.0.0, Culture=neutral, PublicKeyToken=null"
      name="WMI TraceListener"
   />
</listeners>
```

## Configuring the Rolling Flat File Trace Listener

The rolling flat file trace listener is much like the flat file trace listener, but it adds a feature that allows it to create a new log file based on the current date and time or when the file reaches a certain size. This makes searching through a log file much simpler, especially when dealing with log files created by applications that log hundreds, thousands, tens of thousands, or more messages. This way, you can target the logged message you are looking for based on when the log entry was made.

The rolling flat file trace listener has the same properties as the flat file trace listener and adds the following properties:

- RollFileExistsBehavior: Defines whether the rolling flat file trace listener should increment an existing file or overwrite it.

- RollSizeKB: Sets the maximum threshold in kilobytes allowed before a new file is created.

- RollInterval: Defines the time interval that is used to decide when to create a new log file. The following intervals are available:

  - None means that the log file will not be rolled to a new log file based on a time interval.

  - Minute rolls the log every minute.

  - Hour rolls the log every hour.

  - Day rolls the log every day.

  - Week rolls the log every week.

  - Month rolls the log every month.

  - Year rolls the log every year.

- `TimeStampPattern`: Defines the date and time pattern used to append to the log file, thus making it easier to know to which time interval a log file applies. This takes the same format as the date and time pattern of the `ToString` method of a `DateTime` object.

Figure 9-10 shows a rolling flat file trace listener configured in the Configuration Console.

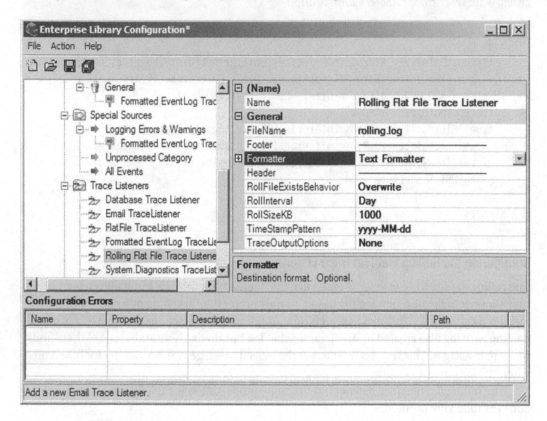

**Figure 9-10.** *Rolling flat file trace listener configuration*

## Configuring the XMLTrace Listener

The XML trace listener is the easiest of them all to configure. It is almost identical to configuring the flat file trace listener, except you don't specify the header, footer, or formatter. All you need to do is specify the filename for the log file. The formatter automatically defaults to `XMLLogFormatter`.

## Configuring a Custom Listener

In order to configure a custom listener, such as the `MessageBoxTraceListener` we created earlier in this chapter, you must add a Custom Trace Listener node to the configuration file. The one required property is the type of the trace listener class.

As with other custom classes within the Enterprise Library, there is an optional name-value pair property called `Attributes`. This is where you can specify the `Title` property to display a custom title for the message box for the sample `MessageBoxTraceListener`

Listing 9-16 contains the configuration data to utilize the custom `MessageBoxTraceListener` with an application, and Figure 9-11 shows it configured within the Configuration Console.

**Listing 9-16.** *Custom Listener Configuration for the MessageBoxTraceListener*

```
<listeners>
  <add
    listenerDataType="Microsoft.Practices.EnterpriseLibrary.Logging.
      Configuration.CustomTraceListenerData,
      Microsoft.Practices.EnterpriseLibrary.Logging, Version=3.0.0.0,
      Culture=neutral, PublicKeyToken=null"
    traceOutputOptions="None"
    type="LoggingDemoLibrary.MessageBoxTraceListener,
      LoggingDemoLibrary, Version=1.0.0.0, Culture=neutral, PublicKeyToken=null"
    name="SQL Server Trace Listener"
    initializeData=""
    formatter="Text Formatter"
  />
</listeners>
```

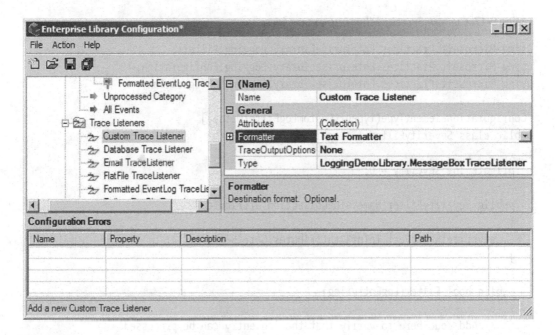

**Figure 9-11.** *Custom trace listener configuration*

## Creating Custom Filters

The Logging Application Block comes with three standard filters, as discussed in the next section. If none of these meets your needs, you can create a custom filter.

Custom filters implement the `ILogFilter` interface. This requires that the new class have a `Filter` method and a `Name` property. The purpose of the `Filter` method is to test if the message that the custom filter receives meets that criteria to be processed.

Follow these steps to create a sample custom filter:

1. Add a new class to the project that is extending the Logging Application Block and name it `SeverityFilter`.

2. Add the following using statements:

   ```
   using Microsoft.Practices.EnterpriseLibrary.Logging
   using Microsoft.Practices.EnterpriseLibrary.Logging.Filters
   using Microsoft.Practices.EnterpriseLibrary.Logging.Configuration
   using Microsoft.Practices.EnterpriseLibrary.Common.Configuration
   ```

3. Inherit the new class from `ILogFilter`.

4. Add the `ConfigurationElementType` attribute to the class.

5. Implement the `Filter` method and `Name` property.

Listing 9-17 shows the implementation of the `SeverityFilter` class.

**Listing 9-17.** *Custom Severity Filter Implementation*

```
using Microsoft.Practices.EnterpriseLibrary.Logging.Filters;
using Microsoft.Practices.EnterpriseLibrary.Logging.Configuration;
using Microsoft.Practices.EnterpriseLibrary.Common.Configuration;

[ConfigurationElementType(typeof(CustomLogFilterData))]
public class SeverityFilter : ILogFilter
{
    private int severity = 0;

    public SeverityFilter(NameValueCollection attributes)
    {
        severity = Convert.ToInt32(attributes.Get("Severity"));
    }

    public bool Filter(LogEntry log)
    {
        // Add code here to verify that the log entry can be processed
        // based on the Severity property
        return Convert.ToInt32(log.Severity) < severity;
    }

    public string Name
    {
        get { return "Severity Filter"; }
    }
}
```

The constructor, which accepts a `NameValueCollection`, allows the class to use the `Attributes` property from the configuration data of the custom filter.

# Configuring Filters

The Logging Application Block ships with category, log-enabled, and priority filters. The following sections describe how to configure each of these, as well as a custom filter. To select a filter, right-click the Filters node and select New ➤ Type.

## Using the Category Filter

The category filter provides the ability to allow or deny individual or groups of categories. This is accomplished by setting the `CategoryFilterExpression` property. The Configuration Console displays a dialog box to help set the values for this property. Behind the scenes, this one property is split into an attribute on the `add` element to define the filter name and one or more `add` elements inside the `categoryFilters` element to define the specific categories to allow or deny.

Listing 9-18 shows an example of a category filter configuration in the `app.config` file, and Figure 9-12 shows the category filter configured in the Configuration Console.

**Listing 9-18.** *Category Filter Configuration*

```
<logFilters>
   <add
      categoryFilterMode="DenyAllExceptAllowed"
      type="Microsoft.Practices.EnterpriseLibrary.Logging.Filters.CategoryFilter,
         Microsoft.Practices.EnterpriseLibrary.Logging, Version=3.0.0.0,
         Culture=neutral, PublicKeyToken=null"
      name="My Category Filter">
      <categoryFilters>
         <add name="Trace" />
         <add name="General" />
      </categoryFilters>
   </add>
</logFilters>
```

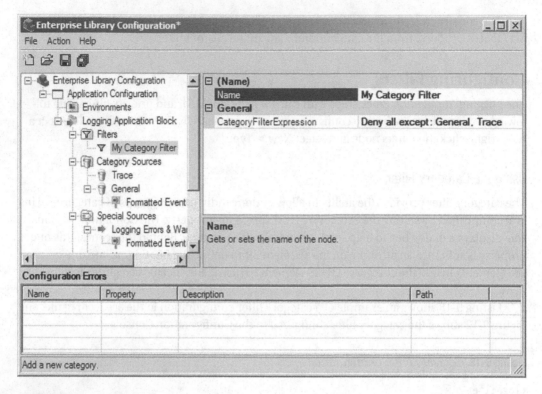

**Figure 9-12.** *Category filter configuration*

## Using a Custom Filter

The custom filter configuration item is meant to allow a development team to create a custom filter, as shown earlier in the chapter, and still have the ease of setup afforded for the standard filters.

You need to set two properties: Type and Attributes. The Type property stores the name of the class that implements ILogFilter. In order to assign this through the Configuration Console, click the ellipse in the properties grid and select the assembly. The Attributes property allows you to construct a list of name-value pairs that will be used by the custom filter. This relies on the fact that the developer who configures the class knows the values from documentation for the filter.

Listing 9-19 shows the configuration data for the custom filter created earlier in Listing 9-17. Figure 9-13 shows the custom filter configured with the severity key-value pair defined.

**Listing 9-19.** *Custom Severity Filter Configuration*

```
<logFilters>
   <add
      Severity="10"
      type="LoggingDemoLibrary.SeverityFilter, LoggingDemoLibrary,
         Version=1.0.0.0, Culture=neutral, PublicKeyToken=null"
      name="Custom Filter"
   />
</logFilters>
```

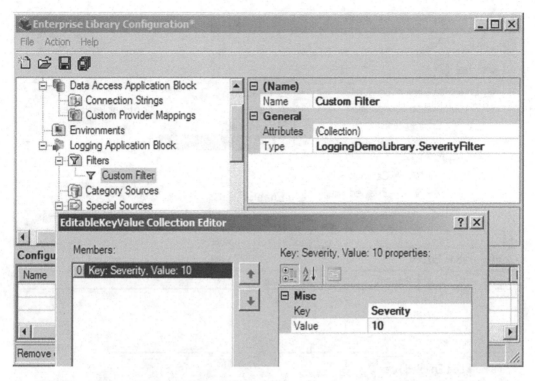

**Figure 9-13.** *Custom filter configuration*

## Using the Log-Enabled Filter

The log-enabled filter is a simple switch. It is set to either allow or deny all LogEntry objects that flow through it.

Listing 9-20 shows an example of a log-enabled filter configuration in the app.config file, and Figure 9-14 shows this configuration in the Configuration Console.

**Listing 9-20.** *Log-Enabled Filter Configuration*

```
<logFilters>
   <add enabled="true"
      type="Microsoft.Practices.EnterpriseLibrary.Logging.Filters.LogEnabledFilter,
      Microsoft.Practices.EnterpriseLibrary.Logging, Version=3.0.0.0,
         Culture=neutral, PublicKeyToken=null"
      name="LogEnabled Filter"
   />
</logFilters>
```

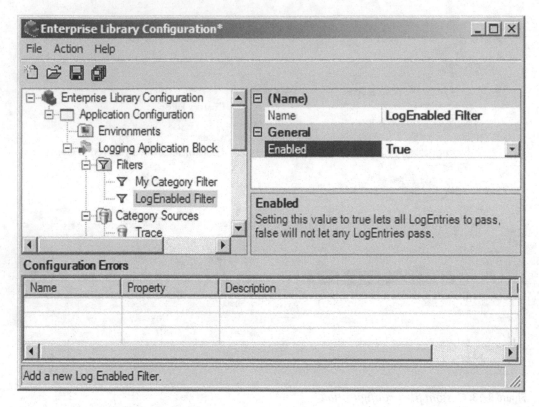

**Figure 9-14.** *Log-enabled filter configuration*

## Using the Priority Filter

The priority filter has two properties that determine the way it functions: MaximumPriority and MinimumPriority. These are compared to the priority of a LogEntry object to determine whether it should be logged. If the minimum setting is omitted, then there is no lower bound on priorities to be logged. Likewise, leaving out a maximum setting allows all priorities above the minimum value. If these values are left blank, the minimum and maximum are set to –1 and 2147483647, respectively.

In the example in Listing 9-21, the priorities are set between 10 and 90. Figure 9-15 shows the filter configured in the Configuration Console.

**Listing 9-21.** *Priority Filter Configuration*

```
<logFilters>
  <add
    minimumPriority="10"
    maximumPriority="90"
    type="Microsoft.Practices.EnterpriseLibrary.Logging.Filters.PriorityFilter,
      Microsoft.Practices.EnterpriseLibrary.Logging, Version=3.0.0.0,
      Culture=neutral, PublicKeyToken=null"
    name="Priority Filter"
  />
</logFilters>
```

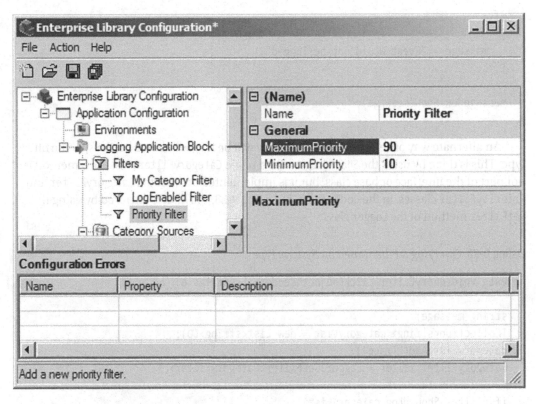

**Figure 9-15.** *Priority filter configuration*

## Querying Filters Programmatically

The reason for polling a filter is to determine if a LogEntry object will be logged before it is passed to the Logger class. This allows the developer to avoid resource-intensive activities that may be required to collect information to be included in the LogEntry object. This task is accomplished by calling the ShouldLog method of the Logger class with a LogEntry object that has been populated with the appropriate categories and the priority of the entry, as shown in Listing 9-22.

**Listing 9-22.** *Querying a Filter Programmatically*

```
private void queryLogSource_Click(object sender, EventArgs e)
{
    LogEntry entry = new LogEntry();
    entry.Priority = 11;
    entry.Categories.Add("Debug");
    string message = string.Empty;

    if (Logger.ShouldLog(entry))
    {
        message = "Event would be logged";
    }
```

```
    else
    {
        message = "Event would not be logged";
    }

    MessageBox.Show(message);
}
```

An alternate way of determining if a category will be logged is based on the specific filter type. This is done by using the ShouldLog method of the CategoryFilter class. This method is not part of the interface or base class, but it is implemented on both the CategoryFilter and PriorityFilter classes. In the code shown in Listing 9-23, the filter is retrieved by using the GetFilter method of the Logger class.

**Listing 9-23.** *Querying a Filter Based on System.Type*

```
private void queryFilter_Click(object sender, EventArgs e)
{
    string message;
    ICollection<string> categoryList = new List<string>(0);
    categoryList.Add("Trace");
    CategoryFilter filter = Logger.GetFilter<CategoryFilter>();

    if (filter.ShouldLog(categoryList))
    {
        message = "Event would be logged";
    }
    else
    {
        message = "Event would not be logged";
    }

    MessageBox.Show(message);
}
```

## Configuring Log Sources

Log sources are configured in the <categorySources> and <specialSources> sections of the application configuration file.

To add a sample new category, follow these steps:

1. Right-click the Category Sources node in the Configuration Console and select New ➤ Category.

2. Select the new Category node.

3. Set the Name property to DAL Trace Event and select Information from the SourceLevels property drop-down list.

4. Add a trace listener reference by right-clicking the new category and selecting New ➤ Trace Listener Reference.

Altering the properties for the trace listener attached to the log source will modify the settings associated with that listener in the <listeners> section. This means that any other log source that references that trace listener will also use the same settings. If you need to have different settings, create a new trace listener.

Listing 9-24 shows an example of a log source configuration.

**Listing 9-24.** *Log Source Configuration*

```
<categorySources>
  <add switchValue="Information" name="DAL Trace Events">
    <listeners>
      <add name="Formatted EventLog TraceListener" />
    </listeners>
  </add>
  <add switchValue="All" name="General">
    <listeners>
      <add name="Formatted EventLog TraceListener" />
    </listeners>
  </add>
</categorySources>
```

Although the special sources are a Logging Application Block default, they do not have listeners associated with them by default. Adding a listener is done the same way as for custom log sources. Listing 9-25 shows an example of configuring special sources.

**Listing 9-25.** *Special Sources Configuration*

```
<specialSources>
  <allEvents
    switchValue="All"
    name="All Events"
  />
  <notProcessed
    switchValue="All"
    name="Unprocessed Category"
  />
  <errors
    switchValue="All"
    name="Logging Errors &amp; Warnings">
    <listeners>
      <add name="Formatted EventLog TraceListener" />
    </listeners>
  </errors>
</specialSources>
```

## Creating Custom Formatters

The Logging Application Block provides only binary and text formatters. If you want to use some other format for an application's log, such as XML, you'll need to create a custom formatter.

To create a new formatter, define a new class that implements the ILogFormatter interface. This interface resides in the Microsoft.Practices.EnterpriseLibrary.Logging. Formatters namespace. The contract for ILogFormatter specifies the method Format, which takes a LogEntry object as an input parameter and returns a string.

Add the following using namespace directives to the code file:

```
using Microsoft.Practices.EnterpriseLibrary.Common;
using Microsoft.Practices.EnterpriseLibrary.Common.Configuration;
using Microsoft.Practices.EnterpriseLibrary.Logging;
using Microsoft.Practices.EnterpriseLibrary.Logging.Configuration;
using Microsoft.Practices.EnterpriseLibrary.Logging.Formatters
```

The next piece of code is your custom formatter class. It is decorated with a ConfigurationElementType attribute, which indicates the configuration object to be used for this class. Finally, the Format method should be overridden.

Listing 9-26 shows an example of a custom formatter.

**Listing 9-26.** *Custom Formatter*

```
using Microsoft.Practices.EnterpriseLibrary.Common;
using Microsoft.Practices.EnterpriseLibrary.Common.Configuration;
using Microsoft.Practices.EnterpriseLibrary.Logging;
using Microsoft.Practices.EnterpriseLibrary.Logging.Configuration;
using Microsoft.Practices.EnterpriseLibrary.Logging.Formatters;

namespace LoggingDemoLibrary
{
    [ConfigurationElementType(typeof(CustomFormatterData))]
    public class MyFormatter: LogFormatter
    {
        public MyFormatter(NameValueCollection attributes)
        {
        }

        public override string Format(LogEntry log)
        {
            StringBuilder builder = new StringBuilder();
            builder.Append("<LogEntry>");
            builder.Append("<Message>");
            builder.Append(log.Message);
            builder.Append("</Message>");
```

```
            builder.Append("<Activity>");
            builder.Append(log.ActivityId.ToString());
            builder.Append("</Activity>");
            builder.Append("</LogEntry>");

            return builder.ToString();
        }
    }
}
```

A token system similar to the text formatter could be used in order to convert properties of a LogEntry instance into XML tags. The implementation for this should be placed within the Format method.

## Configuring Formatters

You can configure a binary or text formatter, as well as a custom formatter, as described in the following sections.

### Using the Binary Formatter

The binary formatter really has only one purpose: to serialize the log entry using a binary format. Everything is output to the log, and there are no options to customize it.

To add this to the list of formatters via the Configuration Console, right-click the Formatters node and select New ➤ Binary Formatter. The resulting XML will look like the configuration data in Listing 9-27.

**Listing 9-27.** *Binary Formatter Configuration*

```
<formatters>
    <add
        type="Microsoft.Practices.EnterpriseLibrary.Logging.Formatters.
            BinaryLogFormatter, Microsoft.Practices.EnterpriseLibrary.Logging,
            Version=3.0.0.0, Culture=neutral,  PublicKeyToken=null"
        name="Binary Formatter"
    />
</formatters>
```

### Using the Text Formatter

To add a text formatter in the Configuration Console, right-click the Formatters node and select New ➤ Text Formatter. You can set options for this formatter based on tokens in the template section. The template is much easier to edit from the Configuration Console than by hand, since the template attribute is one long string value. In the configuration file, line feeds and carriage returns are converted to &#0A and &#0D, respectively. The resulting configuration data will look like the XML in Listing 9-28.

**Listing 9-28.** *Text Formatter Configuration*

```
<formatters>
   <add
      template="
         Timestamp: {timestamp}&#xD;&#xA;
         Message: {message}&#xD;&#xA;
         Category: {category}&#xD;&#xA;
         Priority: {priority}&#xD;&#xA;
         EventId: {eventid}&#xD;&#xA;
         Severity: {severity}&#xD;&#xA;
         Title:{title}&#xD;&#xA;
         Machine: {machine}&#xD;&#xA;
         Application Domain: {appDomain}&#xD;&#xA;
         Process Id: {processId}&#xD;&#xA;
         Process Name: {processName}&#xD;&#xA;
         Win32 Thread Id: {win32ThreadId}&#xD;&#xA;
         Thread Name: {threadName}&#xD;&#xA;
         Extended Properties: {dictionary({key} - {value}&#xD;&#xA;)}"
      type="Microsoft.Practices.EnterpriseLibrary.Logging.Formatters.TextFormatter,
         Microsoft.Practices.EnterpriseLibrary.Logging, Version=3.0.0.0,
         Culture=neutral, PublicKeyToken=null"
      name="Text Formatter"
   />
</formatters>
```

The tokens of the template are delimited by curly braces. The majority of the tokens are handled by the StringBuilder class's Replace method. The template string is replaced by the value of a property in the LogEntry.

Special tokens are converted by a class derived from TokenFunction. An example of this is the TimeStampToken class. This particular token takes a format parameter the same as the standard ToString method of the DateTime data type.

The extended properties are another special case. They are handled by the DictionaryToken class. When the LogEntry instance is processed by this formatter, it is passed to the FormatToken method, where it looks for the tag {dictionary} in the template. It then loops through the extended properties looking for the key and value tags to determine whether to output the key, value, or both.

Enterprise Library 3.0 introduces two enhancements to the tokens. The first enhancement allows for the rendering of local time as opposed to UTC in the log file. (Versions of Enterprise Library prior to 3.0 support only UTC output.) This is done by adding the local: prefix to the timestamp token. The second enhancement is the addition of the ReflectedPropertyToken class. This class will allow you to add log custom properties that are added to classes that derive from LogEntry or from a modified version of the LogEntry class. The syntax for the ReflectedPropertyToken class is as follows:

{property(*MyCustomPropertyName*)}

Replace *MyCustomPropertyName* with the name of a custom property added to a derived instance of the LogEntry class.

### Using a Custom Formatter

A custom formatter requires that the developer designate an assembly that contains the formatter class. The resulting XML will look like the configuration data in Listing 9-29.

**Listing 9-29.** *Custom Formatter Configuration*

```
<formatters>
  <add
    type="LoggingDemoLibrary.MyFormatter, LoggingDemoLibrary,
      Version=1.0.0.0, Culture=neutral, PublicKeyToken=null"
    name="MyXmlLogFormatter"
  />
</formatters>
```

The one optional setting is the Attributes property. This can be used to contain a list of key-value pairs, which the formatter can use as configuration settings. They would be passed to the class through the NameValueCollection parameter of the constructor.

## Logging WCF Messages

Enterprise Library 3.*x* adds functionality to support logging WCF messages. WCF can log only to trace sources found in the System.Diagnostics namespace.

To use the Logging Application Block with WCF, you need to create a custom trace listener that will wrap a message that is received from a trace source, create a LogEntry object, and pass it along to the Logging Application Block. Essentially, this is creating a "logging proxy." This special trace listener is called the EntLibLoggingProxyTraceListener and uses the XMLLogEntry class to package the WCF message and send it to the Logging Application Block

Configuring the Logging Application Block to work with WCF is not a trivial task. The "Integrating the Logging Application Block with WCF Applications" section of the documentation that comes with Enterprise Library 3.*x* goes through detailed steps on how to properly configure the Logging Application Block for WCF.

## Deploying the Logging Application Block

The documentation for the Logging Application Block says that there are two ways to deploy it: either use an xcopy distribution or a strongly named distribution. But this is only part of what needs to be done for deployment. Most of the considerations have to do with operations to support deployment.

If you're using a flat file log, the ID that the application will run under will need to have write access to the directory in which that file will reside. In the case of an ASP.NET application, this means the ASPNET user.

If one of the logging destinations is an event log source, a custom installer must be created and run using installutil.exe. The ID that is used to run the installer must have administrator privileges. For security reasons, this should not be the same ID that runs the application.

Other deployment considerations include the following:

- Configuring queues and setting permissions

- Creating email accounts and setting up SMTP services to send messages

- Making sure that category and priority filters are set to log the minimum amount of information to keep from impacting performance

- Installing EIF on the target server

# Migrating from Prior Versions

Fortunately, the program-facing interfaces of the Logging Application Block are identical between versions 2.0 and 3.*x*, and only some minor changes exist between 1.*x* and 3.*x*. This makes the impact of programming changes fairly small. In all cases, the application block contains LogEntry, Logger, and LogWriter classes with very similar signatures.

It should be a given that the reference to the Logging Application Block assemblies will need to be replaced in all projects that use logging. The configuration files from a 1.*x* implementation of the Logging Application Block will require more manual-intensive conversion. The easiest way to accomplish this is to open the two configuration tools side by side. The June 2005 version used a separate loggingConfiguration.Config file, whereas the current version uses the application configuration file. Open the original file in the 1.*x* version of the configuration tool and the application configuration file for the project in the current version. Attempting to open the original file in the newer tool will not show any of the 1.1 application block information.

The biggest difference between the two versions of the application block is in the removal of the distribution strategies and sinks. Sinks now inherit from TraceListener and are therefore named to reflect this. Since there are no more distribution strategies, this means that when an application that used the Message Queuing distribution strategy is upgraded, it should use the MSMQ trace listener instead.

Another impact of moving to TraceListener-derived sinks is that any existing custom trace listeners now should derive from CustomTraceListener.

The Severity property of the 1.*x* LogEntry class has been changed to a TraceEventType enumeration. Using the enumeration instead of an integer supports interoperability with the System.Diagnostics namespace. If the application requires numeric values to be recorded, the Priority property should be used as an alternate value.

The Correlation Manager is a new feature of the .NET 2.0 Framework which is used by the Logging Application Block in Enterprise Library 2.0 and 3.x. It correlates traces that are part of the same logical transaction by using the activity ID, which is either passed into or created by the constructor of the Tracer class. In the June 2005 version, the Tracer class kept a ThreadStatic variable with a list of activity IDs, which it would use to perform a similar function to that of the Correlation Manager.

# Adding the Logging Application Block to the ACME POS Application

Like any respectable company, ACME Cosmetics wants to ensure that its systems are not used by unauthorized users. Besides having security mechanisms in place, the company wants to log when sales staff or managers request or update data. This way, it can attempt to ensure the system is being used in the manner intended.

In order to accomplish this task, you will arrange for logging events to be captured in the domain (business) layer of the application using the database trace listener provided with the Logging Application Block. It will capture the employee's ID plus the request made by the employee.

If you did not already run the LoggingDatabase.sql script mentioned earlier in the "Adding the Logging Application Block to an Application" section, do that now.

## Configuring the Database Trace Listener for the ACME POS Service

To begin, open the web.config file in the ACME.POS.Service.Host project, and then add the Logging Application Block to it. Configure it as follows:

1. Add a new connection string for the logging database.

2. Create a new database trace listener. You can leave the defaults, but make sure that you select Text Formatter for the Formatter property and the connection string you created for the logging database for the DatabaseInstance property. Figure 9-16 shows this configuration.

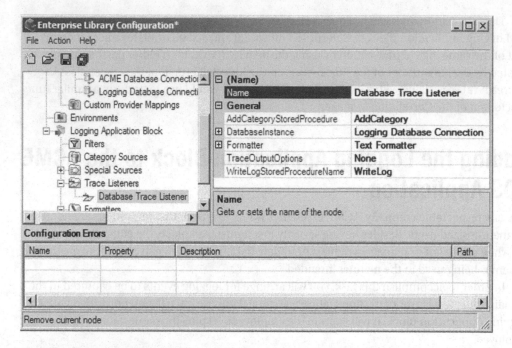

**Figure 9-16.** *Configuring the database trace listener for the ACME POS service*

   **3.** Add a new category source called `Customer` and specify the newly created database
   trace listener for the `ReferencedTraceListener` property, as shown in Figure 9-17.

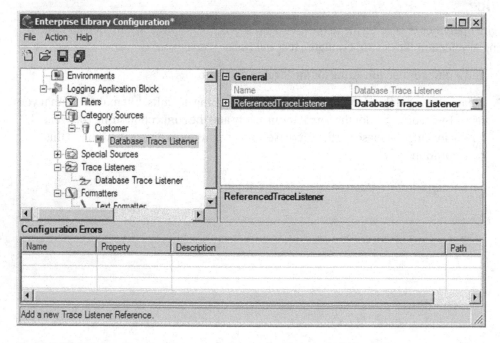

**Figure 9-17.** *Configuring the Customer category for the ACME POS service*

   **4.** Save the configuration file.

# Adding the LogEntry and Logger Classes to the ACME Domain Layer

The next task is to update the ACME.POS.Domain.BusinessRules class to include the proper LogEntry and Logger code to write the log events to the database.

First, open the ACME Domain class and add the code shown in Listing 9-30 to the existing BusinessRules class. Note that in both the SaveCustomerData and GetAllCustomers methods, the Logger class's ShouldLog method is called to determine if it is even necessary to attempt to write the log data to the database.

**Listing 9-30.** *Adding Logging to the BusinessRules Class*

```
using System;
using System.Collections.Generic;
using System.Text;
using ACME.POS.Domain.Entity;
using ACME.POS.Domain.DAL;
using Microsoft.Practices.EnterpriseLibrary.Logging;

namespace ACME.POS.Domain
{
    public class BusinessRules
    {
        public void SaveCustomerData(CustomerList customers)
        {
            CustomerList modifiedCustomers = customers.ModifiedCustomers;

            LogEntry logEntry = new LogEntry();
            logEntry.Message = "Modifying Customers";
            logEntry.Categories.Add("Customer");
            logEntry.ExtendedProperties.Add("UserId", modifiedCustomers.EmployeeId);
            logEntry.TimeStamp = DateTime.Now;
            logEntry.ExtendedProperties.Add("LogData",
                modifiedCustomers.ToXmlString());

            if(Logger.ShouldLog(logEntry))
                Logger.Write(logEntry);

            //Send data to DAL
            CustomersDAL customersDal = CustomersDAL();
            customersDal.SaveCustomers(modifiedCustomers);
        }

        public CustomerList GetAllCustomers(CustomerList customers)
        {
```

```
            LogEntry logEntry = new LogEntry();
            logEntry.Message = "Getting Customers";
            logEntry.Categories.Add("Customer");
            logEntry.ExtendedProperties.Add("UserId", modifiedCustomers.EmployeeId);
            logEntry.TimeStamp = DateTime.Now;

            if (Logger.ShouldLog(logEntry))
                Logger.Write(logEntry);

            //Get customer data from DAL
            CustomersDAL customersDal = CustomersDAL();
            return customersDal.GetAllCustomers();

        }
    }
}
```

And voilà, when the SaveCustomerData or GetAllCustomers are called and it is determined by the application configuration data that calls to those methods should be logged, an entry will be made into the respective Log table of the Logging database.

# Summary

This chapter went over the many features of the Logging Application Block. While the Logging Application Block may seem like the most complex of the application blocks—especially when dealing with custom trace listeners, custom log filters, configuration, and so on—that complexity is necessary. The design of the Logging Application Block allows it to provide the flexibility and robustness that an organization may require during both the development cycle and while the application is in production.

The next chapter covers the Cryptography Application Block. This is where certain data can be encrypted to prevent prying eyes from reading it. This is especially important nowadays, as customer privacy and data security are in the spotlight on a daily basis.

# CHAPTER 10

■ ■ ■

# The Cryptography Application Block

The Cryptography Application Block pulls double duty. It supports the other application blocks, such as the Caching Application Block, as well as providing stand-alone encryption functionality for an application.

This chapter will discuss how the Cryptography Application Block can abstract the implementation of encryption in an application and how to extend the application block. But first let's take a broader look at encryption.

## Types of Encryption

Cryptography is all about keeping secrets. This may be something as simple as protecting a password or as complex as hiding a customer's financial transactions from prying eyes while they are transferred between end points. The technique used to hide the true value of a piece of data, called *encryption*, depends on its intended eventual use and its sensitivity. Encryption falls into three main categories:

*Hashes*: A hash is one-way encryption for a situation where the value needs to be secured but does not need to be decrypted. Hash values are numbers that represent a string or byte array value. In their native format, they are much smaller than the value they represent. They are generated by an algorithm that makes it very unlikely that two strings would result in the same hash value. Hashes are used for items such as passwords, since the user will supply a new copy of the value, which can then be hashed and compared to the previously hashed value. This type of encryption is not appropriate for data that needs to be decrypted at a later time. The Cryptography Application Block makes hashing values and comparing hashed values relatively painless. It also makes it possible to change hash algorithm providers via configuration.

*Symmetrical encryption*: This type of encryption uses the same key to both encrypt and decrypt the data. The danger with symmetrical encryption is that the key must be delivered to the end user before it can be used and might be intercepted. Symmetrical encryption relies on the same key being available to both encrypt and decrypt a piece of data. While the fact that both parties use the same key is its own security risk, this type of encryption does have its benefits. The most obvious advantage is that symmetrical encryption is faster than asymmetrical encryption.

305

*Asymmetrical encryption*: This type of encryption uses a public and private key. This is more secure than the symmetrical alternative, since only the private key can decrypt the message encrypted by the public key; however, it is also slower. The standard example of this type of encryption is Secure Sockets Layer (SSL), which is used for securing HTTP traffic. SSL uses symmetrical keys, which are exchanged via asymmetrical encryption, for a best of both worlds approach. Asymmetrical encryption methods are not covered by the Cryptography Application Block.

The Data Protection API (DPAPI) provides a means of protecting private keys, stored credentials, and confidential data for use by applications. In the case of the Cryptography Application Block, DPAPI is used to protect encryption keys, which it does through *entropy*. Entropy is a secondary key that is used to ensure that users cannot decrypt a key on their own. Since the keys held in DPAPI are accessible to all applications run by the current user, entropy gives an added layer of protection for data specific to an application.

# Understanding the Design of the Cryptography Application Block

Many considerations went into the design of the Cryptography Application Block. These include performance, providing a key protection model, and making it easily configurable and extensible.

The Cryptography Application Block has probably the fewest moving parts of any of the application blocks. There is not a lot of direct inheritance in its design. The design uses interfaces to make it easy to plug in custom-built hashing and symmetrical encryption providers. Figure 10-1 shows the logical class hierarchy of the Cryptography Application Block.

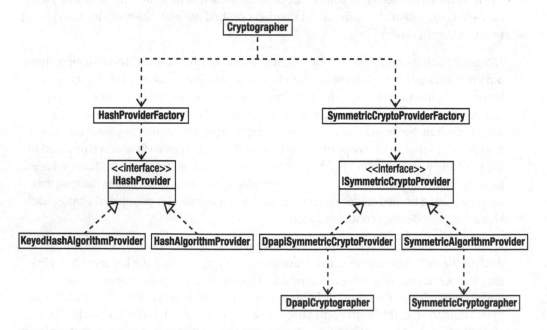

**Figure 10-1.** *Cryptography Application Block logical class hierarchy*

## Cryptographer Façade

The Cryptographer class is a static class that gives an application the ability to create hashes, compare hashes, encrypt data, and decrypt data. In order to maintain consistency with data types, each of the methods has two overloads. One accepts a byte array parameter, and the other accepts a string parameter. The class diagram for the Cryptographer class is shown in Figure 10-2.

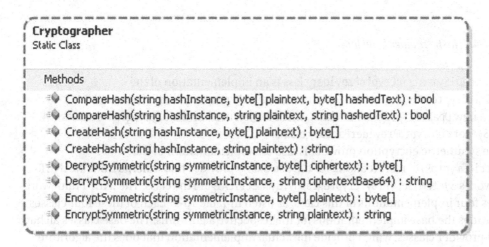

**Figure 10-2.** *Cryptographer class diagram*

## Provider Factories and Providers

The provider factory is a class that uses the Factory pattern, which gives the application block more flexibility. The Cryptography Application Block contains two provider factories: one for creating hash providers and the other for creating symmetric providers. They inherit from the ObjectBuilder's NameTypeFactoryBase generic class. The NameTypeFactoryBase class has two methods: Create and CreateDefault. The Create method allows a named instance to determine the specific instance that should be created. The CreateDefault method allows the default instance that is defined in the configuration file to be instantiated.

Each provider type has its own interface. The symmetric encryption provider has the ISymmetricCryptoProvider interface, shown in Figure 10-3, and the hash provider has the IHashProvider interface, shown in Figure 10-4.

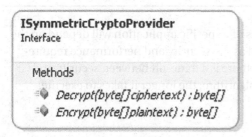

**Figure 10-3.** *ISymmetricCryptoProvider interface*

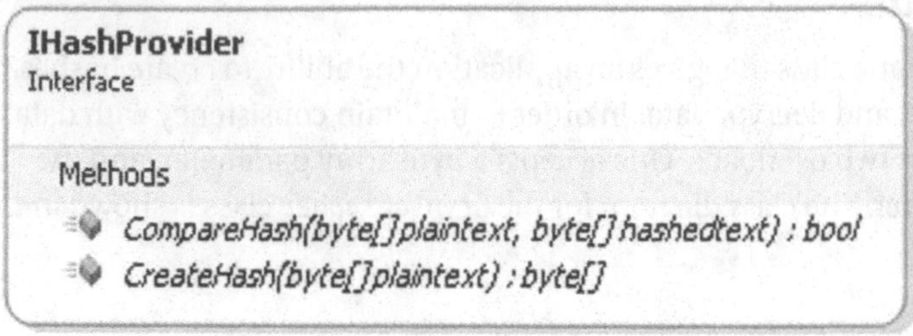

---
**IHashProvider**
Interface

Methods
  ≡♦ *CompareHash(byte[]plaintext, byte[]hashedtext) : bool*
  ≡♦ *CreateHash(byte[]plaintext) : byte[]*
---

**Figure 10-4.** *IHashProvider interface*

The DpapiSymmetricCryptoProvider class is an implementation of the ISymmetricCryptoProvider interface. It has a read-only property that creates and returns a new DpapiCryptographer class, which is then used by the Cryptographer class via the SymmetricCryptoProviderFactory class.

The symmetric encryption provider is also an implementation of the ISymmetricCryptoProvider. It allows for the use of any provider that inherits from the .NET Framework's System.Security.Cryptography.SymmetricAlgorithm class. The .NET Framework provides four implementations of this class, as listed in Table 10-1. Each of these four classes just provides the base implementations for the respective algorithms. The base classes all have derived provider classes, which provide the actual implementation that does the algorithm work, as shown in Table 10-1.

**Table 10-1.** *Symmetric Provider Implementations and Derived Classes*

| Base Implementation | Description | Derived Class |
|---|---|---|
| DES | Provides base functionality for all Data Encryption Standard (DES) algorithm implementations | DESCryptoServiceProvider |
| RC2 | Provides base functionality for all RC2 algorithm implementations | RC2CryptoServiceProvider |
| Rijndael | Provides base functionality for all Rijndael algorithm implementations | RijndaelManaged |
| TripleDES | Provides base functionality for allTriple DES algorithm implementations | TripleDESCryptoServiceProvider |

Which implementation best meets the needs of a specific application will depend on the standards of the company or department, as well as the security and performance requirements of the application. As with all encryption, there is a trade-off between security and speed. Generally speaking, the more secure the algorithm, the longer it takes to execute.

The Cryptography Application Block ships with two hash provider implementations for hashing: the HashAlgorithmProvider and KeyedHashAlgorithmProvider classes. These two provider classes wrap the use of the underlying .NET Framework classes. The HashAlgorithmProvider class handles any classes that derive from System.Security. Cryptography.HashAlgorithm. The KeyedHashAlgorithmProvider class supports any classes that derive from System.Security.Cryptography.KeyedHashAlgorithm.

## Helper Classes

The Cryptography Application Block contains two helper classes that assist in reading and writing keys as well as the encryption process: the KeyManager and CryptographyUtility classes.

The KeyManager class handles utility tasks associated with symmetric algorithm and keyed hash keys. Figure 10-5 shows a class diagram of this class.

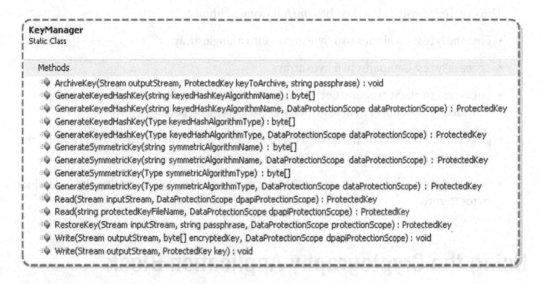

**Figure 10-5.** *KeyManager class diagram*

The ArchiveKey and RestoreKey methods of the KeyManager class are meant for transferring keys between machines by archiving them to or restoring them from a stream. The Read and Write methods have a similar purpose, although in this case, they are not intended for transferring keys between machines. The GenerateKeyedHashKey and GenerateSymmetricKey methods have overloads to create keys based on either the algorithm name or algorithm type.

The CryptographyUtility class includes methods that ease some of the more mundane tasks associated with managing encryption data. As such, this class's functionality can be quite helpful in managing encrypted data. The CryptographyUtility class diagram is shown in Figure 10-6.

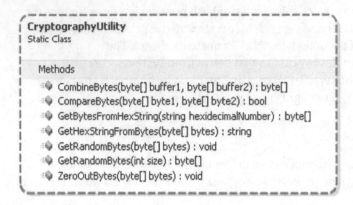

**Figure 10-6.** *CryptographyUtility class diagram*

The CryptographyUtility class has the following methods:

- CombineBytes: Combines two byte arrays into a single array.

- CompareBytes: Compares two byte arrays.

- GetBytesFromHexString and GetHexStringsFromBytes: Convert strings representing hexadecimal numbers to byte arrays and back again, respectively.

- GetRandomBytes: Can be use to fill a memory space with random bytes. This protects the space used to encrypt data from the more serious hacker.

- ZeroOutBytes: Takes a byte array and performs the exciting task of setting the individual bytes to zero.

# Using the Cryptography Application Block

Now that you've learned about the design of the Cryptography Application Block, let's see how to use it in your applications. We'll look at standard usage, configuration, and customization.

## Adding the Cryptography Application Block to an Application

For the examples, you need to create an application that will use the Cryptography Application Block. Follow these steps:

1. Create a new C# Windows project for your application and add the following references to it.

    - Microsoft.Practices.EnterpriseLibrary.Security.Cryptography.dll

    - Microsoft.Practices.EnterpriseLibrary.Common.dll

    - Microsoft.Practices.EnterpriseLibrary.ObjectBuilder.dll

2. In the default Form class (Form1.cs), add the following using clause:

   using Microsoft.Practices.EnterpriseLibrary.Security.Cryptography;

3. Add an app.config file (right-click the project and select Add ➤ New Item, and then select Application Configuration File from the Add New Item dialog box).

4. Open the Enterprise Library Configuration Console and add the Cryptography Application Block (using the Action ➤ New menu item or the context menu of the app.config file in the Explorer pane). The application block will appear in the Configuration Console, as shown in Figure 10-7.

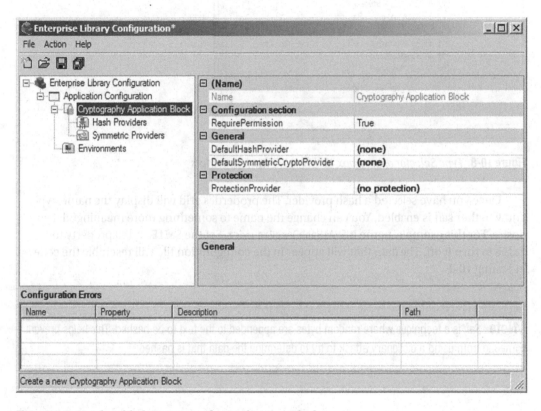

**Figure 10-7.** *Newly added Cryptography Application Block*

## Using a Hash Provider

We'll start by adding a hash provider. Right-click the Hash Providers node and select New ➤ HashAlgorithm Provider. The Type Selector dialog box appears, listing the available providers, which derive from the .NET HashAlgorithm class. For this example, select SHA1Managed, as shown in Figure 10-8.

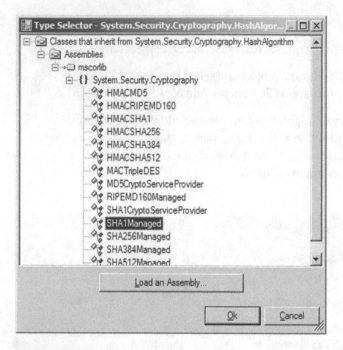

**Figure 10-8.** *Type Selector dialog box listing .NET hash providers*

Once you have selected a hash provider. The properties grid will display the name, type, and whether salt is enabled. You can change the name to something more meaningful if you desire. For this example, name it SHA1HashDemoProvider. Set the SaltEnabled property to false to turn it off. The data that will appear in the configuration file will resemble the code in Listing 10-1.

---

■**Note** *Salt* is a technique where random bytes are appended to the text to be hashed. This helps prevent someone from using a dictionary attack to try to determine the data that is hashed.

---

**Listing 10-1.** *Hash Provider Configuration*

```
<hashProviders>
  <add
     algorithmType="System.Security.Cryptography.
        SHA1CryptoServiceProvider, mscorlib,
        Version=2.0.0.0, Culture=neutral,
        PublicKeyToken=b77a5c561934e089"
     saltEnabled="false"
      type="Microsoft.Practices.EnterpriseLibrary.Security.Cryptography.
      HashAlgorithmProvider,
      Microsoft.Practices.EnterpriseLibrary.Security.Cryptography,
      Version=3.0.0.0, Culture=neutral, PublicKeyToken=null"
      name="SHA1HashDemoProvider" />
</hashProviders>
```

## Hashing a String

As noted earlier, hashes are typically used for passwords, and the next example will demonstrate how that works. In order to show that no smoke and mirrors are involved, the password will be not be hidden from the user.

Before writing the code to create the hash from the password, create a new form that will allow the user to enter the password. The form will need two properties. The first property, StringDescription, will allow for the text of a label to be set at runtime. The second property, ReturnString, will contain the value entered by the user. Follow these steps to create this form:

1. Add a new Windows form to the project and name it StringInput.cs.

2. Add a Label control and a TextBox control to the form, and name them m_StringDescription and m_StringToEncrypt, respectively.

3. Add an Ok button and a Cancel button to the form.

4. Set the DialogResult property of the Ok button to OK, and the same property on the Cancel button to Cancel.

5. Add the following code for the StringDescription and ReturnString properties.

```
using System;
using System.Collections.Generic;
using System.Text;
using System.Windows.Forms;

namespace DGTEL.HashSample
{
    public partial class StringInput : Form
    {
        public string StringDescription
        {
            set { m_StringDescription.Text = value; }
        }

        public string ReturnString
        {
            get { return m_StringToEncrypt.Text; }
        }
    }
}
```

6. Add a button called m_CreatePasswordHash to the main form and place the bolded code shown in Listing 10-2 in the click event.

**Listing 10-2.** *Adding The m_CreatePasswordHash Click Event*

```
using System;
using System.Collections.Generic;
using System.Text;
using System.Windows.Forms;

namespace DGTEL.HashSample
{
    public partial class Form1 : Form
    {

        private void m_CreatePasswordHash_Click
                                    (object sender, EventArgs e)
        {
            string result;
            StringInput inputDialog = new StringInput();
            inputDialog.StringDescription = "Password to Hash";
            if (inputDialog.ShowDialog(this) == DialogResult.OK)
            {
                result = Cryptographer.CreateHash("SHA1HashDemoProvider",
                    inputDialog.ReturnString);
                MessageBox.Show(result);
            }
        }
    }
}
```

The first parameter of CreateHash is the name of the hash provider to be used. This is followed by the string to be hashed. The overload of this method takes a byte array as the second parameter and returns a byte array as a result.

Compile and run the program. Click the Create Password Hash button. When the dialog box appears, enter **Password1!**, and then click the OK button. You should see the message box shown in Figure 10-9.

**Figure 10-9.** *Using a password hash*

## Comparing Hashes

Now that the application can create a hash from a password string, you need to be able to compare the originally hashed result with a user's attempt to authenticate. This is done by using the CompareHash method of the Cryptographer class.

Normally, an application would be pulling this value from a database or some other point of storage. To keep this example simple, we'll save the original hash value to a private variable.

The code for matching the hash values is very compact thanks to the CompareHash method. Add a new button to the Form1 class named m_MatchHash and create the click event. Then implement the hash comparison code in the m_MatchHash button click event handler, as shown in Listing 10-3.

**Listing 10-3.** *Adding the m_MatchHash Click Event*

```
using System;
using System.Collections.Generic;
using System.Text;
using System.Windows.Forms;

namespace DGTEL.HashSample
{
    public partial class Form1 : Form
    {
        private string m_HashValue = string.Empty;

        private void m_CreatePasswordHash_Click(object sender, EventArgs e)
        {
            string result;
            StringInput inputDialog = new StringInput();
            inputDialog.StringDescription = "Password to Hash";
            if (inputDialog.ShowDialog(this) == DialogResult.OK)
            {
                result = Cryptographer.CreateHash("SHA1HashDemoProvider",
                    inputDialog.ReturnString);
                MessageBox.Show(result);
                m_HashValue = result;
            }
        }

        private void m_MatchHash_Click(object sender, EventArgs e)
        {
            StringInput inputDialog = new StringInput();
            inputDialog.StringDescription = "Password to Match";
            if (inputDialog.ShowDialog(this) == DialogResult.OK)
            {
                MessageBox.Show("Compare hashes:" +
                Convert.ToString(Cryptographer.CompareHash
                    ("SHA1HashDemoProvider", inputDialog.ReturnString,
                    m_HashValue)));
            }
        }
    }
}
```

Try entering the original password string. The resulting dialog box will display a value of true. If you enter any other value, the dialog box will display false, as the hash values will not match.

If the SaltEnabled property of the hash provider is set to true, the CompareHash method will extract the salt from the original hash value and use it to hash the new input that is being compared. If you would like to try this, open the application configuration file for this example in the Configuration Console, select the SHA1HashDemoProvider hash provider that you created earlier, select true for the SaltEnabled property, and save the configuration file. Then repeat the preceding steps to try the password comparison with salt enabled.

## Using a Symmetric Encryption Provider

Three types of symmetric encryption providers can be configured: .NET providers that derive from the .NET SymmetricAlgorithm class, DPAPI providers, and custom providers. Figure 10-10 shows the selection of .NET providers that derive from the SymmetricAlgorithm class.

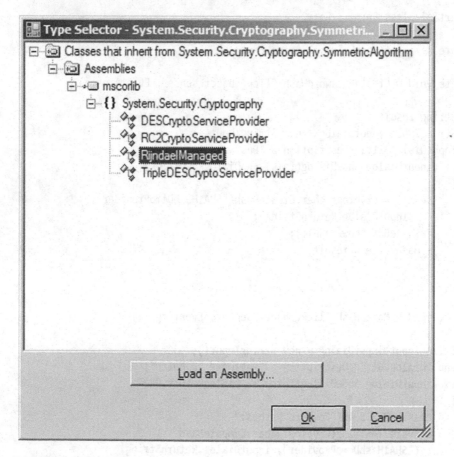

**Figure 10-10.** *Type Selector dialog box listing .NET symmetric encryption providers*

After you've selected a provider, the symmetricCryptoProviders section of the app.config file should look similar to the XML in Listing 10-4.

**Listing 10-4.** *Configuration Section for a Symmetric Cryptography Provider*

```
<symmetricCryptoProviders>
    <add algorithmType="System.Security.Cryptography.
            TripleDESCryptoServiceProvider, mscorlib, Version=2.0.0.0,
            Culture=neutral,
            PublicKeyToken=b77a5c561934e089"
            protectedKeyFilename=
                "C:\Vs2005Projects\CryptographyDemo\
                CryptographyDemo\TripleDEC.key"
            protectedKeyProtectionScope="LocalMachine"
            type="Microsoft.Practices.EnterpriseLibrary.
                Security.Cryptography.SymmetricAlgorithmProvider,
                Microsoft.Practices.EnterpriseLibrary.
                Security.Cryptography,Version=3.0.0.0,
                Culture=neutral, PublicKeyToken=null"
            name="TripleDESCryptoServiceProvider" />
</symmetricCryptoProviders>
```

## Encrypting a String

Many messages can be handled simply as strings. In this example, we will add a new form to the sample application and then see how string encryption works.

1. Create a new Windows project and call it `DGTEL.EncryptStringSample`.

2. Add a new Windows form to the project and call it `EncryptSymmetrical.cs`.

3. Open the application configuration file in the Configuration Console and add the Cryptography Application Block to it.

4. Add a new TripleDES symmetric provider to the Symmetric Providers node and go through the Cryptographic Key Wizard. To make this sample simple, just generate a new key and save it to a file when prompted by the wizard to do so.

5. Save the configuration file.

6. Change the `Program` class (`Program.cs`) so that the `Run` method of the `Application` class instantiates the `EncryptSymmetrical` class, as follows:

   ```
   Application.Run(new EncryptSymmetrical ());
   ```

7. Place two Label controls on the form. Set one control's Text property to `Plain Text` and the other control's Text property to `Encrypted String`.

8. Add two TextBox controls. Both should have their `Multiline` property set to true. Name them `m_PlainText` and `m_EncryptedText`.

9. Add two Button controls. Set their Text properties to `Encrypt` and `Decrypt`, and name them `m_Encrypt` and `m_Decrypt`. The completed form should look like Figure 10-11.

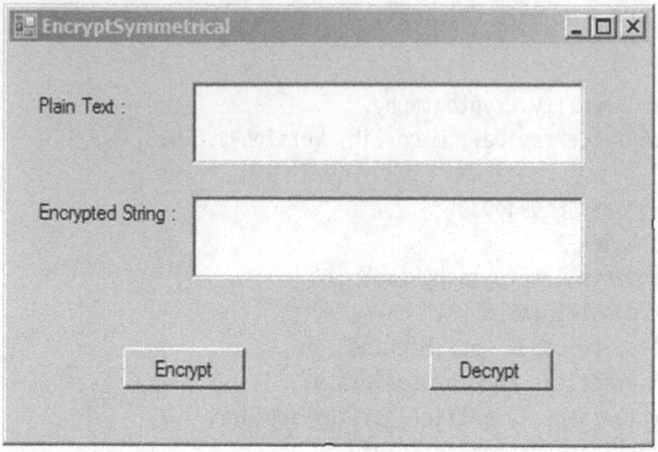

**Figure 10-11.** *Form for encrypting a string*

**10.** Add the encryption implementation for the click event of the m_Encrypt button, as shown in Listing 10-5.

**Listing 10-5.** *Adding the m_Encrypt Click Event*

```
using System;
using System.Collections.Generic;
using System.Text;
using System.Windows.Forms;

namespace DGTEL.EncryptStringSample
{
    public partial class EncryptSymmetrical : Form
    {
        public EncryptSymmetrical()
        {
            InitializeComponent();
        }

        private void m_Encrypt_Click(object sender, EventArgs e)
        {
            string result;
            result = Cryptographer.EncryptSymmetric(
                "TripleDESCryptoServiceProvider",
                m_PlainText.Text);
            m_EncryptedText.Text = result;
        }
    }
}
```

## Decrypting a String

It's great that the data can be secured, but if you cannot retrieve that data, it's not much good. It's similar to saying that if you want to secure your server, unplug it and put it in a closet.

In order to decrypt the value in the m_EncryptedText control, add the click event to the m_Decrypt button, and provide the implementation for decrypting within the click event handler, as shown in Listing 10-6.

**Listing 10-6.** *Adding the m_Decrypt Click Event*

```
using System;
using System.Collections.Generic;
using System.Text;
using System.Windows.Forms;

namespace DGTEL.EncryptStringSample
{
    public partial class EncryptSymmetrical : Form
    {
        public EncryptSymmetrical ()
        {
            InitializeComponent();
        }

        private void m_Encrypt_Click(object sender, EventArgs e)
        {
            string result;
            result = Cryptographer.EncryptSymmetric(
                "TripleDESCryptoServiceProvider", m_PlainText.Text);
            m_EncryptedText.Text = result;
        }

        private void m_Decrypt_Click(object sender, EventArgs e)
        {
            string result;
            result =
                Cryptographer.DecryptSymmetric("TripleDESCryptoServiceProvider",
                m_EncryptedText.Text);
            m_PlainText.Text = result;
        }
    }
}
```

## Encrypting a File

Most times that encryption is discussed, it goes no further than simple strings or byte arrays. Many times, you will find that you need to encrypt whole files. This example demonstrates one solution, as well as the use of the byte array overload of the EncryptSymmetric method.

As you did in the previous section, start by creating a new form and adding controls.

1. Add a new form to the project and name it EncryptSymmetricalToFile.

2. Change the Program class (Program.cs) so that the Run method of the Application class instantiates the EncryptSymmetricalToFile class.

3. Add three Label controls. Set their Text properties to File to Encrypt, Encrypted File, and Decrypted File.

4. Place three TextBox controls on the form. Name them m_FileToEncryptLocation, m_EncryptedFileLocation, and m_DecryptedFileLocation, corresponding to the labels that you added.

5. Next to each of the TextBox controls, add a Button control. Name these with the TextBox control name plus Select (for example, m_FileToEncryptLocationSelect). These will be used to launch an OpenFileDialog instance.

6. For each of the button click events, add the following code, making sure that each button sets the Text property of the correct corresponding TextBox control.

```
OpenFileDialog dialog = new OpenFileDialog();
dialog.ValidateNames = false;
 if (dialog.ShowDialog() == DialogResult.OK)
 {
     m_FileToEncryptLocation.Text = dialog.FileName;
 }
```

7. Add two more Button controls. Set their Text properties to Encrypt File and Decrypt File, and name them m_EncryptFile and m_DecryptFile, respectively. Figure 10-12 shows the completed form.

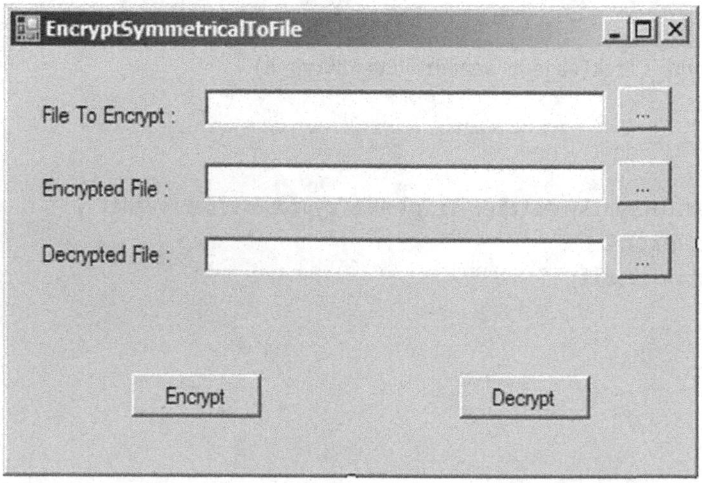

**Figure 10-12.** *Form for encrypting a file*

8. Add the code in Listing 10-7 to the click event of the m_EncryptFile button.

**Listing 10-7.** *Adding the m_EncryptFile Click Event*

```
using System;
using System.Collections.Generic;
using System.Text;
using System.Windows.Forms;
using Microsoft.Practices.EnterpriseLibrary.Security.Cryptography;
using System.IO;

namespace DGTEL.EncryptFileSample
{
    public partial class EncryptSymmetricalToFile : Form
    {
        public EncryptSymmetricalToFile()
        {
            InitializeComponent();
        }

        private void m_EncryptFile_Click(object sender, EventArgs e)
        {
            FileStream inputStream = null;
            FileStream outputStream = null;
            byte[] readBuffer;
            byte[] writeBuffer;
            int inputOffset = 0;
            int outputOffset = 0;
            int count;

            if (m_EncryptedFileLocation.Text.Length > 0 &&
                m_FileToEncryptLocation.Text.Length > 0)
            {
                try
                {
                    inputStream = new FileStream(m_FileToEncryptLocation.Text,
                        FileMode.Open, FileAccess.Read);
                    outputStream = new FileStream(m_EncryptedFileLocation.Text,
                        FileMode.OpenOrCreate);

                    readBuffer = new byte[(int)inputStream.Length];
                    while (inputStream.Length > inputOffset)
                    {
                        count = inputStream.Read(readBuffer, inputOffset,
                            (int)inputStream.Length - inputOffset);
                        inputOffset += count;
                    }

                    if (readBuffer.Length > 0)
                    {
```

```
                    writeBuffer =
                        Cryptographer.EncryptSymmetric(
                        "TripleDESCryptoServiceProvider", readBuffer);
                    outputStream.Write(writeBuffer, outputOffset,
                        writeBuffer.Length);

                    outputOffset += writeBuffer.Length;
                }

                MessageBox.Show("Done");
            }
            catch (Exception ex)
            {
                MessageBox.Show(ex.Message);
            }
            finally
            {
                if (inputStream != null)
                    inputStream.Close();
                if (outputStream != null)
                    outputStream.Close();
            }
        }
    }
}
```

## Decrypting a File

Now we will take the file encrypted with the code in the previous section and decrypt it. The fun part is that the only modification you need to make from the code in the m_EncryptFile button's click event is to change the EncryptSymmetric call to DecryptSymmetric.

Copy the code from the m_EncryptFile button click event to the click event of the m_DecryptFile button. Reverse the controls used for opening the input and output streams. The resulting code should look like Listing 10-8.

**Listing 10-8.** *Adding the m_DecryptFile Click Event*

```
using System;
using System.Collections.Generic;
using System.Text;
using System.Windows.Forms;

namespace DGTEL.EncryptFileSample
{
    public partial class EncryptSymmetricalToFile : Form
    {
```

```
public EncryptSymmetricalToFile()
{
    InitializeComponent();
}

private void m_EncryptFile_Click(object sender, EventArgs e)...


private void m_DecryptFile_Click(object sender, EventArgs e)
{
    FileStream inputStream = null;
    FileStream outputStream = null;
    byte[] readBuffer;
    byte[] writeBuffer;
    int inputOffset = 0;
    int outputOffset = 0;
    int count;

    if (m_EncryptedFileLocation.Text.Length > 0 &&
        m_DecryptedFileLocation.Text.Length > 0)
    {
        try
        {
            inputStream = new FileStream(m_EncryptedFileLocation.Text,
                FileMode.Open,
                FileAccess.Read);
            outputStream = new FileStream(m_DecryptedFileLocation.Text,
                FileMode.OpenOrCreate);

            readBuffer = new byte[(int)inputStream.Length];
            while (inputStream.Length > inputOffset)
            {
                count = inputStream.Read(readBuffer, inputOffset,
                (int)inputStream.Length - inputOffset);
                inputOffset += count;
            }

            if (readBuffer.Length > 0)
            {
                writeBuffer =
                    Cryptographer.DecryptSymmetric(
                    "TripleDESCryptoServiceProvider",
                    readBuffer);
                outputStream.Write(writeBuffer, outputOffset,
                    writeBuffer.Length);

                outputOffset += writeBuffer.Length;
```

```
            }

                MessageBox.Show("Done");
            }
            catch (Exception ex)
            {
                MessageBox.Show(ex.Message);
            }
            finally
            {
                if (inputStream != null)
                    inputStream.Close();
                if (outputStream != null)
                    outputStream.Close();
            }
        }
    }
}
}
```

Now you've seen how to configure both symmetric and hash providers. Another option is to create a custom encryption provider, as discussed next.

## Creating Custom Encryption Providers

This section will demonstrate how to create custom hash and symmetric encryption providers. For the examples, add a new class library to the CryptographyDemo solution and name it CryptographyDemoLibrary. Then add the following references:

- Microsoft.Practices.EnterpriseLibrary.Security.Cryptography.dll

- Microsoft.Practices.EnterpriseLibrary. Security.Cryptography.Configuration.dll

- Microsoft.Practices.EnterpriseLibrary.Common.dll

- System.Configuration.dll

- System.Security.dll

### Creating a Custom Hash Provider

Creating a custom hash algorithm is not for the faint of heart or the mathematically challenged. It is a subject that has entire books and college courses devoted to it. Since this section is meant to demonstrate the creation of a provider and not the implementation of a hashing algorithm, the code will simply wrap the MD5 provider supplied by the .NET Framework.

To begin, add a new class to the CryptographyDemoLibrary project and name it DemoHashProvider.cs. Then add the proper using statements and inherit the IHashProvider interface, as shown in Listing 10-9.

**Listing 10-9.** *Inheriting the IHashProvider Interface*

```
using Microsoft.Practices.EnterpriseLibrary.Security.Cryptography;
using Microsoft.Practices.EnterpriseLibrary.Security.Cryptography.Configuration;
using Microsoft.Practices.EnterpriseLibrary.Common.Configuration;
using System.Security.Cryptography;
using System.Collections.Specialized;

namespace DGTEL.CryptographyLibrary
{
    public class DemoHashProvider: IHashProvider
    {
        public DemoHashProvider(NameValueCollection attributes)
        {
        }

        #region IHashProvider Members

        public bool CompareHash(byte[] plaintext, byte[] hashedtext)
        {

        }

        public byte[] CreateHash(byte[] plaintext)
        {

        }

        #endregion
    }
}
```

Next, add the ConfigurationElementType attribute to the class. Then implement the IHashMembers interface. Listing 10-10 shows these additions.

**Listing 10-10.** *Creating a Custom Hash Provider Class*

```
using Microsoft.Practices.EnterpriseLibrary.Security.Cryptography;
using Microsoft.Practices.EnterpriseLibrary.Security.Cryptography.
   Configuration;
using Microsoft.Practices.EnterpriseLibrary.Common.Configuration;
using System.Security.Cryptography;
using System.Collections.Specialized;

namespace DGTEL.CryptographyLibrary
{
```

```csharp
[ConfigurationElementType(typeof(CustomHashProviderData))]
public class DemoHashProvider: IHashProvider
{
    public DemoHashProvider(NameValueCollection attributes)
    {
    }

    #region IHashProvider Members

    public bool CompareHash(byte[] plaintext, byte[] hashedtext)
    {
        MD5CryptoServiceProvider md5Provider = new
            MD5CryptoServiceProvider();
        byte[] tempHash = md5Provider.ComputeHash(plaintext);

        bool match = false;
        if (hashedtext.Length == tempHash.Length)
        {
            int i = 0;
            while ((i < hashedtext.Length) &&
                (hashedtext[i] == tempHash[i]))
            {
                i += 1;
            }
            if (i == hashedtext.Length)
            {
                match = true;
            }
        }

        return match;
    }

    public byte[] CreateHash(byte[] plaintext)
    {
        MD5CryptoServiceProvider md5Provider = new
            MD5CryptoServiceProvider();
        return md5Provider.ComputeHash(plaintext);
    }

    #endregion
}
}
```

## Creating a Custom Symmetric Encryption Provider

Anyone who has taken a security class has probably created a simple encryption algorithm.
This example will perform an exclusive OR of a single character against the plain text in order
to hide the original value. This is by no means secure, except when dealing with intruders who
are simply curious. However, this example will show the general coding steps required to create a custom encryption provider.

First, add a new class to the CryptographyDemoLibrary project and name it
DemoSymmetricProvider. Then add the proper using statements and inherit the
ISymmetricCryptoProvider interface, as shown in Listing 10-11.

**Listing 10-11.** *Inheriting the ISymmetricCryptoProvider Interface*

```
using Microsoft.Practices.EnterpriseLibrary.Security.Cryptography;
using Microsoft.Practices.EnterpriseLibrary.Security.Cryptography.Configuration;
using Microsoft.Practices.EnterpriseLibrary.Common.Configuration;
using System.Collections.Specialized;
using System;

namespace DGTEL.CryptographyLibrary
{
    public class DemoSymmetricProvider: ISymmetricCryptoProvider
    {
        public DemoSymmetricProvider(NameValueCollection attributes)
        {
        }

        #region ISymmetricCryptoProvider Members

        public byte[] Decrypt(byte[] ciphertext)
        {
        }

        public byte[] Encrypt(byte[] plaintext)
        {
        }

        #endregion
    }
}
```

Next, add the ConfigurationElementType attribute to the class. Finally, implement the
ISymmetricCryptoProvider interface. Listing 10-12 shows these additions.

**Listing 10-12.** *Implementing the ISymmetricCryptoProvider Interface*

```
using Microsoft.Practices.EnterpriseLibrary.Security.Cryptography;
using Microsoft.Practices.EnterpriseLibrary.Security.Cryptography.Configuration;
using Microsoft.Practices.EnterpriseLibrary.Common.Configuration;
using System.Collections.Specialized;
using System;


namespace DGTEL.CryptographyLibrary
{
    [ConfigurationElementType(typeof(CustomSymmetricCryptoProviderData))]
    public class DemoSymmetricProvider: ISymmetricCryptoProvider
    {
        public DemoSymmetricProvider(NameValueCollection attributes)
        {
        }

        #region ISymmetricCryptoProvider Members

        public byte[] Decrypt(byte[] ciphertext)
        {
            byte[] result = new byte[ciphertext.Length];
            // This code is to show where to place code. It is not intended to show
            // an effective encryption algorithm
            for (int idx = 0; idx < ciphertext.Length; idx++)
            {
                result[idx] = (byte)(ciphertext[idx] ^ Convert.ToByte('A'));
            }

            return result;
        }

        public byte[] Encrypt(byte[] plaintext)
        {
            byte[] result = new byte[plaintext.Length];
            // This code is to show where to place code. It is not intended to show
            // an effective encryption algorithm
            for (int idx = 0; idx < plaintext.Length; idx++)
            {
                result[idx] = (byte)(plaintext[idx] ^ Convert.ToByte( 'A' ));
            }

            return result;
        }

        #endregion
    }
}
```

Copy the new assembly to the bin directory of the Enterprise Library installation. Create a reference to the new assembly from the demo application.

### Configuring Custom Encryption Providers

Configuring a custom encryption provider is no different from configuring any other symmetric or hash provider. Just make sure it is accessible to the Configuration Console; either by string naming the custom components and putting them in the GAC or by putting them in the same folder as the Configuration Console executing assembly.

In the Configuration Console, select to add either a new custom hash provider or custom symmetric provider. Then give it a name and specify the assembly, and you should be off to the races.

## Migrating from Prior Versions of Enterprise Library

The object model of the Cryptography Application Block has changed very little from the Enterprise Library 1.1 version. One of the biggest differences is in the configuration. Whereas the previous version required a separate configuration file, the new version stores this information in the application configuration file.

Migrating from version 2.0 to 3.x requires only changing the Enterprise Library assembly version in the configuration file from 2.0.0.0 to 3.0.0.0.

# Encrypting Customer Data in the ACME POS Application

Any company has concerns about security and privacy of data, and ACME is no exception. ACME needs to ensure the privacy of customer data, including personal and financial data.

While the sales team members are on the road, they need to be able to store data locally until they can synchronize with the central ACME servers. While this data is stored locally on the sales users' laptops, it is imperative that this data be protected. The solution to this problem is actually twofold. First, there needs to be a mechanism for storing the offline data, and second there needs to be a mechanism to encrypt it.

The answer, believe it or not, has nothing to do with the Cryptography Application Block—well, at least not directly. In this case, the Caching Application Block (covered in Chapter 7) can be used to store the offline data locally, and the Caching Application Block has the ability to consume the Cryptography Application Block to encrypt the data.

All the cryptography work will be done through configuration files, so there isn't going to be any code required to provide the cryptography functionality. However, it is necessary to add some code to support the online/offline functionality of the ACME POS client.

Before getting knee-deep in the client code, you should make one change in the Customer web service (created in Chapter 8). Open the Customer.cs class file in the ACME.POS.Service.ServiceImplementation project. Locate the System.Web.Service.WebService attribute, above the Customer class. In this attribute, change the Name property from Customer to CustomerServices. This will help distinguish the web service proxy that you will create in this chapter from another class with the same name (autogenerated by the framework).

## Storing Offline Data

First, we need to create the online/offline functionality for the ACME POS client. To begin, open the ACME.POS.Service solution. Right-click the Add References node of the ACME.POS.Service.Client solution and add the following assemblies:

- Microsoft.Practices.EnterpriseLibrary.Caching.dll

- Microsoft.Practices.EnterpriseLibrary.Caching.Cryptography.dll

- ACME.POS.UserInterface.Configuration.dll

Add a web reference to the Customer web service that was created in Chapter 8 to the ACME.POS.Service.Client. Name the class OfflineManager. Within the class, add the following using statements and ensure the class is public.

```
using System;
using System.Collections.Generic;
using System.Net;
using System.Text;

using Microsoft.Practices.EnterpriseLibrary.ExceptionHandling;
using Microsoft.Practices.EnterpriseLibrary.Caching;
using ACME.POS.Service.Client.ACMECustomerWebService;
using ACME.POS.UserInterface.Configuration;

namespace ACME.POS.Service.Client
{
    public class OfflineManager
    {

    }
}
```

Next, add the TestWebServer method and GetUrl property. The TestWebServer method will take a URL and a timeout value. This method will test to ensure the URL exists. This will tell the application whether to save data locally or to the ACME server. The GetUrl property will retrieve the default web service URL from the application configuration file. Listing 10-13 shows these additions.

**Listing 10-13.** *Adding the testWebServer Method*

```
namespace ACME.POS.Service.Client
{
    public class OfflineManager
    {
        private string m_Url ;

        private bool TestWebServer(string Url, int Timeout)
        {
            HttpWebRequest httpRequest = WebRequest.Create(Url) as HttpWebRequest;
```

```csharp
        HttpWebResponse httpResponse = null;
        bool testResult = false;

    try
    {
        //Don't allow infinite timeouts
        if (Timeout > 0)
            httpRequest.Timeout = Timeout;

        // Set resource limits
        httpRequest.MaximumAutomaticRedirections = 4;
        httpRequest.MaximumResponseHeadersLength = 4;

        // Set credentials
        httpRequest.Credentials = CredentialCache.DefaultCredentials;
        httpResponse = httpRequest.GetResponse() as HttpWebResponse;

        testResult = true;
    }
    catch
    {
        //Ignore any exception that occurs
    }
    finally
    {
        if (httpResponse != null)
        {
            httpResponse.Close();
        }
    }

    return testResult;
}

private string GetUrl
{
    get
    {
        if(String.IsNullOrEmpty(m_Url))
        {
            WebServiceSettings settings = new WebServiceSettings();
            m_Url = settings.WebServiceURLs.Get(
                settings.DefaultWebServiceURL).URL;
        }

        return m_Url;
    }
}
}
}
```

The next step is to add the methods for retrieving the data: ReadCustomerData and ReadCustomerDataFromServer. The ReadCustomerData method will determine if the server is available via the TestWebServer, and determine the appropriate way to retrieve the customer data. The ReadCustomerDataFromServer method will create the web service proxy object and retrieve the data from the web service. This is shown in Listing 10-14.

**Listing 10-14.** *Adding the ReadData and ReadDataFromServer Methods*

```
namespace ACME.POS.Service.Client
{
    public class OfflineManager
    {
        private string m_Url;

        private bool TestWebServer(string Url, int Timeout)...

        private string GetUrl...


        public Customer[] ReadCustomerData()
        {
            string url = GetUrl;
            Customer[] customers;

            //check to see if server is available
            if (TestWebServer(url, 10))
            {
                customers = ReadCustomerDataFromServer(url);
            }
            else
            {
                CacheManager cache = CacheFactory.GetCacheManager();
                customers = cache.GetData("customers") as Customer[];
            }

            return customers;
        }

        private Customer[] ReadCustomerDataFromServer(string url)
        {
            CustomerServices service = new CustomerServices();
            service.Url = url;
            return service.GetCustomerList();
        }
    }
}
```

Finally, create the SaveData method. This method will test to see if the web server is available, save the data to the server, and then retrieve all the customers again. This way, any changes made in the back office will be reflected. Listing 10-15 shows the added method.

**Listing 10-15.** *Adding the SaveData Method*

```
namespace ACME.POS.Service.Client
{
    public class OfflineManager
    {
        private string m_Url;

        private bool TestWebServer(string Url, int Timeout)...

        private string GetUrl...

        public List<Customer> ReadData()...

        private List<Customer> ReadDataFromServer(string url)...

        public void SaveData(Customer[] customers)
        {
            string url = GetUrl;

            //check to see if server is available
            if (TestWebServer(url, 10))
            {
                CustomerServices service = new CustomerServices();
                service.Url = url;

                //save data
                for(int i = 0; i < customers.Length; i++)
                {
                    if (customers[i].IsModified)
                    {
                        customers[i] = service.SaveCustomer(customers[i]);
                    }
                }
            }
            else
            {
                CacheManager cache = CacheFactory.GetCacheManager();
                cache.Add("customers", customers);
            }
        }
    }
}
```

## Encrypting Offline Data

In the OfflineManager class, the SaveData and ReadDataFromServer methods both referred to a named cache instance called customers. In order to support that cache, we need to create a named cache instance called customers in the application configuration file, and we want the cache to be encrypted. Creating this encrypted cache instance involves two steps: configuring the Cryptography Application Block and configuring the Caching Application Block.

### Configuring the Cryptography Application Block

The steps for configuring the Cryptography Application Block are similar to those outlined in the earlier examples in this chapter. The four steps are as follows:

1. Open the application configuration file of the ACME.POS.Service.Client project in the Configuration Console.

2. Add the Cryptography Application Block.

3. Add a new TripleDES provider to the Symmetric Providers node.

4. Go through the Cryptographic Key Wizard and name the key file customer.key.

### Configuring the Caching Application Block

With the symmetric encryption provider configured, it is time to configure the customers cache. Follow these steps:

1. Add a new cache manager instance to the Cache Managers node of the Caching Application Block and name it customers.

2. Add an isolated cache store by right-clicking the customers node and selecting New ➤ Isolated Storage.

3. Click the Isolated Storage node and set the PartitionName property value to customerData.

4. Right-click the Isolated Storage node and select New ➤ Symmetric Storage Encryption.

5. Click the Symmetric Storage Encryption node and set the SymmetricInstance property value to the TripleDESCryptoServiceProvider that you created earlier.

That will allow the cached data to be stored locally on the user's machine in an encrypted format. Figure 10-13 shows the encrypted cache configuration in the Configuration Console.

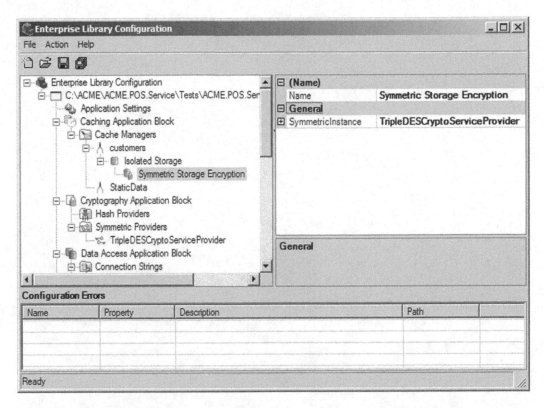

**Figure 10-13.** *Configured customers encrypted cache*

# Summary

This Cryptography Application Block simplifies the use of cryptography. Typically, the only time you will need to use this application block directly is within your own custom solutions that don't involve Enterprise Library directly. Enterprise Library already contains the necessary configurable implementations, thus making cryptography implementation for the Enterprise Library application blocks as easy as configuring them in the Configuration Console.

The next chapter will introduce the Security Application Block and demonstrate how it provides mechanisms to provide common authorization-related functionality.

# CHAPTER 11

■ ■ ■

# The Security Application Block

**S**ecurity tends to be an area of application development that is often overlooked or is implemented poorly. This is partially because of the increasingly constrained project schedules, but also because of the growing complexity of application development. This problem is compounded by the myriad ways in which development teams have historically gone about creating access schemes.

The Security Application Block was created to simplify and standardize the way that applications authorize users and cache security information within an application. It also allows developers to extend the application block to handle more complicated authorization schemes. This chapter describes the makeup of the Security Application Block, how to use it in an application, and how to create custom authorization and security cache providers.

## Understanding the Design of the Security Application Block

The Security Application Block was designed to allow the flexibility required for organizations to implement their own authorization schemes, while also providing implementations for the most common authorization methods.

Another objective of this application block is to cache the profile of a user in such a way as to make it usable throughout the application. This reduces the need to constantly access the authorization provider source to determine if the user has the required privileges.

Like the Cryptography Application Block, the Security Application Block has few moving parts. The public face of this application block consists of the authorization and security caching factories. The heavy lifting is performed by the implementation of individual providers.

Intended to be functional and efficient, the Security Application Block does not include any whizbang features. This application block uses features of the .NET Framework and other application blocks wherever possible. The object model of the Security Application Block is shown in Figure 11-1. It illustrates this relatively simple implementation, including the use of the Caching Application Block to cache authorization information.

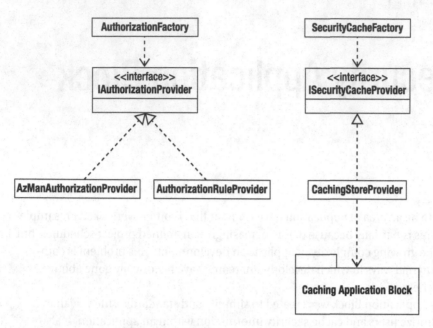

**Figure 11-1.** *Object model of the Security Application Block*

## Authorizing Users in an Application

Microsoft, as well as other vendors, have put a lot of time into various authentication schemes. Unfortunately, authentication only tells an application that users are who they say they are. The system needs to determine what functions a user is authorized to perform. This authorization could be at many levels. One application may handle user access at only a form level, or even at the application level. Other systems may go as far as specifying what type of access each user has to specific components of an application, such as edit or view capabilities on a specific form or control.

### AuthorizationFactory Class

The AuthorizationFactory class works in the same way as the other factories throughout the Enterprise Library application blocks. It allows for an AuthorizationProvider class to be defined in the application's configuration and loaded at runtime.

This particular factory has one main method, GetAuthorizationProvider, which comes in two variations. When it is called without any parameters, the default provider defined in the application configuration file will be instantiated. The other variation takes a string parameter to return a named instance of a provider.

### Authorization Providers

The Authorization Manager (AzMan) is a standard interface for maintaining Active Directory roles, groups, tasks, and operations. It allows for the management of role-based authorization within an application. The Security Application Block supplies an AzMan provider to easily determine if users are authorized for a specific task or operation based on information contained in their identity.

The `AzManAuthorizationProvider` class allows the use of Windows Server 2003 AzMan within the Security Application Block. To use the `AzManAuthorizationProvider` class, you need to install the Windows Server 2003 Administration Tools Pack for Windows XP and Windows 2003 computers. Windows Vista should install AzMan by default.

The other authorization provider class is `AuthorizationRuleProvider`. The `AuthorizationRuleProvider` class allows a rule to be defined for each task, to specify which roles and identities are authorized. It uses a logical equation type of syntax to describe a rule.

## Caching Authorization Profiles

Authenticating a user often requires calls to resources that are not locally available. In a stateless environment, a user should be verified every time a request is made to the server. Unfortunately, these two conditions together can create a significant performance overhead.

The solution that the Security Application Block provides is to use a security cache for caching credentials, and supply clients with a token that they can present as proof that they have been authenticated. This local cache then expedites credential retrieval.

### SecurityCacheFactory Class

The `SecurityCacheFactory` has one static method: `GetSecurityCacheProvider`. As with the `GetAuthorizationProvider` method, the `GetSecurityCacheProvider` method has two possible signatures, which produce a provider base on either the default provider or a specified named provider.

### Security Cache Providers

Each security cache provider derives from the `ISecurityCacheProvider` interface, which provides the ability to save authenticated identities, principals, and profiles that return a token for later retrieval through corresponding methods. It also gives the developer the ability to programmatically expire each of these security items.

The only implementation of a security cache provider provided by the Security Application Block utilizes the Caching Application Block to cache the authorization data.

# Using the Security Application Block

Now that you understand the design of the Security Application Block, you'll learn how to use it in your applications. We'll look at standard usage, configuration, and customization.

## Installing AzMan

Currently, most developers are running Windows XP or Windows Vista as their development platform. In order to use the `AzManAuthorizationProvider` class, the Windows Server 2003 Service Pack 1 Administration Tool Pack and the Windows 2000 Authorization Manager Runtime need to be installed on your Windows XP computer. If you are using Windows Vista, these should already be installed for you. To get these components and learn how to configure AzMan properly, visit http://msdn2.microsoft.com/en-us/library/ms998336.aspx. Follow the instructions in the document to create the AzMan application and objects that we will use in the following examples:

- Operation: Operation 1

- Task: Task 1

- Role: Manager

You also need to give the ASP.NET user access to the XML file.

After you've set up AzMan, load the Enterprise Library solution. Then add the following projects to the solution (located in the src\Security directory of Enterprise Library):

- Security.Azman.csproj

- Security.Azman.Configuration.Design.csproj

Build the solution and run the CopyAssemblies.bat script in the root of Enterprise Library to copy the assembly to the bin directory.

---

**Note** For Windows XP users, it may be easier to create a virtual Windows Server 2003 server that runs IIS, as some of the preconfiguration required for Windows XP can be extensive.

---

## Adding the Security Application Block to an Application

Since the Security Application Block gets its greatest benefit in web applications, we'll create a web application for the examples in this chapter. Before you begin, make sure that you have compiled the Security.Azman and Security.Azman.Configuration.Design projects, mentioned in the previous section. Also, ensure you have IIS 5.1 or greater installed on your computer.

Follow these steps to create the application and add the Security Application Block:

1. Create a new C# web site for your application called SecurityDemo and add the following references to it:

    - Microsoft.Practices.EnterpriseLibrary.Security.dll

    - Microsoft.Practices.EnterpriseLibrary.Security.AzMan.dll

    - Microsoft.Practices.EnterpriseLibrary.Security.Cache.CachingStore.dll

2. Using the IIS Manager, remove anonymous access from the virtual directory.

3. Set the Default.aspx page as the start page.

4. Add a web.config file (right-click the project, select Add ➤ New Item, and choose Web Configuration File in the Add New Item dialog box).

5. Open the Enterprise Library Configuration Console and add the Security Application Block (using the Action ➤ New menu or the context menu of the web.config file in the Explorer pane). The application block should appear in the Configuration Console as shown in Figure 11-2.

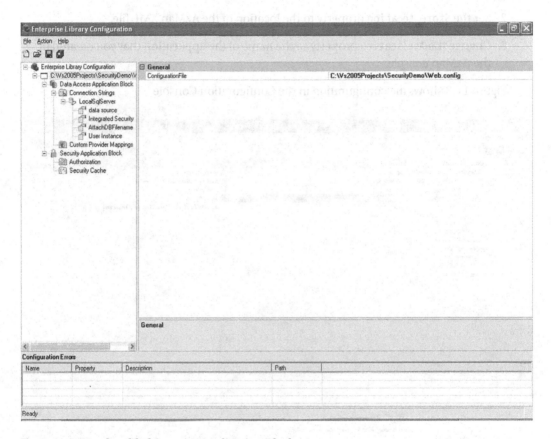

**Figure 11-2.** *Newly added Security Application Block*

The AuthorizationFactory class is one of the two main abstraction points for the Security Application Block. After it has been configured, the factory class can be queried for a provider, which can be used to determine if a user can access a specific operation.

## Using the AzMan Provider

The AzMan provider and authorization rule provider are supplied with the Security Application Block. The following sections describe how to configure them through the Configuration Console and then use them in the demo application.

## Configuring the AzMan Provider

With the Security Application Block added to the demo application, you can now set up the application to use the AzMan provider as an authorization source. Follow these steps to configure the AzMan provider:

1. Right-click the Authorization node of the Security Application Block and select New AzMan Provider.

2. Set the Store Location property to the location of the AzMan XML file.

3. Change the Application property to the name of the application that you created in the AzMan console.

   Figure 11-3 shows the configuration in the Configuration Console.

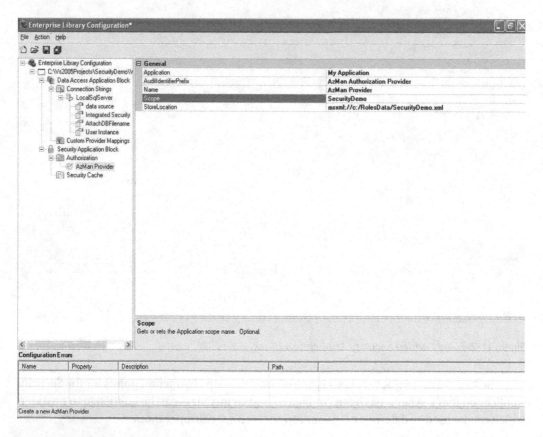

**Figure 11-3.** *Configured AzMan provider*

The Scope parameter allows the application to have different sections that act as individual security areas. Note that in a server environment, the Store Location would normally be Active Directory.

## Verifying That a User Is Authorized with the AzMan Provider

With the AzMan provider configured, you can use it with the demo application. This example will use the current user's identity and a hard-coded role to show how authorization is performed.

First, add the following using statement to the Default.aspx web form's code behind file.

```
using Microsoft.Practices.EnterpriseLibrary.Security;
using System.Security.Principal;
```

Next, add a Label control named m_ResultLabel and a Button control named m_AuthAzMan to the form. Then add the code shown in Listing 11-1 to the click event of the Button control.

**Listing 11-1.** *Using the AzMan Authorization Provider*

```
protected void m_AuthAzMan_Click(object sender, EventArgs e)
{
    IPrincipal principal = new GenericPrincipal(
        User.Identity, new string[] { "Manager" });

    IAuthorizationProvider provider =
        AuthorizationFactory.GetAuthorizationProvider("AzMan Provider");

    if (provider.Authorize(principal, "Task 1"))
    {
        m_ResultLabel.Text = "Authorized to perform Task 1";
    }
    else
    {
        m_ResultLabel.Text = "Not Authorized to perform Task 1";
    }
}
```

If the operation or task that is being authorized against does not exist in the XML store, it will cause an XML missing element exception. This is not a very nice way to treat a missing context, so it is best to surround calls to Authorize in a try/catch block.

---

■**Note**  As with most resources, it is best if access is centralized. Repeated calls to a remote service or file will have serious impacts on performance.

---

## Configuring an Authorization Rule Provider

An authorization rule provider is described entirely by its configuration. The provider is a set of one or more rule definitions. Follow these steps to configure the authorization rule provider:

1. In the Enterprise Library Configuration Console, right-click the Authorization node of the Security Application Block and select New ➤ Authorization Rule Provider.

2. Set the Name property to Task 1 Rule.

3. Right-click the new authorization rule provider and select New ➤ Rule.

4. Set the rule's Name property to DemoRule.

5. Click the ellipsis next to the Expression property. This will open the Rule Expression Editor dialog box.

6. In the dialog box, click the Role button. This adds an R: in the Expression text area. Type Manager after the colon, as shown in Figure 11-4. This rule designates that the identity being authorized must be in the Manager role.

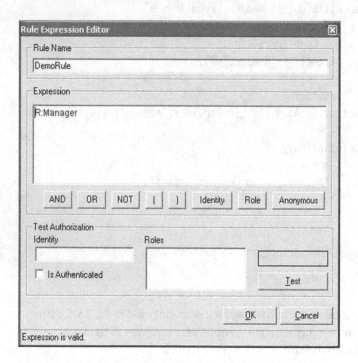

**Figure 11-4.** *Adding a rule in the Rule Expression Editor*

**Note** The Rule Expression Editor does allow you to test that an expression is valid or that it works under specific conditions.

### Verifying That a User is Authorized with the Authorization Rule Provider

Since the demo application already has a form that has the required using statements, to use the new rule, simply add a button to the form. Name it m_AuthRuleProvider and set its Text property to Authorize by Rule Provider. Populate the button's click event with the code shown in Listing 11-2.

**Listing 11-2.** *Using the Authorization Rule Provider*

```
protected void m_AuthRuleProvider_Click(object sender, EventArgs e)
{
    IPrincipal principal = new GenericPrincipal(
        User.Identity, new string[] { "Manager" });

    IAuthorizationProvider provider =
        AuthorizationFactory.GetAuthorizationProvider(
            "Task 1 Rule");

    if (provider.Authorize(principal, "DemoRule"))
    {
        m_ResultLabel.Text = "Authorized by DemoRule";
    }
    else
    {
        m_ResultLabel.Text = "Not Authorized by DemoRule";
    }
}
```

Start the application and click the Authorize by Rule Provider button. Since the configuration specified that the user should be in the Manager role, the "Authorized by DemoRule" message will be displayed on the form.

To test that the code is working, change the call to the GenericPrincipal constructor, so that the context is set to Sales. Rerun the test, and you should see the "Not Authorized by DemoRule" message.

## Using a Security Cache

Using the caching store provider supplied with the Security Application Block, you can save and retrieve security objects from the cache.

### Configuring a Caching Store Provider

To configure a caching store provider, in the Configuration Console, right-click the Security Cache node of the Security Application Block and choose New ➤ Caching Store Provider. When you add a caching store provider, the Caching Application Block is automatically added to the configuration file, because this provider is dependent on that application block.

For this demonstration, all the defaults for the caching store provider are sufficient. If the application requires that the cache survive longer than the default 60 minutes, you can set the AbsoluteExpiration property to the desired duration. The SlidingExpiration property defines the duration of time an object was last accessed to the time it expires. This should be a shorter time interval than the AbsoluteExpiration property, since the object will be removed from cache by the time the AbsoluteExpiration value is reached.

## Saving an Object to the Cache

As mentioned earlier, you can save identities, principals, and profiles using the SecurityCacheProvider class. The basic code is the same for saving an IIdentity, IProfile, or IPrincipal object. In order to accomplish this, the code must first get an instance of the SecurityCacheProvider defined in the configuration for the application. The appropriate save method is then called to place the object in cache. This example demonstrates saving an identity with the SaveIdentity method and storing the token that is returned in the session.

Add a button to the form. Name it m_SaveIdentity and set its Text property to Save an Identity to Cache. Place the code shown in Listing 11-3 in the click event of the new button.

**Listing 11-3.** *Saving an Identity to the Cache*

```
protected void m_SaveIdentity_Click(object sender, EventArgs e)
{
    // Get a caching provider based on configuration
    ISecurityCacheProvider provider =
    SecurityCacheFactory.GetSecurityCacheProvider(
        "Caching Store Provider");

    // Get a token representing the authenticated
    // user so that the identity can be retrieved later
    IToken securityToken = provider.SaveIdentity(User.Identity);

    // Save the token for the next visit
    Session["token"] = securityToken;
    m_ResultLabel.Text = "Token : " + securityToken.Value;
}
```

When you click the button on the web form, you will see a globally unique identifier (GUID) for the token representing the authenticated user.

## Retrieving an Identity from the Cache

Once a security object has been placed in the cache, it can be retrieved in subsequent calls to the application using the token generated at the point it was saved. To do this, you must create an instance of SecurityCacheProvider and call the corresponding Get method with the token as a parameter. To demonstrate, we will continue working with an IIdentity-derived object that needs to be retrieved from cache.

Add a button to the form with an ID of m_CacheProvider and a Text property of Authorize with Cache Provider. Place the code shown in Listing 11-4 in the click event of the new button.

**Listing 11-4.** *Retrieving an Identity from the Cache*

```
protected void m_CacheProvider_Click(object sender, EventArgs e)
{
    // Get a caching provider based on configuration
    ISecurityCacheProvider provider =
    SecurityCacheFactory.GetSecurityCacheProvider("Caching Store Provider");

    // Get a token from session
    IToken securityToken = (IToken)Session["token"];

    if (securityToken != null)
    {
        // Retrieve the identity for the supplied token
        IIdentity identity = provider.GetIdentity(securityToken);
        m_ResultLabel.Text = "Identity : " + identity.Name;
    }
    else
    {
        m_ResultLabel.Text = "Token was not available in session";
    }
}
```

Run the application and click the Save an Identity to Cache button, then the Authorize with Cache Provider button. The first event will save the token to cache so that it can be retrieved on the click of the second button. The final result will be that the user's login will be displayed in the label at the top of the page.

# Adding a Custom Authorization Provider

Your application may require that authorization rules reside in a database table or have complex logic. In this case, the best approach is to create a custom authorization provider.

## Creating a Custom Authorization Provider

For a custom authorization provider, you must implement the Authorize method. This method takes two parameters:

- An IPrincipal-derived object that gives the user's information.

- A string that gives context for the user being authorized. This context is generally a role name.

For this example, we will use an XML file to store a cross-reference of user IDs and roles. This will also serve as a good example of using attributes within a custom provider, as the XML store file will be designated in the configuration. Listing 11-5 shows the format of the file.

**Listing 11-5.** *XML File of User IDs and Roles*

```
<?xml version="1.0" encoding="utf-8" ?>
<Users>
  <User Name="EntLib\jsmith" Role="Manager"/>
  <User Name="EntLib\jsmith" Role="Admin"/>
  <User Name="EntLib\mjones" Role="Sales"/>
</Users>
```

Perform the following steps to create a sample custom authorization provider:

1. Add a new class library to the SecurityDemo solution and name it SecurityDemoLibrary. Add the following references:

   - Microsoft.Practices.EnterpriseLibrary.Security.dll

   - Microsoft.Practices.EnterpriseLibrary.Security.Cache.CachingStore.dll

   - Microsoft.Practices.EnterpriseLibrary.Common.dll

   - Microsoft.Practices.EnterpriseLibrary.Caching.dll

   - System.Configuration.dll

2. Add a new class to the SecurityDemoLibrary project and name it DemoAuthorizationProvider.

3. Add the following using statements:

   ```
   using Microsoft.Practices.EnterpriseLibrary.Security;
   using Microsoft.Practices.EnterpriseLibrary.Common.Configuration;
   using Microsoft.Practices.EnterpriseLibrary.Security.Configuration;
   using System.Xml;
   using System.Collections.Specialized;
   using System.Configuration;
   ```

4. Define the class that derives from AuthorizationProvider. You should see a SmartTag that gives the option to implement the abstract AuthorizationProvider class. Select this option.

5. Create a private string variable to hold the XML store path and name it xmlPath.

6. Define a constructor that takes a NameValueCollection as a parameter and sets the xmlPath value, as follows:

```
public DemoAuthorizationProvider(NameValueCollection attributes)
{
    xmlPath = attributes.Get("XmlStore");
}
```

7. Add the following attribute to the class so that the class can be loaded via the AuthorizationFactory class.

```
[ConfigurationElementType(typeof(CustomAuthorizationProviderData))]
```

8. Add the code shown in Listing 11-6 to the Authorize method.

**Listing 11-6.** *Adding the Authorize Method*

```
public override bool Authorize(
    System.Security.Principal.IPrincipal principal,
    string context)
{
    string name = principal.Identity.Name;
    bool authorized = false;

    if (xmlPath == string.Empty)
    {
        throw new ConfigurationErrorsException
            ("Configuration Error: XML Store " +
            "Path Not Set");
    }

    // Open the role store
    XmlTextReader reader = new XmlTextReader(xmlPath);

    // Check if the username is in the role
    // specified by the context parameter
    while (reader.Read())
    {
        if (reader.Name.Equals("User"))
        {
            if (reader.GetAttribute("Name") == name &&
                reader.GetAttribute("Role") == context)
            {
                authorized = true;
            }
        }
    }
    return authorized;
}
```

## Configuring a Custom Authorization Provider

To configure a custom authorization provider through the Enterprise Library Configuration Console, you need to first copy the assembly to the `bin` folder of the Enterprise Library project. After you've copied the assembly, follow these steps to configure the new provider:

1. Right-click the Authorization node of the Security Application Block and choose New ➤ Custom Authorization Provider.

2. Click the ellipsis next to the `Type` property. This will bring up the Type Selector dialog box, as shown in Figure 11-5. Click the name of the provider, and then choose OK.

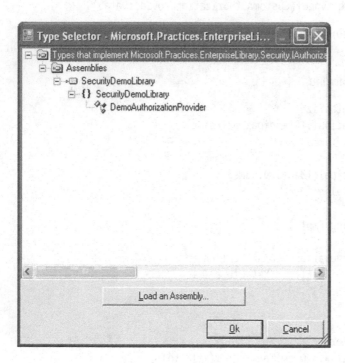

**Figure 11-5.** *Choosing an authorization provider from the Type Selector dialog box*

3. Click the ellipsis next to the `Attributes` property to open the EditableKeyValue Collection Editor dialog box.

4. Click the Add button to add a key and value. Type `XmlStore` in the Key field and the path to the XML file containing the roles in the Value field, as shown in Figure 11-6. Click OK to complete the configuration.

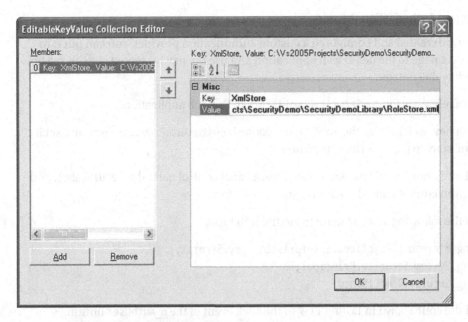

**Figure 11-6.** *Using the EditableKeyValue Editor dialog box*

The new authorization provider should appear in the Configuration Console, as shown in Figure 11-7.

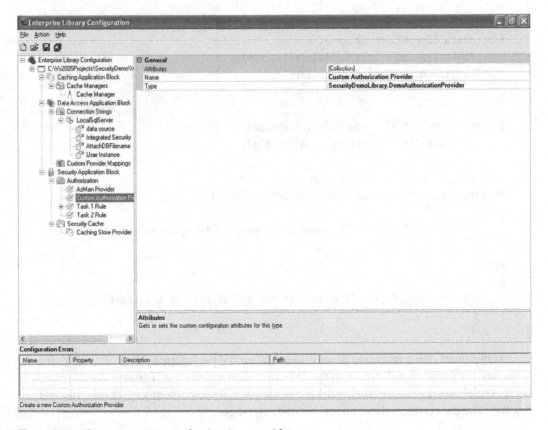

**Figure 11-7.** *The new custom authorization provider*

## Using a Custom Authorization Provider

Now that you've created and configured a custom authorization provider, you can put it to use. You'll add a page to the demo web application and use the newly created class to see how it works. Follow these steps:

1. Add a reference for the SecurityDemoLibrary to the web application.

2. Add a new web form to the application. Name it CustomAuthProvider.aspx and set it as the startup page for the application.

3. Add a TextBox control named m_RoleName, a Label control named m_ResultLabel, and a Button control named m_AuthUser to the web form.

4. Add the following using statements to the web form:

   ```
   using Microsoft.Practices.EnterpriseLibrary.Security;
   using System.Security.Principal;
   using SecurityDemoLibrary;
   ```

5. Add the code shown in Listing 11-7 to the click event of the m_AuthUser button.

**Listing 11-7.** *Adding the m_AuthUser Click Event*

```
protected void m_AuthUser_Click(object sender, EventArgs e)
{
    // Get an instance of the custom provider
    IAuthorizationProvider provider =
        AuthorizationFactory.GetAuthorizationProvider
        ("Custom Authorization Provider ");


    IPrincipal principal = new GenericPrincipal
        (User.Identity,new string[]{"Manager"});

    // Check if the user is authorized
    if (provider.Authorize(principal, roleName.Text))
    {
        m_ResultLabel.Text = "The user is authorized for this role";
    }
    else
    {
        m_ResultLabel.Text = "The user is not authorized for this role";
    }
}
```

At this point, the application is ready to go. When the page appears, type the role that is associated with the logged-in user in the XML store. You will see the "The user is authorized for this role" message in the label at the top of the page. If you enter any other role, you will see the "The user is not authorized for this role" message.

# Adding a Custom Security Cache Provider

Your application might need functionality beyond that of the CachingStoreProvider class. It is just for that reason that the Caching Application Block allows for custom security cache providers to be created.

The example in this section takes the functionality of the CachingStoreProvider class and adds the ability to save a SecurityCacheItem instance to it. This is a class built into the application block that is used by the provider to hold an instance of IIdentity, IPrincipal, and IProfile for caching. The new class will add the ability to accept an instance of SecurityCacheItem and save it in the cache.

## Creating a Custom Security Cache Provider

A lot of functionality must be implemented for a custom security cache provider. It inherits abstract methods to save, retrieve, and set as expired IIdentity, IPrincipal, and IProfile objects. Each of the save methods also has an overload, which takes a token to identify that the security item has previously been saved.

Much of the code you'll use in this example is borrowed from the CachingStoreProvider class. It inherits from the SecurityCacheProvider class, which is an abstract implementation of the ISecurityCacheProvider and IInstrumentationEventProvider interfaces. The example in this section demonstrates how to create a provider that will use the Caching Application Block as backing store, with the addition of storing a SecurityCacheItem object.

Follow these steps to create the custom security cache provider:

1. Add a new class to the SecurityDemoLibrary project and name it DemoSecurityCacheProvider.

2. Add the following using statements to the new class:

   ```
   using Microsoft.Practices.EnterpriseLibrary.Caching;
   using Microsoft.Practices.EnterpriseLibrary.Caching.Expirations;
   using Microsoft.Practices.EnterpriseLibrary.Common.Configuration;
   using Microsoft.Practices.EnterpriseLibrary.Security;
   using Microsoft.Practices.EnterpriseLibrary.Security.Cache.CachingStore;
   using Microsoft.Practices.EnterpriseLibrary.Security.Configuration;
   using System.Collections.Specialized;
   ```

3. Define the class so that it derives from SecurityCacheProvider. You will see a SmartTag that gives the option to implement the abstract SecurityCacheProvider class. Select this option.

4. Add the following attribute to the class definition:

   ```
   [ConfigurationElementType(typeof(CustomSecurityCacheProviderData))]
   ```

5. Define the following private class level variables. They will be used to create and maintain the cache manager used by the provider.

   ```
   private int slidingExpiration;
   private int absoluteExpiration;
   private CacheManager securityCacheManager;
   ```

6. Add a constructor that accepts a NameValueCollection parameter so that attributes can be added during configuration. It should contain the code shown in Listing 11-8.

**Listing 11-8.** *Defining the DemoSecurityCacheProvider Constructor*

```
public DemoSecurityCacheProvider(NameValueCollection attributes)
{
    int.TryParse(attributes["slidingExpiration"],out
        this.slidingExpiration);
    int.TryParse(attributes["absoluteExpiration"],out
        this.absoluteExpiration);
    this.securityCacheManager =
    CacheFactory.GetCacheManager(
        attributes["securityCacheManager"]);
}
```

7. Add the ExpireSecurityCacheItem and ClearCacheItem methods, as shown in Listing 11-9.

**Listing 11-9.** *Adding the ExpireSecurityCacheItem and ClearCacheItemEntity Methods*

```
private void ExpireSecurityCacheItem(IToken token,
    SecurityEntityType entityType)
{
    SecurityCacheItem item = GetSecurityCacheItem(token);
    if (item != null)
    {
        ClearCacheItemEntity(item, entityType);

        if (item.IsRemoveable)
        {
            securityCacheManager.Remove(token.Value);
        }
    }
}

private void ClearCacheItemEntity(SecurityCacheItem item,
    SecurityEntityType entityType)
{
    switch (entityType)
    {
        case SecurityEntityType.Identity:
            item.Identity = null;
            break;

        case SecurityEntityType.Principal:
            item.Principal = null;
            break;
```

```
        case SecurityEntityType.Profile:
            item.Profile = null;
            break;
    }
}
```

8. Replace the default exception throw statements in the ExpirePrincipal, ExpireIdentity, and ExpireProfile methods. They will all make the same method call. The difference will be the SecurityEntityType enumeration value.

```
public override void ExpirePrincipal(IToken token)
{
    ExpireSecurityCacheItem(token, SecurityEntityType.Principal);
}
```

9. Implementing the SavePrincipal, SaveIdentity, and SaveProfile methods gives the provider the ability to place the respective security items in the cache. Each has two versions defined by the ISecurityCacheProvider interface. The difference is that one signature returns an IToken after the save and the other accepts an IToken parameter. An example of each is shown in Listing 11-10.

**Listing 11-10.** *Versions of SavePrincipal*

```
public override void SavePrincipal(
    System.Security.Principal.IPrincipal principal,
        IToken token)
{
    SaveSecurityCacheItem(new SecurityCacheItem(principal),
        token);
}

public override IToken SavePrincipal(
    System.Security.Principal.IPrincipal principal)
{
    return SaveSecurityCacheItem(new
        SecurityCacheItem(principal);
}
```

10. Implement the GetPrincipal, GetIdentity, and GetProfile methods in order to retrieve the appropriate security information from the cache. Follow the pattern used in the following example, changing the property being returned for each method.

```
public override System.Security.Principal.IPrincipal
    GetPrincipal(IToken token)
{
    return GetSecurityCacheItem(token).Principal;
}
```

11. You need to create several supporting private methods. These handle the actual access to the cache manager. Copy the code in Listing 11-11 and add it to the class definition.

**Listing 11-11.** *Adding the GetSecurityCacheItem, GetCacheExpirations, and ConvertExpirationToSeconds Methods*

```
public SecurityCacheItem GetSecurityCacheItem(IToken token)
{
    return GetSecurityCacheItem(token, false);
}

private SecurityCacheItem GetSecurityCacheItem(
    IToken token, bool createIfNull)
{
    SecurityCacheItem item = null;
    item = securityCacheManager.GetData(token.Value)
        as SecurityCacheItem;

    if (item == null && createIfNull)
    {
        item = new SecurityCacheItem();
        securityCacheManager.Add(token.Value,
            item, CacheItemPriority.Normal, null,
            GetCacheExpirations());
    }

    return item;
}

private ICacheItemExpiration[] GetCacheExpirations()
{
    ICacheItemExpiration[] cachingExpirations =
        new ICacheItemExpiration[2];
    cachingExpirations[0] = new AbsoluteTime(
        new TimeSpan(0, 0,
        ConvertExpirationTimeToSeconds(absoluteExpiration)));
    cachingExpirations[1] = new SlidingTime(
        new TimeSpan(0, 0,
        ConvertExpirationTimeToSeconds(slidingExpiration)));
    return cachingExpirations;
}

private int ConvertExpirationTimeToSeconds(
    int expirationInMinutes)
{
    return expirationInMinutes * 60;
}
```

**12.** The code for the SaveSecurityCacheItem method and its overload differ from the other save methods in that they do not call the GetSecurityCacheItem method to save their data. The second version of the method actually calls the cache manager directly. Copy the code in Listing 11-12 into the class to implement this functionality.

**Listing 11-12.** *Adding the SaveSecurityCacheItem Methods*

```
public IToken SaveSecurityCacheItem(SecurityCacheItem item)
{
    IToken token = new GuidToken();
    SaveSecurityCacheItem(item, token);
    return token;
}

public void SaveSecurityCacheItem(
    SecurityCacheItem item, IToken token)
{
    SecurityCacheItem cacheItem = null;
    cacheItem = securityCacheManager.GetData(token.Value)
        as SecurityCacheItem;

    if (cacheItem == null)
    {
        securityCacheManager.Add(token.Value, item,
        CacheItemPriority.Normal, null,
        GetCacheExpirations());
    }
    else
    {
        cacheItem.Identity = item.Identity;
        cacheItem.Principal = item.Principal;
        cacheItem.Profile = item.Profile;
    }
}
```

Compile the code and copy the new assembly to the bin directory of the Enterprise Library installation. Create a reference to the new assembly from the demo application.

## Configuring a Custom Security Cache Provider

The hardest part is complete, and now it is time to configure the new security cache provider. The unfortunate part about creating a custom provider is that the easiest implementation requires that any properties be added as attributes. Since the sample security cache provider uses the same cache manager as the default caching store provider, you will need to add attributes to the configuration.

The few steps listed here will set up the DemoSecurityCacheProvider class to be used with the cache manager that was configured earlier in the chapter.

1.  Open the demo application's web.config file in the Enterprise Library Configuration Console.

2.  Right-click the Security Cache node and select New ➤ Custom Security Cache Provider. This will create a new provider node.

3.  Click the ellipsis next to the Type property. The Type Selector dialog box will appear. As long as the new security cache provider is in the bin folder of the Enterprise Library installation, it should be available for selection, as shown in Figure 11-8.

**Figure 11-8.** *The Type Selector dialog box lists the new DemoSecurityCacheProvider*

4.  Click the ellipsis next to the Attributes property to open the EditableKeyValue Collection Editor dialog box. Add the following keys and values, as shown in Figure 11-9:

    •   slidingExpiration: 10

    •   absoluteExpiration: 60

    •   securityCacheManager: Cache Manager

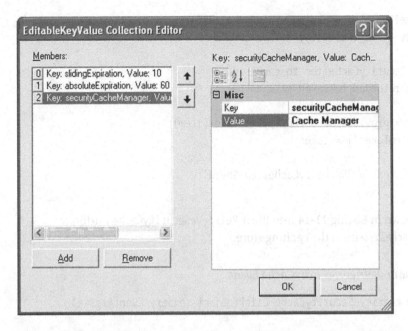

**Figure 11-9.** *Adding custom cache provider attributes through the EditableKeyValue Collection Editor dialog box*

## Using a Custom Security Cache Provider

Now that the new security cache provider has been developed and configured, you can use it from a web page.

Since the demo application already has a reference to the assembly, you can skip that step. Add a new web form to the demo application called CustomSecurityCache and make it the startup page. Add the following using statements:

```
using Microsoft.Practices.EnterpriseLibrary.Security;
using Microsoft.Practices.EnterpriseLibrary.Security.Cache.CachingStore;
using SecurityDemoLibrary;
```

On the form, place a label named m_ResultLabel, a button named m_SaveSecurityCache, and a button named m_RetrieveSecurityCache. Add the code shown in Listing 11-13 to the click event of the m_SaveSecurityCache button.

**Listing 11-13.** *Adding the m_SaveSecurityCache Event*

```
protected void m_SaveSecurityCache_Click(object sender, EventArgs e)
{
    // Get an instance of the custom security cache provider
    DemoSecurityCacheProvider provider =
        SecurityCacheFactory.GetSecurityCacheProvider(
        "Custom Cache Provider") as DemoSecurityCacheProvider;

    // Create a new SecurityCacheItem and set its Identity property
```

```
        SecurityCacheItem item = new SecurityCacheItem();
        item.Identity = User.Identity;

        // Save the SecurityCacheItem to cache and
        // place the returned token in session

        IToken token = provider.SaveSecurityCacheItem(item);
        Session["CustomToken"] = token;

        m_ResultLabel.Text = "SecurityCacheItem Saved";
    }
```

Insert the code shown in Listing 11-14 into the m_RetrieveSecurityCache button to
retrieve the SecurityCacheItem from the caching store.

**Listing 11-14.** *Adding the m_RetrieveSecurityCache Event*

```
    protected void m_RetrieveSecurityCache_Click(object sender, EventArgs e)
    {
        // Get an instance of the custom security cache provider
        DemoSecurityCacheProvider provider =
        SecurityCacheFactory.GetSecurityCacheProvider(
            "Custom Cache Provider") as DemoSecurityCacheProvider;

        // Retrieve the SecurityCacheItem denoted by the token saved in session
        SecurityCacheItem item =
            provider.GetSecurityCacheItem(
            (IToken)Session["CustomToken"]);

        m_ResultLabel.Text = item.Identity.Name;
    }
```

Compile and execute the application. When the page appears, click the save button. You
will see a message indicating that the save was completed. Next, click the retrieve button, and
the currently logged-in user's name will be displayed.

## Migrating from Prior Versions of Enterprise Library

The biggest difference between the current and previous versions of the Security Application
Block is the removal of authentication functionality. This is now a feature of the
System.Web.Security namespace in .NET 2.0 and 3.0.

Another change is the location of the configuration for the application block. In the
previous version, it was in a separate securityConfiguration.config file. Now it is in the
application configuration file by default.

■**Note**  In order to keep the ACME POS application as simple as possible the Security Application Block was left out of the application. This is due to the amount of effort it would take to implement a solid security infrastructure to support the application. I do not want to distract from the purpose of this book.

## Summary

As shown in this chapter, the Security Application Block can be a very capable tool. In most of today's applications, the ability to authorize users at some level or another is a must. The next chapter will focus on the Validation Application Block, which allows for the validation of data that is passed through an application.

# CHAPTER 12

■■■

# The Validation Application Block

In this chapter, you'll learn how the Enterprise Library can facilitate the implementation of domain (business) rules within an application. With Enterprise Library 2.0, you were on your own when figuring out how to implement this kind of functionality, but Enterprise Library 3.0 has a solution to help complete the puzzle for you. The Validation Application Block allows you to provide validators for .NET Framework data types. These validators apply specific validation rules to objects and determine whether the objects pass validation. This can be useful in many parts of any application, such as validating a tax identification number entered into a text box or validating data passed into a web service.

The Validation Application Block also targets the following technologies:

- ASP.NET, for validating data in web controls

- Windows forms, for validating data in windows controls

- Windows Communication Foundation (WCF), for validating data passed into a WCF service

This chapter covers the design of the Validation Application Block, using the built-in validators, and creating a custom validator.

## Looking Inside the Validation Application Block

The Validation Application Block provides the functionality necessary to validate .NET Framework data types. The data type validation is performed by a series of classes called *validators*.

### Validator Class

The core component of the Validation Application Block is the Validator class. This class is the base class from which all validators inherit. The Validator class provides functionality for logging the results so the appropriate action(s) can take place. The Validator class diagram is shown in Figure 12-1.

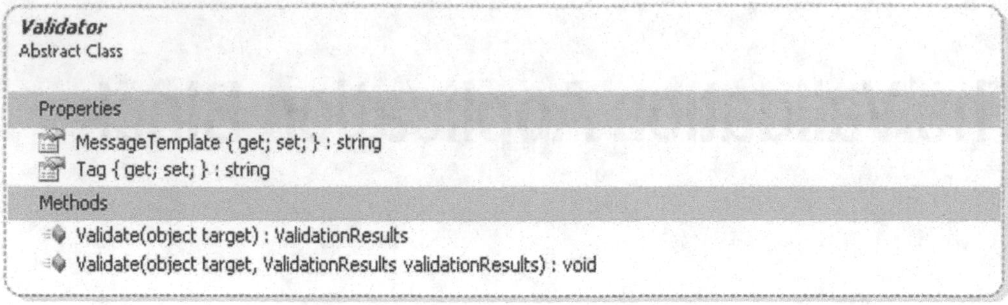

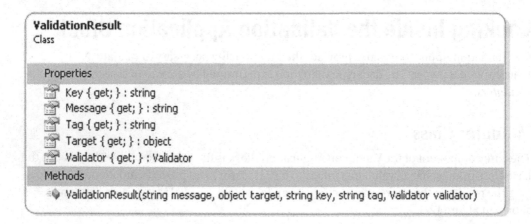

**Figure 12-1.** *Validator class diagram*

The Validator class contains an overloaded method called Validate. The purpose of the Validate method is to validate a given object and determine whether or not it passes validation based on the rules of the validator. This method contains two overloaded signatures, as shown in Figure 12-1. The first signature will create a ValidationResults object for you and return it back to the caller. The second method expects an instance of the ValidationResults class to be passed in as one of the method parameters. Both overloads require an object that is to be validated to be passed in as well.

The Validator class also contains two public properties that are used to define how and what will be logged in the ValidationResults collection: MessageTemplate and Tag. The MessageTemplate property defines a template that will be used to create a message in the event a ValidationResult object is created. The Tag property is used to filter or categorize a particular validation result.

## ValidationResult Class

The ValidationResult class represents specific results returned by a Validator instance. The ValidationResult class diagram is shown in Figure 12-2.

**Figure 12-2.** *ValidationResult class diagram*

When a Validator instance determines that a rule is violated, a new instance of ValidationResult is created and added to the ValidationResults collection. The parameters of the ValidationResult constructor are the message to be logged or shown to a user, the object that was tested, a key that shows the location of the validation result within a collection, a tag value that describes the validation result (usually used for filtering or categorizing ValidationResult objects), and the validator object itself. As shown in Figure 12-2, the ValidationResult object also contains five read-only properties for getting the values that were passed into the constructor.

## ValidationResults Class

The ValidationResults class provides a collection of validation results that were processed during the validation of an object. If validation results were returned, then one or more rules were broken during the validation process. Figure 12-3 shows the ValidationResults class diagram.

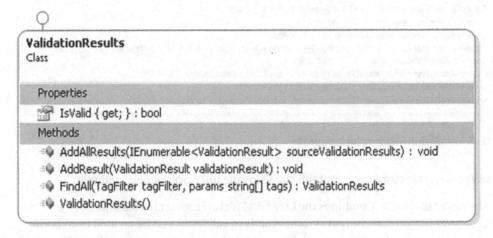

**Figure 12-3.** *ValidationResults class diagram*

The ValidationResults class provides a property called IsValid, which determines if any validation results exist. The IsValid property determines the total count of validation results and returns true if the count is zero, or false if the count is not equal to zero.

The ValidationResults class also contains the following three methods:

- AddAllResultsMethod: Takes a parameter of type IEnumerable<ValidationResult>. This allows the validation results of another ValidationResults object to be added to the current collection.

- AddResult: Takes a parameter of type ValidationResult. This allows one validation result to be added to the current collection.

- FindAll: Returns a new ValidationResults instance based on the tags created by the user. This allows specific processes to run based on the validation results of a particular user-defined category or filter. The FindAll method takes on two parameters: tagFilter, which defines whether to include or exclude the tags specified, and tags, which defines one or more strings to search for via a string array.

## ValidationFactory Class

The ValidationFactory class is a static class whose responsibility is to return a specific Validator class instance. Figure 12-4 shows the class diagram for the ValidationFactory class.

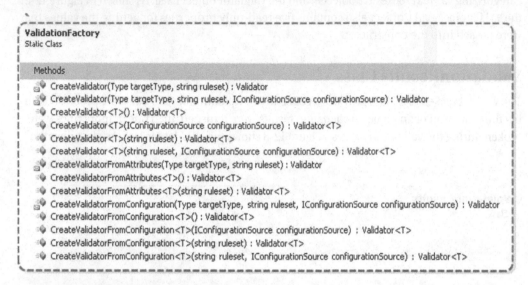

**Figure 12-4.** *ValidationFactory class diagram*

The ValidationFactory class contains the following three overloaded methods:

- CreateValidator<T>: Combines the CreateValidatorFromAttributes and CreateValidatorFromConfiguration methods so validators can be created from both sources based on the <T> specified. Listing 12-1 shows an example of using this method.

- CreateValidatorFromAttributes<T>: Creates a validator instance based on the validation attributes that are defined for a particular type defined by <T>.

- CreateValidatorFromConfiguration<T>: Creates a validator instance based on the configuration data specified by either the configurationSource parameter or the default configuration source of the application for a particular type defined by <T>.

**Listing 12-1.** *Creating an Instance of the Validator Class via the ValidationFactory Class*

```
public class ProcessOrders
{
    public bool ValidateOrders(Order myOrder)
    {
        Validator<Order> v = ValidationFactory.CreateValidator<Order>();
        ValidationResults r = v.Validate(myOrder);
        return r.IsValid;
    }
}
```

---

■**Note**  The ValidationFactory class also has three internal methods—CreateValidator, CreateValidatorFromAttributes, and CreateValidatorFromConfiguration–which take a parameter of System.Type. These methods are marked as internal, and are to be used by the Validation Application Block for internal purposes only.

---

Each method can contain a combination of one of the two parameters or none at all. The ruleset parameter allows validation rules to be grouped, so they may be processed together. For example, you would use ruleset if you wanted to apply specific rules for orders by businesses as opposed to orders by consumers, as demonstrated in Listing 12-2. The other parameter, configurationSource, is of type IConfigurationSource, and it allows you to define the configuration data to be used to configure the particular validator.

**Listing 12-2.** *Using the ruleset Parameter to Define Groups of Rules*

```
public class ProcessOrders
{
    public bool ValidateOrderItem(OrderItem myOrderItem, bool isBusiness)
    {
        Validator<Order> v;

        if( isBusiness )
        {
            v = ValidationFactory.CreateValidator<OrderItem>("BusinessOrder");
        }
        else
        {
            v = ValidationFactory.CreateValidator<OrderItem>("ConsumerOrder");
        }

        ValidationResults r = v.Validate(myOrderItem);
        return r.IsValid;
    }
}

public class OrderItem
{
    private int m_Quantity;
    private int m_ItemNumber;
    private decimal m_UnitCost;

    [Int32RangeValidator(10, RangeBoundaryType.Inclusive, 0,
        RangeBoundaryType.Ignore,
        Ruleset="BusinessOrder")]
```

```
[Int32RangeValidator(100, Ruleset="ConsumerOrder")]
[Int32RangeValidator(0, RangeBoundaryType.Inclusive,
    0, RangeBoundaryType.Ignore)]

public int Quantity
{
   get { return m_Quantity; }
   set { m_Quantity = value; }
}


[Int32RangeValidator(1000, RangeBoundaryType.Inclusive, 9999,
    RangeBoundaryType.Inclusive)]
public int ItemNumber
{
   get { return m_ItemNumber; }
   set { m_ItemNumber = value; }
}


public decimal UnitCost
{
   get { return m_UnitCost; }
   set { m_UnitCost = value; }
}
}
```

As shown in Listing 12-2, any order that is defined as a business order, by setting the isBusiness parameter of the ValidateOrderItem method to true, will apply all rules that are defined as BusinessOrder; otherwise, the ConsumerOrder rules are applied. So if a business order item comes in and has a quantity of only 5 items, it will fail validation. If an order comes in as a customer order item and has a quantity of 120 items, it will also fail validation. However, if a customer order item came in with a quantity of –1, it would actually pass validation. This is because the two validators created specified either the BusinessOrder or ConsumerOrder ruleset. The Int32RangeValidator that does not specify a ruleset would not be invoked by either ruleset. The range validators are discussed in the "Basic Validators" section later in this chapter, and combining validators is discussed in the "Composite Validators" section.

## Validation Class

The Validation class is a façade class that creates a façade layer so that you can create the proper instance of a Validator class and get the ValidationResults back in one line of code. Figure 12-5 shows the Validation class diagram.

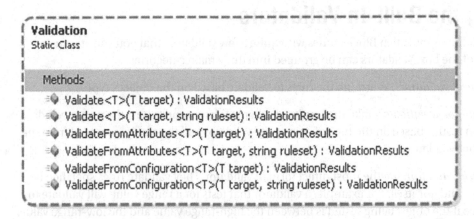

**Figure 12-5.** *Validation class diagram*

The following line of code shows how the Validation class can be used.

```
ValidationResults results = Validation.Validate(myOrderItem);
```

## The Behaviors of Attribute-Based Validation

It is important to understand the behaviors and limitations of attribute-based validation. In the Table 12-1 the different targets that can be used with the Validation Application Block are listed with how the Validation Application Block behaves when using attribute-based validation with them.

**Table 12-1.** *Attribute-Based Validation Behavior*

| Target Type | Behavior |
|---|---|
| Class | Only the NonNullValidator, ObjectCollectionValidator and Composite validators may be used at the class level, all others must be used on the member level. |
| Field | The value of the field is validated. |
| Property | Only the value of the get property is validated. |
| Method | Attribute-based validation of methods will validate the returned object of a method and the method must not contain any arguments. |
| Parameter | The Validation Application Block can only support attribute-based validation of parameters via Policy Injection Application Block which is discussed in Chapter 13. |

# Using the Built-In Validators

The Validation Application Block comes with quite a few validators that you can start using right out of the box. Validators can be grouped into three main categories:

- *Object validators* determine the rules to validate based on the object's type.

- *Composite validators* take the results of other validators and return the proper validation results based on the type of composite validator and the results returned from the other validators.

- *Basic validators* are the most direct form of validator. They validate rules specified by the validator itself. For example, a validator that tests for a range value will validate to true if the object being tested is between the high-range value and the low-range value.

## Object Validators

Object validators make it easy to pass in an object and apply rules based on the object's type. Typically, these types of rules are defined in the configuration file or by attributes placed on members of the object, but it is also possible to have the object self-validate, by using the SelfValidation and HasSelfValidation attributes.

### Self Validation

Self validation allows an object to call specific methods within itself to perform validation on the object. This can be useful when values must be compared to non-static data sources, such as a table within a database. In order for an object to use self validation, it must be decorated with the HasSelfValidation attribute. Then any method marked with the SelfValidation attribute will be called during validation of the object.

The methods decorated with the SelfValidationAttribute class must pass in a parameter of ValidationResults; otherwise, an exception will occur. The SelfValidationAttribute contains one public property called Ruleset, which allows you to categorize the rule for validation purposes. Figure 12-6 shows the class diagram of public members for the SelfValidationAttribute class.

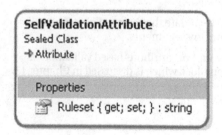

**Figure 12-6.** *SelfValidationAttribute class diagram of public members*

During validation, any method with the SelfValidation attribute will create an instance of the SelfValidationValidator class. The SelfValidationValidator class has a public constructor that passes in a `System.Reflection.MethodInfo` object, so that the validator knows which method to call from the validated object. Listing 12-3 shows an example of using the `SelfValidationAttribute` class.

**Listing 12-3.** *Using Self Validation*

```
[HasSelfValidation]
public class MyClass
{
    [SelfValidation]
    public void AmIValid(ValidationResults validationResults)
    {
        //Do some validation
    }
}
```

■ **Caution**  While it is possible to use the `SelfValidationValidator` class directly in code, it is generally not suggested. This is because the validator itself does not determine which methods are self-validating. It simply attempts to execute the method. Hence, any change to the validated class's members could produce unexpected results.

## Object Validation

Objects can be validated based on their type. This allows a base class to have specific rules to validate differently based on classes that inherit from it. This can be accomplished either on a single object basis via the `ObjectValidator` class or on a collection basis via the `ObjectCollectionValidator` class. Figure 12-7 shows the `ObjectValidator` public members, and Figure 12-8 shows the `ObjectCollectionValidator` members.

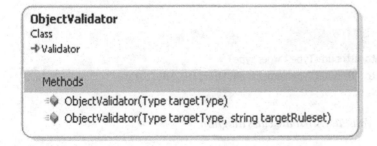

**Figure 12-7.** *ObjectValidator class diagram of public members*

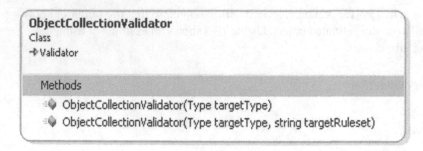

**Figure 12-8.** *ObjectCollectionValidator class diagram*

The ObjectValidator and ObjectCollectionValidator classes have two constructors: one that takes just a System.Type parameter, and one that takes a System.Type parameter and ruleset (string) parameter.

The ObjectValidator class and ObjectCollectionValidator class each has a corresponding attribute class to support attribute-based validation: ObjectValidatorAttribute and ObjectCollectionValidatorAttribute. These two classes are shown in Figures 12-9 and 12-10.

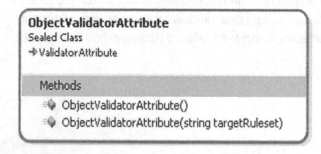

**Figure 12-9.** *ObjectValidatorAttribute class diagram*

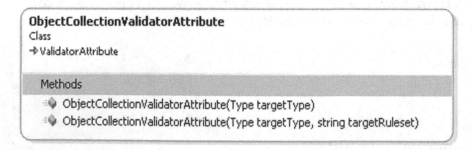

**Figure 12-10.** *ObjectCollectionValidatorAttribute class diagram*

## Property Comparison Validation

The PropertyComparisonValidator class allows two properties of a class to be compared. Like the other validators, it has an attribute variation that takes the property name and type of comparison that should be performed. Listing 12-4 shows how this validator is used.

**Listing 12-4.** *Using the EnumConversionValidatorAttribute Class*

```
public class MyClass
{
    private int m_MyMinValue;
    private int m_MyCurrentValue;

    public string MyMinValue
    {
        get { return m_MyMinValue; }
        set { m_MyMinValue = value; }
    }

    [PropertyComparisonValidator("MyMinValue",
        ComparisonOperator.GreaterThanEqual)]
    public string MyCurrentValue
    {
        get { return m_MyCurrentValue; }
        set { m_MyCurrentValue = value; }
    }

}
```

## Conversion Validators

The two conversion validators included with the Validation Application Block attempt to convert a specific type to another type. If the conversion is successful, the object passes validation. The two conversion classes are EnumConversionValidator and TypeConversionValidator.

### EnumConversionValidator

The Validation Application Block supports a validator called EnumConversionValidator, which determines if a string representation of an enumerator can be converted to a specific enumerator type. For example, it could test to see if "Friday" can be converted to the System.DayOfWeek enum type. Figure 12-11 shows the class diagram of the EnumConversionValidator public members.

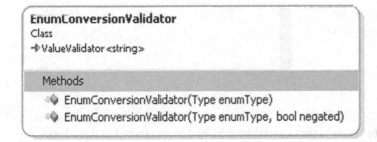

**Figure 12-11.** *EnumConversionValidator class diagram of public members*

> **Note** Since the EnumConversionValidator inherits from Validator<string>, it can be applied only to values that are of type System.String.

The EnumConversionValidator class also supports attribute-based validation via the EnumConversionValidatorAttribute class. Like EnumConversionValidator, EnumConversionValidatorAttribute has two overloads. One overload takes the enum type you want to test. The other overload takes an enum type and a Boolean parameter, negated, indicating whether validation results should be produced if the condition is met. By setting the negated parameter to true, the positive condition will produce validation results. This is inverse of the default behavior. Figure 12-12 shows the class diagram of public members for the EnumConversionValidatorAttribute class.

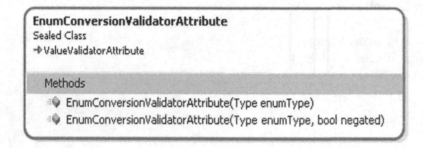

**Figure 12-12.** *EnumConversionValidatorAttribute class diagram of public members*

Listing 12-5 shows an example of using EnumConversionValidatorAttribute.

**Listing 12-5.** *Using the EnumConversionValidatorAttribute Class*

```
public class MyClass
{
    private string m_MyEnumValue;

    [EnumConversionValidator(typeof(System.DayOfWeek))]
    public string MyEnumValue
    {
        get { return m_MyEnumValue; }
        set { m_MyEnumValue = value; }
    }
}
```

### TypeConversionValidator

The TypeConversionValidator class is very much like the EnumConversionValidator class. It takes a string and attempts to convert it to a specific type of object using the TryParse method of that specific object type. Figure 12-13 shows the public constructors available

for the TypeConversionValidator class. The associated attribute class,
TypeConversionValidatorAttribute, contains only one constructor that takes a specific
type as a parameter.

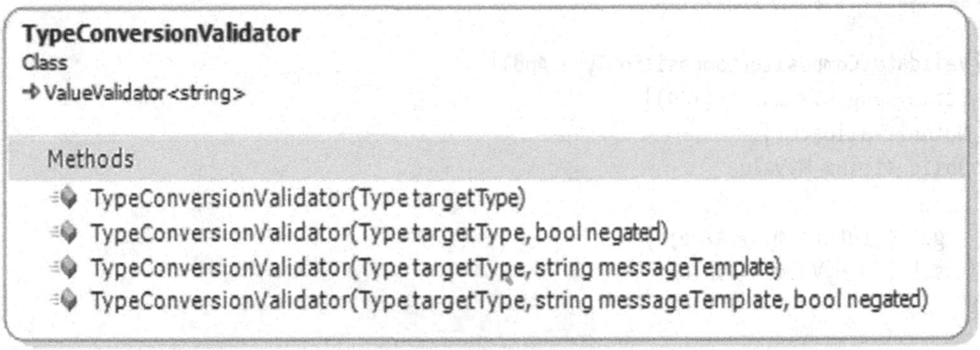

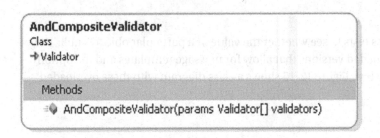

**TypeConversionValidator**
Class
→ ValueValidator<string>

Methods
≡● TypeConversionValidator(Type targetType)
≡● TypeConversionValidator(Type targetType, bool negated)
≡● TypeConversionValidator(Type targetType, string messageTemplate)
≡● TypeConversionValidator(Type targetType, string messageTemplate, bool negated)

**Figure 12-13.** *TypeConversionValidator class diagram*

## Composite Validators

The two composite validators provided in the Validation Application Block are
AndCompositeValidator and OrCompositeValidator, which correspond to the AND and
OR logical operators. Their use is identical, but they cannot be used directly by attribute-
based validation. Only configuration and direct validation are supported.

The AndCompositeValidator and OrCompositeValidator classes both have a public
constructor that takes one or more validator classes as parameters. Figure 12-14 shows the
AndCompositeValidator class diagram.

**AndCompositeValidator**
Class
→ Validator

Methods
≡● AndCompositeValidator(params Validator[] validators)

**Figure 12-14.** *AndCompositeValidator class diagram*

When using attribute-based validation, there is not a corresponding AndCompositeValidator
or OrCompositeValidator attribute class. Instead, you will find a class called
ValidatorCompositionAttribute. This class has one constructor that takes the enum type
of CompositionType (And or Or). By simply decorating a class's member with this, all other
validators will use the ValidatorCompositionAttribute class to determine the final outcome
of pass or fail. Listing 12-6 shows an example of using ValidatorCompositionAttribute.

**Listing 12-6.** *Using the ValidatorCompositionAttribute Class*

```
public class MyClass
{
    private string m_MyValue;

    [ValidatorComposite(CompositionType.And)]
    [StringLengthValidator(100)]
    [NotNullValidator]
    public string MyValue
    {
        get { return m_MyValue; }
        set { m_MyValue = value; }
    }
}
```

# Basic Validators

The bulk of the validators provided by the Validation Application Block are of the basic variety, where they simply test the value of a property, field, parameter, and so on, and determine if the conditions are met. These types of validators break down into three subcategories: value validators, range validators, and everything else.

## Value Validators

The value validators are designed to assess the value of an object and determine if the object's value is valid based on the validator's rules and parameters. The three types of value validators are NotNullValidator, DomainValidator, and ContainsCharactersValidator.

### NotNullValidator

The NotNullValidator class tests to see whether the value of a particular object is null. The constructor has four overloaded versions that allow for message templates and the option to negate the results of the test. Figure 12-15 shows a class diagram with these overloaded constructors.

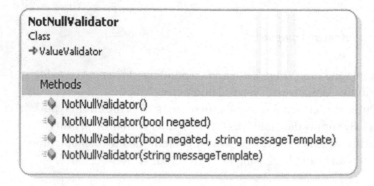

**Figure 12-15.** *NotNullValidator class diagram*

The NotNullValidator class also has a corresponding class to support attribute-based validation, called NotNullValidatorAttribute. Figure 12-16 shows its public constructors.

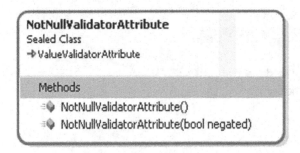

**Figure 12-16.** *NotNullValidatorAttribute class diagram*

Using the constructor with the negated parameter will allow you to test to see if the parameter is null, as opposed to being not null. Listing 12-7 shows an example of this usage of NotNullValidator.

**Listing 12-7.** *Using NotNullValidator to Test for Nulls*

```
public class MyClass
{
    private string m_MyValue;

    [NotNullValidator(true)]
    public string MyValue
    {
        get { return m_MyValue; }
        set { m_MyValue = value; }
    }
}
```

### DomainValidator

The DomainValidator class checks to see that a value is contained within a specific set of values. For instance, you could check to see if an integer is 1, 5, 7, or 11, or that a string is either "yes" or "no". This class can also be used for determining equality by simply specifying one value to compare against. Figure 12-17 shows the available public constructors.

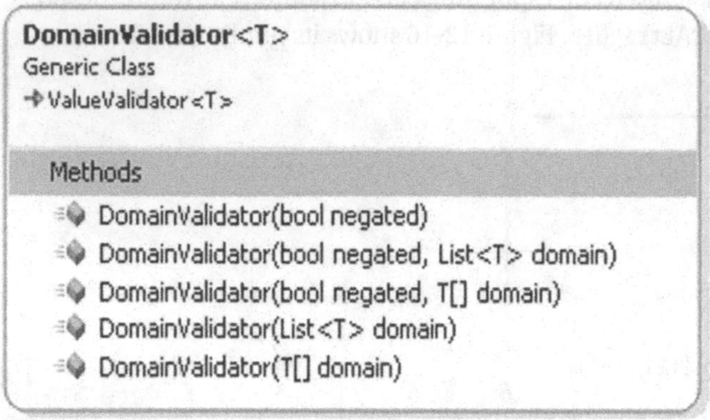

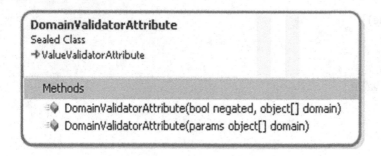

**Figure 12-17.** *DomainValidator class's constructors*

As shown in Figure 12-17, the DomainValidator class contains five overloaded constructors. Four of these constructors take an object for comparison purposes, either by providing an array of objects or by using the generic List class. The one constructor that does not take an object list takes just a Boolean value for the negated parameter. This specific constructor tests for null values.

The DomainValidatorAttribute class works along with the DomainValidator class to support attribute-based validation. Figure 12-18 shows the DomainValidatorAttribute class's constructors.

```
DomainValidatorAttribute
Sealed Class
→ ValueValidatorAttribute

Methods
≡♦ DomainValidatorAttribute(bool negated, object[] domain)
≡♦ DomainValidatorAttribute(params object[] domain)
```

**Figure 12-18.** *DomainValidatorAttribute constructors*

Listing 12-8 shows how to use the DomainValidatorAttribute class to test for equality between two values and to test for equality between multiple values.

**Listing 12-8.** *Using the DomainValidatorAttribute Class to Test for Equality*

```
public class MyClass
{
    private string m_MyValue;
    private int m_IntValue;

    [DomainValidator("success")]
    public string MyValue
```

```
    {
        get { return m_MyValue; }
        set { m_MyValue = value; }
    }

    [DomainValidator(0, 1, 3, 5)]
    public string IntValue
    {
        get { return m_IntValue; }
        set { m_IntValue = value; }
    }
}
```

**ContainsCharactersValidator**

The ContainsCharactersValidator class allows a string to be tested to see if it contains any or all of the characters contained within another string. When testing for all characters, it is not important that both sets of strings match. For instance, Listing 12-9 shows how ContainsCharactersValidator can be used to test to see if certain vowels are contained within a sentence.

**Listing 12-9.** *Using the ContainsCharactersValidator Class to Test for Sentence Contents*

```
public class MyValidationClass
{
    public static bool validateAll(string toValidate)
    {
        ContainsCharactersValidator valid = ContainsCharactersValidator("aeiou",
            ContainsCharacters.All);

        ValidationResults results = valid.Validate(toValidate);

        return results.IsValid;
    }

    public static bool validateAny(string toValidate)
    {
        ContainsCharactersValidator valid = ContainsCharactersValidator("aeiou",
            ContainsCharacters.Any);

        ValidationResults results = valid.Validate(toValidate);

        return results.IsValid;
    }
}

public class MyClass
```

```
{
    public void doValidation()
    {
        Console.Write("The cat jumped over the bin.");
        Console.Write(MyValidationClass.validateAll("The cat jumped over the bin."));
        Console.Write(MyValidationClass.validateAny("The cat jumped over the bin."));

        Console.Write("The dog chased the cat.");
        Console.Write(MyValidationClass.validateAll("The dog chased the cat."));
        Console.Write(MyValidationClass.validateAny("The dog chased the cat."));
    }
}
```

The results of Listing 12-9 are as follows:

```
The cat jumped over the bin.
true
true
The dog chased the cat.
false
true
```

In the sentence "The dog chased the cat," the character *u* is not present, so the validation rule that tests for all vowels will fail.

The ContainsCharactersValidator class contains three overloaded constructors, as shown in Figure 12-19. The first constructor automatically defaults the containsCharacters parameter to ContainsCharacters.Any. This class also has a corresponding class to support attribute-based validation, called ContainsCharactersValidatorAttribute, which has the exact same constructors as the ContainsCharactersValidator class.

**ContainsCharactersValidator**
Class
→ ValueValidator <string>

Methods
- ○ ContainsCharactersValidator(string characterSet)
- ○ ContainsCharactersValidator(string characterSet, ContainsCharacters containsCharacters)
- ○ ContainsCharactersValidator(string characterSet, ContainsCharacters containsCharacters, bool negated)

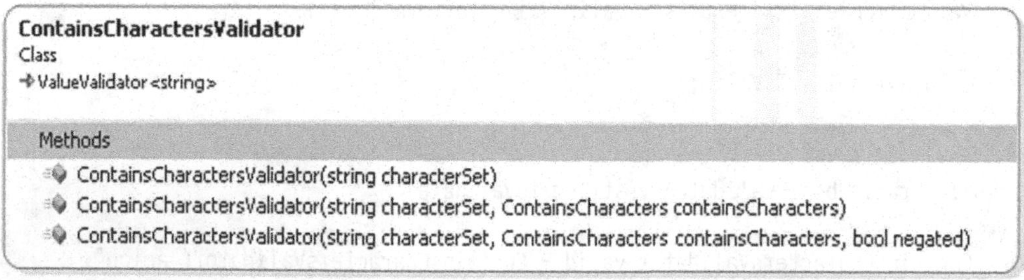

**Figure 12-19.** *ContainsCharactersValidator constructors*

## Range Validators

The range validators work somewhat like the value validators, but instead of testing for one or more values, they test for a range of values. In this case, a developer will specify a high range and a low range, and the validator will determine if a value fits in between the range.

The Validation Application Block comes with four range validators: RangeValidator, DateTimeRangeValidator, Int32RangeValidator, and StringRangeValidator.

### RangeValidator

The RangeValidator class is the base class from which all the other range validators inherit. It contains four overloaded constructors that allow you to specify upper and lower bounds of an object, as well as the behavior of how the range will be validated. It is important to note that any type used by the RangeValidator object must implement the IComparable interface.

The behavior of the RangeValidator class is defined via the upperBoundType and lowerBoundType parameters of the constructor. These two parameters are RangeBoundaryType enums, and the values are Inclusive, Exclusive, and Ignore. Figure 12-20 shows the available constructors for the RangeValidator class. Any constructor that does not specify a RangeBoundaryType parameter will default to Inclusive for the respective upper-bound and lower-bound objects.

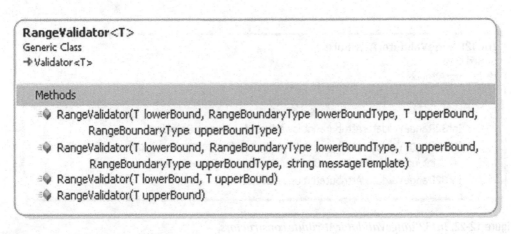

**Figure 12-20.** *RangeValidator constructors*

Unlike the other validator classes, the RangeValidator does not have a class that supports attribute-based validation. However, the three classes that inherit from RangeValidator—DatetimeRangeValidator, Int32RangeValidator, and StringRangeValidator—do have classes that support attribute-based validation.

### StringRangeValidator, Int32RangeValidator, and DatetimeRangeValidator

The StringRangeValidator, Int32RangeValidator, and DatetimeRangeValidator classes have the same constructors as the RangeValidator class, except that parameter T is a string, int, or DateTime object, respectively.

The DateTimeRangeValidatorAttribute, Int32RangeValidatorAttribute, and StringRangeValidatorAttribute classes essentially have the same three constructors, with the exception of the DateTimeRangeValidatorAttribute class, which has six constructors (three for handling string representations of date and time, and three for handling DateTime objects directly). The public constructors for these classes are shown in Figures 12-21, 12-22, and 12-23. These three constructors allow you to specify upper-bound and lower-bound values, as well as RangeBoundaryType values.

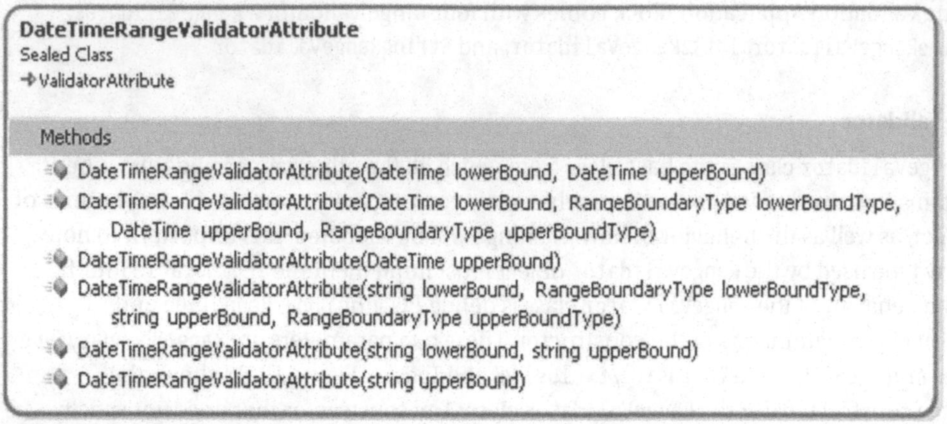

**DateTimeRangeValidatorAttribute**
Sealed Class
↪ValidatorAttribute

Methods

▪◈ DateTimeRangeValidatorAttribute(DateTime lowerBound, DateTime upperBound)
▪◈ DateTimeRangeValidatorAttribute(DateTime lowerBound, RangeBoundaryType lowerBoundType,
        DateTime upperBound, RangeBoundaryType upperBoundType)
▪◈ DateTimeRangeValidatorAttribute(DateTime upperBound)
▪◈ DateTimeRangeValidatorAttribute(string lowerBound, RangeBoundaryType lowerBoundType,
        string upperBound, RangeBoundaryType upperBoundType)
▪◈ DateTimeRangeValidatorAttribute(string lowerBound, string upperBound)
▪◈ DateTimeRangeValidatorAttribute(string upperBound)

**Figure 12-21.** *DateTimeRangeValidatorAttribute constructors*

**Int32RangeValidatorAttribute**
Sealed Class
↪ValidatorAttribute

Methods

▪◈ Int32RangeValidatorAttribute(int lowerBound, int upperBound)
▪◈ Int32RangeValidatorAttribute(int lowerBound, RangeBoundaryType lowerBoundType,
        int upperBound, RangeBoundaryType upperBoundType)
▪◈ Int32RangeValidatorAttribute(int upperBound)

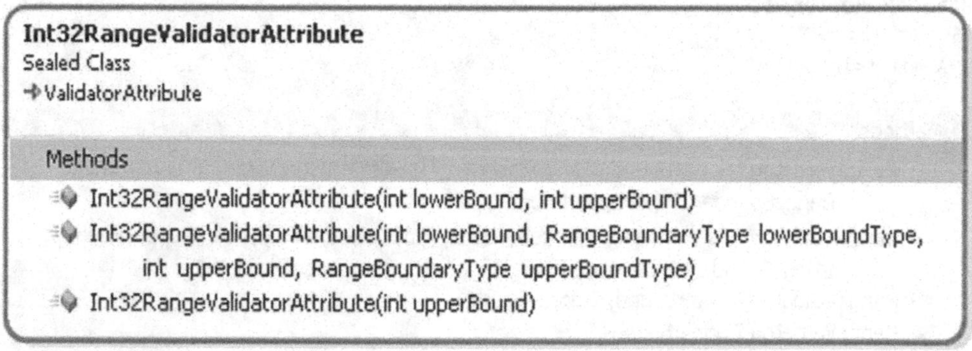

**Figure 12-22.** *Int32RangeValidatorAttribute constructors*

**StringRangeValidatorAttribute**
Sealed Class
↪ValidatorAttribute

Methods

▪◈ StringRangeValidatorAttribute(string lowerBound, RangeBoundaryType lowerBoundType,
        string upperBound, RangeBoundaryType upperBoundType)
▪◈ StringRangeValidatorAttribute(string lowerBound, string upperBound)
▪◈ StringRangeValidatorAttribute(string upperBound)

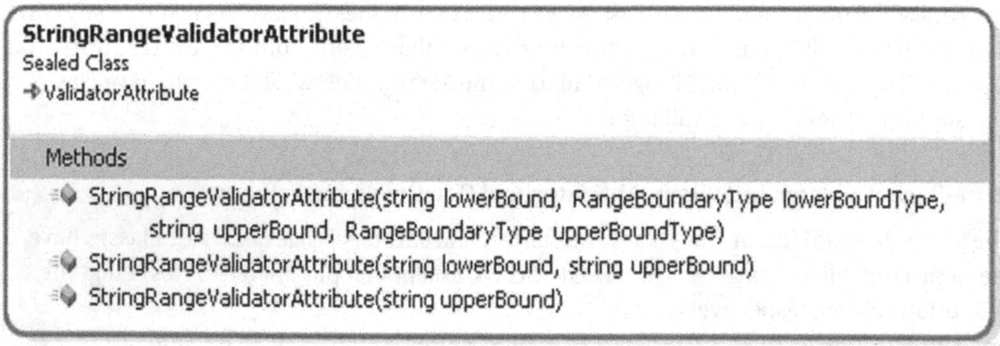

**Figure 12-23.** *StringRangeValidatorAttribute constructors*

Listing 12-10 shows an example of using the Int32RangeValidatorAttribute class to validate a value between 0 and 10, but to ensure that the value is not between 5 and 7.

**Listing 12-10.** *Using the Int32RangeValidator to Validate an Integer Range*

```
public class MyClass
{
   private int m_IntValue;

   [Int32RangeValidator(0, RangeBoundaryType.Inclusive, 10 ,
      RangeBoundaryType.Inclusive)]
   [Int32RangeValidator(5, RangeBoundaryType.Inclusive, 7 ,
      RangeBoundaryType.Inclusive, Negated=true)]

   public string IntValue
   {
      get { return m_IntValue; }
      set { m_intValue = value; }
   }
}
```

## Everything Else

The "everything else" subcategory contains the StringLengthValidator and RegexValidator classes. These validators differ from the value validators in that they don't test for a particular value, but test for a particular characteristic of the object being validated.

### StringLengthValidator

The StringLengthValidator class provides the ability to determine if a string meets a minimum and/or maximum string-length requirement. The class itself contains four overloaded constructors that allow you to validate the string's length. These constructors are shown in Figure 12-24.

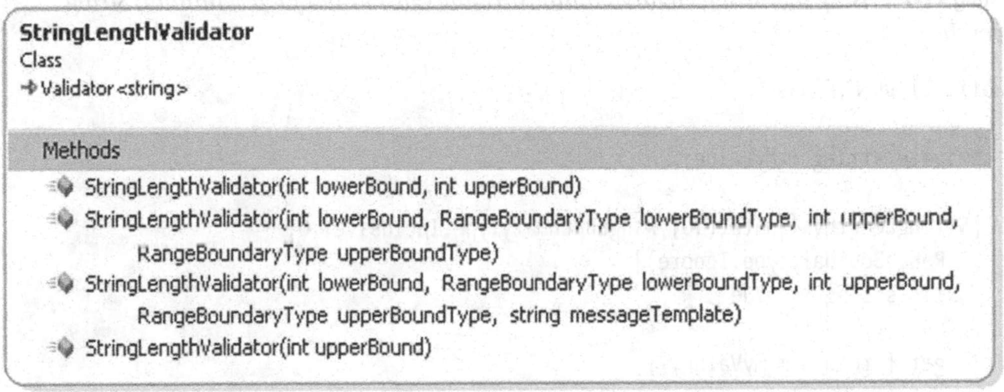

**StringLengthValidator**
Class
⇥ Validator <string>

Methods
=◈ StringLengthValidator(int lowerBound, int upperBound)
=◈ StringLengthValidator(int lowerBound, RangeBoundaryType lowerBoundType, int upperBound,
        RangeBoundaryType upperBoundType)
=◈ StringLengthValidator(int lowerBound, RangeBoundaryType lowerBoundType, int upperBound,
        RangeBoundaryType upperBoundType, string messageTemplate)
=◈ StringLengthValidator(int upperBound)

**Figure 12-24.** *StringLengthValidator constructors*

The StringLengthValidator class validation scheme matches that of the range validators by having upper-bound and lower-bound parameters, so it is important to understand the default behaviors. For instance, the constructor that specifies only the upper and lower bounds will always test inclusively within those bounds. In other words, if the constructor were coded as follows:

```
StringLengthValidator stringLen = new StringLengValidator(5, 10);
```

testing the values of 5 and 10 would both pass validation. If it were exclusive, 5 and 10 would fail validation.

The StringLengthValidator also supports attribute-based validation. The StringLengthValidatorAttribute class constructors are shown in Figure 12-25.

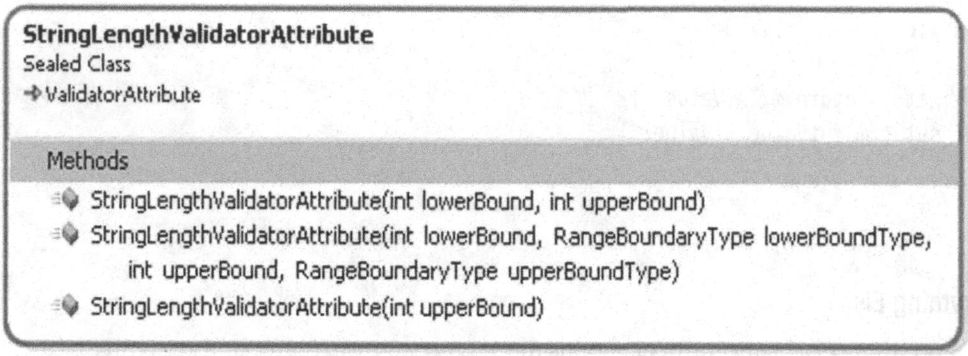

---

**StringLengthValidatorAttribute**
Sealed Class
↪ ValidatorAttribute

Methods

■◆ StringLengthValidatorAttribute(int lowerBound, int upperBound)
■◆ StringLengthValidatorAttribute(int lowerBound, RangeBoundaryType lowerBoundType,
        int upperBound, RangeBoundaryType upperBoundType)
■◆ StringLengthValidatorAttribute(int upperBound)

---

**Figure 12-25.** *StringLengthValidatorAttribute constructors*

Testing for a minimum value can also be tricky. At first glance, it appears that there are not any constructor overloads for testing a minimum string length. However, if you use the constructor that has the lower bound, lower bound range type, upper bound, and upper bound range type parameters, it is possible to ignore the upper bound by specifying the RangeBoundaryType.Ignore enum in the constructor. Listing 12-11 shows how this is done.

**Listing 12-11.** *Using the StringLengthValidatorAttribute Class to Test for a Minimum String Length*

```
public class MyClass
{
    private string m_MyValue;

    [StringLengthValidator(10, RangeBoundaryType.Inclusive, 0,
        RangeBoundaryType.Ignore)]
    public string MyValue
    {
        get { return m_MyValue; }
        set { m_MyValue = value; }
    }

}
```

RegexValidator

The RegexValidator class lets you use regular expressions to test a string. If a match is found, it will pass validation. It is important to note that this validator does not provide the ability to validate for a value that fails the regular expression via a Negate property.

The RegexValidator class provides four overloaded constructors, as shown in Figure 12-26. Figure 12-27 shows the RegexValidatorAttribute class's constructors. If you have used the Regex class in the .NET Framework, you should be pretty comfortable with this validator.

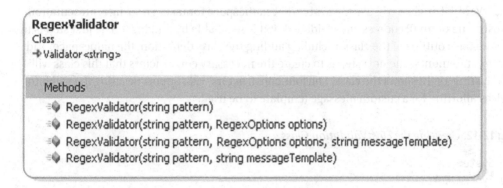

**Figure 12-26.** *RegexValidator constructors*

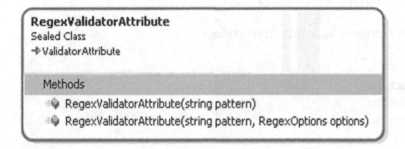

**Figure 12-27.** *RegexValidatorAttribute constructors*

# Creating a Custom Validator for the ACME POS Application

Creating a custom validator involves three steps:

- Create the validator class.

- Create the attribute-based validator to support attribute-based validation.

- Create the necessary configuration components to support validation via configuration data.

For the ACME POS application, we will create a validator that will validate the hostname that the application will use to communicate with the web service. This will allow the user to know if the web service is available. This task will be accomplished by attempting to "ping" the web service. Since this validator will need to be only attribute-based for this example, we will create only the validator and its corresponding attribute support class.

## Creating the HostValidator Class

The HostValidator class will use the System.Net namespace for taking a string representation of a hostname or an IP address and validate that it is reachable by pinging it. The first step is to create the base outline of the class, including adding the class definition, the namespace, and the using statements. The next step is to create the necessary constructors that this class will utilize. Listing 12-12 shows the class. The four constructors will support negating the validator as well as allowing for a custom message template to be used.

**Listing 12-12.** *Creating the HostValidation Class*

```
using System;
using System.Net;
using System.Net.NetworkInformation;
using Microsoft.Practices.EnterpriseLibrary.Validation.Validators;

namespace DGTEL.Samples.Validation.Validators
{
    public class HostValidator : ValueValidator<string>
    {
        //constuctors
        #region constructors…
        public HostValidator()
            : this(null)
        { }

        public HostValidator(bool negated)
            : this(null, negated)
        { }

        public HostValidator(string messageTemplate)
            : base(messageTemplate, null, false)
        { }

        public HostValidator(string messageTemplate, bool negated)
            : base(messageTemplate, null, negated)
        { }
        #endregion
    }
}
```

Since the ValueValidator abstract class was inherited from, three members must be implemented: the DoValidate method, the DefaultNegatedMessageTemplate property, and the DefaultNonNegatedMessageTemplate property. Listing 12-13 shows these three members implemented. There is also another method called IsValidHost for validating whether a hostname is valid.

**Listing 12-13.** *Implementing the Required Members for the HostValidation Class*

```
using System;
using System.Net;
using System.Net.NetworkInformation;
using Microsoft.Practices.EnterpriseLibrary.Validation.Validators;
using Microsoft.Practices.EnterpriseLibrary.Validation;

namespace DGTEL.Samples.Validation.Validators
{
    public class HostValidator : ValueValidator<string>
    {
        //constructors go here...


        protected override void DoValidate(string objectToValidate,
            object currentTarget,
            string key,
            ValidationResults validationResults)
        {
            IPAddress ip = null;

            if (!string.IsNullOrEmpty(objectToValidate)
                && (IPAddress.TryParse(objectToValidate, out ip)
                    || IsValidHost(objectToValidate)))
            {
                Ping ping = new Ping();
                PingReply reply = ping.Send(objectToValidate);

                if (reply.Status != IPStatus.Success)
                {
                    string message = this.MessageTemplate;
                    LogValidationResult(validationResults, message, currentTarget, key);
                }
            }
            else
            {
                string message = this.MessageTemplate;
                LogValidationResult(validationResults, message, currentTarget, key);
            }
        }
```

```
        private bool IsValidHost(string hostName)
        {
            IPHostEntry host;

            try
            {
                host = Dns.GetHostEntry(hostName);

                if(host.AddressList.Length > 0)
                    return true;
                else
                    return false;
            }
            catch
            {
                return false;
            }
        }

        protected override string DefaultNegatedMessageTemplate
        {
            get { return "Host Name or IP Address is valid."; }
        }

        protected override string DefaultNonNegatedMessageTemplate
        {
            get { return "Host Name or IP Address is not valid."; }
        }
    }
}
```

That is all there is to creating the HostValidator class. The next step is to create the class to support attribute-based validation.

## Creating the HostValidatorAttribute Class

Implementing the HostValidatorAttribute class is even easier than implementing the HostValidator class. Since the purpose of the HostValidator class is to determine that a given property or parameter is a valid host or IP address, it won't be necessary to create any constructor overloads for this class. Since the ValueValidatorAttribute class is inherited from, it will be necessary to implement the DoCreateValidator method. Listing 12-14 shows the implemented HostValidatorAttribute class.

**Listing 12-14.** *Implementing the HostValidatorAttribute Class*

```
using System;
using Microsoft.Practices.EnterpriseLibrary.Validation;
using Microsoft.Practices.EnterpriseLibrary.Validation.Validators;
```

```
namespace DGTEL.Samples.Validation.Validators
{
    [AttributeUsage(AttributeTargets.Property
        | AttributeTargets.Field
        | AttributeTargets.Method
        | AttributeTargets.Parameter,
        AllowMultiple = true,
        Inherited = false)]
    public sealed class HostValidatorAttribute : ValueValidatorAttribute
    {
        public HostValidatorAttribute ()
        { }

        protected override Validator DoCreateValidator(Type targetType)
        {
            return new HostValidator();
        }
    }
}
```

In the next chapter, we will use this new HostValidator class as well as other validators via policy injection in the ACME POS application.

# Summary

The new Validation Application Block in Enterprise Library 3.0 adds a wide range of possibilities for dealing with simple domain (business) rules in most applications. The ability of this application block to implement validation logic via attributes or via a configuration file can ease the development and maintenance of an application.

The next chapter covers a new application block called the Policy Injection Application Block. It allows developers to declaratively handle common functions—such as validation, exception handling, logging, and so on—via policies, by simply declaring, via attributes, which objects, methods, or properties should use specific policies.

# CHAPTER 13

■ ■ ■

# The Policy Injection Application Block

For years, the software development community has used procedural programming and object-oriented programming in the development of software applications. Over time, the need for scalable applications that can communicate with heterogeneous systems has inspired development architectures, such as service-oriented architecture.

Around the turn of the millennium, a new type of development methodology has been emerging: *aspect-oriented programming*. The Microsoft patterns & practices group has embraced this new development paradigm and created the Policy Injection Application Block, which is covered in this chapter. However, before diving into this new application block, it is important for you to understand what aspect-oriented programming is.

## Introducing Aspect-Oriented Programming

Aspect-oriented programming attempts to aid in the separation of concerns. While procedural and object-oriented programming have taken steps to modularize this separation, aspect-oriented programming takes it to a new level.

### Separating Concerns

The separation of concerns is a major consideration for any programming language. In the simplest terms, a *concern* is a modular unit of code that has a specific purpose. All programming methodologies, in some way or another, handle the separation of concerns by encapsulating them into some entity. In procedural languages, concerns are defined within procedures. In object-oriented languages, concerns are defined within classes. However, some concerns cannot be bound to these constructs.

For example, most applications require some ability to capture and handle exceptions. Typically, a developer needs to go into each method and block of code and attempt to handle exceptions that may arise. Listing 13-1 shows an example of a class with exception handling, which uses the Exception Handling Application Block in each of its methods.

**Listing 13-1.** *Class with Exception Handling*

```
public class MyClass
{
    //adds two numbers and returns a value
    public int AddTwoNumbers(int firstNumber, secondNumber)
    {
        try
        {
            return firstNumber + secondNumber;
        }
        catch (Exception ex)
        {
            If(ExceptionPolicy.HandleException("MyExceptionPolicy",
                ex))
            {
                throw;
            }
        }
    }

    //subtracts two numbers and returns a value
    public int SubtractTwoNumbers(int firstNumber, secondNumber)
    {
        try
        {
            return firstNumber - secondNumber;
        }
        catch (Exception ex)
        {
            If(ExceptionPolicy.HandleException("MyExceptionPolicy",
                ex))
            {
                throw;
            }
        }
    }
}
```

As you can see in Listing 13-1, it was necessary to repeat the exception-handling code in both the SubtractTwoNumbers and AddTwoNumbers methods. This type of concern is known as a *cross-cutting concern*, or an *aspect*.

Cross-cutting concerns can be found in many parts of an application—along with exception handling, they can occur in logging, validation, authorization, caching, and instrumentation. All these can require the repetitive use of essentially identical code for each concern. In other words, handling exceptions in the user interface layer of an application isn't going to be much different, if different at all, than handling exceptions in the data access layer. The same could be said for logging, validation, and authorization.

Another issue with the code in Listing 13-1 is the intertwining of domain logic and the cross-cutting concern in each method. Mixing these together makes code harder to read and maintain. It would be easier if the code within the `SubtractTwoNumbers` and `AddTwoNumbers` methods simply contained the necessary domain logic and nothing else.

Aspect-oriented programming attempts to address cross-cutting concerns and eliminate the problems of repetition and intermixing.

---

■**Note** Aspect-oriented software *development* differs from aspect-oriented *programming*. Aspect-oriented software development takes the language concepts that support aspect-oriented programming to the next level by adding an environment and methodology to the development process. While the Policy Injection Application Block contains many of the concepts of aspect-oriented programming, it is not a true aspect-oriented software development framework.

---

## Implementing Aspect-Oriented Programming in .NET

*Weaving* is essentially injecting instructions into the application. Another way to put it is that weaving is changing the original intended behavior of the application. In the .NET environment, two approaches can be taken in aspect-oriented programming:

- *Compile-time weaving:* Code is injected into the source code of an application to address the cross-cutting concerns.

- *Runtime weaving:* Instructions are injected at runtime, typically through the use of a proxy object that the consuming object sees as the original object. This works much the same way as .NET Remoting does.

In order to be able to modify the behavior of an application, it is necessary to define what behavior needs to be performed. The definition of behaviors is known as an *advice*. An advice is an interceptor placed between the caller and the callee that will perform some action when the entry, exit, or exception occurs while processing some code, such as a method.

With the behavior defined, we next need to specify where it will be placed. This can be done in a variety of ways, such as reflection or by decorating the target callee with an attribute. When using reflection, there can be multiple variants of defining where to place the behavior; some may include programming tips and the use of an external definition file such as an application configuration file.

# Understanding the Design of the Policy Injection Application Block

The purpose of the Policy Injection Application Block is to separate the core concerns of an entity, such as domain logic, from the cross-cutting concerns that are required to develop an application. The block does this through the use of handlers that define the specific behaviors that should be performed on a specific member of a class, such as a method or property. A handler can be defined in one of two ways:

- By decorating class members with an attribute that will declaratively define the handler to be used

- By defining the class type and class member on which the handler will act

Let's look at each of these techniques.

## Defining Handlers via Attributes

Defining handlers via attributes is relatively self-explanatory. By decorating a method or property you intend to target, it defines where the behavior will be placed, and the contents of the attribute itself can define the behavior to perform. Listing 13-2 shows an example that takes the class defined in Listing 13-1 and uses attributes to define the handlers.

**Listing 13-2.** *Class with Policies to Define Exception Handling*

```
public class MyClass : MarshalByRefObject
{
    //adds two numbers and returns a value
    [ExceptionCallHandler("MyExceptionPolicy")]
    public int AddTwoNumbers(int firstNumber, int secondNumber)
    {
        return firstNumber + secondNumber;
    }

    //subtracts two numbers and returns a value
    [ExceptionCallHandler("MyExceptionPolicy")]
    public int SubtractTwoNumbers(int firstNumber, int secondNumber)
    {
        return firstNumber - secondNumber;
    }
}
```

Notice that Listing 13-2 has a lot less code than Listing 13-1. Specifically, the try-catch blocks are now gone. Instead, two attributes that decorate the AddTwoNumbers and SubtractTwoNumbers methods define an ExceptionCallHandler, which specifies the MyExceptionPolicy exception policy to use in the event an exception occurs within their respective methods.

While using attributes may seem like the easiest way to handle cross-cutting concerns, this approach can have some drawbacks. If you wanted to change the name of the exception policy used, you would need to do it everywhere in your code. Also, if you wanted to remove the exception policy completely, you would also need to go through all of your code and remove the ExceptionCallHandler handler attributes. However, there is a way to define specific handlers to use on a class's members without needing to define them in code. This technique is described in the next section.

# Defining Handlers by Intercepting Target Classes

The other way to define handlers is by targeting a specific class and applying the policies to that class's members. Targeting a class's members is accomplished by defining a named policy. This named policy contains matching rules and handlers. If the matching rules return a positive match, the handlers defined for the named policy will be applied to that class member. Table 13-1 lists the rules that are provided with the Policy Injection Application Block.

**Table 13-1.** *Rules Provided with the Policy Injection Block*

| Matching Rule | Description |
| --- | --- |
| Assembly | Allows the targeting of classes based on the name of the assembly |
| Custom attribute | Allows the targeting of a class and/or its members based on the custom attribute type |
| Member name | Allows the targeting of a class's member based on its member name |
| Method signature | Allows the targeting of a class's method based on its name and method signature |
| Namespace | Allows the targeting of a class and/or its members based on the class's namespace |
| Parameter type | Allows the targeting of a class's member based on member's type |
| Property | Allows the targeting of a class's property based on the property name |
| Return type | Allows the targeting of a class's member based on member's return type |
| Tag attribute | Allows the targeting of a class and/or its members based on the name of an attribute of type Tag |
| Type | Allows the targeting of a class based on its type (namespace and class name) |

It is possible to define multiple rules at one time. This grouping of rules is defined as a *ruleset*. For one or more handlers to be applied to a class's members, all of the rules within a ruleset must return true. A named policy may contain only one ruleset; hence, if you want to create an "or" condition, you will need to create two named policies with the different matching rules but the same handlers.

## Creating and Configuring Custom Rules

Creating a custom rule involves implementing the IMatchingRule interface. The IMatchingRule interface contains one method called Matches, which takes an instance of System.Reflection. MethodBase as a parameter and returns a Boolean value. The MethodBase parameter is the class's member that must be checked in order to determine if the specified rule matches. The Boolean value should return true only if the rule is satisfied. An example of an IMatchingRule implementation is shown in Listing 13-3.

**Listing 13-3.** *Creating a Custom Rule*

```
[ConfigurationElementType(typeof(CustomMatchingRuleData))]
public class MyTimeOfDayRule : IMatchingRule
{

    private TimeSpan m_BeginTimeSpan;
    private TimeSpan m_EndTimeSpan;

    // time span values should be in hh:mm:ss or hh:mm:ss.ff
    // hh = hours, mm = minutes, ss = seconds, ff = fractions of a second
    public MyTimeOfDayRule(NameValueCollection configValues)
    {
        m_BeginTimeSpan =
            TimeSpan.Parse(configValues["BeginTimeSpan"]);

        m_EndTimeSpan =
            TimeSpan.Parse(configValues["EndTimeSpan"]);
    }

    //ignore MethodBase parameter
    public bool Matches(MethodBase member)
    {
        TimeSpan currentTimeOfDay = DateTime.TimeOfDay;

        return (currentTimeOfDay >= m_BeginTimeSpan &&
            currentTimeOfDay <= m_EndTimeSpan);
    }

}
```

As shown in Listing 13-3, unlike the matching rules provided with the Policy Injection Application Block (see Table 13-1), this rule has nothing to do with the member that is being targeted. Instead, it determines if the handlers specified will be processed based on the time of day. This can be helpful, for example, if caching should be applied to a class's member during only peak times of the day.

To configure a matching rule, you can use the more generic name-value pair method via the CustomMatchingRuleData class, or you can define your own design-time components to support the configuration of your custom matching rules. While the latter may provide a prettier user interface, using the CustomMatchingRuleData class is much simpler to implement—you just need to decorate your matching rule class with the ConfigurationElementType attribute, as shown in Listing 13-3.

## Using Predefined Call Handlers

The Policy Injection Application Block comes with a series of call handlers that can be used within your own application. Table 13-2 lists these call handlers.

**Table 13-2.** *Available Call Handlers*

| Class Name | Description |
|---|---|
| AuthorizationCallHandler | Uses the Security Application Block for authorizing the user to specific features of an application, such as accessing or setting a property value or being able to call a method. |
| CachingCallHandler | Provides caching functionality. |
| ExceptionCallHandler | Uses the Exception Handling Application Block to provide exception-handling services. This gives you the ability to handle exceptions without needing to write try-catch blocks. |
| LogCallHandler | Uses the Logging Application Block to provide tracing functionality for the call to a target. You can specify whether the beginning and/or ending of the call should be logged. |
| PerformanceCounterCallHandler | Gives the ability to record performance data when calling a target. |
| ValidationCallHandler | Allows for a target's parameters to be validated before the target is called. |

## Creating and Configuring Handlers

Creating handlers is about as simple as creating matching rules, but you do need to be aware of a few more things.

You need to implement the ICallHandler method for any custom handler. This interface has a method called Invoke, which must be implemented. The Invoke method takes two parameters: an instance of the IMethodInvocation interface and an instance of the GetNextHandlerDelegate class. The Invoke method also will return an instance of IMethodReturn.

Before digging into creating a custom handler, you should understand the purposes of the IMethodInvocation and IMethodReturn interfaces, as well as the GetNextHandlerDelegate class.

The GetNextHandlerDelegate class contains a reference to the next handler to be processed in the chain of handlers. The IMethodInvocation instance will contain all the details about the current method that was invoked or the property that was accessed. Figure 13-1 shows the details about the IMethodInvocation interface.

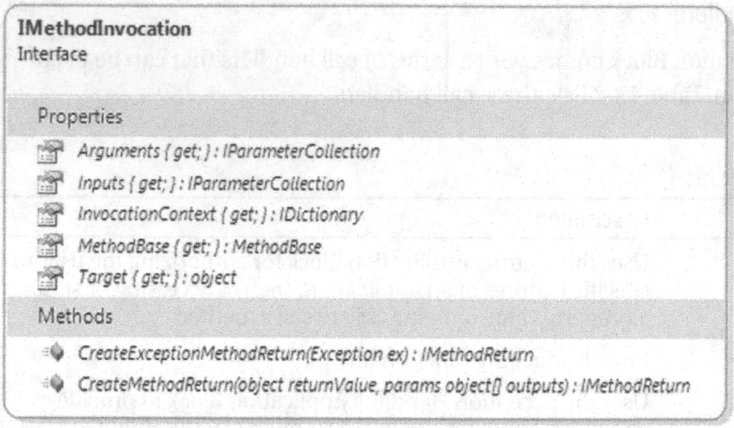

**Figure 13-1.** *IMethodInvocation interface members*

The IMethodInvocation interface has the following properties:

- Arguments: Contains an IParameterCollection of all of the input, output, and by reference parameters.

- Inputs: Also contains an IParameterCollection, with only input parameters.

- InvocationContext: Contains an implementation of IDictionary that allows data to be passed between handlers.

- MethodBase: An instance of the MethodBase for the actual target.

- Target: The target object for which you are calling the member.

The IMethodInvocation interface has two methods that will return an instance of IMethodReturn: CreateExceptionMethodReturn and CreateMethodReturn. The CreateExceptionMethodReturn method is used to return an exception to the caller. The CreateMethodReturn method will return the results of the target to the caller. The CreateMethodReturn method could be used to intercept a call to the target, such as when caching is desired.

An example of how a handler can be created is shown in Listing 13-4.

**Listing 13-4.** *Creating a Custom Handler*

```
[ConfigurationElementType(typeof(CustomCallHandlerData))]
public class CreateFileHandler : ICallHandler
{

    private string m_Filename;

    public CreateFileHandler(NameValueCollection configValues)
    {
        m_Filename = configValues["FileName"];
    }

    public IMethodReturn Invoke(IMethodInvocation input,
```

```
        GetNextHandlerDelegate getNext)
    {

        System.IO.FileStream fileStream = File.Create(m_Filename);

        input.InvocationContext["CreatedFileStream"] = fileStream;

        IMethodReturn msg = getNext()(input, getNext);

        System.IO.FileStream returnedStream =
            msg.InvocationContext["CreatedFileStream"] as
            System.IO.FileStream;

        //clean up file resources if any exist
        if (returnedStream != null)
        {
            try
            {
                returnedStream.Close();
            }
            catch {}
        }

        if (fileStream != null)
        {
            try
            {
                fileStream.Close();
            }
            catch {}
        }

        return msg;
    }
}
```

The ICallHandler's Invoke method allows for preprocessing and postprocessing of the
target. Another way to put it is that parameters can be modified before the target member is
actually called, and the returned results can also be modified before they are returned to the
caller.

The IMethodReturn interface is shown in Figure 13-2. It contains four properties that
return the necessary data to the caller and policy handlers:

- Exception: Returns an exception if one occurred.

- InvocationContext: Returns an IDictionary instance that contains any data that may
  have been passed around between the handlers in the pipeline.

- Outputs: Contains all the parameters that were passed in, including the input parameters.

- ReturnValue: Returns the resulting return value from the target callee, if there was one.

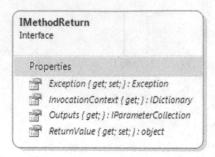

**Figure 13-2.** *IMethodReturn properties*

Configuring a custom handler is no different than configuring a matching rule. If you want to use the `NameValueCollection`, use the `CustomCallHandlerData` with the `ConfigurationElementType` attribute above your class. Otherwise, you can create your own design-time components.

## Understanding the Chain of Events

So now that the matching rules and handlers are defined, how do they fit in when calling a target member of an object from a caller? Figure 13-3 shows a high-level view of how a caller makes a call to the target object.

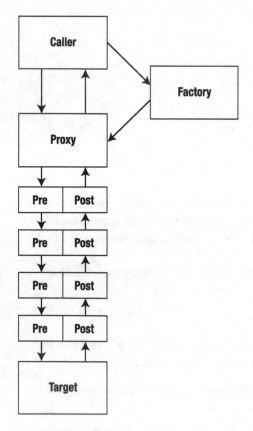

**Figure 13-3.** *High-level view of a policy call stack*

As you can see in Figure 13-3, the actual object is never presented to the caller. Instead, a proxy is created from a factory. This proxy then walks down the handlers until it reaches the target, and then walks back up the handlers until it reaches the proxy. In order to allow this to occur, a target class must be made targetable.

## Making and Using Targetable Classes

To make a class targetable, it can either inherit from MarshalByRefObject or implement an interface. If you use an interface, only the defined members of the interface can be injected with policies. Either method incurs the same amount of overhead, so it's really more a matter of personal preference (personally, I'm more of a fan of using the interface). Listing 13-5 shows two classes: one that inherits from MarshalByRefObject and one that inherits from a defined interface.

**Listing 13-5.** *Making a Class Targetable*

```
Namespace TargetableClasses
{
    //class is targetable by inheriting from MarshalByRefObject
    public class MyFirstTargetableClass : MarshalByRefObject
    {
        //class implementation
    }

    //interface used to make MySecondTargetableClass targetable
    public interface MySecond
    {
        //interface definition
    }

    //class is targetable by inheriting from MySecond interface
    public class MySecondTargetableClass : MySecond
    {
        //class implementation
    }
}
```

## Creating or Obtaining Object Instances with the PolicyInjection Class

Now that the class is targetable, the next step is to determine the method to use the policies. The PolicyInjection class is used to apply the policies to the call from the caller to the target callee member. You can set up policies during the creation of the object, or you can have the PolicyInjection class wrap an existing targetable class. The corresponding methods that can perform these functions are the Create and Wrap methods, as shown in Figure 13-4.

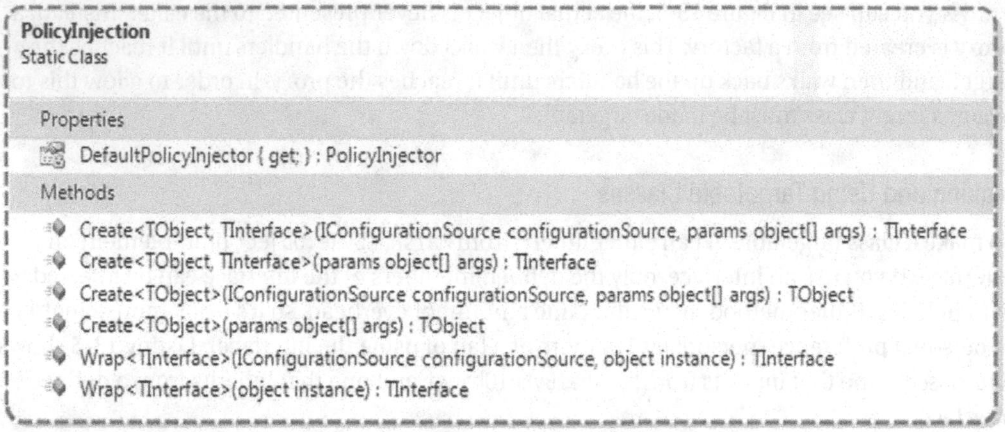

**PolicyInjection**
Static Class

Properties

⬛ DefaultPolicyInjector { get; } : PolicyInjector

Methods

◆ Create<TObject, TInterface>(IConfigurationSource configurationSource, params object[] args) : TInterface

◆ Create<TObject, TInterface>(params object[] args) : TInterface

◆ Create<TObject>(IConfigurationSource configurationSource, params object[] args) : TObject

◆ Create<TObject>(params object[] args) : TObject

◆ Wrap<TInterface>(IConfigurationSource configurationSource, object instance) : TInterface

◆ Wrap<TInterface>(object instance) : TInterface

**Figure 13-4.** *PolicyInjection class public members*

Both the Wrap and Create methods contain overloads for defining a custom
IConfigurationSource. The Create method also contains overloads that allow you to specify
constructor parameters, as well as an interface, if the targetable object was implemented by
inheriting from an interface as opposed to inheriting from MarshalByRefObject.

---

**Note** If you plan on using the Wrap method to add policies after a targetable object is created, you must
use the Create factory to create the targetable object, even if no policies exist during the time of creation.

---

## Determining the Priority of Handlers

With the ability to add policies via attributes or by creating matching rulesets, an order of
precedence must be determined. This order must understand the behavior of how each policy
will be processed. The order of precedence for the discovery and application of handlers is as
follows:

1. If the class or type, or any class or type it derives from, has the [ApplyNoPolicies]
   attribute, the discovery process is canceled and the application block does not apply
   any policies to that class or type.

2. If the member (property or method) of the class, or in a class that it derives from, has
   the [ApplyNoPolicies] attribute, the discovery process is canceled and the application
   block does not apply any policies to that member.

3. If the class or type, or any class or type in its inheritance hierarchy, has any of the
   standard Policy Injection Application Block handler attributes, the application
   block applies these handlers and continues the discovery process. The final order
   of individual handlers is always unspecified.

4.  If the member (property or method) of the class (or the same member in a class within its inheritance hierarchy) carries a handler attribute, the application block applies this handler and continues the discovery process. The final order of individual handlers is always unspecified, although handlers for property accessors (get and set) usually occur earlier in the handler pipeline.

5.  If the configuration for the Policy Injection Application Block contains matching rules that select the class or member, the application block applies these handlers. However, it will not overwrite, change, or replace any handlers defined at higher precedence. The application block applies policies defined later in the configuration closer to the target (later in the handler pipeline) and applies handlers within each policy in the order they occur in the configuration.

## Understanding Policy Injection Block Limitations

The Policy Injection Application Block has some limitations due to its design of using handlers to address cross-cutting concerns, as opposed to using custom application code:

*   Other business logic routines cannot be called from a handler. For example, the code in a handler that logs method calls cannot handle additional context information that is not in the call message—at least not without significant effort.

*   The Policy Injection Application Block cannot inject policies for class constructors or non-public members of classes.

*   The Policy Injection Application Block can intercept and inject policies only for objects that meet the requirements of the built-in interception mechanism. The built-in mechanism supports classes that either inherit a known interface or inherit from the abstract base class. However, it is possible to replace a built-in interception mechanism with a custom mechanism.

*   Matching rules cannot use runtime information, such as parameter values, to target classes and members.

*   Matching rules cannot contain dynamic logic that changes over time, since the Policy Injection Application Block caches policies as it initializes, as opposed to reevaluating them on each call.

*   The Policy Injection Application Block cannot store state between calls. If it did so, multithreaded applications could have issues.

## Configuring and Using Policies

As an example of using the Policy Injection Application Block, we'll return to the simple class that was implemented in Listing 13-2 and add a new attribute-defined policy to validate the inputs. Then we'll create a policy via the application configuration file, which will have an instrumentation handler as well.

## Adding Attribute-Based Policies

To start off, add ValidationCallHandlerAttribute attributes under the
ExceptionCallHandlerAttribute attributes to each of the two methods in the MyClass
class, as shown in Listing 13-6.

**Listing 13-6.** *Adding ValidationCallHandlerAttribute Attributes*

```
using Microsoft.Practices.EnterpriseLibrary.PolicyInjection.CallHandlers;
using Microsoft.Practices.EnterpriseLibrary.Validation.Validators;

public class MyClass : MarshalByRefObject
{
    //adds two numbers and returns a value
    [ExceptionCallHandler("MyExceptionPolicy")]
    [ValidationCallHandler]
    public int AddTwoNumbers(int firstNumber, int secondNumber)
    {
        return firstNumber + secondNumber;
    }

    //subtracts two numbers and returns a value
    [ExceptionCallHandler("MyExceptionPolicy")]
    [ValidationCallHandler]
    public int SubtractTwoNumbers(int firstNumber, int secondNumber)
    {
        return firstNumber - secondNumber;
    }
}
```

The next task is to add the actual validation attributes to the AddTwoNumbers and
SubtractTwoNumbers method's parameters. The validation attributes will ensure the values
of each parameter are above 0. Listing 13-7 shows these methods with their parameters
decorated with the RangeValidatorAttribute attribute.

**Listing 13-7.** *Ensuring Parameter Values Are Above Zero*

```
public class MyClass : MarshalByRefObject
{
    //adds two numbers and returns a value
    [ExceptionCallHandler("MyExceptionPolicy ")]
    [ValidationCallHandler]
    public int AddTwoNumbers(
```

```
        [RangeValidator(typeof(Int32), "0",
        RangeBoundaryType.Inclusive, "0", RangeBoundaryType.Ignore,
        MessageTemplate = "Value must be greater than zero." )]
        int firstNumber,
        [RangeValidator(typeof(Int32), "0",
        RangeBoundaryType.Inclusive, "0", RangeBoundaryType.Ignore,
        MessageTemplate = "Value must be greater than zero." )]
        int secondNumber)
    {

        return firstNumber + secondNumber;
    }


    //subtracts two numbers and returns a value
    [ExceptionCallHandler("MyExceptionPolicy ")]
    [ValidationCallHandler]
    public int SubtractTwoNumbers(
        [RangeValidator(typeof(Int32), "0",
        RangeBoundaryType.Inclusive, "0", RangeBoundaryType.Ignore,
        MessageTemplate = "Value must be greater than zero." )]
        int firstNumber,
        [RangeValidator(typeof(Int32), "0",
        RangeBoundaryType.Inclusive, "0", RangeBoundaryType.Ignore,
        MessageTemplate = "Value must be greater than zero." )]
        int secondNumber)
    {

        return firstNumber - secondNumber;
    }
}
```

Now that the MyClass class contains both exception handling and validation policies defined via attributes, it is time to configure the instrumentation.

## Configuring the Policy Injection Block

You configure the instrumentation through the application file. Follow these steps:

1. In the Configuration Console, open or create an application file. Then add the Policy Injection Application Block (right-click the Application Configuration file node and select Policy Injection Application Block). Figure 13-5 shows the newly added Policy Injection Application Block. It has two nodes: Policies and Injectors.

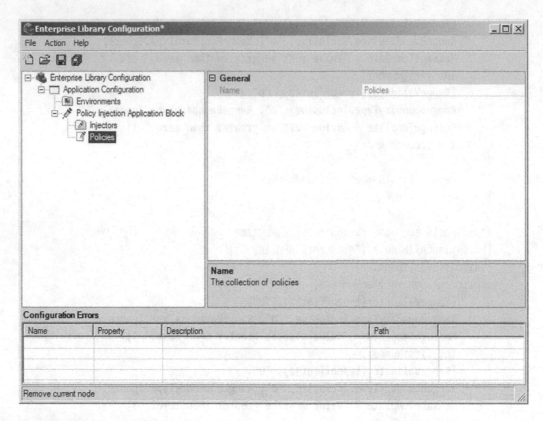

**Figure 13-5.** *Adding the Policy Injection Application Block*

2. To create the policy, right-click the Policies node and select New ➤ Policy. This adds a new node named Policy with two child nodes called Matching Rules and Policies. Select the Policy node and change the Name property to InstrumentationPolicy, as shown in Figure 13-6.

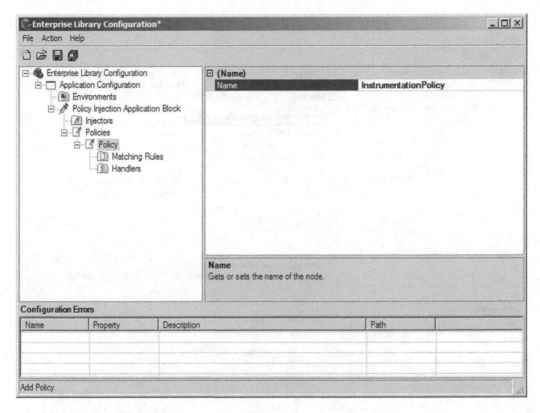

**Figure 13-6.** *Adding the InstrumentationPolicy policy*

3. To create the performance counters handler, right-click the Handlers node and select
   New ► Performance Counters Handler. Change the Name property to MyClass Perf
   Handler. Set the CategoryName property to MyPerformance, the InstanceName property
   to MyClass Performance, and the IncrementAverageCallDuration property to false (all
   we want to do is count the number of times a method is called). Figure 13-7 shows the
   configured MyClass Perf Handler performance counters handler.

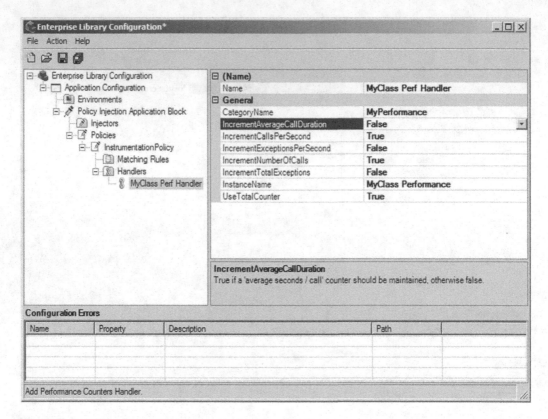

**Figure 13-7.** *Adding the performance counters handler*

4. The last task in configuring this policy is to add a member name matching rule. Right-click the Matching Rules node and select New ➤ Member Name Matching Rule. Select the new matching rule and click the ellipsis next to the Matches property. In the Match Collection Editor dialog box, add the AddTwoNumbers and SubtractTwoNumbers methods to that list, as shown in Figure 13-8.

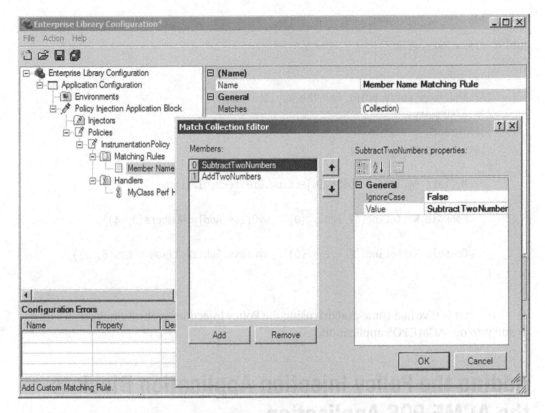

**Figure 13-8.** *Adding the SubtractTwoNumbers and AddTwoNumbers methods to the matching rule*

5. Save this application configuration file.

To finish the example, create a new Windows console application project. The project should reference the following Enterprise Library assemblies:

- `Microsoft.Practices.EnterpriseLibrary.ExceptionHandling.dll`

- `Microsoft.Practices.EnterpriseLibrary.Validation.dll`

- `Microsoft.Practices.EnterpriseLibrary.PolicyInjection.dll`

- `Microsoft.Practices.EnterpriseLibrary.PolicyInjection.CallHandlers.dll`

Once those references are added, the next task is to add the `Main` method and its code, as shown in Listing 13-8.

**Listing 13-8.** *MyProgram Class*

```
public class MyProgram
{
    /// <summary>
    /// The main entry point for the application.
    /// </summary>
    [STAThread]
    static void Main()
    {
        MyClass myClass = PolicyInjection.Create<MyClass>;

        Console.WriteLine("2 + 4 = {0}" ,myClass.AddTwoNumbers(2, 4));

        Console.WriteLine("8 - 2 = {0}" ,myClass.SubtractTwoNumbers(8, 2));
    }
}
```

Now that you've had some practice using the Policy Injection Application Block, it's time to add it to our ACME POS application.

# Adding the Policy Injection Application Block to the ACME POS Application

The web services for the ACME POS application are practically completed, and the web service proxy is in place. The next task will be to create the UI for the application. We will also add basic validation to the domain logic layer.

## Creating the ACME POS UI

In the ACME.POS.Service.Client project of the ACME.POS solution, if there are any Windows forms classes, go ahead and remove them now. Create two new Windows forms classes: SearchForm.cs and CustomerForm.cs. Change the Text property of the SearchForm class to Search for Customer. and the Text property of the CustomerForm class to Customer.

Add the Windows controls listed in Table 13-3 to the SearchForm form. Figure 13-9 shows the layout of these controls.

---

■**Tip**    If you do not feel like building these Windows forms, you can find prebuilt versions within the solution located in the Chapter 13\Begin directory of this book's downloadable source code.

---

**Table 13-3.** *Windows Controls for the SearchForm Form*

| Type | Name Property | Other Properties |
| --- | --- | --- |
| System.Windows.Forms.ListView | m_CustomerListView | View = Detail |
| System.Windows.Forms.Button | m_CreateCustomerButton | Text = Create Customer |
| System.Windows.Forms.Button | m_EditCustomerButton | Text = Edit Customer |
| System.Windows.Forms.Button | m_DeleteCustomerButton | Text = Delete Customer |

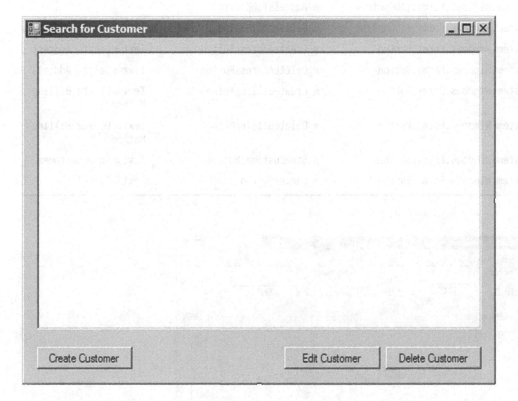

**Figure 13-9.** *SearchForm control layout*

Add the controls listed in Table 13-4 to the CustomerForm form. Figure 13-10 shows the layout of these controls.

**Table 13-4.** *Windows Controls for the CustomerForm Form*

| Type | Name Property | Other Properties |
| --- | --- | --- |
| System.Windows.Forms.Label | m_FirstNameLabel | Text = First Name : |
| System.Windows.Forms.Label | m_LastNameLabel | Text = Last Name : |
| System.Windows.Forms.Label | m_BirthDateLabel | Text = Birth Date : |
| System.Windows.Forms.Label | m_MemberSinceLabel | Text = Member Since : |
| System.Windows.Forms.TextBox | m_FirstNameTextBox | |

*Continued*

**Table 13-4.** *Continued*

| Type | Name Property | Other Properties |
| --- | --- | --- |
| System.Windows.Forms.TextBox | m_LastNameTextBox | |
| System.Windows.Forms.DateTimePicker | m_BirthDateDateTimePicker | Format = Short |
| System.Windows.Forms.DateTimePicker | m_MemberSinceDateTimePicker | Format = Short |
| System.Windows.Forms.GroupBox | m_AddressGroupBox | -- |
| System.Windows.Forms.GroupBox | m_BillingMethodGroupBox | -- |
| System.Windows.Forms.TabControl | m_AddressTabControl | -- |
| System.Windows.Forms.TabControl | m_BillingMethodTabControl | -- |
| System.Windows.Forms.Button | m_CreateAddressButton | Text = Create Address |
| System.Windows.Forms.Button | m_DeleteAddressButton | Text = Delete Address |
| System.Windows.Forms.Button | m_CreateBillingMethod | Text = Create Billing Method |
| System.Windows.Forms.Button | m_DeleteBillingMethod | Text = Delete Billing Method |
| System.Windows.Forms.Button | m_SaveCustomerButton | Text = Save Customer |
| System.Windows.Forms.Button | m_CancelButton | Text = Cancel |

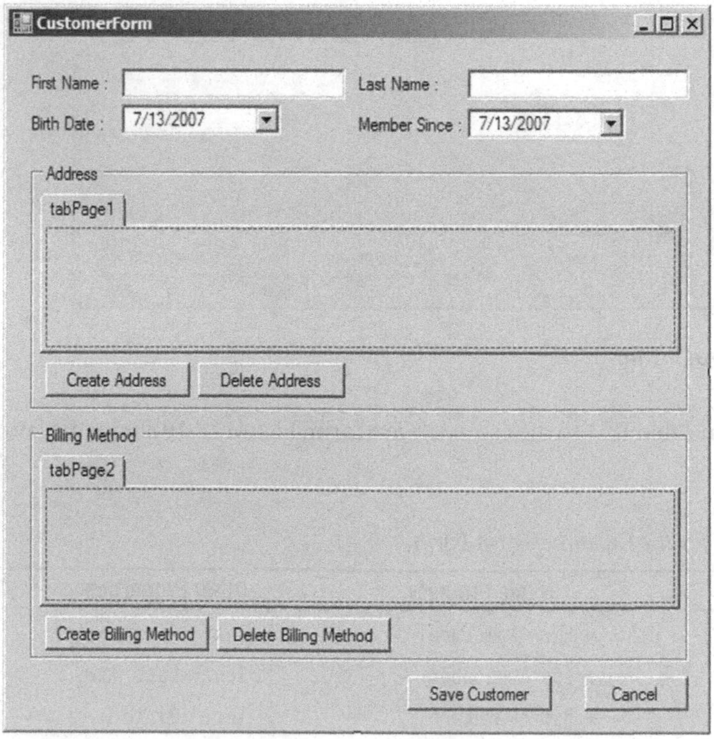

**Figure 13-10.** *CustomerForm control layout*

In Figure 13-10, I left the tab pages in each of the tab controls so you can see that the tab controls are placed inside the Address and Billing Method GroupBox controls. You will want to remove these tab pages. Also, the Address and Billing Method tab controls should be placed in their respective group boxes.

The next task is to create the ICustomer interface. This interface will contain one member called Save. This will be used so the Policy Injection Application Block can inject policies in the customer save routine. Listing 13-9 shows this interface.

**Listing 13-9.** *ICustomer Interface*

```
using System;
using System.Collections.Generic;
using System.Text;

namespace ACME.POS.Service.Client
{
    interface ICustomer
    {
        void Save();
    }
}
```

Next, add the ICustomer interface to the CustomerForm class, create the SaveCustomerButton click event, and have that event call the ICustomer interface's Save method. Listing 13-10 shows this code.

**Listing 13-10.** *Implementing the ICustomer Interface*

```
using System;
using System.Collections.Generic;
using System.ComponentModel;
using System.Data;
using System.Drawing;
using System.Text;
using System.Windows.Forms;

namespace ACME.POS.Service.Client
{
    public partial class CustomerForm : Form, ICustomer
    {
        public CustomerForm()
        {
            InitializeComponent();
        }

        private void m_SaveCustomerButton_Click(object sender,
            EventArgs e)
        {
```

```
            Save();
        }

        #region ICustomer Members

        public void Save()
        {
            throw new Exception(
                "The method or operation is not implemented.");
        }

        #endregion
    }
}
```

The next task is to add a reference to the Policy Injection Application Block assembly and the Policy Injection Application Block Call Handler assembly to the ACME.POS.Service.Client project. Also, add the following using statement to the top of the CustomerForm class with the other using statements.

```
using Microsoft.Practices.EnterpriseLibrary.PolicyInjection.CallHandlers;
```

Now add an ExceptionCallHandler attribute to the Save method with the policy name of "ACMEClientExceptionPolicy". (We created the ACMEClientExceptionPolicy in Chapter 8.) Listing 13-11 shows the Save method decorated with the ExceptionCallHandler attribute.

**Listing 13-11.** *ExceptionCallHandler Added to the Save Method*

```
[ExceptionCallHandler("ACMEClientExceptionPolicy")]
public void Save()
{
    throw new Exception(
        "The method or operation is not implemented.");
}
```

Now if you try running the application and an error should be generated and then handled via the injected exception policy with no try-catch code involved. (Of course, you still need to implement the actual Save method.)

## Adding Validation to the Domain Logic Layer

The next step in creating the ACME POS application is to add basic validation to the domain logic layer. This helps ensure what gets passed in from the web service layer is valid. In Listing 13-12, the Policy Application Block's ValidationCallHandler and the Validation Application Block's NotNullValidator are used to validate that the collection passed into the SaveCustomerData method of CustomerBusinessRules is not null.

**Listing 13-12.** *Validating the CustomerList Object*

```
public class CustomerBusinessRules
{
    [ValidationCallHandler]
    public void SaveCustomerData(
        [NotNullValidator]CustomerList customers)
    {

        CustomerList modifiedCustomers = customers;

        LogEntry logEntry = new LogEntry();
        logEntry.Message = "Modifying Customers";
        logEntry.Categories.Add("Customer");
        logEntry.TimeStamp = DateTime.Now;

        if (Logger.ShouldLog(logEntry))
            Logger.Write(logEntry);

        //Send data to DAL
        CustomerDAL customerDal = new CustomerDAL();
        customerDal.SaveCustomers(modifiedCustomers);
    }


    public CustomerList GetAllCustomers() ...

}
```

# Summary

With the Policy Injection Application Block, you can manage cross-cutting concerns without complicating your application code. However, it is still important to decide when to use the Policy Injection Application Block. If performance is a consideration, then the overhead may be too much of a hindrance.

This completes the coverage of the Enterprise Library 3.0 and 3.1 application blocks. The next chapter explains how to create your very own application block.

# CHAPTER 14

# The Application Block Software Factory

This chapter covers a new software factory created by the Microsoft patterns & practices team that helps you build the skeleton for your own application block. This software factory is appropriately named the Application Block Software Factory. The Application Block Software Factory is installed with the default installation of Enterprise Library 3.0 and 3.1.

The Application Block Software Factory allows you to create providers for the existing Enterprise Library application blocks. It also comes bundled with a set of tools and resources that provide tutorials, guidance on best practices, and automated guidance packages known as *recipes*. The tutorials are provided as help documentation. The best practices are provided both as help documentation and by the automated guidance packages. Together, this solution and accompanying information make it easier to create your own providers with minimum effort.

## Introducing the Guidance Navigator

While it is great to offer content that provides the best practices and recipes to develop an application block, it would be counterproductive to neglect to put the information and tools in a manageable format. This is where the Guidance Navigator comes into play.

The Guidance Navigator, shown in Figure 14-1, provides a central location for navigating the tools and resources bundled with the Application Block Software Factory.

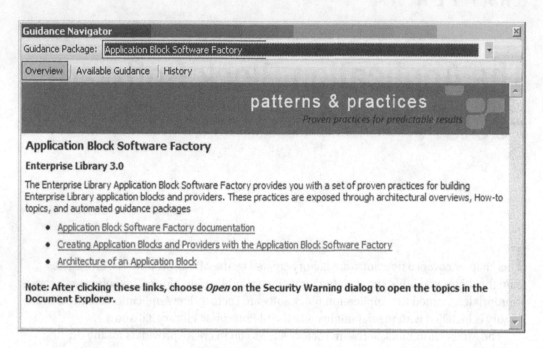

**Figure 14-1.** *Overview tab of the Guidance Navigator*

The Guidance Navigator can be found under the View ➤ Other Windows menu option in Visual Studio. Since the Guidance Navigator is a Windows form hosted in Visual Studio, it is possible to dock this window. This allows you to keep the Guidance Navigator handy as you are developing an application block.

The Guidance Navigator's Overview tab (see Figure 14-1) contains links to examples and other forms of guidance.

The Available Guidance tab contains guidance in the form of recipes for stubbing out your code. The recipes are for creating an application block and the providers that it uses, as well as creating providers for the existing Enterprise Library application blocks. To use a recipe, expand one of the available guidance entries and click the Run This Recipe link, as shown in Figure 14-2.

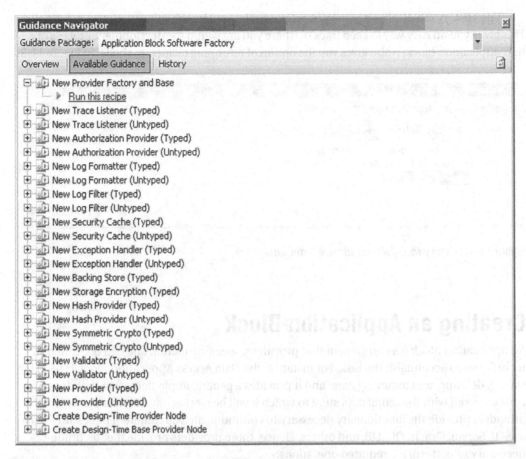

**Figure 14-2.** *Available Guidance tab of the Guidance Navigator*

As you can see, quite a few recipes are provided by the Application Block Software Factory. However, only a handful of them are used to create a custom application block; the rest are used for creating providers for the existing Enterprise Library application blocks. Table 14-1 lists the recipes used for creating a custom application block.

**Table 14-1.** *Recipes for Creating a Custom Application Block*

| Recipe | Description |
| --- | --- |
| New Provider Factory and Base | Creates the provider factory and base classes used to provide the proper base functionality and proper provider instantiation for the application block |
| New Provider (Typed) | Provides a typed provider |
| New Provider (Untyped) | Provides an untyped provider |
| Create Design-Time Provider Node | Allows for the creation of design-time provider nodes for configuring an application block with the Configuration Console |
| Create Design-Time Base Provider Node | Provides the necessary base provider node for design-time configuration via the Configuration Console |

The History tab displays a history of actions performed for the software factory solution. This gives you an easy way to keep track of where you are within the development process of a new application block. It also gives you the option of rerunning recipes, as shown in Figure 14-3.

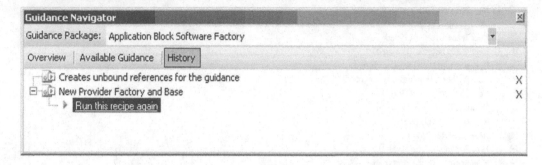

**Figure 14-3.** *History tab of the Guidance Navigator*

# Creating an Application Block

An application block is a component that provides a specific function and can use different techniques to accomplish the task. For instance, the Data Access Application Block is used for saving, deleting, and retrieving data, and it provides a generic implementation that does not concern itself with the actual data store to which it will be storing data. The data access providers provide the functionality necessary to communicate with different data stores such as SQL Server, Oracle, OLEDB, and others. Hence, these providers provide the "technique" necessary to perform the required operations.

An application block can be configured to use any provider dynamically at runtime through a configuration file using the out-of-the-box features, or it could be wired up manually through some other mechanism in code. This feature also allows for other providers that adhere to the necessary provider interface to be created to provide functionality that did not come with Enterprise Library.

To demonstrate using the Application Block Software Factory, this section goes through the steps of creating an application block that will perform simple math functions. Here, the focus is on the creation of an application block, rather than developing complex functionality within it.

## Creating the Application Block Solution

The first step in creating a new application block is to create the actual solution that will contain the necessary projects for the application block. When you select a new project in Visual Studio, you will see the standard New Project dialog box. In the Project Types list, expand the Guidance Packages node, and then select Application Block Software Factory. The templates available give you the following choices:

- Use C# or VB .NET

- Create an application block or just a provider library

- Create the project with or without unit tests

---

■**Note**  The unit tests that come with the Application Block Software Factory are only for Visual Studio Team System.

---

Follow these steps to create the application block solution:

1. In the New Project dialog box, select the template labeled Application Block (C#), as shown in Figure 14-4. Type in a name in the Name text box, and then click OK.

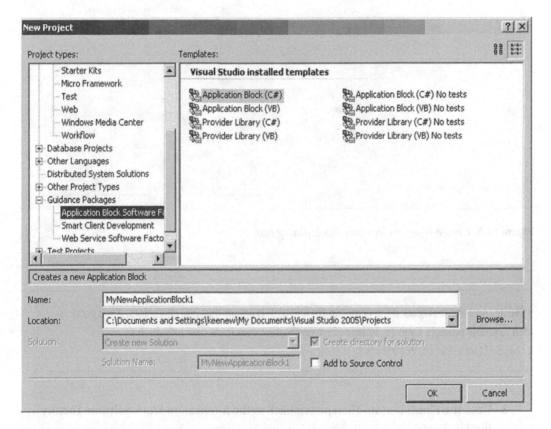

**Figure 14-4.** *Choosing to create an application block using C#*

2. The Create New Application Block dialog box appears. Enter the name, friendly name, namespace, and author in the text boxes, as shown in Figure 14-5. The name is SampleAB in this example.

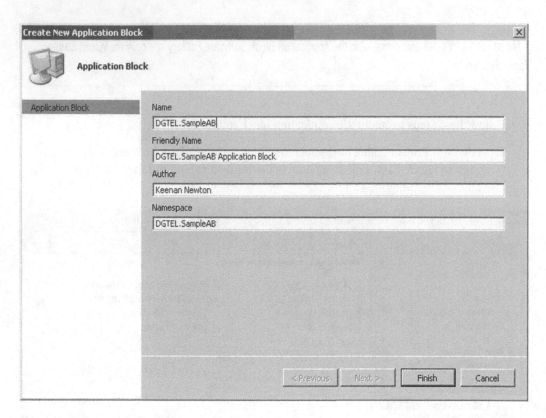

**Figure 14-5.** *Create New Application Block dialog box*

---

**Note** An error can occur if the complete file and path is longer that 260 characters. It is a good idea to create projects involving software factories in their own route directory, such as `c:\mySoftwareFactoryProjects\`.

---

**3.** Click the Finish button. Then just sit back as the Application Block Software Factory does its magic.

Your solution should look similar to Figure 14-6. Notice that the design-time configuration project, unit test projects, and application block project have been stubbed out for you.

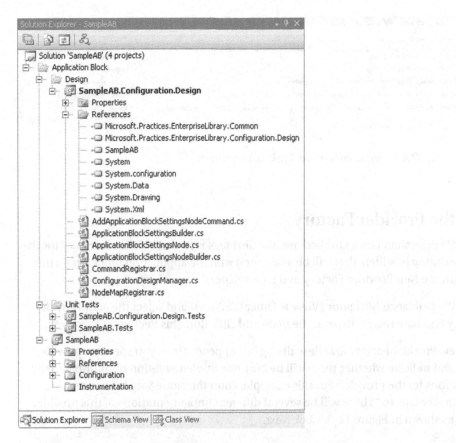

**Figure 14-6.** *New application block solution in the Solution Explorer*

The created class files are mostly just empty shells that need the guts created for them. To assist in this process, a series of TODO comments have been inserted in the files, as reminders of what still needs to be done to complete the application block. To simplify searching for all the TODO comments within an application, open the Task List window, and then select Comments in the drop-down list. All of the TODO comments will then be listed in the task list, as shown in the example in Figure 14-7.

---

**Note** The TODO comments are not a complete list of what must be done to complete your specific custom application block, of course. You may need to take into account architecture and development considerations as well.

---

| | Description ▲ | File ▲ | Line ▲ |
|---|---|---|---|
| | TODO: Verify that the plural property value is correct. | ApplicationBlockSettings | 29 |
| | TODO: Specify the API for the SampleProvider Provider | ISampleProvider.cs | 13 |
| | TODO: Use the SampleProviderData object to set runtime values for the SampleProvider. | SampleProvider.cs | 17 |
| | TODO: Decide whether the SampleProvider constructor with discrete arguments is neccesary. | SampleProviderCustomF | 31 |
| | TODO: Add the configuration properties for SampleProviderData. The snippet for creating configuration properties would be useful. | SampleProviderData.cs | 30 |

*Task List - 6 tasks* · Comments

Error List | Task List | Output | Pending Checkins | Find Symbol Results

**Figure 14-7.** *Viewing TODO comments in the Task List window*

## Creating the Provider Factory

With the initial application block stubbed out, the next task is to provide the necessary mechanism for consuming providers that will be associated with the application block. To do this, you need to run the New Provider Factory and Base recipe.

1. Open the Guidance Navigator (View ➤ Other Windows) and select the New Provider Factory and Base recipe. Expand the node and click Run This Recipe.

2. The New Provider Factory and Base dialog box appears. Here, you specify a provider name and indicate whether there will be only one implementation or multiple implementations for the provider. For this example, enter the name SampleProvider and set the provider type to "There will be several different implementations of this provider type," as shown in Figure 14-8. Click Next.

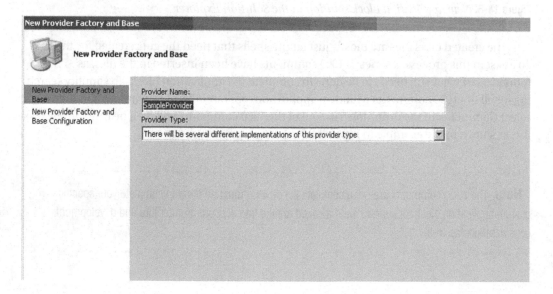

**Figure 14-8.** *Creating the provider factory*

**3.** Because you selected to have several different implementations of the provider type, the next dialog box requests the name of the default instance. Set the default instance name to defaultMath for this example. Then click Finish.

If you make a mistake while running a recipe, you can always run it again. Just look in the History tab of the Guidance Navigator. Figure 14-9 shows an example of the History tab after running the New Provider Factory and Base Recipe.

---

■**Caution** Rerunning a recipe will automatically undo any changes you already made to the code.

---

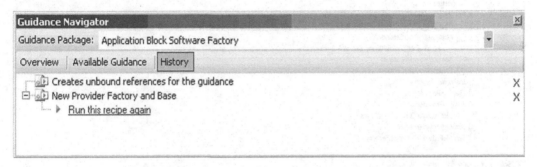

**Figure 14-9.** *History tab after creating a provider factory*

After running the New Provider Factory and Base recipe, a series of files will be created to support the instantiation and wiring up of a new instance of the provider. These include the provider factories, provider interface, and provider base class, as shown in Figure 14-10.

Now you need to work with two files:

- I*<Provider Name>*.cs will contain an interface to which all the providers will adhere. This file is named ISampleProvider.cs in the example.

- *<Provider Name>*.cs provides a base class implementation for the interface. This file is called SampleProvider.cs in the example.

You can see these files toward the bottom of the Solution Explorer window in Figure 14-10.

**Figure 14-10.** *Solution Explorer after running the New Provider Factory and Base recipe*

## Implementing the Provider Interface

The ISampleProvider.cs file is shown in Listing 14-1. Notice that the appropriate attributes to support the ObjectBuilder are already provided, as well as any necessary using statements (imports for VB .NET).

**Listing 14-1.** *The ISampleProvider Class File*

```
using SampleAB.Configuration;
using Microsoft.Practices.EnterpriseLibrary.Common.Configuration.ObjectBuilder;

namespace SampleAB
{
    /// <summary>
    /// Defines the basic functionality of an SampleProvider
    /// </summary>
    [ConfigurationNameMapper(typeof(SampleProviderDataRetriever))]
    [CustomFactory(typeof(SampleProviderCustomFactory))]
    public interface ISampleProvider
    {
```

```
        // TODO: Specify the API for the SampleProvider Provider
    }
}
```

Also notice the TODO comment in Listing 14-1. You will want to replace this with your implementation code. Since this is an interface, you will simply define the members that must be implemented by other providers that will inherit from this interface.

For this example, create a method called DoMath that takes two integers and outputs the result as an integer. Listing 14-2 shows this method added to the ISampleProvider interface.

**Listing 14-2.** *Adding the DoMath Method to ISampleProvider*

```
using SampleAB.Configuration;
using Microsoft.Practices.EnterpriseLibrary.Common.Configuration.ObjectBuilder;

namespace SampleAB
{
    /// <summary>
    /// Defines the basic functionality of an SampleProvider
    /// </summary>
    [ConfigurationNameMapper(typeof(SampleProviderDataRetriever))]
    [CustomFactory(typeof(SampleProviderCustomFactory))]
    public interface ISampleProvider
    {
        int DoMath(int x, int y);
    }
}
```

## Implementing the Provider Base Class

You also need to implement the abstract base class, called SampleProvider in this example. The base class allows you to implement common functionality, such as performing validation. In this example, the SampleProvider class will ensure that the result is never less than zero. Listing 14-3 shows this implementation.

**Listing 14-3.** *SampleProvider Base Class Implementation*

```
using Microsoft.Practices.EnterpriseLibrary.Common.Instrumentation;
using SampleAB.Configuration;

namespace SampleAB
{
    /// <summary>
    /// Abstract implementation of the <see cref="ISampleProvider"/> interface.
    /// </summary>
    public abstract class SampleProvider : ISampleProvider
    {
        #region ISampleProvider Members
```

```
        public int DoMath(int x, int y)
        {
            int z = Calculate(x, y);

            if(z < 0)
                z = 0;

            return z;
        }

        #endregion

        protected abstract int Calculate(int x, int y);

    }
}
```

## Creating Providers

With the provider factories, provider interface, and base classes created, the next step is to actually create the providers.

The Application Software Application Block provides two mechanisms for configuring a provider:

- A *typed* implementation allows for strongly typed configuration settings to be defined. This mechanism is demonstrated throughout the Enterprise Library application blocks.

- An *untyped* implementation allows for simple name-value pairs to be defined.

You can choose an untyped or a typed provider when you create the provider. It is generally a good idea to implement an untyped provider first until you get the application block working, and then convert it to a typed provider later.

You can create a provider using the Guidance Navigator or from the Solution Explorer. For this example, we'll use the Solution Explorer to create two providers: AddProvider and SubtractProvider.

1. Build the project. (You will find out why this is necessary later, when you create the design-time configuration nodes).

2. Right-click the `SampleAB` project in the Solution Explorer and select Application Block Software Factory ➤ New Provider (Untyped), as shown in Figure 14-11.

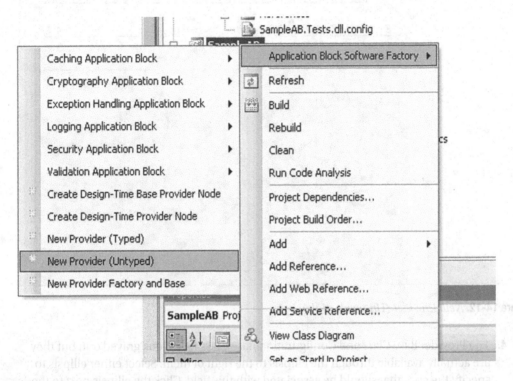

**Figure 14-11.** *Selecting to create an untyped provider*

3. The New Provider (Untyped) dialog box appears. The first field requires the name of the provider. For this example, enter `AddProvider` as the name, as shown in Figure 14-12.

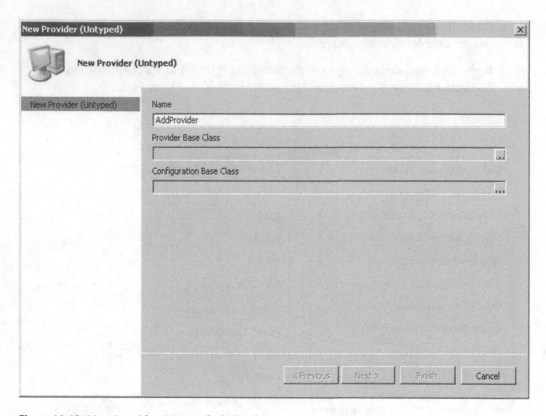

**Figure 14-12.** *New Provider (Untyped) dialog box*

4. The Provider Base Class and Configuration Base Class fields look grayed out, but they are actually available through the ellipsis to the right of them. Select either ellipsis to specify the class that should be associated with this field. Click the ellipsis next to the Provider Base Class field for this example.

5. The Browse and Select a .NET Type dialog box appears. Select the SampleProvider class, as shown in Figure 14-13, and then click OK.

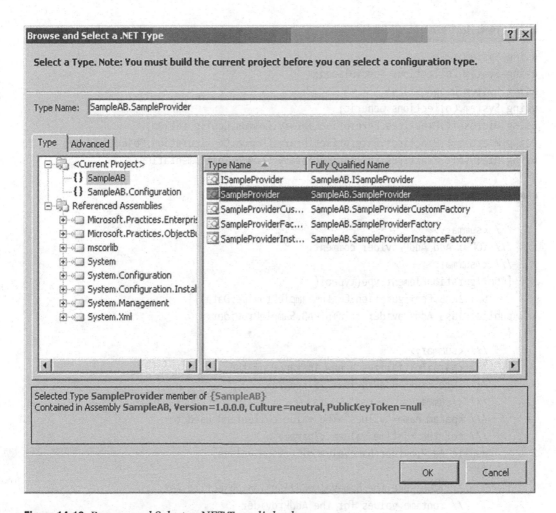

**Figure 14-13.** *Browse and Select a .NET Type dialog box*

6. The New Provider dialog box will now not only have the Provider Base Class field filled in, but it will also have the Configuration Base Class filled in (the recipe searched the same project to determine the appropriate configuration base class to use). In this case, you should see SampleAB.SampleProvider in the Provider Base Class field and SampleAB.Configuration.CustomSampleProviderData in the Configuration Base Class field. Click the Finish button.

A new class called AddProvider has been created, as shown in Listing 14-4.

**Listing 14-4.** *AddProvider Class*

```
using System;
using System.Collections.Specialized;
using System.Diagnostics;
using System.Collections.Generic;
using Microsoft.Practices.EnterpriseLibrary.Common.Configuration;
using Microsoft.Practices.EnterpriseLibrary.Common.Configuration.ObjectBuilder;
using Microsoft.Practices.EnterpriseLibrary.Common.Instrumentation;

namespace SampleAB
{
    /// <summary>
    /// TODO: Add AddProvider comment.
    /// </summary>
    [ConfigurationElementType(typeof(
        SampleAB.Configuration.CustomSampleProviderData))]
    public class AddProvider : SampleAB.SampleProvider
    {
        /// <summary>
        /// <para>Initializes a new instance of the
        /// <see cref="AddProvider"/>.</para>
        /// </summary>
        /// <param name="values">The value collection used to
        /// set the runtime values.</param>
        public AddProvider(NameValueCollection values)
        {
            // TODO: Use the NameValueCollection object to set
            // runtime values for the AddProvider
        }

        // TODO: Implement SampleAB.SampleProvider methods on AddProvider

    }
}
```

The new class contains three TODO comments. The first is to provide a summary of what the class is for, the second is to read in name-value configuration settings, and the third is to implement the AddProvider methods.

Since this provider inherits from the SampleProvider class, it will be necessary to implement the Calculate method. Listing 14-5 shows the implemented AddProvider class.

**Listing 14-5.** *AddProvider Class Implementation*

```
using System;
using System.Collections.Specialized;
using System.Diagnostics;
using System.Collections.Generic;
```

```
using Microsoft.Practices.EnterpriseLibrary.Common.Configuration;
using Microsoft.Practices.EnterpriseLibrary.Common.Configuration.ObjectBuilder;
using Microsoft.Practices.EnterpriseLibrary.Common.Instrumentation;

namespace SampleAB
{
    /// <summary>
    /// This provider adds two numbers and returns the result.
    /// </summary>
    [ConfigurationElementType(typeof(
        SampleAB.Configuration.CustomSampleProviderData))]
    public class AddProvider : SampleAB.SampleProvider
    {
        /// <summary>
        /// <para>Initializes a new instance of the
        /// <see cref="AddProvider"/>.</para>
        /// </summary>
        /// <param name="values">The value collection used to
        /// set the runtime values.</param>
        public AddProvider(NameValueCollection values)
        {
            // TODO: Later. Use the NameValueCollection object
            // to set runtime values for the AddProvider
        }

        protected override int Calculate(int x, int y)
        {
            return x + y;
        }
    }
}
```

Now to create `SubtractProvider`, repeat the same procedure as used to create `AddProvider`, except the implementation will be to subtract y from x.

## Creating the Design-Time Configuration Nodes

One of the great features of creating an application block is the ability to use the Enterprise Library Configuration Console to define the configuration settings that will be used with the application block. The Application Block Software Factory contains recipes that will help with building these design-time configuration features.

Two nodes are typically created for a particular application block:

- The base provider node, which specifies which provider will be used

- The provider node, which specifies configuration settings for the provider itself

We'll create both of these nodes for our sample application block.

## Creating the Design-Time Base Provider Node

Follow these steps to create a design-time base provider node:

1. Run the Create Design-Time Base Provider Node recipe. You can do this using the Guidance Navigator or by right-clicking the design-time project within the Solution Explorer and selecting Application Block Software Factory ➤ Create Design-Time Base Provider Node.

2. The Create Design Time Base Provider Node dialog box appears, as shown in Figure 4-14. In the Node Name field, enter Math, and then click the ellipsis next to the Runtime Configuration Type field.

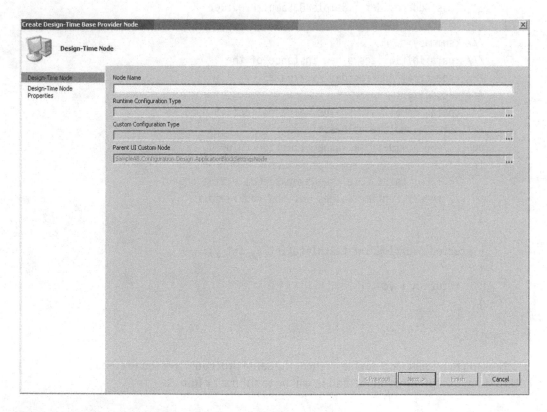

**Figure 14-14.** *Create Design-Time Base Provider Node dialog box*

3. In the dialog box, you will see the SampleAB project that is referenced in the design-time project. It is important that you select the base class and not the custom class. In this example, select the SampleProviderData class, which is the base class, and then click OK.

---

**Note** Remember earlier when I mentioned it was necessary to build the SampleAB project. That is because the Application Block Software Factory uses reflection to determine the provider base and configuration base types of the referenced projects. So if the projects were not built, they will not show up when you are adding a design-time base provider node.

---

4. The Create Design-Time Base Provider Node dialog box will display not only the `Sample`-`ProviderData` class in the Runtime Configuration Type field, but also the `CustomSampleProviderData` class in the Custom Configuration Type field. Click Next to continue.

5. The next dialog box shows any properties that were defined in the configuration run-time components. There are none in this example. Click the Finish button to complete this recipe.

Now would be a good time to check out how this node is starting to shape up within the Enterprise Library Configuration Console. Copy the design-time binaries `SampleAB.dll` and `SampleAB.Configuration.Design.dll` to the executing folder of the Configuration Console. Then start the Configuration Console, create a new configuration file, and add the SampleAB Application Block to the newly created configuration file, as shown in Figure 14-15.

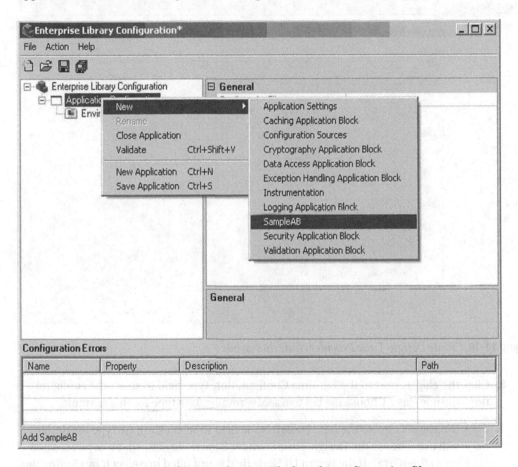

**Figure 14-15.** *Adding the SampleAB Application Block to the configuration file*

You will notice some generic naming that was put in place that should be edited later. For now, go ahead and close the Enterprise Library Configuration Console without saving the configuration file.

## Creating the Design-Time Provider Node

The design-time provider node provides specific configuration settings for a particular provider. Follow these steps to create the node:

1. Right-click the design-time configuration project in the Solution Explorer and select Application Block Software Factory ➤ Create Design-Time Provider Node.

2. The Create Design-Time Provider Node dialog box appears, as shown in Figure 14-16. In the Node Name field, enter AddMath.

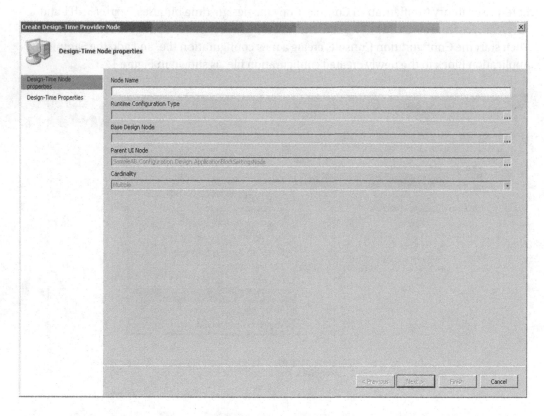

**Figure 14-16.** *Create Design-Time Provider Node dialog box*

3. Click the ellipsis next to the Runtime Configuration Type field to select the configuration runtime class. Choose the CustomSampleProviderData type for this example.

4. Click the ellipsis next to the Base Design Node field to select the base type the design node will use. Choose the Design-Time Provider Base node class that was just created (SampleProviderData). If the Parent UI Node field is not filled in, select it by clicking the ellipsis and choose the parent class node.

5. The Cardinality drop-down list lets you select single or multiple instances. Choose Single for this example.

6. Click Next. Once again, there aren't any design-time properties specific to this provider. Click the Finish button.

Now you need to repeat the same process to add the design-time provider node for SubtractProvider. Name it SubtractMath.

And that completes the creation of the new application block.

# Using the Sample Application Block

Now with everything built, it is time to use your new application block. Create a new Windows application with two text boxes, a label, and a button. Label the button DoMath. Then add the code for the click event of the DoMath button, as shown in Listing 14-6.

*Listing 14-6. DoMath Click Event*

```
using System;
using System.Collections.Generic;
using System.ComponentModel;
using System.Data;
using System.Drawing;
using System.Text;
using System.Windows.Forms;
using SampleAB;

namespace SampleABTestHarness
{
    public partial class TestForm : Form
    {
        public TestForm()
        {
            InitializeComponent();
        }

        private void m_DoMathButton_Click(object sender, EventArgs e)
        {
            ISampleProvider math = SampleProviderFactory.CreateSampleProvider();

            int result = math.DoMath(Convert.ToInt32(m_XTextBox.Text, 10),
                Convert.ToInt32(m_YTextBox.Text, 10));

            m_ResultLabel.Text = result.ToString();
        }
    }
}
```

The next step is to configure the application configuration file. Add SampleAB to the configuration file, and finally select AddProvider as the default.

**Note**  The completed application block and sample application shown in this chapter can be downloaded from the Source Code/Download section of the Apress website (http://www.apress.com).

# Summary

With the addition of the Application Block Software Factory, creating new application blocks in Enterprise Library 3.0 has become a lot easier. The sample application block created in this chapter was a very simple arithmetic example, but it demonstrated the process. You can see how your own specific business components could be modified into application blocks to be inserted in your own applications. It would then be relatively easy to swap out providers to meet specific business needs. Or you could create application blocks to be consumed by the developers in your enterprise for general needs surrounding application architecture and development.

The final chapter of this book will look into application blocks and providers that are outside Enterprise Library, as well as some advanced configuration settings that can be used in the Enterprise Library Configuration Console.

# CHAPTER 15

∎∎∎

# Other Application Blocks and Advanced Configuration Features

The Enterprise Library is not the only source of application blocks. Other application blocks have been created by the development community, third-party vendors, and the Microsoft patterns & practices group.

The Microsoft patterns & practices group has created application blocks that focus on user interface (UI) development and mobile applications, including the following:

- Composite UI Application Block
- Connection Monitor Application Block
- Endpoint Catalog Application Block
- Disconnected Service Agent Application Block
- Composite Web Application Block
- Page Flow Application Block
- Updater Application Block
- Mobile Client Software Factory application blocks, including the Mobile Composite UI Application Block, Mobile Data Access Application Block, Mobile Configuration Application Block, and more

In this chapter, you'll learn more about these application blocks. Also, you'll be introduced to some of the more advanced features of the Enterprise Library Configuration Console.

## Composite UI Application Block

The UI of an application can be one of the most difficult components to design and develop, yet it's also arguably the most critical, since it's how the end user will interact with the application. Therefore, when designing the UI of an application, you need to understand the audience of that application.

For instance, if you're developing a business application, you'll want to fully understand the type of business in which the application will be used. Are the users customer service representatives who will perform routine tasks over and over again? Or do they perform back-office types of duties, such as data analysis and reporting? Also, are the users used to using applications such as Microsoft Word, Excel, and PowerPoint? And will the application be used by people from different parts of the world? If so, you need to take into account both the different languages and cultures. The last thing you want to do is insult the users of your application because you accidentally used the wrong color scheme.

You also need to learn more about the specific tasks the users desire to perform with the application you are designing. You might interview the users and even monitor them as they go about their daily tasks. Make sure that you interview many different cross sections of users to obtain a complete understanding of the tasks at hand before moving forward with the UI design. At the same time, you should steer clear of relying on your users to actually design the interface. Try to discern common user themes and goals, and then design your application around that information.

So now that you know your users, what they do, and how they do it, you're ready build the killer UI for the application. The design goals should center around creating a simplistic and intuitive interface while enhancing user productivity. Don't be afraid to draw the application on paper first or create simple HTML mock-ups to be used for user review. Try to get a user consensus regarding the interface's flow and look and feel before writing even one line of code. It will save you time and effort in the long run.

For simple UIs, such as an address book application, it may make sense just to go ahead and drag and drop some controls onto a Windows form and proceed from there. However, for more complex endeavors, such as a customer relationship or order management application, you will likely need a very robust infrastructure to support your application and its complex UI. This is where the Composite UI Application Block comes into the picture. Although this application block is not included with the core Enterprise Library set, it is still built on the overall design principles of Enterprise Library.

**Note** The Composite UI Application Block can be downloaded as part of the Smart Client Software Factory, which is available at `http://www.codeplex.com/smartclient`. The May 2007 release of the Smart Client Software Factory contains a version of the Composite UI Application Block that supports Windows Presentation Foundation (WPF).

## Uses of the Composite UI Application Block

The Composite UI Application Block was meant for use within applications requiring a robust UI, where many pieces can interact with each other to provide a fluid, consistent experience to the user. The interaction between the UI components is provided by the Composite UI

Application Block's modular plug-in design. The following types of robust applications are targeted by the Composite UI Application Block:

- Online transaction processing (OLTP) applications

  - Point-of-sale

  - Employee time clock

  - Electronic banking

  - Accounting applications

- Portal applications

  - Insurance claim adjustment

  - Investment research

  - Intranets

- UI-intensive applications

  - Customer relationship management

  - Software development

  - Help desk

  - Personal finance

When designing your UI and deciding if a particular architecture will suit your needs, make sure you do your homework. Like the rest of the components developed by the Microsoft patterns & practices group, the Composite UI Application Block represents just one approach, and other UI frameworks or design patterns may meet your needs better.

UI architectures (also called *interactive software architectures* or *UI management systems*) are based on the notion that the application part contains the software functionality—what the system does—and the UI part contains the representation of this functionality to the user(s) of the system. The motivation behind UI architectures is to improve extensibility, adaptability, portability, complex functionality, and separation of concerns of interactive software. Some of these UI architecture patterns include Model-View-Controller (MVC), Model-View-Presenter (MVP), and Presenter-Abstraction-Control (PAC). The Composite UI Application Block supports all of these and many more UI architectures. This allows application developers the greatest flexibility in choosing the right architectural approach for the Windows application they are going to build.

The Composite UI Application Block is one of the first application blocks that was designed with a large amount of input from the developer community. This is a somewhat new development paradigm for the Microsoft patterns & practices group, and Microsoft in general, and the end result has been quite impressive to date.

Besides making the application block easy to work with, its modular design provides another benefit to the application team as a whole. It allows developers who specialize in creating UIs to specifically work on the shell and components of an application, while other developers can focus on developing the application logic, such as its domain and validation logic. Because the developers can work within their specialized areas, they should be more productive in developing the application, thus reducing the overall time it takes to build and deploy it.

# Core Components of the Composite UI Application Block

The Composite UI Application Block consists of five core components:

- *SmartParts* provide the building blocks of the UI.

- *Workspaces* provide the containers to display UI components such as SmartParts.

- *WorkItems* provide the building blocks for performing tasks.

- The *application shell* is the container of the application.

- *Modules* contain the SmartParts and WorkItems within an assembly to be used by the application shell.

## SmartParts

The history of the SmartPart actually extends back to the introduction of Microsoft Share-Point. In the beginning days of SharePoint, developers had the option of creating custom controls called *WebParts*. A WebPart is a little pluggable ASP.NET server control that can do more than simply be collapsed or hidden. You can also configure it with parameters and values, save them, and have them restored when the user returns to the page. You can find this type of technology used on many websites today, mainly to customize the users' experience by displaying information that is relevant to them, such as news headlines, stock quotes, weather, and/or sports.

Microsoft saw the potential of using the WebPart in its ASP.NET 2.0 offering, so now you can create WebParts in ASP.NET 2.0. However, unlike the SharePoint WebParts, the ASP.NET version also supports building WebParts with user controls, which makes the design and development easier than needing to create server controls. Here's an example of creating an ASP.NET WebPart:

```
Public class MyWebPart : WebPart
{
    // Implementation goes here
}
```

---

**■Note** The one downside to the ASP.NET 2.0 WebParts is that they are not compatible with the SharePoint WebParts. So you will be forced to rework some of your existing SharePoint WebParts to make them work with ASP.NET 2.0.

---

These WebParts have been a great concept for web-based UIs, and the Microsoft patterns & practices team created SmartParts to bring the idea to the Windows forms world. Like their web counterparts, SmartParts allow you to create customized, pluggable controls that allow for interaction between the Composite UI Application Block and other SmartPart components.

SmartParts have taken the overall design to a new level. Unlike the WebParts, which must inherit from a base class, SmartParts uses the ObjectBuilder subsystem (discussed in Chapter 4) to create and inject objects into the application during runtime. This gives you a great amount of flexibility in the design and development of your application. Listing 15-1 shows an example of creating a SmartPart.

**Listing 15-1.** *Creating a SmartPart*

```
[SmartPart]
public partial class MySmartPart : UserControl
{
    public MySmartPart()
    {
        InitializeComponent();
    }

    // Implementation goes here
}
```

The ApplicationShell class is abstracted from the SmartPart. This abstraction is accomplished with the use of attribute-based dependency. One of the many features this allows for is the use of multiple types of Windows UI components, such as using the Windows Presentation Foundation (WPF) components (formerly known as Avalon) and Windows forms components within the same application.

## The WorkItem Class

The WorkItem class is the container of components that work together to perform a specific function within an application. More technically speaking, a WorkItem instance will represent a specific use case for an application. Typically, the WorkItem object will contain SmartParts, UIElements, controllers, services, child WorkItem objects, and other components to accomplish the tasks necessary to complete the use case.

When using WorkItems, you should be careful not to mimic use cases at a granular level. Instead, a WorkItem object should represent a set of related use cases together. For example, you might have a Customer WorkItem class that handles the viewing and editing of customer data. Making the WorkItem classes too granular can result in an unnecessarily complex application that is very difficult to maintain.

The WorkItem classes make it easy to implement the MVC and MVP patterns. In the case of these patterns, the WorkItem class will contain the view (SmartParts or other visual UI components) and controller components. The controller (or presenter) will typically be another child WorkItem object that will manage the calls between the SmartParts and business logic, as well as manage the state for the parent WorkItem object (model).

The Composite UI Application Block allows for extensions to be created for the WorkItem classes, which can provide new or modified capabilities and behaviors within the WorkItem instance. A WorkItem extension allows for code that can be run during specific points within the life cycle of the WorkItem instance. Some of these points (or events) are listed in Table 15-1.

**Table 15-1.** *Some WorkItem Life Cycle Events*

| Event | Description |
| --- | --- |
| Initializing | Fires when the WorkItem is initializing |
| Initialized | Fires when the WorkItem is initialized |
| Activating | Fires when the WorkItem status has been changed to active |
| Activated | Fires when the WorkItem is finished activating |
| DeActivating | Fires when the WorkItem status has been changed to inactive |
| DeActivated | Fires when the WorkItem has finished deactivating |
| RunStarted | Fires when the WorkItem's Run method is called |
| Terminating | Fires when the WorkItem is terminating |
| Terminated | Fires when the WorkItem is finished terminating |

WorkItem extensions offer a lot of extensibility to an application, especially since WorkItem extensions do not need to exist in the same module as the WorkItem object.

## Application Shell

The application shell is the core of the Composite UI Application Block. It handles the initialization of all the standard services provided in the Composite UI Application Block. The application shell comes in two flavors:

- The ApplicationContextApplication class, which allows you to control the application context

- The FormShellApplication class, which allows you to have a main shell Windows form

Using the FormShellApplication class, when you close the main shell form, the entire application will close. In contrast, the ApplicationContextApplication class allows you to control the life of the application. With the ApplicationContextApplication class, you need to explicitly exit the application. This can be useful when creating applications that can have multiple forms open, or when the user can run other programs, such as task scheduler, in the background. Just make sure to provide some mechanism for the application to shut down, such as a system tray icon. Also, make sure that multiple instances of the application cannot be opened. Otherwise, you may find your computer coming to a grinding halt due to a lack of system resources.

Both the ApplicationContextApplication and FormShellApplication classes can be found in the Microsoft.Practices.CompositeUI.WinForms namespace. They inherit from the WindowsFormsApplication class, which is also found in the Microsoft.Practices.CompositeUI.WinForms namespace. This class contains all the logic necessary to handle Windows forms-style applications. For example, it knows when to call specific builder strategies and services needed for any Windows forms-based applications.

The WindowsFormsApplication class inherits from the CabShellApplication class. The CabShellApplication class is responsible for supporting any application requiring a shell in which to run. It adds a parameter that allows the retrieval of the type of shell that is used by the application. It also provides the virtual methods BeforeShellCreated and AfterShellCreated, which can be overridden to perform before-shell-creation and after-shell-creation tasks. They occur before and after creation of the shell in the OnRootWorkItemInitialized event handler of the CabApplication class.

The core of the whole operation is the CabApplication class, which is inherited by the CabShellApplication class and is basically where the rubber meets the road. This class has a main public method called Run, which is responsible for calling all of the necessary services and ObjectBuilder strategies to get the application shell up and running. The Run method performs the following tasks:

- Register the unhandled exception handler.

- Create the ObjectBuilder Builder object and add any specified builder strategies.

- Create the root WorkItem.

- Create visualizers.

- Add required services:
    - TraceSourceCatalogService, which manages TraceSource objects
    - WorkItem ExtensionService, which handles the registration of WorkItemExtension objects
    - WorkItemTypeCatalogService, which manages WorkItem objects that are instantiated when the module is initialized
    - SimpleWorkItemActivationService, which ensures that only one WorkItem object is active at one time
    - WindowsPrincipalAuthenticationService, which provides authentication services
    - ModuleLoaderService, which loads modules
    - FileCatalogModuleEnumerator, which processes module assemblies based on a solution profile
    - CommandAdapterMapService, which maps CommandAdapters objects
    - UIElementAdapterFactoryCatalog, which manages UIElementAdapter factory classes
    - DataProtectionCryptographyService (on demand only), which provides cryptography services via the Windows Data Protection API (DPAPI)

- Add services specified in the configuration file.

- Provide the AddServices virtual method so that required services can be specified in the application.

- Authenticate the user.

- Process and load any WorkItem extensions or services present in the executing assembly.

- Call the BuildUp method of the root WorkItem instance.

- Load any necessary modules as defined in the ProfileCatalog.xml file.

- Initialize the WorkItem extensions that pertain to the root WorkItem instance.

- Call the Run method on the root WorkItem instance.

- Call the Start method, which must be overridden by the developer.

- Call the Dispose method of the root WorkItem to properly clean up the application.

As you can see, the CabApplication class's Run method is truly central to the initialization, running, and teardown of the application. This method could be modified to add in your own special behaviors if you so desire, but typically, you would not use the CabApplication, CabApplicationShell, or WindowsFormsApplication class directly.

## Modules

The Composite UI Application Block modules allow for the customization of an application based on the assemblies that are specified and deployed with the application. A file called ProfileCatalog.xml contains the list of modules that can be used by a particular application. For example, using this feature, you could deploy WorkItem extensions to a user's computer to allow for detailed instrumentation of an application to discover potential performance problems. You can also use it to allow specific features of an application to be present or absent, based on whether it was deployed to the user's computer.

## Workspaces

Workspaces specify where the SmartParts and other visual elements are displayed. They can define the look and feel, control placement constraints, and provide other options on how components are activated in an application. This design allows controls contained within a Workspace to be consistent in enabling, disabling, showing, or hiding components independently of the SmartParts hosted within it. Table 15-2 lists the five types of Workspaces that come with the Composite UI Application Block.

**Table 15-2.** *Composite UI Application Block Workspace Types*

| Type | Description |
| --- | --- |
| WindowWorkspace | Enables the displaying and hiding of SmartPart controls within a windowed frame |
| MdiWorkspace | Inherits from the WindowWorkspace and displays SmartPart controls as MDI child forms |
| TabWorkspace | Enables the displaying and hiding of SmartPart controls inside a tabbed page |
| DeckWorkspace | Enables the displaying and hiding of SmartPart controls in an overlapping manner without windowed frames (like a deck of cards) |
| ZoneWorkspace | Enables the displaying and hiding of SmartPart controls in a tiled layout, like the look and feel of the Visual Studio IDE itself |

Each of the five Workspace types implements a common interface called IWorkspace, which allows the Composite UI Application Block components to interact with it. This interface contains members for activating, showing, hiding, and closing SmartPart controls. The IWorkspace interface also provides a collection of SmartPart objects through the SmartParts property, which specifies the active SmartPart control and events for handling the activation and closing of SmartPart objects.

When developing a Workspace, you might want granular control of how specific controls appear within it. This is done through the ISmartPartInfo interface and the default SmartPartInfo class implementation that is provided with the Composite UI Application Block. The SmartPartInfo base class provides an implementation that supports the Visual Studio design interface with a SmartPart control. You can simply drag and drop it from your toolbox onto the SmartPart control designer. Currently, three SmartPartInfo classes support the TabWorkspace, WindowWorkspace, and ZoneWorkspace components. Table 15-3 lists the features that these SmartPartInfo classes support.

**Table 15-3.** *Workspace Features Supported by SmartPartInfo*

| Workspace | Feature | Description |
|---|---|---|
| WindowWorkspace | ControlBox | When set to true, the control box will be visible in the window |
| | Height | Sets the height of the window |
| | Icon | Sets the icon to display in the title bar of the window |
| | Location | Sets the location of the window |
| | MaximizeBox | When set to true, the maximize box will be visible in the window |
| | MinimizeBox | When set to true, the minimize box will be visible in the window |
| | Title | Sets the title in the window's title bar |
| | Modal | When set to true, makes the window shown a modal window |
| | Width | Sets the width of the window |
| TabWorkspace | ActivateTab | When set to true, the tab will get the focus when shown |
| | Position | Specifies whether the tab will be at the beginning or end of the page |
| ZoneWorkspace | Dock | Sets the dock style of the control within the ZoneWorkspace |
| | ZoneName | Sets the name of the zone where the SmartPart control should be displayed |

With the design of the Composite UI Application Block, you can build your own custom Workspaces and SmartPartInfo implementations to meet your application's specific needs. This flexibility can allow for great control of the look and feel of any application.

# Composite UI Application Block Event Handling

The Composite UI Application Block provides a robust, loosely coupled communication infrastructure to allow the components within an application to communicate with one another. This lets SmartParts or other classes within a WorkItem communicate with one another without needing to know about the other SmartPart's or class's implementation. In other words, you can create a WorkItem that is set up to subscribe to a particular published event, but if the event is not available, the application will still run without any hiccups (except, of course, the event will never be fired).

Events within the Composite UI Application Block are handled by three main components: events marked as EventPublishers, methods marked as EventSubscribers, and the EventTopic class. Together, these three components compose the Event Broker service. This design allows you to manage event publications, subscriptions, and topics programmatically.

The critical piece in the Event Broker service is the EventTopic class. The EventTopic class provides the means to publish events from the event publishers to the event subscribers. EventTopic objects are contained in the WorkItem.EventTopics collection class. The EventTopic class uses the assistance of a helper class called EventInspector. The EventInspector is responsible for examining components and registering any event subscriptions or publications to the EventTopic, and adding those topics to the EventTopics collection. The EventInspector also handles unregistering EventTopics when the application disposes of a component.

## Creating Event Publications

You can easily create event publications with the EventPublication attribute. All that you need to specify is a unique topic name, such as topic://MyApplication/MyEvent. Optionally, you can also specify one of the following three publication scopes:

- *Global*: The events that are a part of the EventTopic class should be fired on all WorkItem instances. This is the default scope if a publication scope is not specified.

- *Descendants*: The events that are part of the EventTopic class should be fired on only the WorkItem instances where the event publication was fired and all of the WorkItem's descendant WorkItem instances.

- *WorkItem*: The events that are part of the EventTopic class should be fired on only the WorkItem instance where the event publication was fired.

## Creating Event Subscribers

Creating event subscribers is as easy as creating event publications. Simply use the EventSubscription attribute, specifying the topic name to which to subscribe. Optionally, you can also specify one of the three following threading options:

- BackGround: Specifies that the event handler should be called on a separate background thread.

- Publisher: Specifies the event handler should be called on the same thread as the thread on which the event was published.

- UserInterface: Specifies the event handler should be called on the same thread as the UI is running. This allows for safe interaction with the UI components.

■**Note**  The Event Broker service was not designed to broadcast or send messages outside the application domain on which it is executing.

## State Maintenance

The Composite UI Application Block allows for the state of an application to be kept, even if the application is closed by the user. The WorkItem class contains a State property, which holds a loose collection of name-value pairs. When the State property is changed, the StateChanged event is fired. This gives the application the ability to respond to state changes, such as persisting the state to a file in case of an unexpected application failure.

The state of an application can be kept even if the application is shut down by the user. This is handled by the State Persistence service. The State Persistence service provides an interface called IStatePersistenceService, which defines the interface for performing state persistence duties. Also included with the Composite UI Application Block are two state persistence implementations: the FileStatePersistenceService class and the IsolatedStorageStatePersistenceService class. Both of these classes provide similar functionality in storing the state of an application to a file and retrieving it.

## UIElements

Almost all UIs use common elements throughout an application. In order to simplify the use and interaction of these common elements, the Composite UI Application Block supports the development of user interface components called UIElements. UIElements include menus, status bars, progress bars, toolbars, notification tray icons, and so on. Typically, the shell developer will create the UIElement component, and the module developers will use it.

To handle the manipulation of a UIElement, a specialized adapter called the IUIElementAdapter must be defined. The IUIElementAdapter contains the members that a UIElement adapter should support. The IUIElementAdapter contains two methods that must be implemented: the Add and Remove methods. An implementation class named UIElementAdapter provides generic methods for satisfying this interface. Currently, the Composite UI Application Block contains two UIElement adapters:

* ToolStripItemOwnerCollectionUIAdapter: Provides an adapter where new System. Windows.Forms ToolStripItems will be added to an existing ToolStripItems collection.

* ToolStripItemCollectionUIAdapter: Provides an adapter for wrapping the System. Windows.Forms.ToolStripCollection class for use by an instance of the IUIElementAdapter interface.

UIExtensionSites are a collection of elements contained within a WorkItem class that allow you to access and manage UIElements through their registered adapters. You must specify the name of the site (typically a URI string) when registering adapters. Other components and code will use the site name to reference the UIElements contained within a UIExtensionSite.

## Commands

Many applications have common functionality that can be invoked from more than one component within an application. To simplify these tasks, the Composite UI Application Block provides commands that work hand and hand with UIElements. These commands provide a simplified interface to invoke UIElements. You can specify that one command event handler can be associated with more than one UIElement or vice versa.

The use of the CommandHandlerAttribute attribute associates a command with a specific method. The WorkItem class contains a property called Commands. This property is a collection of commands that are registered and handled by the framework. The Command object contains an AddInvoker method that allows you to wire up an event to that specific command.

Here is an example of creating a command:

```
[CommandHandler("ShowError")]
public void ShowName(object sender, EventArgs e)
{
  MessageBox.Show("Sorry you are not allowed to do this.");
}
```

And here is how you could add an event to the preceding command:

```
MyWorkItem.Commands["ShowName"].AddInvoker(item, "MouseOver");
```

# Connection Monitor Application Block

The Connection Monitor Application Block was developed to help application developers determine changes in network connectivity. This way, developers can handle both online and offline scenarios within their applications.

Using the Connection Monitor Application Block, you can determine if a particular network resource is available. The application block can determine the availability of resources on both physical and logical networks. A logical network could be a corporate intranet or home network. A physical network consists of the actual network adapters.

The core component of the Connection Monitor Application Block is the ConnectionMonitor class. This class contains a collection of Connection and Network objects that are to be monitored. You create an instance of the ConnectionMonitor class via the ConnectionMonitorFactory class. This factory class allows you to specify a string indicating the correct configuration section within an application configuration file to use to determine which network resources to monitor. If a string is not specified, the default configuration section will be used.

## Monitoring Networks

The ConnectionMonitor class contains a NetworkCollection property called Networks. This NetworkCollection contains all of the networks that are to be monitored. The NetworkCollection class allows for a network strategy to determine how it will determine the connection availability. By default, the HttpPingStatusStrategy is used to determine connection availability, but it is also possible to create a custom strategy. The named ConnectionMonitor can then be configured within the application configuration file to use the custom network strategy.

The NetworkCollection class consists of a collection of Network classes. Each Network class contains three properties to determine the network resource name, network resource address, and whether that network resource is connected.

## Monitoring Connections

The ConnectionMonitor class also has a ConnectionCollection property called Connections. The ConnectionCollection class contains a collection of Connection classes. Each Connection class has a property called IsConnected, which determines if that specific connection is available. Table 15-4 lists these connection types.

**Table 15-4.** *Connection Types That Can Be Monitored*

| Type | Description |
| --- | --- |
| NicConnection | Provides the capability to detect if the application has a connection to a network via any type of connection |
| WiredConnection | Allows the application block to monitor connectivity to Ethernet adapters |
| WirelessConnection | Allows the application block to monitor connectivity to wireless network adapters |
| DesktopConnection | Allows the application block to monitor connectivity to local services |

## Handling Connectivity Changes

Each Connection and Network class contains an event called StateChanged. The StateChanged event passes in an instance of the StateChangedEventArgs class. This class contains a property called IsConnected, which allows you to determine how the current state of a connection has changed.

# Endpoint Catalog Application Block

The Endpoint Catalog Application Block manages the physical address and authentication data for the web service endpoints that will be used by a smart client application. This application block consists of three core classes: EndpointCatalog, EndpointCatalogFactory, and Endpoint.

## EndpointCatalog Class

The EndpointCatalog class allows for the management of the Endpoint classes. Using this class, you can retrieve endpoints and credentials for a named network, and also set endpoints. An instance of the EndpointCatalog class is created via the CreateCatalog method of the EndpointCatalogFactory class.

The EndpointCatalog class contains two methods for retrieving credentials and addresses and one method for setting an endpoint:

- GetAddressForNetwork: Takes a single argument of type string to determine which address to return based on the specified network. If the string does not match any networks within the endpoint catalog, the default address is returned; otherwise, the address corresponding to the network name provided is returned.

- GetCredentialForNetwork: Works in the same manner as the GetAddressForNetwork method, but returns an instance of the .NET Framework's System.Net. NetworkCredential class for the specified network name.

- SetEndpoint: Takes an argument of the Endpoint class and adds that to its own internal catalog.

## Endpoint Class

The Endpoint class contains the actual details about an endpoint. It has two public properties that allow you to retrieve the address and retrieve or set the credentials required for the endpoint. The Endpoint class also has the methods listed in Table 15-5.

**Table 15-5.** *Public Methods for the Endpoint Class*

| Method | Description |
|---|---|
| ContainsConfigForNetwork | Determines if the network specified exists in the endpoint. |
| GetAddressForNetwork | Gets the endpoint address for a specified network. If the network not found, the default address is returned. |
| GetCredentialForNetwork | Gets the credentials necessary for authenticating against an endpoint. If the network is not found, the default credential is returned. |
| SetConfiguration | Adds the network name and an instance of the EndpointConfig class to the Endpoint class. |

The EndpointConfig class is used in conjunction with the Endpoint class's SetConfiguration method to add a new named network to the Endpoint class. It contains two properties, which specify the credentials and network address used to define a specific named network.

# Disconnected Service Agent Application Block

The Disconnected Service Agent Application Block provides management services for using web services from smart client applications. The application block allows a queue of web service requests to be held offline. When a web service is available again, it will "replay" these web service requests.

The Disconnected Service Agent Application Block consists of three core classes:

- RequestManager: Manages the request queues. It stores failed or pending requests in a SQL Server 2005 Compact Edition database via an implementation of the IRequestQueue interface called the DatabaseRequestQueue class. It uses the RequestDispatcher class to send messages to the web services. You can create a custom storage implementation for requests by inheriting from the IRequestQueue interface and specifying it within the application configuration file.

- Request: Contains the actual web service request. The data includes the endpoint that will handle the request, the arguments of the request, and the metadata on how the dispatcher should handle the request. The Request class uses the EndPointCatalog class, which is part of the Endpoint Catalog Application Block, to know which endpoints are available for receiving requests.

- ConnectionMonitorAdapter: The liaison between the Request class and the ConnectionMonitor class of the Connection Monitor Application Block. It raises necessary events when connection statuses change and also provides the necessary detailed information on network resources.

# Composite Web Application Block

The Composite Web Application Block is part of the Web Client Software Factory. This application block is conceptually the web version of the Composite UI Application Block, as described earlier in this chapter.

---

■**Note**  The Web Client Software Factory can be downloaded from http://www.codeplex.com/websf.

---

## Uses of the Composite Web Application Block

Like the Composite UI Application Block, the Composite Web Application Block takes UI components and combines them together to create a web application. These UI components, known as *modules*, typically consist of UI elements and tasks that can be performed on them. Some examples include a login module, credit card verification module, and email verification module. The modules are then hosted in an application shell that allows for a cohesive web client solution.

## Core Components of the Composite Web Application Block

The Composite Web Application Block consists of modules, as well as the following components to support the application block:

- *Global application class*: A class called WebClientApplication, which is the entry point of the web client application,

- *Composition containers*: Containers that manage services and objects through their life cycle.

- *Services*: Objects that provide functionality to other components.

- *Authorization*: A component that provides authorization services for the Composite Web Application Block.

- *Module site map provider*: A component that provides an in-memory representation of the navigation structure for the site.

## Modules

Modules encapsulate a set of concerns within an application. Two types of modules are supported by the Composite Web Application Block:

- A *business module* handles the UI and logic required for a specific task. Business modules are usually independent of each other and do not expose functionality to other modules.

- A *foundational module* handles functionality that is shared across the application. A foundational module will not contain web pages.

Three types of components compose a module:

- *Module web pages*: The ASP.NET web pages displayed for the module.

- *Module assembly*: A class library that contains the domain logic for the module.

- `Web.config` *file*: An ASP.NET configuration file used to identify the module assembly and the location of the web pages.

---

**Note** A module can have a separate `Web.config` file, or you can add the entries required for a module to the website's `Web.config` file.

---

When a web client application starts, the Composite Web Application Block uses the `Web.config` file for the website to determine the current modules that should be loaded.

## Global Application Class

The global application class is the entry point for an application. In the `Global.asax` file, you can declare a directive called `Application`, which allows you to specify compiler options, language used, a code behind file, and which `HttpApplication`-derived class the web application can use.

When using the Composite Web Application Block, the `Inherits` attribute must specify the `WebClientApplication` class, as in this example:

```
<%@ Application Language="C#" Inherits="CompositeWeb.WebClientApplication" %>
```

The `WebClientApplication` class provides various web application startup and page preprocessing features that are used by the Composite Web Application Block. The web application startup tasks are as follows:

- Create instances of the ObjectBuilder classes and add builder strategies as required.

- Create the root composition container (described in the next section).

- Add any required global services (described in the "Services" section).

- Load and configure modules.

- Run any required application-specific startup code.

The web page processing tasks involve injecting dependencies for web page requests prior to the execution of the ASP.NET page, as well as teardown functionality for the postexecution of the ASP.NET page.

## Composition Containers

Composition containers are runtime components that manage the lifetime of services and managed objects. The WebClientApplication class contains a root composition container that holds all of the other containers. The root container will contain a composition container for each business module, and each business module will have its own container for keeping managed objects alive.

## Services

Services are objects that provide shared functionality to other components. The WebClientApplication class initializes services at startup and hands them to its root composition container to keep them alive throughout the application. Table 15-6 lists some of the services available.

**Table 15-6.** *Some Composite Web Application Block Services*

| Service | Description |
| --- | --- |
| ModuleConfigurationLoaderService | Locates the configuration information for a module |
| VirtualPathUtilityService | Contains functionality for handling virtual paths and URLs |
| AuthorizationRulesService | Registers and returns rules for a specific URL |
| SessionStateLocatorService | Provides access to the System.Web.HttpContext.Current.Session instance |
| HttpContextLocatorService | Provides access to the System.Web.HttpContext.Current instance |
| ModuleLoaderService | Loads modules |
| WebModuleEnumerator | Finds module information from Web.config files for a given website |
| ModuleContainerLocatorService | Finds the composition container for a given module |

All services can be located in the ServicesCollection object of a composition container. When the Composite Web Application Block attempts to find a service, it first looks in the container of the module for the particular service. If the service is not found in that container, the application block will search the root composition container for the service. This gives you the ability to override the global functionality for particular modules.

## Authorization

The Composite Web Application Block contains functionality for setting up rules that define which users can access specific pages. For instance, you may want only administrators to have access to the admin.aspx page of a web application while allowing general access to the rest of the site.

The Composite Web Application Block uses two interfaces to implement authorization functionality:

- IAuthorizationRulesService provides mapping rules to URLs.

- IAuthorizationService provides the authorization check for a given rule.

The Composite Web Application Block also provides an implementation of IAuthorizationService that allows the Enterprise Library Security Application Block (discussed in Chapter 11) to authorize users. Using this approach, any authorization provider, including AzMan, could provide these services.

---

**Note** ASP.NET also provides authorization services via an access control list. You can find out more about this subject on the MSDN website (search for "ASP.NET Authorization").

---

## Module Site Map Provider

The last major component of the Composite Web Application Block is the ModuleSiteMapProvider class. This class is responsible for keeping an in-memory representation of the web site navigation. The ModuleSiteMapProvider class supports an implementation of the IAuthorizationService to determine if a particular user has access to a particular module.

# Page Flow Application Block

The Page Flow Application Block is another application block that comes with the Web Client Software Factory. The Page Flow Application Block uses the Windows Workflow Foundation (WF) for providing the page flow via the WF page flow provider.

A web application will have only a single instance of a page flow provider. You define the page flow provider for an application in the configuration file for that application. The Page Flow Application Block creates a catalog that registers page flow definitions for an application. Page flow definitions specify how pages will flow between each other. Each page contains a collection of possible transitions it can make based on the page flow definition. The page flow definition is defined by the IPageFlowDefinition interface, which contains a collection of pages involved in the page flow.

When the Page Flow Application Block processes a web page request, the page flow provider determines if the page belongs to a particular page flow definition. If it does, the page flow definition is used to process the request.

When a web page request is received for a page that belongs to a page flow definition, a page flow instance is created by the application block. The application block contains an interface called IPageFlow, which is used to begin a page flow, transition between web pages, and end the page flow.

To handle page flows that span multiple requests, the Page Flow Application Block provides an instance store to save and retrieve instance data.

# Updater Application Block

The Updater Application Block has been around since the original release of the application blocks for .NET Framework 1.0 and 1.1—even before the introduction of Enterprise Library. This application block allows an application to update itself when new application components become available. This simplifies an application's ongoing deployment and maintenance tasks.

When Enterprise Library 1.1 was released, the Updater Application Block was updated to version 2.0 to keep it in line with Enterprise Library. .NET Framework 2.0 included a technology called ClickOnce, which essentially performs the same tasks as the Updater Application Block. However, Updater Application Block version 2.0 was updated for .NET Framework 2.0. Currently, the Microsoft patterns & practices team has archived the Updater Application Block. At the time of this writing, there are no plans for updating it.

---

■**Note** The Updater Application Block can be found on the CodePlex website at http://www.codeplex.com/ smartclient/wiki/view.aspx?title=Updater%20Application%20Block.

---

The Updater Application Block consists of four core logical subsystems that are used to manage the application update process, as listed in Table 15-7.

**Table 15-7.** *Updater Application Block Core Subsystems*

| Subsystem | Description |
| --- | --- |
| Update management system | Responsible for determining if any updates are available and downloading those updates as necessary. It is composed of the ApplicationUpdaterManager, RegistryManager, and UpdaterTask classes. |
| Manifest management system | Responsible for containing the configuration information for an application's components. It tells the application block which components are available and the version. The application block then makes the necessary updates based on the information it contains. |
| Downloader subsystem | Responsible for downloading the updates from a server. |
| Activation subsystem | Performs any processing necessary for the updated application, such as moving files to a specific location, deleting files, performing Windows registry entry tasks, and so on. |

The classes that make up the update management subsystem are the core components and work as follows:

- `ApplicationUpdateManager`: A singleton class that is responsible for calling to the `ManifestManager` class to determine which updates are needed, if any. (The `ManifestManager` class is responsible for getting the manifest from the server and deserializing it.) The `ApplicationUpdateManager` class is the one primarily used by an application.

- `UpdaterTask`: Contains the state of an update. This way, if an update is stopped mid-cycle, it can be picked up where it left off.

- `RegistryManager`: Basically, behaves like a traffic cop. It manages the execution of the updates and ensures only one update at a time is executing.

# Application Blocks for Mobile Applications

Mobile applications for Windows Mobile 5.0 Pocket PCs and smartphones have the same issues and concerns as other types of applications. Some of these concerns include how to architecturally lay out the components of an application and simplify cross-cutting concerns such as data access, exception handling, tracing, authorization, and so on. The Microsoft patterns & practices team has created the Mobile Client Software Factory to address the needs of mobile applications.

The Mobile Client Software Factory contains guidance and application blocks for creating applications for Windows Mobile 5.0 devices. Many of the application blocks you might find in Enterprise Library and the Smart Client Software Factory can also be found here—in a lighter, optimized form, but with all of the core functionality. The Mobile Client Software Factory even includes a mobile version of ObjectBuilder. Table 15-8 lists the application blocks that are available with the Mobile Client Software Factory.

**Table 15-8.** *Mobile Client Software Factory Application Blocks*

| Application Block | Description |
| --- | --- |
| Mobile Composite UI | Core component used alongside the Mobile ObjectBuilder for creating mobile-based application UIs; similar to the Composite UI Application Block |
| Mobile Data Access | Provides data-access functionality similar to the Data Access Application Block (discussed in Chapter 6) |
| Mobile Configuration | Provides configuration management services comparable to the Enterprise Library's configuration components |
| Mobile Data Subscription | Provides services to support data replication to SQL Server databases from a mobile device |
| Orientation Aware Control | Provides UI services to help determine the orientation and resolution of a Windows Mobile device's screen |
| Password Authentication | Provides password-authentication services as well as data-encryption services |
| Mobile Connection Monitor | Monitors connections to network resources, much like the Smart Client Software Factory's Connection Monitor Application Block |

| Application Block | Description |
|---|---|
| Mobile Disconnected Service Agent | Allows for the storage of web service requests offline, and executes them when the proper network resource is available, similar to the Smart Client Software Factory's Disconnected Service Agent Application Block |
| Mobile Endpoint Catalog | Manages physical addresses and other metadata required to connect to remote services, similar to the Endpoint Catalog Application Block |

As with any other software factory, you must have the Guidance Automation Extensions installed in order to install the Mobile Client Software Factory. Additionally, some other prerequisites are required for the Mobile Client Software Factory:

- Windows Mobile 5.0 Pocket PC SDK

- SQL Server 2005 (for data replication)

- Guidance Automation Toolkit (later than the June 2006 CTP release)

The following sections discuss each of the Mobile Client Software Factory application blocks in more detail, focusing on their differences from their desktop counterparts discussed earlier in this chapter. The most noticeable differences involve configuration, since the .NET Compact Framework does not contain the System.Configuration namespace. Also, tracing features from the System.Tracing namespace are not supported in the .NET Compact Framework. Another difference is that the .NET Compact Framework does not support the System.Runtime.Serialization namespace, so serialization features will not be available.

## Mobile Composite UI Application Block

The Mobile Composite UI Application Block is the mobile version of the Composite UI Application Block, discussed earlier in this chapter, and it contains many of the same features as its desktop counterpart. The following are some of the major features that are different:

- The StateElement class is not thread-safe in the mobile version.

- The CabApplication class does not support the visualizer feature in the mobile version.

- Isolated storage features are not supported in the mobile version.

- The mobile version includes the FormWorkspace control, which is derived from the Workspace control. This control allows for easier creation of menus for a form.

## Mobile Data Access Application Block

The Mobile Data Access Application Block specifically targets SQL Server 2005 Mobile Edition databases. However, you can create new providers to support other database platforms as well.
This application block has two core classes:

- DbProviderFactory: An abstract class that contains three methods for creating connections, creating commands, and creating parameters. The SQL Server 2005 Mobile Edition implementation of this class is called SqlClientFactory.

- Database: An abstract class that provides the necessary methods for accessing the data from the database. This includes executing a command with no results returned, executing a command with a scalar value returned, and executing a command with a DataReader returned. The SQL Server 2005 Mobile Edition implementation of this class is called SqlDatabase. The SqlDatabase class adds a method called ExecuteResultSet, which is used for getting an updatable, scrollable, and bindable cursor called SqlCeResultSet back from the database.

## Mobile Configuration Application Block

The Mobile Configuration Application Block provides application configuration features that are not available in the .NET Compact Framework. It allows read-only access to configuration data, and provides only the basic set of features that would be required for a mobile application. So don't expect to see appSettings section support.

This application block was designed based on the classes found in the .NET Framework's System.Configuration namespace. This means you will find ConfigurationManager, ConfigurationSection, ConfigurationElement, and ConfigurationPropertyAttribute classes, just as in the .NET Framework's System.Configuration namespace.

The ConfigurationManager class contains a GetSection method that is used for deserializing configuration data into an object. The ConfigurationSection, ConfigurationElement, and ConfigurationPropertyAttribute classes can be used to define the data stored for a particular configuration section in much the same way as is done in the .NET Framework.

The Mobile Configuration Application Block also contains features for handling encrypted sections within a mobile application configuration file. You can use a tool named ConfigSectionEncrypt.exe, located in the <Mobile Client Software Factory Install Root>\Tools\ConfigSectionEncrypt folder, to encrypt configuration sections of a configuration file.

## Mobile Data Subscription Application Block

The Mobile Data Subscription Application Block is one of the unique Mobile Client Software Factory application blocks, in that it does not have a desktop counterpart. This application block is used for retrieving a local copy of data from a database. This way, an application can access the latest available application data without needing to always be connected to a database.

The Mobile Data Subscription Application Block contains four main classes to support its features: SqlSubscriptionManager, Subscription, SubscriptionParameters, and SubscriptionCredentials.

The SqlSubscriptionManager class manages a collection of Subscription class instances. The SqlSubscriptionManager instance will also contain credential information via a class derived from SubscriptionCredentials. Adding subscriptions is done via the Add method of the SqlSubscriptionManager class, which takes an argument of a SubscriptionParameters instance that will define the subscription. The SqlSubscriptionManager class uses the SqlCeReplication class from the System.Data.SqlServerCe namespace to start, stop, and show the status of subscriptions via the methods listed in Table 15-9.

**Table 15-9.** *SqlSubscriptionManager Methods*

| Method | Description |
|---|---|
| Add | Adds a new subscription by passing in an instance of the SubscriptionParameters class |
| BeginSynchronize | Begins an asynchronous data synchronization |
| CancelSynchronize | Cancels an asynchronous data synchronization |
| ClearCache | Clears and refreshes the synchronizations from the list of subscription information in the database |
| Drop | Removes a subscription from both the local database and the internal synchronization list or just the local database, based on which overload is used |
| EndSynchronize | Ends an asynchronous data synchronization when completed |
| ReloadSubscriptions | Gets the synchronization information from the database and reloads the Subscriptions collection of the SqlSubscriptionManager instance |
| Synchronize | Performs a synchronous data synchronization |

## Orientation Aware Control Application Block

The Orientation Aware Control Application Block is a custom base control for handling control layout for different screen configurations. It allows for awareness of the following:

- Screen orientation, such as landscape or portrait

- Aspect ratio, such as 16:9 or 4:3

- Dot sensitivity (dots per inch), such as 240 by 320 or 480 by 640

The Orientation Aware Control Application Block is used like a user control. It uses resource files to determine how controls will be displayed based on attributes of the display screen such as orientation, dots per inch, and aspect ratio.

## Password Authentication Application Block

The Password Authentication Application Block provides functionality to authenticate users and create encryption keys based on personal identification numbers entered by a user.

The two main classes in this application block are the PasswordIdentity class and the AuthenticationToken class. The PasswordIdentity class takes the username, password, and an instance of the RsaAesCryptographyProvider class. The AuthenticationToken class allows either a PasswordIdentity instance or a username and password to be passed into its constructor. It will then look at the stored token for that user and determine if the user is authenticated.

## Mobile Connection Monitor, Disconnected Service Agent, and Endpoint Catalog Application Blocks

The Mobile Connection Monitor and Mobile Disconnected Service Agent, and Mobile Endpoint Catalog Application Blocks work in much the same manner as their desktop counterparts.

For the Mobile Connection Monitor Application Block, one difference is that the available networks are determined by the mobile device's Settings section, as opposed to a configuration file. Another difference is that the types of connections available are DesktopConnection, NicConnection, and CellConnection.

For the Mobile Disconnected Service Agent Application Block, the difference is that the request queue is stored in a SQL Server 2005 Mobile Edition database, as opposed to the SQL Server 2005 Compact Edition database.

The Mobile Endpoint Catalog Application Block does not have any differences from its desktop counterpart.

# Advanced Configuration Features

The Enterprise Library 3.0/3.1 Configuration Console and Visual Studio 2005 Configuration Editor have features that go beyond simply configuring the application blocks themselves. These features allow for the following:

- Partial trust support

- Configuration data encryption

- Environment-specific configurations

- Definition of the location of the configuration assemblies

## Partial Trust

In Enterprise Library 3.0/3.1, the application blocks allow for applications that have partial trust to run by isolating permission demands to only the code that truly requires it. However, you may need to grant additional permissions by creating a custom security policy based on the application blocks and providers that are used.

In order to implement this feature, you need to grant the application ConfigurationPermission, or you can add the requirePermission attribute to the relevant sections of the application's configuration file and set it to false. The example in Listing 15-2 allows the Logging Application Block to read configuration information in a partial trusted environment.

**Listing 15-2.** *Setting the requirePermission attribute*

```
<configuration>
    <configSections>
        <section name="loggingConfiguration"
            type="Microsoft.Practices.EnterpriseLibrary.Logging.
            Configuration.LoggingSettings,
            Microsoft.Practices.EnterpriseLibrary.Logging"
            requirePermission="false"/>
    <configSections>
<configuration>
```

You can change the value of the requirePermission attribute in the Configuration Console or Configuration Editor by selecting the application block node. This value is now saved by the Configuration Console or Configuration Editor, rather than overwritten, as it was in prior versions of the Configuration Console.

## Data Encryption and Decryption

Data can be encrypted or decrypted in the configuration file's configuration sections. The Configuration Console and Configuration Editor allow you to select from the encryption providers that are specified in the Machine.config file. Typically, you can choose from the following two providers:

- DataProtectionConfigurationProvider: Uses DPAPI. If the encrypted configuration file is going to be on only a single server, you can use the DataProtectionConfigurationProvider.

- RsaProtectedConfigurationProvider: Uses RSA. If it is necessary to deploy the same encrypted configuration file on multiple servers, you should use the RsaProtectedConfigurationProvider. This provider makes it easy for you to encrypt the data on one server, and then export the RSA private key to decrypt the configuration data on the other servers.

To encrypt the file, follow these steps:

1. Open the Configuration Console or the Configuration Editor.

2. Either create a new application configuration file or open an existing one.

3. Click the name of the application block whose configuration information is to be encrypted.

4. In the properties grid, click ProtectionProvider. Select either DataProtectionConfigurationProvider or RsaProtectedConfigurationProvider, as shown in Figure 15-1.

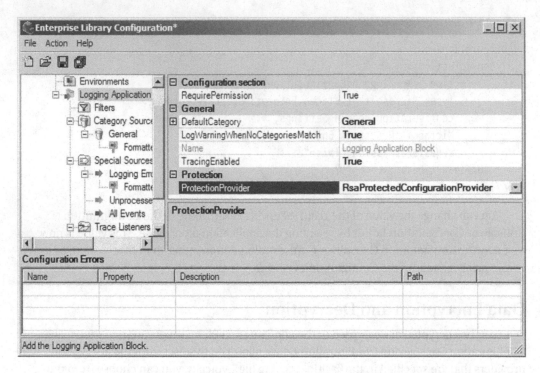

**Figure 15-1.** *Selecting the ProtectionProvider property in the Configuration Console*

---

■**Note** All the settings for the protection providers are also in the `Machine.config` file. You cannot change this file with the Configuration Console or Configuration Editor. Instead, the file must be manually modified.

---

Decryption of the configuration file is automatic. When you open the file in the Configuration Console or Configuration Editor, it will be decrypted.

## Environmental Overrides

You can use the Configuration Console or Configuration Editor to customize the runtime settings of your configuration to suit a particular environment. This feature is useful if you have multiple environments that share the same basic configuration but require different property settings. For example, you may have a development environment that uses one connection string for the Data Access Application Block and a test environment that uses another connection string.

Instead of maintaining multiple configuration files or having to change a file manually or programmatically, you can create a base configuration file (`.config`) and a delta file that contains the differences (`.dconfig`). Here is the procedure:

1. Open the Configuration Console or the Configuration Editor.

2. Open an existing application configuration file or create a new one.

3. Add any application blocks that you plan on using in your application and configure them.

4. Right-click the Environments node and select New ➤ Environment.

5. Set the following properties:

   - Name: Environment name

   - EnvironmentConfigurationFile: Merged configuration filename

   - EnvironmentDeltaFile: Delta filename

6. Repeat steps 4 and 5 for each environment.

7. Click a node of an application block whose properties need to be customized on a per-environment basis. Click in the Overrides on [*name of environment*] property field, and then select the Override Properties option.

8. Expand the Overrides on [*name of environment*] node and modify the properties as necessary for that environment.

9. Repeat steps 7 and 8 for each node that needs customizing.

10. Save the file.

11. Right-click the environment node, and then click Save Merged Configuration in the context menu.

During the build process of each environment, you can run an executable called MergeConfiguration.exe, which will merge the configuration files for a particular environment, as follows:

```
MergeConfiguration.exe configFile deltaFile [mergedFile]
```

The three MergeConfiguration.exe parameters work as follows:

- configFile: Specifies the main configuration file that will be merged with the delta file.

- deltaFile: Specifies the environment delta file that contains the environment-specific data.

- mergedFile: An optional parameter that specifies the output configuration file from the merged delta and configuration files. If a mergedFile parameter is not specified, the filename stored in deltaFile is used.

## Assembly Sets for the Configuration Editor

Since Enterprise Library 1.0, the configuration assemblies had to be in the same location as the Enterprise Library Configuration Console executable. In the latest version, that has not changed. However, since the new Configuration Editor is a Visual Studio 2005 add-in, it is necessary to somehow determine where the configuration components are located for the Configuration Editor. To do this, a registry key determines where to find the assemblies.

When Enterprise library is installed, two assembly sets are created: the Microsoft Signed set, which points to the strong-named binaries located in the main Enterprise Library installation folder, and the EntLib3Src set, which points to the Enterprise Library's source bin.

### Overriding the Assembly Set for a Specific Solution

By default, every configuration file opened with the Configuration Editor uses the default assembly set. To override this for a specific solution, the SelectedEnterpriseLibraryConfigurationSet property on the solution root element can specify an alternative configuration set that will be associated with all application configuration files in the solution. The list of alternative configuration sets is stored in the Windows registry.

### Specifying Assembly Sets in the Registry

To modify assembly sets, the ConfigurationEditor registry key must be changed. To change the registry key, open Registry Editor (Regedit.exe), and then navigate to the following key for computer-wide settings:

HKEY_LOCAL_MACHINE\SOFTWARE\Microsoft\VisualStudio\8.0\Packages\
{488366a4-630c-4a0e-a6a2-b019cee13bea}\ConfigurationEditor

or this key for per-user settings:

HKCU\Software\Microsoft\Practices\EnterpriseLibrary\ConfigurationEditor

Each assembly set is defined in a key below one of these root keys. For example the Microsoft Signed registry key resides under this folder and each assembly set will have its own key. The following are the assembly set keys that need to be modified:

- ConfigurationUIAssemblyPath: This key contains the path of an assembly that implements Microsoft.Practices.EnterpriseLibrary.Configuration.Design.HostAdapter. ISingleHierarchyConfigurationUIHostAdapter.

- ConfigurationUIAdapterClass: This key points to the namespace-qualified name of a class that implements Microsoft.Practices.EnterpriseLibrary.Configuration.Design.HostAdapter. ISingleHierarchyConfigurationUIHostAdapter.

- ConfigurationUIPluginDirectory: This key specifies the directory that contains the design-time and runtime configuration assemblies of the custom assembly set.

# Advanced Configuration in Enterprise Library 2.0

The Enterprise Library 2.0 Configuration Console did not support specifying environmental overrides, application settings, and protection providers. These features were not added to Enterprise Library until 3.0. However, the development community has found a way to add these features to Enterprise Library 2.0.

Olaf Conijn created a tool for Enterprise Library 2.0 to support these features. He even added the ability to configure the System.Web setting of a Web.config file using the Configuration Console. This tool is named the .NET Configuration Manager, and it can be downloaded from http://www.codeplex.com/Wiki/View.aspx?ProjectName=CoMan.

After you have downloaded the .NET Configuration Manager, you need to copy its assemblies into the Configuration Console's execution folder. If you downloaded just the source, as opposed to the binaries, you will need to compile the project first. Once the .NET Configuration Manager assemblies are in the Configuration Console's execution folder, all that is left to do is run the Configuration Console.

---

■**Note** The .NET Configuration Manager comes configured to be run independently of Enterprise Library by having its own instance of the Configuration Console. Combining the .NET Configuration Manager and Enterprise Library configuration assemblies is purely optional.

---

When you first start up the Configuration Console, you won't see any new features. However, when you open an existing application or create a new one, you can right-click the configuration file to see a list of configuration nodes that can be added, as shown in Figure 15-2. The following are the new root configuration nodes:

- Application Settings

- Configuration Protector

- Environmental Overrides

- SystemWeb Settings

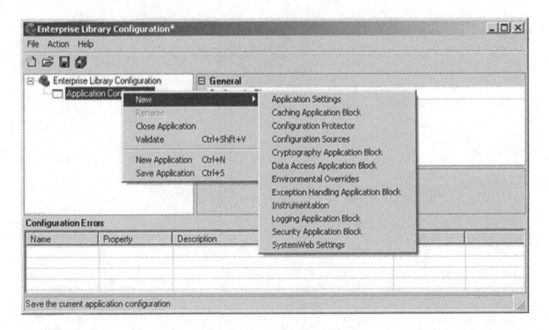

**Figure 15-2** *.NET Configuration Manager root configuration nodes*

The .NET Configuration Manager is a very neat tool, and it shows just how extensible Enterprise Library can be.

■**Note**  You can find more information about the .NET Configuration Manager on the CodePlex website
(http://www.codeplex.com/).

# Summary

With the community and the Microsoft patterns & practices team behind Enterprise Library,
expect to see new features and components keep popping up. As .NET grows, so will the
continual need to provide best practices and guidance in developing .NET applications.
As .NET 3.5 is around the corner, expect new and exciting features to be included in the next
version of Enterprise Library, as well as other application blocks provided by the Microsoft
patterns & practices group.

# Index

# You Need the Companion eBook

**Your purchase of this book entitles you to buy the companion PDF-version eBook for only $10. Take the weightless companion with you anywhere.**

We believe this Apress title will prove so indispensable that you'll want to carry it with you everywhere, which is why we are offering the companion eBook (in PDF format) for $10 to customers who purchase this book now. Convenient and fully searchable, the PDF version of any content-rich, page-heavy Apress book makes a valuable addition to your programming library. You can easily find and copy code—or perform examples by quickly toggling between instructions and the application. Even simultaneously tackling a donut, diet soda, and complex code becomes simplified with hands-free eBooks!

Once you purchase your book, getting the $10 companion eBook is simple:

❶ Visit **www.apress.com/promo/tendollars/**.

❷ Complete a basic registration form to receive a randomly generated question about this title.

❸ Answer the question correctly in 60 seconds, and you will receive a promotional code to redeem for the $10.00 eBook.

THE EXPERT'S VOICE™

2855 TELEGRAPH AVENUE | SUITE 600 | BERKELEY, CA 94705

**Offer valid through 5/26/08**

Printed in the United States
By Bookmasters